W9-AYX-238

Protest and Popular Culture

Women in the U.S. Labor Movement, 1894–1917

Mary E. Triece

UNIVERSITY OF AKRON

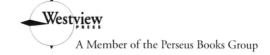

A Member of the Perseus Books Group

Copyright © 2001 by Westview Press, a Member of the Perseus Books Group

Published in 2001 in the United States of America by Westview Press, 5500 Central Avenue, Boulder, Colorado 80301-2877, and in the United Kingdom by Westview Press, 12 Hid's Copse Road, Cumnor Hill, Oxford OX2 9JJ

Find us on the World Wide Web at www.westviewpress.com

 Library of Congress Cataloging-in-Publication Data
Triece, Mary E.
    Protest and popular culture : women in the U.S. labor movement, 1894–1917 / Mary E. Triece.
      p.   cm.
    Includes bibliographical references and index.
    ISBN 0-8133-6819-7
    1. Women in the labor movement—United States—History.   2. Women—Employment—United States—History.   3. Women consumers—United States—History.   I. Title.

HD6079.2.U5 T75   2000
331.4'78'0973—dc21

                                                                00-043708

The paper used in this publication meets the requirements of the American National Standard for Permanence of Paper for Printed Library Materials Z39.48-1984.

10   9   8   7   6   5   4   3   2

To the women and girls of the Uprising of 30,000.
May their fighting spirits live on in
the hearts and minds of workers the world over.

Contents

Acknowledgments

As is the case with most creative endeavors, *Protest and Popular Culture* has been a product of many influences. I am most grateful to have had Dr. Dana Cloud of the University of Texas at Austin as a dissertation adviser and mentor. As both a teacher and as a role model, Dr. Cloud has greatly influenced my work and she has inspired me to stick to my argument even when it proved unpopular. Dr. Roderick Hart of the University of Texas at Austin has been another scholarly mainstay whose guidance and support I could not have done without. From Dr. Hart's example, I developed a passion for rhetorical studies and a commitment to the discipline. I would also like to thank Dr. John Rodden, who from the beginning encouraged me to develop a potential in myself that I had not yet recognized. I am especially thankful for Dr. Rodden's scholarly insights and personal empathy, which shaped me as a scholar and as a human being. I would also like to thank those who served on my disser tation committee at the University of Texas at Austin in addition to Drs. Cloud and Hart: Dr. Richard Cherwitz, Dr. Ronald Greene, and Dr. Deslie Deacon. My colleagues in the School of Communication at the University of Akron have also provided tremendous support and have given me the encouragement necessary to complete this project.

A special thanks goes to those who put their efforts into the production of this book, especially the anonymous reviewers who took their time with initial drafts, provided invaluable feedback, and remained optimistic about the manuscript's potential to become a book. Also, thank you to the editors at Westview Press, especially Andrew Day and David McBride, who worked on this project. Barbara Morley at Cornell University's Kheel Center for Labor-Management Documentation and Archives, Susan Boone at Smith College's Sophia Smith Collection, and Tom Featherstone at Wayne State University's Archives of Labor and Urban Affairs helped me find photographs for the book and I am grateful for their support and expertise.

Before I met the teachers, mentors, and colleagues who have greatly influenced my scholarship, my parents, William J. Triece and Eleanor Trautman Triece, instilled qualities that have led me to become the scholar and teacher I am today. My father taught me determination and persistence, qualities that enabled me to overcome a vocal disability and to reach the goals I set for myself. My mother taught me compassion and a concern for others, which sparked my interest in social justice and women's issues. I am forever thankful for their influence and unending support of my endeavors.

Finally, I thank my life partner and friend, Peter A. Velasquez, for his daily influence on my life. From him I have learned the importance of seeing art in everyday life. Our conversations remain a source of inspiration and invigoration as we both continue our quests to write more fully, read more deeply, play more passionately, and live more creatively while striving to shape a better world.

Mary E. Triece
Akron, Ohio
October 2000

Introduction:
Understanding Popular and
Protest Rhetorics

In the winter of 1909–1910, women and girls led the "Uprising of 30,000," a walkout of thousands of women and men in shirtwaist factories in New York City. It was the inspiration of numerous labor uprisings for years to come. On November 22, 1909, at a crowded meeting of shirtwaist makers headed by the well-known American Federation of Labor (AFL) leader Samuel Gompers, and a wealthy reformer, Mary Dreier, a young working girl stood up before the gathering and made a simple but impassioned statement for an immediate general strike: "I have listened to all the speeches. I am one who thinks and feels from the things they describe. I, too, have worked and suffered. I am tired of the talking. I move that we go on a general strike!" (Clark and Wyatt, 1910b, 81).

The popular magazine *McClure's* covered the remarkable event, noting its dramatic beginning with the words of one working girl. The article then concluded reassuringly how "[w]onderful to know that, after her [a shirtwaist worker's] very bones had been broken by the violence of a thug of an employer, one of these girls could still speak for perfect fairness for him [the employer] with an instinct for justice truly large and thrilling" (Ibid., 86). The description of a generous and compassionate striker provides an interesting example of how these militant actions were tempered and interpreted in a manner palatable for a middle-class audience. Actions motivated by anger and inspired by a belief in economic and political justice were transformed into an experience in character cultivation and an opportunity for mutual understanding between the classes. Material differences were elided; thus, rhetorical consensus was achieved.

Into the 1890s and early 1900s, magazines such as *McClure's* (as well as newspapers and dime novels) grew in popularity as various technological advances and cheaper prices made these entertainment forms available to readers of all classes. These cultural texts thus played an increasingly important role in constructing meanings and framing events—such as the Uprising of 30,000—enabling their readers to make sense of social gains and ills as well as the rapid change that industrial capitalism was introducing into American life.

Protest and Popular Culture explores early-twentieth-century popular and protest rhetorics in order to understand the relationship between the discourse and goals of social movements, more specifically, the labor and suffrage movements, and of the popular media that frame and constrain the actions of the protesters. The following chapters examine popular magazine portrayals of women's daily experiences in the home, at the factory, and on the picket line and ask: How were early-twentieth-century readers encouraged to understand women's lives as mothers, as income providers, and as activists? What stories were told and how? And what narratives remained unspoken and why?

Popular magazines were not the only outlet for learning about the needs and concerns of women struggling for equality. This book also gives voice to the thousands of women who participated in labor and suffrage struggles firsthand and expressed their own viewpoints and self-definitions through speeches, rallies, and testimonies. The following analysis examines "traditional" rhetorical relics such as speeches in addition to less-known and less frequently accessed sources in order to uncover the voices of women labor activists and suffragists. Alternative labor organs and papers of the Women's Trade Union League, the Industrial Workers of the World, and female union locals, in addition to notes, diaries, and letters of well-known labor activists provide rich sources for coming to a fuller understanding of the ways that subordinate groups struggled to speak on their own behalf even as popular media outlets were increasingly addressing their concerns as a disenfranchised group. Largely untapped by scholars of rhetoric, these sources are provocative, for they point to the influence of material and cultural conditions that both motivate and constrain attempts at social change.

Examining early-twentieth-century protest and popular rhetorics can tell us much about contemporary discourses and attempts for social justice. *Protest and Popular Culture* argues that the ideological strategies of popular media of the early 1900s pioneered the ways that contemporary popular culture responds to social movements and represents the voices of subordinate groups in the late twentieth century. The overarching rhetorical frames in early-twentieth-century high-brow and muckraking magazines, as well as periodicals targeted specifically to the working class, laid the groundwork for contemporary media and the ways they portray social movements that challenge the status quo.

Despite these continuities, much has changed since the early 1900s with regard to communication outlets and their influences on the ways people live, work, and come to understand themselves and their relations to the broader community. In present-day society, information is distributed to a wider audience, more rapidly, and in a more fragmented form than in the early 1900s. Consider that nearly 100 percent of U.S. households have either a telephone, radio, television or all three. Consider how Internet transmission, satellite hookups, and real-time chat rooms have influenced public knowledge of the Clinton sex scandal, shaped warfare in the hills of Chiapas, and fostered interpersonal relationships that span the globe. And consider that the act of television viewing, characterized by segmentation, soundbite presentation, and consumer orientation, has fundamentally shaped the realm of politics and public affairs. Yet, *Protest and Popular Culture* argues that, despite these technological changes and the changes they have wrought for better or for worse on social relations, fundamental persuasive principles have remained by and large the same. As the following pages demonstrate, popular media outlets past and present strive to preserve unequal relations through naturalization (Chapter 1), gain consensus through universalization (Chapter 2), and quell dissent through domestication (Chapter 3). As such, *Protest and Popular Culture* cautions scholars who would herald a new age of communication technologies while overlooking persistent persuasive strategies that reinforce class, race, and gender inequalities.

Recent popular-culture scholarship has taken an interest in the ways readers resist the dominant ideologies found in popular texts. In many ways, these works represent a concession to the pervasive influence of mass communication and a shift to the micro-politics of resistance (Brown, 1994; Fiske, 1987, 1989; Radway, 1984; Brummett and Duncan, 1992; Grossberg, 1984, 1989; McRobbie, 1994). That is, the goal has become examining how subordinate groups "make do" within dominant constraints. These studies focus on individuals as *agents of consumption* in that they examine the ways that members of subordinate groups view/read, i.e., consume, hegemonic discourses in resistant ways, such as through transgressive readings and/or by exploiting the text's semiotic excess. *Protest and Popular Culture* intervenes in these contemporary studies, arguing that despite the prevalence of popular culture in people's lives today, the traditional forms of resistance in which people construct and engage themselves as *laboring agents* still play a fundamental role in social change and thus warrant continued (or renewed) scholarly attention.

In short, the argument in *Protest and Popular Culture* is twofold. First, this book examines early-twentieth-century popular ideological strategies, arguing that though contemporary communication technologies have transformed the production, transmission, and reception of mediated messages since the early 1900s, there remain notable parallels between past and present persuasive strategies that reinforce class, gender, and race inequalities. Second, as communication scholars we can learn much about the roles of rhetoric in resistance and social change by examining the ways that subordinate groups construct themselves rhetorically as laborers in contradistinction to popular ideologies that address and define them as consuming agents. *Protest and Popular Culture* represents a case study exploring what Aune (1994) describes as the complex relationship between "subjective agencies and objective structures," or the use of rhetoric in encouraging an audience to envision and struggle against objective structures that are entrenched but not inalterable. But taking Aune's insights one step further, the following chapters also examine how women engaged themselves physically as laboring agents in order to resist popular ideologies but also, and not least important, to alter the material conditions (e.g., industrial factory system) that benefited from divisive ideologies in the first place.

Women's Activism and Popular Framings: Past and Present

The lives of well-known labor activists such as Leonora O'Reilly and Rose Schneiderman and middle-class reformers such as Jane Addams and Inez Milholland who joined hands with their wage-earning sisters were not altogether different from those of women today. In the early 1900s, wage-earning women worked for lower wages than their male coworkers, faced sexual harassment from foremen, and went home in the evening to do the second shift—housecleaning, meal preparation, and childcare. Middle- and upper-class women, confined by prevailing gender norms dictating domesticity, were denied participation in the public sphere and in decision making in the home. The early twentieth century also witnessed a great boom in the growth and circulation of various forms of popular culture, in particular, newspapers and magazines. To facilitate circulation and attract advertisers, these entertainment outlets increasingly targeted their female readers, devoting ample space to narratives of women's daily lives, their experiences as mothers, their desires for sexual freedom, and even their involvement in the burgeoning feminist and Progressive Era reform movements.

From historical accounts of social activism, we are aware of the ways in which women publicly voiced their concerns through the temperance and women's suffrage movements.[1] However, women and girls also played a central role in numerous labor uprisings between 1909 and 1916. The Women's Trade Union League played a central role in many of these strikes and represents to this day the most significant example of cross-class organizing on behalf of women's rights. The League defined itself as the "women's branch of the labor movement and the industrial branch of the women's movement" and sought to organize working women into trade unions and to address the sexism faced by working women (Jacoby 1975, 126). Though class conflicts within the League were substantial, the group assisted in advancing the material gains of working women in important ways.[2]

Perhaps most significant, labor strikes between 1909 and 1916, in which women played a defining role, resulted in remarkably improved pay and working conditions for thousands of men and women, and served as the foundation for labor laws existing today. Further, new union locals were organized and occupied by women, and the nearly defunct International Ladies' Garment Workers' Union (ILGWU) Local no. 25 was revitalized, as nearly 20,000 new members joined after the Uprising of 30,000 (Foner 1979, 339). Furthermore, from these strikes women and girls gained experience in organizing and speaking *on their own behalf* and they learned the power of solidarity. As one woman asserted: "This is not just a strike for self. Only by standing together can we get better conditions for all" (quoted in Foner 1979, 344).

Through testimonies and speeches, wage-earning women and girls did not mince words when expressing their anger toward workplace injustice and their dedication to achieving a "square deal." Yet popular magazine portrayals, such as the one that opened this chapter, often took a quite different tack when discussing the struggles of wage-earning activists. In the story of the Uprising of 30,000 referenced earlier, readers were encouraged to focus on the prevailing goodness of individuals rather than on material disparities stemming from the prevailing economic system. The image of the striker who could still speak for her employer "with an instinct for justice truly large and thrilling" implicitly discredited worker anger and collective confrontation, two key elements that enabled the workers to improve their conditions. *McClure's* magazine employed a universalizing frame in which character was shown to overcome class conflict, thus reaffirming the current arrangement of social relations under industrial capitalism, i.e., no need to transform the system when a kind heart is enough to better conditions.

Three quarters of a century later, there remain striking similarities in both popular culture and women's status in the workplace. Like their sisters of the early twentieth century, women and girls who labor in present-day factories around the world face sexual harassment, deplorable work conditions, and below-poverty-level wages. Women and girls in Nike plants in Vietnam earn $1.60 a day—not even enough for three meals—and are regularly harassed and worked to exhaustion. Garment sweatshops in New York City and Los Angeles employ Latina women who are paid below minimum wage and labor in dark unventilated factories for sixty hours a week. In small towns throughout Guatemala and Puerto Rico and on the U.S.-Mexico border, women work endless hours for U.S. companies such as Ford, Zenith, and Emerson, making parts that are then shipped back to the United States. Workers earn as little as thirty-four dollars a week and live in shantytowns that are surrounded by untreated sewage.

And like their predecessors, present-day women workers do not passively accept the abuses of bosses; they organize and fight back. In the Guatemalan "maquiladora zone" women workers in the U.S.-owned Phillips Van Heusen plant formed their own union, STECAMOSA. Led by Maria Marroquin and marked by the dedication, solidarity, and militance of her and her fellow workers, STECAMOSA halted production one morning at 10:00 to protest the company's withholding of bonuses and wages due to workers. As Marroquin relates the outcome, "by two P.M. that day, we had gotten the rest of the bonuses they owed us!" (O'Connor 1997, 12).

How are audiences encouraged to view the experiences of women such as Maria Marroquin? Since the heyday of muckraking magazines such as *McClure's*, the influence of various cultural texts has steadily grown as television shows, movies, magazines, and books continue to shape the ways that readers/viewers understand the experiences, needs, and concerns of women as wage earners, mothers, and activists. On the one hand, since the 1970s television shows and films have more willingly depicted women in "nondomestic" occupations and have openly tackled controversial concerns and issues confronting women in contemporary society.[3] In 1992, viewers watched as the popular television character Murphy Brown gave birth to a baby out of wedlock. Five years later, millions of viewers tuned in to celebrate the comedian-actor Ellen Degeneres' announcement of her lesbian sexuality on her popular television show, *Ellen*. Not confined to fiction accounts, issues that women have struggled with for decades, if not centuries, frequently make headline news. Sexual harassment in the military and in corporations, domestic violence, and unequal work and pay conditions are regular features of the daily paper and the nightly news.

Though the form and content of popular media outlets have changed since Progressive Era days, it remains of interest and importance for scholars of communication and culture to explore the assumptions and underpinnings of popular portrayals and the ways these ideologies have changed or remained consistent over time. In the face of women's protests against political discrimination and labor exploitation, contemporary popular magazines and television shows have taken to cultivating a "friendlier" face for feminism. Music Television presented a "She Thing Weekend" in 1995 focusing on "women's contributions to music and society" and providing a "surprising take on fashion's coexistence with feminism" (Sajbel 1995).[4] The March 1998 issue of the widely read magazine *Cosmopolitan* informed readers of "Fifteen fun, fearless, female ways to celebrate International Women's Day," one of which includes "purchas[ing] ten bottles of nail polish and donat[ing] them to the nearest nursing home" (Duffy 1998, 170). And present-day "she-ros" and "tough girls" (Inness 1999) provide viewers with hyper-sexualized versions of female heroes who display moxie in little more than a bikini. In short, not unlike many early-twentieth-century portrayals, contemporary media often present women, work, and resistance in a manner that popularizes "feminism" (the movement is not inconsistent with haute couture); personalizes "feminist" protest (feminism is giving nail polish to the local nursing home); and/or objectifies strong female characters, thus reifying their status as objects for the male gaze. The conclusion of *Protest and Popular Culture* bridges past and present popular portrayals to demonstrate how early-twentieth-century magazines paved the way for contemporary persuasive strategies such as those found in popular television shows, magazines, and movies.

Likewise, in the midst of postmodern discourses that have called for new concepts, theories, and understandings in an era understood as post-Fordist (post-Fordism is a term used to indicate what is perceived to be a fundamental shift in the nature of capitalist production, away from a production-driven economy to a consumption-driven one) or postfeminist (Hall and Jacques 1989; see also Best and Kellner 1991; Clarke 1991), we may do well to turn to past democratic efforts, which, I argue, have much to teach us about struggles in an age that is witnessing the emergence of new media technologies as well as the entrenchment of "old" relations of exploitation and domination. The conclusion contrasts past and present-day workplaces and elaborates on worker struggles from the 1970s to the present in order to argue for the continued relevance of rhetorical and extra-discursive actions that are labor-based, collectively engaged, and confrontational in nature. As scholars and students interested in communication, power, and social transformation, we have much to learn from the words and actions of activists such as Clara Lemlich and Leonora O'Reilly, who in the early 1900s provided alternative voices to challenge popular hegemonic ideologies and who joined hands with fellow workers in actions that affected objective structures and systems shaping physical well-being.

Throughout this project, communication, both popular and vernacular, is examined as it is embedded within and shaped by the specific historical context. Thus, the following chapters not only present critical analyses of popular and protest rhetorics but also explore the ways these documents were shaped in part by and were responses to various economic and political events such as the rise of industrial capitalism, Progressive Era reformism, the entrance of women in the political realm and the workplace, and changes within the magazine industry. Yet, as this book seeks to demonstrate, despite changes over time regarding the nature of capitalism and forms of communication, early-twentieth-century protest and popular culture still have much to say to us as communication scholars today.

Debating Culture and Social Transformation: Dawn of a New Era?

Protest and Popular Culture can be located within contemporary debates surrounding communication and technological change in the late twentieth century. The sweeping influence of postmodern and poststructuralist theories in the academy has shaped many of these studies with scholarship proclaiming a fundamental break in capitalism's regime of production and accumulation and a concomitant shift in the nature of communication.[5] More specifically, emerging communication technologies are viewed by many as radically altering the ways people live and work, and the ways that ordinary people resist and/or carve a space for themselves within the constraints of liberal capitalist society.

Further, the "discursive turn"—or the move to place language or discourse front and center as the predominant influence in social life—which is characteristic of postmodernism has led scholars to rethink and/or reconceptualize basic ontological and epistemological questions regarding truth, reality, and how we come to know. Philosophers and cultural critics have announced the end of the grand narrative and have denounced the "tyranny of theory." Explanatory critique stemming from an analysis of specific social relations has given way to discursive indeterminacy and the instability of signifiers. Collective confrontation rooted in class relations has yielded to localized "strategic strikes," "rules of thumb," or popular alliances. Within this context, meanings are unstable, selves are multiple, and the philosophical quest for truth is at an at end. The Sign predominates as studies focus on how groups and cultures construct meanings, realities, and practices of domination and resistance through language.

For communication scholars more specifically, the sway of postmodern perspectives on capitalism and communication prompted studies of the ways that communication technologies have shaped the exercise of domination and resistance through language. In many regards these studies offer a needed antidote to a field that heretofore had focused primarily on the "great speeches of great men." Contemporary scholarship has sought to uncover the lives of marginalized groups in order to discover the ways they employ language to resist dominant constraints and to make a better life for themselves within liberal capitalist society.

Additionally, in the spirit of postmodernism with its emphasis on playful subversions, celebrations of the sign, parodic imitation, desire, and jouissance, the language-centered approach in communication studies has produced projects that take an affirmative stance toward popular culture texts and practices. Scholars have variously studied the "self-production of culture" and the ways that subordinate groups empower themselves through various cultural and consumptive practices such as resistant readings (Brown 1994; Fiske 1986, 1987, 1989; Radway 1984), symbolic identifications and pastiche (Brummett 1991; Ono and Sloop 1995), plurivocality (Condit 1994), and identity and micro-politics (Butler 1990; Laclau and Mouffe 1985; McRobbie 1994).

In the "Age of Information," where average citizens are confronted with hundreds of messages each day exhorting them to behave and buy in prescribed ways, scholars have taken up the task of examining what people "do" with this multitude of texts and how they deploy them toward their own ends. Texts as diverse as television dramas, soap operas, game shows, and romance novels have been examined for "semiotic excess," multiple meanings, or "unresolved contradictions" that allow oppressed groups "to take the signifying practices and products of the dominant, to use them for different social purposes, and to return them from where they came, stripped of their hegemonic powers" (Fiske, 1986, 406; see also Fiske 1987, 1989). Fiske (1987) examines soap operas as a genre that validates more traditional "feminine" ways of seeing and knowing and thus carries subversive potential for female viewers. Radway studies women and romance novels, asserting that not only the content of these books but also the act of reading carries potential for female resistance (1984). Studies that celebrate the potentials of popular culture texts for subordinate groups often acknowledge that such reading or viewing pleasures may not directly challenge patriarchal domination, yet conclude optimistically that texts such as novels and television shows provide a "locus of protest" (Radway 1984) or a "masculine-free zone from which a direct challenge may be mounted" (Fiske 1987, 197).

Other perspectives have seized upon the increasingly fragmented nature of communication in contemporary society in order to explore the ways that readers and viewers take bits and pieces from various cultural texts in order to form an understanding of themselves and various social issues. Brummett explains how viewers form "mosaics" from various media texts in order to understand and make decisions regarding complex social issues (1991). Ono and Sloop study "vernacular" discourse, or the language of the oppressed, noting the ways it is constructed from pieces of popular culture to form a pastiche that "challenges the mainstream discourse" (1995, 23). These studies exemplify a larger trend in communication studies, one that emphasizes the positive roles popular culture plays in raising awareness and fostering public understanding of social issues in an era of hypermediation and soundbite politics.

On a theoretically parallel track run communication studies grounded in the notion that the nature of capitalism has fundamentally changed; hence, so too have forms of resistance to domination. Radical alteration through collective confrontation is deemed "outmoded" in light of the contemporary context characterized by flexible labor processes and a predominance of service and information-sector jobs. In its place, scholars advance discursive "concordance," identity politics, and various theories of locality that explain power and resistance as contingent and textualized. As one scholar puts it, "[C]urrent conditions suggest that [a] model of revolutionary change . . . is not necessary" (Condit 1994, 210). Rather, the goal should be "concord" or accommodation of all perspectives within a polyvocal public discourse that represents "the best that can be done under the circumstances" (211).

In the area of organizational communication, scholars have begun to study the "plurivocality" of language and the ways that competing interests struggle to get their voices heard. For example Deetz and Mumby ask: "Do different interests have an equal opportunity for impact on decision making?" (1990, 29). Similarly, Mumby views narrative theories in organizational communication as a way to explore the "infinitude of discourse" or the ways that dominant constructions of social reality are contested and thrown into ideological crisis, thus opening a space for alternative narratives to assert themselves (1993, 1–12).

Influential in the discursive shift in communication studies, Laclau and Mouffe offer a new program for "radical democracy" based on a textualization of concepts such as society, power, and struggle (1985). Their theory departs from the base-superstructure as an explanatory model for social relations, power, and exploitation. Instead, Laclau and Mouffe view the relation between economics and political ideologies as contingent or indeterminate. As such, a plurality of antagonisms characterizes late-twentieth-century capitalism. Social relations are no longer viewed in terms of specific historical conditions and society itself is no longer a "valid object of discourse" (1985, 111). Rather, subjects are "decentered," affected by a "multiplicity of relations of subordination" (Mouffe 1993, 12), and struggle stems not from a particular material position but is bound by ideological and/or political alliances.

Like the scholarship just discussed, *Protest and Popular Culture* is interested in issues surrounding domination, resistance, and communication within the context of capitalist relations. Though *Protest and Popular Culture* is a historical study, this book argues that the insights gained from

examining early-twentieth-century popular magazines and social movement rhetoric can be informative for scholars of present-day communication. As Fiske, Radway, and others have demonstrated, the reception and
viewing of popular culture is unavoidable, stands as a predominate
mode of leisure, and often serves as an activity over which subordinate
groups can exercise an amount of control (e.g., through ironic or subversive interpretations of hegemonic narratives). Yet this book encourages
scholars to refocus attention on the overarching and persistent persuasive strategies that continue to mark popular texts and delimit the range
of meanings within a given text. Brummett's study of popular metonymic images as the prevailing means by which citizens come to understand complex social issues provides a provocative account of how contemporary communication's fragmented form has influenced public
participation and democracy. Similarly, *Protest and Popular Culture* examines popular metonymic images and the ways they shape readers' understandings. But in contrast to Brummett, the following argument reminds
us that popular texts, past and present, are not the only means by which
the public can inform itself on social issues. Rather than resign ourselves
to the fragmented nature of soundbites, slogans, and popular icons,
Protest and Popular Culture reclaims the voices of subordinate groups as
expressed in rally speeches, testimonies, diaries, and pamphlets.

Finally, contemporary studies of capitalism and new communication
technologies inform us of the ways that living and working conditions
have changed since early-twentieth-century industrial capitalism. While
not denying important differences between early- and late-twentieth-
century workplace arrangements, *Protest and Popular Culture* underscores
fundamental similarities across time with regard to persuasive hegemonic
ideologies and the nature of capitalist domination and resistance. It is
true, as recent communication and cultural studies have emphasized, that
workers continue to struggle over meaning-making and interest representation within a "polyvocal" public discourse. But past and present examples of worker struggles demonstrate that the "value of labor and the production process" have not lost significance, as some suggest (Deetz and
Mumby 1990), but are still of quintessential importance. As such, the following critical analyses are underpinned by a theory that highlights the
roles of material institutions and structures in shaping and delimiting the
production and interpretation of political and popular ideologies.

Materialist Feminism:
Bringing the Class Factor Back into Cultural Studies

The historical-materialist perspective that undergirds the following critical analyses emphasizes the necessity of distinguishing between dis-

course and an extra—discursive world, or a context that exists independent of human language. "Materiality" is used here in a classical Marxist
sense to refer to a reality existing external to, though understood through,
human language and consciousness. Historical materialism understands
the relationship between language and the material world as dialectical
(each influences the other), but not indeterminate (their respective forces
are not equal). Discourse shapes social relations as when advertisements
contribute to a consumer ethos that encourages mass consumption and
thus supports the continued mass production of goods. Or to take another
more optimistic example, language impinges on material reality when
workers organize and convince employers to pay a living wage. Language has consequences in the material world, but this is not to say that
language is material in the same way that machinery and food are material—one cannot eat a menu, as Clarke (1991) points out. A dialectical perspective understands economic forces—those that enable a society to feed,
clothe, and shelter its people so as to survive and reproduce itself—as the
most influential in the last instance. "We make our history ourselves, but,
in the first place, under very definite assumptions and conditions" (Engels [1890] 1978, 761). The material base will "set limits" and "exert pressures" that delimit and/or circumscribe cultural meanings (Williams
1977, 83–89). The interaction between an economic base and various discourses is an interaction between two "unequal forces" with "the economic being by far the strongest, the primary and most decisive" force
(Engels, quoted in Rees 1994, 71). In addition to textual analyses, the following chapters explore the contextual factors that shaped how and under what conditions certain discourses gained credence and played a role
in the lives of early twentieth-century workers.

To understand the relationship between popular ideologies and material conditions, consider as an example an ideology that prevailed in medical, religious, and popular texts through the mid–1800s. The "cult of True
Womanhood" ascribed to women the qualities of piety, purity, submissiveness, and domesticity (Welter 1966). According to this discourse,
women were naturally suited for the roles of mother and homemaker and
thus should remain in the home as moral guardians for the family (Welter
1966). This popular ideology justified women's exclusion from full political and economic participation and naturalized the sexual division of labor both within and outside of the home. In these ways, the rhetoric of
True Womanhood affected women's lives in very concrete ways.

Yet it is important to remember that True Womanhood and discourses
sentimentalizing the family arose at a specific time in history in response
to changes in society's economic structure.[6] The rise of industrial capitalism and the subsequent removal of production from the home necessitated a different role for the newly privatized family and women's duties

therein. No longer a site of production, the family became a place of emotional and physical replenishment for the next day's labor in the impersonal world of factory production. As homemakers and mothers, women fed and clothed husbands and children, thus ensuring the reproduction and welfare of workers needed to fill the growing number of positions in factories across the country. At the same time, as the primary purchasers of mass-produced goods for family use, women as consumers provided a regular source of demand for factory output. In addition, the family became a place where children were taught the appropriate behaviors and values that would win them success as adults and where husbands could be rejuvenated for the next day's labor. In short, the values and activities that were made to appear naturally fitting for a family were, in fact, central for the perpetuation and growth of capitalism. Matthaei explains it well: "Since the husband centered his life around self-seeking competition in the economy, women as wives became complements to this process of masculine self-seeking, and family life itself became oriented around his struggle in the economy. . . . Furthermore, given that success in the economy was gained through loyal service to capitalists and capital, one could say that family life had begun to order itself according to capital's need for [its own] expansion" (1982, 118, 119). Various discourses such as the cult of domesticity emerged to support and justify the changing role of the family and women's duties.

As economic conditions have changed over time, so too have the outlines of these discourses. Nevertheless, as the following chapters argue, though popular ideological strategies do adjust and respond to changes in the historical context, in fact the strategies found in early-twentieth-century popular magazines provided the foundation for contemporary popular responses to evolving gender and work relations that challenge prevailing norms. Though the average purveyor of contemporary popular culture may find ample stories of women who succeed in the paid labor force—of single mothers, and of mothers who work outside the home—these images compete in a swirl of prevailing discourses, popular and political, that continue to sentimentalize and naturalize womanhood.

A materialist feminist approach encourages an examination of the ways groups challenge dominant ideologies but also provokes an analysis of the ways that disenfranchised groups sought to alter extra-discursive institutions and systems through collective actions that impacted objective structures and systems. Throughout this project, "extradiscursive" refers to actions and events that exist external to human language and involve material structures ostensibly constituted in culture. Humans understand these phenomena *through* discourse—representations, descriptions, framings—but these events and individuals are not *created* by human language. In particular, wage-earning activists engaged in mass pickets, strikes, and walkouts that were material in origin and had material effects. Many of the working class knew that challenging restrictive gender norms (domesticity, submissiveness) by voicing their grievances, even collectively, often produced little tangible change such as improved wages or reduced hours unless backed with action or the threat of action that carried material consequences, for example, machine stoppage and subsequent loss of profit for owners. Through walkouts and strikes the collective absence of women and girls from factories materially influenced factory owners, who relied on labor to keep machines running. Moreover, the mere presence of female activists engaging in such public protests upended notions of True Womanhood and thus also challenged gender norms.[7] Thus, women struggled rhetorically in order to get their voices heard in the workplace and in order to disrupt popular ideologies that perpetuated their social marginalization. But just as central to their fight were extra-discursive actions such as strikes and walkouts, in which these activists acted collectively in order to resist objective structures that constrained their lives.

Uncovering the protest tactics and rhetorical strategies of the early-twentieth-century activists, *Protest and Popular Culture* seeks to intervene in contemporary cultural debates that focus on consumptive agency and instead urges scholars to renew attention to the ways that people engage themselves as producers in attempts to challenge not just oppressive images but exploitative work conditions.

Situating and Analyzing Popular and Protest Discourses

Establishing the Context

This book analyzes popular texts for the persuasive strategies employed in portrayals of labor, womanhood, and women's involvement in the labor and suffrage movements. As part of the critical analysis, the following chapters incorporate the role of the socioeconomic context in shaping and influencing both popular-culture discourse and protest rhetoric. The economic context was most notably characterized by the continued growth of industrial capitalism and women's entrance into the paid labor force. By 1900, over five million women were in the labor force (Foner 1979, 257) working in factories, department stores, and office jobs. Viewed as an important source of cheap, docile labor, women filled the many unskilled jobs resulting from increased mechanization and rationalization of production. Most were paid below poverty wages, labored in dangerous and unsanitary conditions, were regularly subjected to harassment, and faced layoffs during slack seasons (Tentler 1979, 3–57).

Politically speaking, the 1894–1917 time period was marked by peaks and lulls in suffrage agitation, Progressive Era reformism, anarchist and socialist activism, and World War I. In the late 1800s and early 1900s, middle- and upper-class women entered the public sphere through temperance, labor, and suffrage activities and crafted a unique women's public culture centered on their concerns as homemakers and mothers. Suffragists, by the early 1900s in their third decade of struggle, were increasingly relying on "arguments of expediency," which relied on a notion of women's moral superiority, to justify votes for women (see Kraditor 1965). Also during these years, Progressive Era activists established settlement houses, engaged in muckraking journalism, formed consumer protection leagues, and initiated factory inspections to uncover child labor and other unsafe labor practices. By 1916, as U.S. involvement in World War I became inevitable, labor and suffrage agitation took a conservative turn or was suppressed altogether.

Industrial capitalism, Progressive Era politics, and women's involvement in the labor force and in social reform were events that shaped and were in turn shaped by a number of cultural changes. Perhaps most notably, American culture witnessed a shift from a "producer ethic" to a "consumer ethic" (Fox and Lears 1983). Industrial capitalism's ability to saturate the national market with goods now required consumption on a basis never before experienced. Workers had to be transformed into consumers, hence the birth of advertising as an indispensable corporate tool. In addition, the early twentieth century saw the emergence of a "new middle class," a social class who produced not things but ideas (Deacon 1989; see also Horowitz 1985; Lears 1983; Ohmann 1996). The "new middle class" (Deacon 1989) or "professional managerial class" (Ohmann 1996) "supervise, record and keep track of what others produce" (Deacon 1989, 4). As writers, managers, office workers, teachers, media personnel, and reformers, this group served as a "moral liaison" between the working class and the owners of production. These individuals made their living by legitimating the values and actions of the upper classes while acting as a salve for the lower classes. As activists and as muckraking journalists, middle-class reformers touched the lives of working women in complex ways; thus, their voices in both popular and protest discourses will be explored.

The late eighteen and early nineteen hundreds were also noteworthy for the growth of various popular media forms facilitated by specific economic conditions in the early 1900s. According to the media historian Luther Mott, "[N]one experienced a more spectacular enlargement and increase in effectiveness than the magazines" (1957, 4:2). Though various "quality magazines" such as the *Atlantic Monthly* and *Harper's* had always been available to the wealthy, the changes in the publishing industry made possible the publication of higher-quality magazines at cheaper prices. Beginning in the 1880s, publishing companies replaced their slow flatbed presses with rotary presses and employed conveyor belts and assembly lines, which increased magazine output to levels not known before (Peterson 1956, 5). A new photoengraving technique allowed the production of higher-quality magazines for lower prices (Mott 1957, vol. 4). Finally, decreased mailing rates affected the spread of magazines favorably around the early 1900s. In contrast to the smaller local markets that characterized preindustrial capitalism from 1880 through the turn of the century, the United States witnessed the growth of large national markets and the development of retailing, which were also conducive to the spread of popular magazines (Peterson 1956, 4, 5). Middle- and working- class populations residing in the new cities formed an audience ready to buy the new, cheaper magazines.

By the mid-1890s, then, magazines became a form of entertainment now available to the upper, middle, and working classes. "Ten-cent monthlies" such as *McClure's*, *Cosmopolitan*, and *Muncey's* were directed toward middle-class readers, whereas the working class read "cheap 'family' papers" (Mott 1957, vol. 4) and mail-order journals such as *Comfort*, *Home Life*, and *The People's Home Journal*.

The rhetorical strategies and frames examined in *Protest and Popular Culture* gained widespread popularity and influence in the early 1900s, but their origins lie further back in time. In magazines of the late 1700s and early 1800s we can find similar approaches to portraying women and their roles in society. Though limited to a relatively small audience of well-to-do readers, magazines such as *The Ladies Magazine*, *The American Magazine*, and *The Weekly Magazine* were significant for their content directed toward or relating to women and their roles in post-Revolutionary America (List 1986; 1994). In an examination of these three periodicals, List reveals the presence of the True Womanhood ideology that would continue to prove so pervasive in magazines of the late eighteen and early nineteen hundreds. Though the magazines occasionally delicately broached issues surrounding women's roles in politics and education, they most often discussed women in terms of their relations to husbands and sons. Women were to remain "subservient to their husbands" and "they were responsible for maintaining a pleasant and agreeable relationship with their spouses" (1986, 68). According to List, these texts laid the "groundwork" for media backlash against women insofar as the "media since that time have often conveyed the same thinking on women's place that appeared in these publications 200 years ago" (1994, 110).

By the mid-1800s, over one hundred magazines were targeting a female audience and were addressing themselves to "gender specific topics" (Zuckerman 1998). Among these, the *Ladies Magazine* (to be distinguished from *The Ladies Magazine* of the late 1700s) and *Godey's Lady's Book* were the most popular. Sarah Josepha Hale edited the *Ladies Magazine* in the early 1830s and advanced her vision of separate spheres for the sexes throughout the periodical. Women were encouraged to exert their moral influence on the secular world but to remain in the private sphere of the home (Scanlon 1995, 2; Woloch 1994, 98–113). "Home is her world. We want patterns of virtue, of piety, of intelligence and usefulness in private life," explained Hale in 1830 (Woloch 1994, 102).

In 1837, Hale became editor of *Godey's Lady's Book* after Louis Godey bought out the *Ladies Magazine*. *Godey's Lady's Book* offered readers a "revised definition of womanhood" (Scanlon 1995, 3), one that incorporated women's new role as consumers. It is notable that between the 1830s to the 1850s, images of heroines in *The Lady's Book* changed dramatically in response to the 1848 Seneca Falls Convention for woman suffrage (Hume 1997). Hume notes that in contrast to portrayals in the late 1830s of female characters as pious, selfless, "melancholy victims," heroines in the magazine's late–1850s issues were "cheerful, resourceful and brave" (1997, 9, 10). Noting that "[s]trength, resourcefulness and bravery became common characteristics" for the magazine's female characters, Hume concludes that present-day women can look to these images for "national heroines from early America" (18).

Mid- and late-nineteenth-century magazines targeting female readers also played a major role in crafting the female consumer. Garvey explores how advertisements and short fiction worked in conjunction to create the female reader-buyer of the late 1800s: "[T]he magazine invited the reader to interrupt reading a story about a marriage proposal to consider how she would look in an attractive jacket . . . " (Garvey 1996, 5). *Ladies' World*, a mail-order magazine heavily reliant on advertising, published captivating adventure stories in hopes of drawing in potential consumers (Enstad 1999, 161–200). And not to be forgotten, the *Ladies' Home Journal*, the most popular women's magazine of the early twentieth century, played a significant role in crafting the female consumer by "developing and promoting a domestic ideology that defined editors as experts, advertisers as prophets, and, most importantly, women as consumers" (Scanlon 1995, 3).

Continuing this line of scholarship, *Protest and Popular Culture* details the development of popular portrayals of women as mass media outlets extended their influence through the first decades of the twentieth century. The following chapters also examine the ways that popular images changed in response to the growth of industrial capitalism and women's continued fight for suffrage in the early twentieth century. In contrast to the above-mentioned studies, *Protest and Popular Culture* examines magazines with cross-gender appeal but considers the class-specificity of the target audience. Though many similarities can be found in magazines of the early and mid–1800s, popular periodicals of the early twentieth century increasingly responded to women's demands for economic and political equality and they acknowledged the growing discontent of the underclasses. The rhetorical conventions of these magazines are particularly significant given their widespread availability and the extent to which they influenced the popular imaginary.

Chapters 1–3 explore how and why magazines targeting readers of different class positions employed contrasting rhetorical framings of and responses to their subject matter. The media scholar Todd Gitlin explains media frames as "persistent patterns of cognition, interpretation, and presentation, of selection, emphasis, and exclusion, by which symbol-handlers routinely organize discourse, whether verbal or visual" (1980, 7). This process of selection and exclusion implies certain views of what society is and how it functions, or, as I argue, a specific ideological stance. Whereas *McClure's* readily addressed issues surrounding women's suffrage and factory abuses, the *Atlantic Monthly* maintained an air of propriety, by and large distancing itself from the grit and grind of daily life. Still other popular magazines addressed worker discontent in order to *personalize* solutions to workplace poverty and despair at key historical moments, even while workers outside the magazines' pages were demonstrating the necessity and success of *solidarity*.

Preservation, Accommodation, Realignment, and Resistance

The following analysis of popular magazines explores the ways these texts frame women's labor and reform activities, specifically from 1894 to 1917. In particular, each magazine will be examined for the overarching rhetorical frame that binds the various images, narratives, and viewpoints together even as the discourses negotiate and accommodate challenges in the socioeconomic context. This frame can also be viewed as the "ideological problematic," or the "field of representational possibilities offered . . . and the structuration of issues in particular ways" (White 1987, 182).

Media frames were shaped, in part, by journalistic conventions developing in the context of mid-nineteenth-century America. Scholars have located the origin of the journalistic imperative of "objectivity" in the penny press of the 1830s (Schudson 1978; Schiller 1981). Schudson explains the links between the emergence of the penny press, the growth of a "democratic market society," and the move toward objectivity in newspaper stories (1978, 57). The six-penny papers of the pre-Jacksonian Era were self-consciously partisan and served the interests of political parties and elite circles. In contrast, the penny press bore the spirit of Jacksonian democracy and sought a wide and diverse readership. The penny papers "claimed to represent, colorfully but without partisan coloring, events in the world" (Schudson 1978, 25). Diverging somewhat from Schudson's explanation, Schiller locates the success of the penny press in its ability to speak to "republican tradesmen" as opposed to an identifiable middle class (1981). In their "positive commitment to cheap, value-free information," penny papers expressed the "belief of many republican tradesmen that knowledge, like property, should not be monopolized for exclusive use by private interests" (Schiller 1981, 10). The development of science as a discipline and the increasing belief in and reliance on empirical inquiry also contributed to the growing pervasiveness of objectivity as a journalistic norm into the late 1800s (Schiller 1981, 10; Schudson 1978, 71–77).

But media outlets of the early and mid–1800s saw as their function not only the conveyance of "facts" but also the telling of a compelling story. Journalistic narratives parallel the growth of the novel in the early 1800s (Halttunen 1993, 79). Through character development and detailed plot elaboration, newspaper stories enabled readers to make sense of their lives and their roles within their communities in a swiftly evolving industrial landscape. Enlightenment ideals of liberal humanitarianism shaped the ways that stories were told, particularly those dealing with the evil or horrific. For a society increasingly secular in orientation, religious interpretations and admonitions were no longer adequate for explaining unfamiliar events and surroundings (Schudson 1978, 106). Journalistic storytelling filled the void. Halttunen examines the ways that murder narratives changed under the influences of "liberal Enlightenment" (1993). "The Gothic view of evil at work in the cult of horror was . . . an indispensable corollary to Enlightenment liberalism which ultimately served to protect the liberal view of human nature" as that of "basically good, free, and capable of self-government in the light of an innate moral sense" (1993, 99).

Journalism's twin goals of providing facts and telling a story are not neutral but are ideologically imbued and play a role in the maintenance of cultural hegemony. Hegemony refers to the ways in which dominant groups maintain their position through various symbolic or ideological processes. Consent on the part of subordinate groups is gained and constantly negotiated through certain views, beliefs, narratives, and frames of meaning that reinforce class privilege. Word choices, metaphors, argumentative form, tone, stylistic markers, formatting decisions, and visual images can all be examined for the ways they reinforce a specific worldview and support the continuation of the prevailing economic and political system. Likewise, journalistic conventions such as objectivity operate to regulate the presentation of ideas in concordance with dominant values and interests. The notion of objectivity disguises its partiality, i.e., its ideological component. Objectivity is an "invisible frame" that "ostensibly precludes the very presence of conventions and thus masks the patterned structure of news" (Schiller 1981, 2). Reese notes that "by accepting valueless reporting as the norm, the media accept and reinforce the boundaries, values and ideological 'rules of the game' established and interpreted by elite sources" (Reese 1990, 395). Similarly, storytelling diverts attention from itself and hence its ideological inflection through its very format. Character and plot development involve listeners in the storyline while anesthetizing them to the underlying political assumptions. Like objectivity, storytelling is an "invisible frame." The persuasive power of a narrative comes from its ability to argue "with a hidden bottom line" (Hart 1997, 93).

When alternative or oppositional viewpoints are recognized in various media outlets, they are reconciled within the existing frame of meaning. As Gitlin observes, "[H]egemonic ideology is extremely complex and absorptive; it is only by absorbing and domesticating conflicting definitions of reality and demands on it, in fact, that it remains hegemonic" (1979, 264). Indeed, this quality is what makes hegemony a process of negotiation rather than a static, one-time occurrence. In order to uncover the interaction between popular and protest rhetorics, this book focuses on hegemonic negotiation through analysis of the leaks and gaps available for potential exploitation by readers. In Gramscian terms, the book explores how subordinate groups overcome or resist the contradictions found in "non-organic" ideologies through "organic" ideologies that "'organize' human masses . . . form the terrain on which men move, acquire consciousness of their position, [and] struggle" ([n.d.] 1988, 197, 199).

Magazines targeting different class audiences were chosen for analysis so that class differences in the framing of women's public activities could be explored. The ideological stance of each magazine's writers and owners, combined with the commercial imperative to attract advertisers, appeal to an audience, and remain in business, led to contrasting rhetorical frames in each magazine. And as Robert Entman argues, "Comparing media narratives of events that could have been reported similarly helps to reveal the critical textual choices that framed the story but would otherwise remain submerged in an undifferentiated text" (1991, 6).

Three time periods were chosen for study, each one with particular significance in the labor and woman's movement. Each chapter looks at all three periods. First, the years 1894–95 witnessed increasing class distinctions and labor unrest, which culminated in the Pullman strike of 1894. At the same time, there was an increase in middle-class concern for the conditions of the working class. In particular, the depression of 1893 brought working-class women and middle-class suffragists close together as each realized the benefits to be gained through such an alliance for women's economic and political rights (Foner 1979, 237). During this period, how did magazines—emerging as a popular new source for information and entertainment—recognize, incorporate, or ignore social unrest and women's increasing involvement in the suffrage and labor causes?

As previously mentioned, by the early 1900s, over five million women were active in the labor force, predominantly in sex-typed jobs that paid low wages. Despite their general lack of organization, women continued to participate in various small strikes, even in the face of hostility from bosses as well as fellow male workers. It is at this time, 1903, that the Women's Trade Union League was formed in order to organize women into unions and to fight sex discrimination. Also in this year, the well-known Socialist and labor activist Mary Harris Jones (Mother Jones) was in the spotlight as she led a march of children textile workers from Philadelphia to New York in order to publicize their plight. The second time period, 1903–4, is examined for portrayals of women, work, and protest as these activists were becoming more successful and were gaining substantial national attention.

Finally, the definitive years between 1909 and 1917 will be analyzed in each magazine. These were the peak years of labor unrest as thousands of women participated—and in many cases organized and led—hundreds of strikes in numerous states. Exploring different magazines during key periods that span nearly two decades provides a way to note changes over time as they relate to changes in the socioeconomic context. The primary goal of this analysis is to demonstrate the prevailing characteristics of the popular persuasive strategies and to examine how female activists variously resisted or seized upon leaks in popular narratives in order to construct and engage themselves collectively in contrast to confining gender and work relations. In a fashion similar to that employed by the magazines examined here, contemporary media reflect popular ideologies that seek to reinforce the status quo through a rhetoric of naturalization, gain consensus among social groups through a rhetoric of universalization, and minimize or ignore dissent through a rhetoric of domestication.

Preservation Through Naturalization.   The critical analysis begins in Chapter 1 with an examination of the *Atlantic Monthly*, a well-established magazine targeted toward the upper classes and distinguished by a tone of cultivation and prestige.[8] Though it began as a primarily literary magazine, the *Atlantic* turned to social and political issues around the early twentieth century (Mott 1957, 4:44). The magazine refrained from directly addressing the women's labor activism that was a prominent feature of public life outside it's pages between 1909 and 1917; nevertheless, the *At-*

lantic Monthly's fiction and nonfiction articles probed gender and work relations, the construction of womanhood, and what is referred to as "the ladies' battle," or the struggle for suffrage, and these articles are examined in Chapter 1.

As a framing device, the *Atlantic Monthly* used a *naturalizing* strategy: in this strategy, capitalist as well as unequal gender relations are portrayed as common sense, and thus beyond question, or inevitable. Such a frame discredited attempts at social change by associating change with irrationality or the unnatural. For example, numerous articles throughout *Atlantic Monthly* accepted as an unspoken premise women's predominance in the home, indicating the persistent and hence inevitable status of gender norms or roles dictated by the cult of domesticity—even during key periods in which thousands of women were publicly protesting in their workplaces.

Naturalizing images and narratives were not static, however; they altered in response to various contextual factors, including the growing popularity of Progressive reformism and an increasing presence of upper-class women in the suffrage movement. Writers warned of the "chaos" and "cataclysmal confusion" that would result from women's increased political involvement, and alternately celebrated women's moral influence in politics. Chapter 1 charts these conflicting narratives and advances a theory as to when and why more liberating or oppressive stories and images were included. Ultimately, the *Atlantic Monthly*'s portrayals of gender and work relations were structured within a limited frame and constrained by a tone of propriety, which emphasized self-control, stability, and adherence to dominant norms and behaviors of the time period. Propriety is tied to decorum, which Hariman describes as a "code of etiquette" that regulated the political experiences of those under its control (1992, 155). In the *Atlantic*, propriety necessitated the exclusion of wage-earning women's perspectives and thus did not allow for a deeper critique of a system that shaped the lives of women of different classes in quite different ways.

Accommodation Through Universalization.   *McClure's*, the focus of Chapter 2, was arguably the best known muckraking magazine of the Progressive period and was well received by the middle classes. In contrast to the more reserved *Atlantic Monthly*, *McClure's* did not hold back in exploring controversial issues of the day, including political corruption, factory exploitation, and the need for adequate social support for the growing population. Given its oftentimes sympathetic portrayals of the needs and concerns of subordinate groups, *McClure's* represents an interesting text to explore the complexities surrounding popular culture and its role in providing readers with liberating images, narratives, and viewpoints. This chapter demonstrates how *McClure's* employed a rhetoric of *universalization:* this frame homogenizes class differences, assumes an acceptance of certain beliefs and values, and holds up pursuit of certain ideals—such as positive attitude, good character, and kind spirit—as that which could improve workers' lives. Universalization gains rhetorical consensus by focusing on values and ideals that appear to transcend the material and thus constitute a common humanity. It proved effective for muckraking magazines, some of the earliest mass media outlets to address the difficulties faced by disenfranchised groups.

Within this frame, articles in *McClure's* detailed women's struggles in the laundry and shirtwaist factories of New York City, advocated women's suffrage, and even supported more controversial issues such as birth control and divorce. To convey working-class hardships, *McClure's* relied on metonymic images or biographical pieces that focused on a few "representative" workers. This chapter explores the use of metonymy as a trope for universalization, noting how this rhetorical strategy created reader identification by focusing on seemingly transcendent values and morals. But the use of metonymy was at the expense of a critique of the conditions that necessarily shaped and limited one's abilities to live a fulfilling life. As in the passage from *McClure's* story about the Uprising of 30,000 excerpted at the beginning of this Introduction, the actions of and the resources available to individuals were described with no contextualization of a larger economic system that affected people's behaviors in identifiable patterns of discrimination. In short, *McClure's* rhetoric of universalization allowed the magazine to address work and gender relations while remaining silent on the differences and conflicts upon which these relations rest.

Realignment Through Domestication.   Although they had little money for leisure activities, the working classes around the early 1900s enjoyed cheap papers and mail-order magazines. Chapter 3 is a study of articles, advice columns, and advertisements found in three popular mail-order magazines, *Comfort*, *Home Life*, and *The People's Home Journal*. Working-class experiences and concerns such as limited budgets, tenement living, and factory life were covered in these magazines, yet were controlled through a frame of *domestication*. The domestication frame personalized problems and solutions that were necessarily tied to (and originated within) public institutions and practices such as the factory system, two-party politics, and immigration policies. The rhetoric of domestication can be studied as a response to working-class difficulties and dissent, issues that were widely discussed by reformers, writers, politicians, and businessmen throughout these years. Yet at a time when tens of thousands of women and men were demonstrating their solidarity in the streets, these magazines exhorted readers to turn inward—to home and inner self—in order to cope within their present economic and political environment. In particular, though images of Womanhood were multi-faceted—female characters were clever, strong, or independent-minded—the magazines were significantly silent on wage-earning women's protests. This chapter explores the rhetorical significance of these silences as they related to the magazines' framings and the experiences of readers outside of the magazines' pages.

Resistance Through Collectivization. While gender relations and women's roles in industrial capitalism were being addressed throughout the popular media, working-class as well as middle- and upper-class women were making their own arguments for political and economic change. Chapter 4 examines the rhetoric of the Women's Trade Union League and the Industrial Workers of the World as well as speeches, diaries, and letters of wage earners and asks: How do these activists create their own voices amidst the popular texts that framed their experiences and at times asserted that they spoke on these women's behalf? Carefully identifying class differences among the arguments of activists, this chapter demonstrates how these women variously employed a rhetoric of *collectivization* in their struggles for women's equality. In particular, this chapter highlights the voices of wage earners such as Leonora O'Reilly and Rose Schneiderman and the ways that they emphasized class conflict and created a collective identity based on common class-based experiences.

O'Reilly and Schneiderman were two of the many young girls who worked fifty-six to sixty hours a week in factories, some of whom gave detailed testimonies to middle- and upper-class reformers. They described their work conditions in vivid detail, which initiated a critique of the factory system and their place within it and in the process built up their confidence in speaking in their own behalf for equality. The testimonies explored in this chapter are just one form of cross-class organizing that provide a way to analyze the impact of class position on persuasive style and tactics. Equally important, this chapter examines the persuasive force of walkouts and strikes in which tens of thousands of women participated and which played a crucial role in winning fair wages and shorter work hours. Examining both rhetoric and physical confrontation sheds light on the ways that female activists subverted popular portrayals and engaged a laboring agency in attempts to alter objective working conditions that constrained their lives.

Rethinking What's "New" in the "Postmodern Age"

Chapter 5 more pointedly makes a case for important material and discursive similarities between industrial and "late" capitalism. Recent trends in cultural, sociological, philosophical, and rhetorical scholarship have argued that a postmodern era characterized by post-Fordist production, new media technologies, and social fragmentation require that we develop "new theories and conceptions" and new "values and politics to overcome the deficiencies of modern discourses and practices" (Best and Kellner 1991, 30). *Protest and Popular Culture* seeks to illustrate important continuities between past and present hegemonic strategies in the face of changes in communication technologies. In addition, it encourages attention to the ways that subaltern groups engage themselves as laborers both rhetorically and physically in order to resist popular ideologies and economic conditions that perpetuate social divisions.

The concluding chapter draws two important lessons from the previous chapters' historical analyses. First, we can learn much about contemporary media strategies that accommodate voices of dissent by turning to some of the earliest attempts on the part of mass media outlets to neutralize challenges to the status quo. Popular magazines of the early 1900s laid the groundwork for mass media strategies that can speak to an audience's needs and concerns while absorbing threats to the prevailing system. The strategies of naturalization, universalization, and domestication persist through their very ability to respond to changes in the historical context while maintaining a worldview that leaves social disparities unchallenged. We may even view new media technologies and contemporary postmodern discourses as playing into the hands of, or exacerbating, hegemonic strategies that continue to naturalize, universalize, and domesticate in an era increasingly marked by a sense of ahistoricity, hypermediation, and fragmentation.

Parallels to the *Atlantic Monthly's* frame of naturalization can be found in recent magazine advertisements and Hollywood movies that balance tensions between the traditional True Woman and the new Tough Girl. In an effort to appeal to readers and to boost advertising revenues, women's magazines such as *Good Housekeeping* have promoted the image of the "New Traditionalist," a twenty-first-century True Woman (Darnovsky 1991/92). Echoing the sentiments of a 1911 *Atlantic Monthly* article that lamented the disappearance of the "old fashioned lady . . . dauntless and sweet . . . witty but tender" (Comer 1911, 722), the early–1990s "New Traditionalist" campaign describes a "contemporary woman who finds her fulfillment in traditional values that were considered 'old-fashioned' just a few years ago" (Darnovsky 1991/92, 81).

Contemporary media outlets also rely heavily on the framework of universalization, which muckraking magazines had used so effectively. Television shows, magazine advertisements, and popular movies provide space for voices of dissent through portrayals that point to the power of values and ideals that enable individuals to transcend material disparities. Relegating social oppression and resistance to the realm of the metaphysical leaves material structures and systems unnamed and unscathed. The basic rhetorical vehicle for universalization remains the Horatio Alger myth; it can also be seen in popular discourses on the lives of women such as Oprah Winfrey (Cloud 1996) and Billie Holiday (Paul and Kauffman 1995). Universalization also continues to have a hand in contemporary portrayals of feminism, which are most often aligned with liberal feminism, a perspective that emphasizes freedom of choice and autonomy and downplays material structures that constrain and delimit options and opportunities (Dow 1996). The intensification of cultural commodification since the early 1900s further fuels universalization, as the pervasive logic emphasizes unlimited choice in the marketplace and equates freedom with consumption.

As some of the few media outlets targeting a working-class audience, *Comfort, Home Life,* and *The People's Home Journal* provide a window into the ways that controversial issues are presented (or silenced) to audiences who have the most to gain from radical social transformation. The strategy of domestication—which redirects pain and anger away from social structures and onto personal spaces—continues to provide a persuasive method for addressing social disparities in the media and in public affairs. Domestication has arguably made great strides in the late twentieth century with the predominance of television (an intimate medium by nature) and the persuasiveness of therapeutic discourses that came to the surface in response to unrest in the 1960s and '70s (Cloud 1998a). As corporate "downsizing," plant shutdowns, and layoffs become a regular part of the economic landscape, domestication, through discourses that personalize social problems and atomize possible solutions, undermines the need for collective confrontation. The popularity of the home-improvement guru Martha Stewart—touted as "America's greatest cultural influence since Thomas Jefferson" (Cheng 1997)—and the continued prevalence of self-help and pop psychology discourses points to the continued persuasiveness of domestication.

The second insight to be gained from a historical analysis of protest and popular rhetorics concerns the continued relevance of a historical materialist understanding of social relations and transformation. This understanding maintains the importance of collective, labor-based struggles, which not only provide an alternative voice to popular hegemonic strategies but also represent a challenge to social structures that can have material (extra-discursive) effects. Clarke reminds us that a traditional Marxist analysis does not assume a static or monolithic perspective toward the economy and culture but rather has always conceptualized capitalism as "relational, processual and problematic" (1991, 49). Amidst postmodern musings and obfuscations, some scholars continue to point out that although the nature of capitalist production has indeed changed (e.g., deindustrialization and increases in high-tech and service jobs; "flexible" labor), the nature of workplace relations is still grounded in the exploitation of labor for profit (Ebert 1996; Harvey 1989; Wood 1986). Still, one need not rely on scholarly arguments debating the shape of capitalism, but can turn to "real-world" examples of workplace experiences in the 1990s.

At the time of this writing, a "wave of corporate mergers" is occurring, with new mergers proposed on a near daily basis. Eleven of the largest mergers in history were announced or completed between July 1998 and November 1999. Nineteen ninety-nine alone saw $3.4 trillion in mergers and acquisitions (Knox 2000, C10). On January 10, 2000, America Online announced its plan to buy Time Warner for an estimated $165 billion. And just two weeks later, word had it that Time Warner was working on a deal to merge with the British music company EMI Group. In one day alone, November 23, 1998, ten mergers were announced, including deals between B. F. Goodrich and Coltec, Deutsche Bank AG and Bankers Trust Corp, and America Online Inc. and Netscape Communications Inc. (Glanton 1998, G2).

As a direct result of merger maneuvering, thousands of white- and blue collar workers will lose their jobs while corporate executives will continue to reap 115 times what the average employee is paid. Perhaps the most disquieting merger is that of Mobil Oil and Exxon Corp., which represents an effective re-merging of John D. Rockefeller's Standard Oil, a monopoly that was broken up in the early 1900s. In late 1998, rumors of the alleged merger sent Mobil and Exxon stocks rising, while the picture remained bleak for the estimated 20,000 workers analysts predict will be laid off (Quinones 1998, D7).

In the northeastern United States, where steel, auto, garment, and other industries are historically rooted, layoffs, hiring freezes, and "downsizing" affecting both white- and blue-collar workers have become a staple of the contemporary economic landscape. For example, in 1998–99 in Ohio alone the following closures occurred or were announced: British Petroleum announced the closure of a Cleveland research unit, costing the Warrensville Heights area 230 jobs; Uniroyal Chemical Co. announced it would close its Painesville Township, Ohio, plant in May 1999, idling 125 workers; Geon Company announced it would purchase Synergistic Industries, resulting in the closing of two Synergistics plants in Ontario and Texas and eliminating 250 jobs; Camelot Music Holdings, Rubbermaid Inc., Caliber System Inc., and Revco D.S. Inc. all moved from the Northeast Ohio area, leaving 2,500 white-collar workers jobless; Northeast Ohio–based Lubrizol announced it would cut 250 jobs by the end of March 1999; and the steel manufacturer Timken Co. laid off 224 workers in Canton, Ohio.

Economic changes and trends exemplify capitalism's dynamic nature, the system's tendencies or abilities to overcome "blockages" that interrupt the capitalist process.[9] In short, corporate mergers, NAFTA, "flexible" labor processes, and technology-based manufacturing and distribution systems are not manifestations of a fundamental break from the traditional capitalist mode, but rather represent adaptations that allow the continued accumulation of surplus value off the backs of workers. The words of Leonora O'Reilly, an outspoken labor activist of the early 1900s, are strikingly appropriate in today's context. O'Reilly described industrial "efficiency" [then: scientific management; now: corporate mergers] as "slick means of getting the best of Organized Labor which while they increase profits for the share holders, give the poor wage dupe a crumb of the loaf he has made for the army of loafers" (1915, 35).

The workplace environment and corporate activities just described are pertinent to this project as they too contribute to the broader argument of this book; namely, that there are important material and linguistic similarities between the early twentieth century and today. Although this project is about correspondence in persuasive popular and vernacular strategies across time, these discourses cannot be divorced from the material context and its influence on the production, interpretation, and struggle against hegemonic ideologies. Despite changes in the contours of communication and capitalism—changes brought about in part by evolving communication technologies—the following analysis uncovers strikingly similar persuasive strategies used to respond to challenges to the status quo.

As a case study in continuities across time, *Protest and Popular Culture* draws on the past as a rich source that can illuminate the ways that hegemonic ideologies and strategies for resistance interact in struggles for social justice. It highlights the ways that oppressed groups continue to struggle against popular ideologies by seizing upon the contradictions within them. And not least important, this project, drawing on past experiences and struggles of heroic men and women, returns attention to the ways subordinate groups have struggled against oppressive living conditions through confrontational rhetorics that upend popular hegemonic discourses and through extra-discursive actions such as halting machinery or walking out of the factory en masse that often speak louder than words.

Notes

1. The following is a partial list of books documenting women's public and reform activities roughly from the mid-1800s to the early 1900s: Bordin 1981; Buhle 1981; Campbell 1989; DuBois 1978; Epstein 1981; Flexner 1959; Foner 1979, 1980; Kessler-Harris 1981; Matthaei 1982; Matthews 1992; Ryan 1990.

2. See Dye 1980, 1975a, 1975b; Payne 1988; Foner 1979, 290–373; and Jacoby 1975.

3. This observation is not intended to imply optimism regarding the media's relationship to women and women's concerns. I find convincing, and remain aligned with, arguments that emphasize the quite paltry gains made by women in terms of media representation. See Ferguson (1990) for an extensive account of studies of media representations of women. As Ferguson points out, studies quite consistently conclude that "women continue to be outnumbered, continue to be cast in supportive roles, and continue to have family and romance as their major objectives, even when their professions are salient" (218).

4. Lee Blake Sebastian, the producer of the MTV special "A She Thing Weekend," asserted that he "didn't want to create the impression that a feminist is dour and without sex" (Sajbel 1995, 6).

5. This approach to communication and cultural studies is elaborated in the book, *New Times: The Changing Face of Politics in the 1990s* (Hall and Jacques 1989). As the editors explain, "The 'New Times' argument is that the world has changed . . . [that] advanced capitalist societies are increasingly characterized by diversity, differentiation and fragmentation . . . " (11). Further, "the ambition of the 'New Times' project is . . . to unravel the emergent postmodern culture, to understand the new identities and political subjects in society . . . [and] to provide the parameters for a new politics of the Left" (15).

6. See Coontz 1992 for analysis of the ways that popular and political discourses sentimentalized and commercialized the family and prescribed for women the roles of caretaker, homemaker, and consumer.

7. As Campbell notes, the mere act of speaking publicly was a radical move for females during this time period because it challenged cultural norms dictating the domestic and submissive woman (1973, 78). Public speaking is neither domestic nor submissive.

8. The definition of class adhered to throughout this project will be addressed in the subsequent chapters. In short, this project takes a Marxist perspective that views class in terms of one's position in relation to the means of production.

9. Clarke uses the term "blockages" to explain capitalism's dynamic and processual nature (1991). Clarke explains that Marx viewed the capitalist mode of production as "messy and complicated," a process that includes "gaps, interruptions, blockages, tensions and contradictions, which need to be overcome before the circuit can be completed" (48).

1

Propriety in a Period of Upheaval

Women of color and poor women have always worked outside the home. Yet only since the 1970s have magazines, television shows, and popular films addressed the problems and concerns facing women who juggle work and motherhood. In her study of portrayals of women in Holly-wood movies, Kaplan notes that a "concern discourse" arose surrounding the impact of women's work on child rearing only when white women were beginning to assume careers of their own outside the home (1994). She explains, "Underlying all these films about white mothers and chil-dren is anxiety in relation to white women and cultural changes in sex, family, and work spheres that are emerging in tandem with changes in the technological, economic, and industrial spheres" (258). Throughout the 1980s and into the 1990s, cultural narratives reinventing the Domestic Woman have arisen as a way to talk about social anxieties surrounding women and work. Within this tightly prescribed image, women are "nat-urally" inclined to choose motherhood over a career (material needs are taken care of), and they find sole fulfillment in motherhood (desires for accomplishment or fulfillment outside the home are not present).

A similar phenomenon dominated the pages of women's magazines in the 1970s and 1980s. In the late 1970s, as approximately 45 percent of women with pre-school-aged children were part of the labor force, jour-nals such as *Good Housekeeping* and *McCall's* introduced the "modern Madonna"—a career woman in her mid-thirties who, after giving birth to her first child, chose home and motherhood over work (Keller 1994, 97). And into the 1990s, a "New Traditionalist" discourse emerged depicting a contemporary version of the early twentieth century's "New Woman" (Hennessy 1993; see also Darnovsky 1991/92). Aimed at potential maga-zine advertisers, New Traditionalist discourses "make sense of woman primarily as mother," and "invite their readers to equate 'good house-keeping' with woman's work at a time when housekeeping as a woman's domain . . . is being challenged" (Hennessy 107).

In short, a cult of domesticity that prevailed in the early 1900s lauding women's natural mothering abilities is not absent from contemporary discourses. Albeit in different form, this rhetoric reemerges during periods of great economic and political change as a response to the historically specific needs of the economic and political spheres. We may view such discourses as a reinstallment of propriety and control over women's bodies when the reality beyond the representation belies the gentilities of Womanhood. Within the present-day context of global capitalism, in which women and girls continue to be exploited the world over as cheap labor—whether in Nike plants in Indonesia, or the maquiladoras in Mexico, or the garment sweatshops of New York City—an understanding of the *Atlantic Monthly*'s naturalizing rhetoric provides a grounding for explorations of contemporary constructions of "natural" motherhood.

Justifying the Status Quo:
The Rhetoric of Naturalization in the *Atlantic Monthly*

In her examination of popular and religious texts of the mid-nineteenth century, Welter uncovered the origins of a rhetoric of natural womanhood that she called the "cult of True Womanhood." The late 1800s and early 1900s marked a period of remarkable social, political, and economic change. Examining popular texts during these years opens the way to understanding how rhetorics of naturalization operated to maintain a sense of propriety during periods of change and upheaval. How did images of True Womanhood respond to women's entrance into the labor force and widespread participation in strikes and suffrage parades at the turn of the century? More broadly, how does a rhetoric of naturalization reinforce or bend in response to the socioeconomic context in which it is embedded?

One magazine in particular was renowned in the early 1900s for its genteel presentations of life and culture. In describing the venerable tradition surrounding the *Atlantic Monthly*, the magazine historian Luther Mott proclaims, "[T]he *Atlantic* may be said to have enjoyed a perpetual state of literary grace, so that for a large section of the American public, whatever the *Atlantic* printed was literature" (1938, 2:494). Mott's statement hints at the original intent, tone, and underpinnings of the *Atlantic,* which was founded as a literary magazine geared toward the tastes of the New England upper classes.

Between 1894 and 1917 the magazine contained fiction and nonfiction articles that focused primarily on timeless issues—"great writers" and "great artists." However, between 1902 and 1917, social and political problems received increased attention, although interspersed between articles centering on art, literature, and "high" culture.[1] This chapter explores how the *Atlantic Monthly* approached and presented potentially controversial, complex, or otherwise confrontational topics through a rhetoric of naturalization. Naturalizing ideologies "render their beliefs . . . self-evident"; they encourage readers to "identify them with the 'common sense' of a society so that nobody could imagine how they might ever be different" (Eagleton 1991, 58). The rhetorical frame of naturalization allowed magazines to address controversial issues of the day while prescribing the bounds of social change and providing a filter through which these issues could be controlled. More specifically, through naturalization, existing social and workplace relations and systems were framed as being inevitable and therefore immutable—like nature itself. Stories surrounding labor and women's suffrage were bound by the values of propriety and self-control; they were rhetorically tethered by an acquiescence to the "natural" order of social relations and conditions.

To understand the *Atlantic*'s rhetorical framings one must consider the magazine's target audience as well as the writers, editors, and financial concerns connected to the enterprise. The *Atlantic Monthly* targeted an upper-class, educated readership—individuals who by and large benefited from justifications of the status quo. I use the term "upper-class" to refer to a group who occupies a particular position vis-à-vis the means of production. The concept of class is a contested one, with scholars disagreeing on how class should be defined or on what it should be based. For example, a Marxist view defines class as one's relation to the means of production, whereas a Weberian approach sees class in terms of one's "life chances" or "possession of goods and opportunities for income."[2] In this project, the "upper classes" refers to those who own the means of production and thus benefit from the labor power of others.

I do not argue that the *Atlantic* was read exclusively by the upper classes. However, through its content, tone, and style—its rhetorical frame—the magazine constructed and presented itself as a magazine that was "a cut above the rest." Readers who enjoyed the *Atlantic* were constituted by the magazine as occupying the same "class" the magazine claimed for itself; that is, through a tone of cultivation and prestige, the *Atlantic Monthly* rhetorically created the persona of the refined reader.[3] It provided a utopian vision of cultural distinction in which struggle was replaced by social refinement as the solution to society's ills.

The "working class," which is the subject of Chapter 3, consists of those who must sell their labor power in order to survive. In industrial capitalism, factory workers and other wage earners produced surplus value, which translated into profit for the upper classes. The concept "middle class"—perhaps the most ambiguous concept within the class debate—will be further elaborated in Chapter 2. Pertinent to this study is the emergence, in the early 1900s, of a "new middle class" consisting of managers, office workers, administrators, and teachers, who can be described as managing or facilitating production through the organization and exchange of symbols (Deacon 1989). It was, by and large, members of the middle class who were the writers and editors of popular magazines such as the *Atlantic Monthly*. In order to maintain substantial circulation and stay in business, these writers promoted the values and worldviews of their *readership*—in this case, the upper classes.[4]

This chapter examines a popular magazine that targeted an audience made up largely of individuals from the upper classes who had an interest in perpetuating industrialization and wage labor, and whose privileged economic and political position was most threatened by the mass labor uprisings, unionization, and women's increased involvement in the public realm. In particular, separate spheres for the sexes and the development of the private family were important for the successful perpetuation of industrial capitalism and, likewise, the maintenance of class privilege. Through an ideology of domesticity, women were defined exclusively as mothers and caregivers, thus ensuring the reproduction and maintenance of workers for continued production at no cost to the system. Women's challenges to the public/private split posed a threat particularly to the upper classes, who most clearly benefited from the sexual division of labor. Cultural artifacts such as the *Atlantic Monthly* responded to such protests in part through a rhetoric of naturalization, which posed issues surrounding labor and gender in terms of dichotomous alternatives—order versus chaos, reason versus irrationality. This approach simultaneously discredited arguments for change and defended current conditions as the natural, and thus only, choice.

The magazine's political economy—the editors, publishers, and the *Atlantic*'s economic history—also influenced the content of the magazine. Before we critically examine the fiction and nonfiction stories in the *Atlantic*, it is crucial to understand how central figures shaped and directed the magazine that "stood for culture."[5]

The Magazine that "Stood for Culture"

In 1857 Moses Dresser Phillips, a principal in a Boston publishing firm, Phillips, Sampson & Company, founded the *Atlantic Monthly* with the help of the American writers Ralph Waldo Emerson and Henry Wadsworth Longfellow. The magazine started as a literary endeavor presenting articles, stories, and poetry by well-known American literary figures.

Although the *Atlantic* referred to itself as a "Magazine of Literature, Science, Art, and Politics," through the 1870s it largely ignored politics and maintained a narrow emphasis on literary works. The magazine enjoyed a prominent reputation, and Mott points out that such a distinction was perhaps its downfall as it appealed to such a marginal and elite group of readers. Even through most of the 1890s, in the midst of great social change and upheaval, the *Atlantic* "continued its genteel way, parochial and academic, its circulation dwindling, its profits negligible" (Peterson 1956, 355). By 1898, the *Atlantic*'s circulation fell to an all-time low of about 7,000 (Mott 1957, 4:44).

At this time Walter Hines Page took over the *Atlantic* as editor, a post he held from 1898 to 1899. Page was a successful businessman and journalist who was known for his aggressive editing practices (see Rusnak 1982). Under Page's leadership, the *Atlantic* began to dabble in social and political issues. Yet the concerns addressed were still decidedly upper class. For example, despite the fact that women were active as suffragists and participated in labor uprisings in the mid–1890s, in the *Atlantic* women's concerns seemed to center on social clubs and luncheons.

After Page's brief tenure, in 1899, Bliss Perry, a professor at Princeton, took over. He continued the *Atlantic*'s shift toward more timely issues, in part as a response to growing competition from the "ten-cent monthlies," which focused on contemporary issues and day-to-day affairs. Circulation slowly began to rise. In 1909, Ellery Sedgwick purchased the magazine from the book-publishing company Houghton Mifflin, formed the *Atlantic Monthly* Publishing Company, and assumed the editor's position. At that point the content of the *Atlantic* substantially changed and the stability of the magazine was secured. Sedgwick's previous experiences came from middle-class magazines such as *McClure's* and *American Magazine* and he brought the muckraking practices that were common in these magazines to the pages of the *Atlantic*. Between 1909 and 1920, the *Atlantic* regularly contained articles on contemporary social problems and directly addressed issues such as unionism, socialism, specific labor strikes, and women's influence in the public sphere. By expanding the magazine's content, the *Atlantic* broadened its appeal, thus boosting circulation and ensuring its future success.

Peterson points out that Sedgwick "relied for manuscripts mainly on new writers and on authorities in various fields who were drawn to the *Atlantic* by its prestige, not by its rates of payment, which were low" (1956, 356). Most writers did not rely on their contributions to the *Atlantic* to make a living. Rather, they wanted to benefit from the magazine's reputation. Thus, although the *Atlantic*'s content changed with this editorial shift, its distinct tone did not. The magazine strove to uphold its prestigious reputation by maintaining a distinctly bourgeois tone in presenting timely issues. So, for example, in discussing unionism or women's suffrage, writers maintained an aloof stance and presented stories with an air of restraint and self-control.

More specifically, the work of the *Atlantic*'s editors and writers revealed a naturalizing frame in which systems, institutions, and relations were presented as static, immutable—in short, always-existent like nature itself. The *Atlantic*'s distinct tone and ideological bent made good business sense to the editors and publishers, who strove to appeal to their target audience. Moreover, the worldviews and values inherent in a rhetoric of naturalization played into the genteel bourgeois reading experience prevalent during these years.

Naturalization and the Bourgeois Reading Experience

Naturalization is not a static or otherwise monolithic framing device organizing gender and work relations in a straightforward manner. Rather, as the surrounding economic and political contexts changed over the period, the *Atlantic*'s framings of labor and women's struggles responded to and were shaped by these events. In the *Atlantic Monthly*, issues surrounding labor and women's struggles were presented through the frame of naturalization, which portrayed historical relations and conditions as permanent and enduring. Constantly changing and evolving historical events, institutions, and relations were made to appear timeless and inevitable like nature itself.

In his book *Mythologies*, Roland Barthes explains the naturalizing effect of myths. Barthes refers to myths as "innocent speech," in that, as sign systems, they do not "hide" or "flaunt" meaning (1957, 131, 129). Instead, myths "distort" meaning by "transform[ing] history into nature" (129). Through naturalization, the material motivations behind certain discourses (for example, the ideology of domesticity; an ideology of a natural social order) are eclipsed by *justifications* for the rhetorics. This was a particularly effective ideological strategy for the upper classes because it transformed material interests into inalterable (hence innocent—"I can't do anything about it") reasons. In the *Atlantic Monthly*, historically constructed systems and institutions that privileged certain groups over others were naturalized through a rhetoric that provides justifications for their immutable existence. This rhetorical strategy was further reinforced by an authorial persona that emphasized reason and assured the audience that "just the facts" would be presented.

The ideological strategy of naturalization coincided with the concept of the late-Victorian "gentle reader" and various bourgeois values that prevailed around the early 1900s. The gentle reader was above all a *genteel* reader—detached, calm, and reasonable. For middle- and upper-class individuals of the mid- to late 1800s, the reading experience engendered this type of reader and connected her or him to a specific cultural tradition whose values supported the status quo.[6] In short, reading was a lesson in cultivation. Further, reading served as an escape for members of the upper classes from the enormous political and economic unrest that threatened to disrupt a system that worked to their benefit. Schneirov states that "[l]ike the middle-class home, reading was both a haven and a moral nursery" (1994, 51).

Through its naturalizing strategy and its emphasis on reason and propriety, the *Atlantic* created a genteel reading experience and constructed a world of order, permanence, and self-control. On occasion, the voices of Progressive Era reformers addressing themselves to social ills stemming from industrial capitalism run amok reached the pages of the *Atlantic*. More often, however, the magazine conveyed growing upper-class fears of social chaos and class rebellion. Increasingly throughout the teens, writers echoed the beliefs of well-known scientists, psychologists, and theorists such as Walter Lippmann and Gustave Le Bon, who viewed the social sciences as a viable avenue for establishing social control. It was believed that "social engineers, social scientists, armed with their emerging expertise, would provide the modern state with a foundation upon which a new stability might be realized" (Ewen 1996, 64).

Also influential during these years was a growing view of the media's role in crafting "public opinion" (Ewen 1996, 70–73). In contrast to the "mob" or "crowd," the "public . . . seemed more receptive to ideas, to rationalization, to the allure of factual proof." The "public" was an "audience of readers," they were "spectators" who were "subject to the influences of editorial control" (Ewen 1996, 73). Motivated by a desire to craft the calm and deliberating "public," *Atlantic* writers relied on naturalization, a frame that emphasized the immutability of facts and upheld empirical inquiry as a method for reestablishing social order. Naturalization provided a vehicle through which *Atlantic* writers could craft and direct a very specific "public," one that agreed with norms and values supporting stability, i.e., the status quo. Even into the teens, when the *Atlantic* delved into more controversial social issues, propriety and decorum were the framing tones which bound the limits of what could be communicated and sustained the overarching frame of naturalization. Communicating to the refined reader required a reconciliation between gentility and reality outside the pages of the magazine.

During the period of this study, naturalizing framings in the *Atlantic* responded to controversy surrounding labor-versus-capital disputes and women's struggles for equality by diffusing the issues in one of two ways. Magazine articles often associated change with chaos and irrationality, thus presenting it as an undesirable alternative to stability. In other articles, change was equated with the unnatural, and thus as impossible to attain in contrast to the status quo. The emphases were slightly different but the intended effects were the same, namely, to justify the status quo and place it beyond critique. Other articles employed naturalization to support social change. By framing new gender or work relations as a natural part of human evolution, controversial issues were broached in the calm and reassuring tone befitting the genteel character of the magazine.

The naturalization frame was not monolithic, however, but gave way to events outside the magazine's pages. As the first decade of the twentieth century progressed, support for Progressive Era reform challenged the inevitability of the status quo and made its way into the *Atlantic*. During these years, the *Atlantic*'s decorous identity was more ambivalent. At times the magazine sounded less like a haven of moral repose and more akin to the muckraking magazines of the early 1900s, which exposed political and corporate graft.

Nonetheless, naturalization remained the magazine's overarching ideological frame and remained a presence in the magazine's pages throughout the teens. A 1908 article, "Competition," exemplifies the naturalization frame as it was often employed in the service of upper-class privilege. The author defended the existence of competition by applying a capitalist logic to certain aspects of nature: "When animal life began, the very amoebas, the lucky ones and lively ones and wise ones, floated into the best places, and kept the unlucky ones and lazy ones and stupid ones out. When tadpoles and fish were evolved . . . [they] kept up the game, and made it livelier, perhaps, than ever before or since, even down to the days of Standard Oil" (Holt, 518). Here as well as throughout the magazine, writers responded to public protests against the system in part by naturalizing competition, commercialism, and other controversial byproducts of industrial capitalism. The exploits of Standard Oil were just as natural (and inevitable) as those of the wise amoebas who won out over the lazy ones.

Similarly, the *Atlantic* relied heavily on the cult of True Womanhood in order to justify women's relegation to the home. In the early 1900s, as women continued their struggle for the vote, *Atlantic* articles appealed to women's and men's supposed innate characteristics and capabilities in order to argue that social chaos would inevitably ensue if women went against the roles for which they were "naturally" suited, i.e., if women received the vote (Abbott 1903; Seawell 1910). This rhetorical strategy persisted well into the twentieth century. As the United States gradually became more involved in World War I, numerous articles appeared encouraging women to stay in the home as mothers. As one author explains, "She is the one who, through the serenity and wisdom of her own nature, is dew and sunshine to growing souls" (Key 1913, 51). As will be seen, such exhortations were an essential element of wartime propaganda, which relied on woman as symbol of the home front, which men and boys were recruited to defend in the name of all things American and capitalist.

The following pages examine the *Atlantic* between 1894 and 1917 for the ways that cultural narratives of naturalization responded to and interacted within a material context that belied the magazine's very premises. At a time when well-to-do women were organizing and agitating for woman suffrage, and tens of thousands of workers—many of them women and girls—were striking for workplace rights, the *Atlantic* privileged the self-controlled, private individual, thus discrediting confrontation and collective action. Further, a calm, detached, allegedly factual presentation diffused anger and emotional involvement. Beginning with the mid–1890s, as women continued to press for the vote and as working-class men and women alike struggled within and rebelled against industrial capitalism, the *Atlantic Monthly* presented a world composed predominantly of popes, Da Vincis, and Dantes.

1894-1895: The *Atlantic Monthly* Evades

The mid–1890s marked a time of substantial upheaval in the history of industrial America. Cities were growing at unprecedented rates, and as industry expanded, class divisions became more prominent. Many among the working class lived in tenements and slums and worked sixty-to-seventy-hour weeks under the worst of conditions. Frequently, entire families worked in order to survive. But workers did not passively accept their position within the hierarchy. Throughout the 1800s, workers challenged systemic inequalities frequently and militantly through mass organizations and strikes. The historian Howard Zinn notes that approximately five hundred strikes took place each year from 1881 to 1885 (1980, 267). Women workers played a central role in these strikes, often demonstrating more militancy and persistence than their male coworkers.

The depression of 1893-1894 hit workers hard and took a toll on union membership. But jobless workers continued to demonstrate, oftentimes having to fight not only hunger but federal troops who were unleashed to quell dissent. In one of the most notorious instances, in Chicago in July 1894, President Cleveland released federal troops on railway workers who were striking against the Pullman Palace Car company. As rocks were thrown by strikers, the state militia, assisted by local police, fired on and beat the strikers with clubs. The *Chicago Times* described the scene: "The ground over which the fight had occurred was like a battlefield. The men shot by the troops and police lay about like logs" (quoted in Zinn 1980, 275). In short, says Zinn, "[T]he eighties and nineties saw bursts of labor insurrection. . . . There were now revolutionary movements influencing labor struggles, the ideas of socialism affecting labor leaders. Radical literature was appearing, speaking of fundamental changes, of new possibilities for living" (1980, 275–276).

Also during this decade, wealthy and working women alike participated in labor and suffrage causes. Foner explains that a renewed interest in union organizing among women spread as new organizations among different occupations emerged (1979, 241). The actions of women in Massachusetts and Wisconsin were representative. In 1893, female silk workers in Newton Upper Falls, Massachusetts, with some assistance from the upper-class feminist Hannah Parker Kimball, won a strike to restore hours and wages. Five years later, wives of strikers of a woodworking mill in Oshkosh, Wisconsin, were arrested and jailed after taunting scabs. By the late 1890s, wealthy and working-class women were working together "to improve the lot of the woman worker and to bring about her enfranchisement" (Foner 1979, 238).

In the midst of this activity, the *Atlantic* remained a haven of relative tranquillity and refinement for its readers. Though the *Atlantic*'s readership surely did not go untouched by these events, the reality they encountered as reflected in the pages of the *Atlantic* was characterized by the likes of prime ministers, early Latin poetry, and the encyclicals of Pope Leo XIII. In short, the magazine revealed what Lears refers to as "evasive banality," a way of seeing the world that "provided both a source of escape from unprecedented conflict and a means of legitimizing continued capitalist development" (Lears 1981, 25). Particularly in the mid- and late 1890s, the *Atlantic* avoided dealing with the reality of social conflict, industrial ills, and women's participation in the public sphere through a rhetoric of naturalization that established boundaries for "acceptable" gender and workplace behaviors.

Evading Women Workers

In the pages of the *Atlantic*, women of all classes displayed the enduring qualities of the True Woman: piety, purity, submissiveness, and domesticity. For example, in "Old Boston Mary," a gypsy woman was described by the author as a "men's woman," i.e., a mannish woman (Flynt 1894). At the same time, however, Old Mary was widely known for the "home" that she had established in her countryside shanty, which she opened to other vagrants—males—for shelter. Her gypsy friends looked upon Mary "as a sort of guardian angel" (321). She cooked and cleaned for her men, bandaged their wounds, and listened intently to their stories. Despite her status as tramp, Mary was still considered the "mistress of [the] house." As the writer explained, "[T]here was something about her which certainly quieted and softened the reckless people she gathered together" (322). The association of traditional feminine qualities with a nontraditional woman, a tramp, made the cult of True Womanhood appear enduring. That is, domesticity was portrayed as a natural quality that was to be found in upper-class women and tramps alike. Furthermore, it was a trait that could be easily expressed, regardless of material means. Without money, Old Mary was still successful at transforming a shanty in the woods into a home of which she was the "mistress."

Not all women were as angelic as Old Mary. Within the pages of the *Atlantic*, if women were not domestic and pure, they were dangerous and out of control. "Philip and His Wife" was a serial appearing in the *Atlantic* from 1894–95 that provides a good example of the contrasting images of women at this time (Deland 1894). Philip's wife, Cecil, was a demanding and cold woman who neglected her children and mistreated her servants. Cecil was beautiful and, most important, she was rich. In fact, it was Philip who was financially dependent on his wife. In this story, the reader was invited to identify with and feel sorry for Philip, the kindhearted husband. The story relayed a subtle message regarding excessive leisure and wealth in the hands of a woman. Cecil's face was described as showing a "peculiar brutality one sees sometimes in refined and cultivated faces which have known nothing but ease: faces which have never shown eagerness, because all their desires are at hand: nor pity, because they have never suffered" (11). In other words, Cecil's beauty and wealth (which has granted her power over her husband) have taken away from her ability to act as a True Woman.

In addition, this story echoes the upper-class fears of "overcivilization" that circulated around the mid–1890s. According to Lears, many members of the bourgeoisie criticized the comfort and leisure of wealthy families as sapping vigor and vitality from this class (1981). Underlying these feelings were fears of working-class unrest, which was out in the open at this time. According to critics of the period, "An overcivilized bourgeoisie was vulnerable to 'race suicide' on the one hand, revolutionary overthrow on the other" (Lears 1981, 28). So even though the working class as a group was, by and large, absent from the *Atlantic Monthly*'s world, "Philip and His Wife" displayed an undercurrent of fear that tacitly acknowledged its existence.

Within the *Atlantic*, domesticity was framed as the most crucial quality of femininity. When a woman stepped outside her role as wife, mother, or home-dweller, she created misfortune for herself or for others. "The Queen of Clubs" (White 1894) relayed this lesson to young female readers at a time when many upper-class women were becoming more involved outside the home.

One of the more acceptable ways for wealthy women to be publicly involved was through the club movement. Beginning in the 1860s, women formed various social and literary organizations that allowed them to escape the confines of the home. The number of clubs grew substantially over the decades and included local community clubs as well as larger organizations such as the New England Women's Club and Sorosis. Sklar notes that by 1900, the General Federation of Women's Clubs comprised 2,675 clubs with a total membership of over 150,000 (1995, 48). The historian Eleanor Flexner points out the importance of women's involvement in the club movement: "By the 1890s these activities would broaden to include the settlement-house movement and the organization of women as consumers with social responsibilities; in the long run they would be a potent force in making the political enfranchisement of women inevitable" (1959, 181).

"The Queen of Clubs" offered the reader a view into the life of a popular single woman who was involved in numerous clubs. Eleanor, the "queen of clubs," was superficial and self-centered. Her gravest transgression, however, was that her busy club involvement blinded her to the affections of a kind gentleman, who nevertheless persisted in winning her hand. The story effectively forewarned upper-class female readers of the dangers that public life (via clubs) may bring: her True Womanhood will be marred and she may wind up a spinster.

Despite the *Atlantic Monthly*'s consistent construction of a world consonant with dominant values, progressive themes emerged from time to time. The critical approach taken in this book does not assume that popular discourses are uniformly hegemonic. Rather, a variety of views may be expressed, but they remain within what Cloud refers to as a "structured meaning system in which instances of multivocality are complementary parts of the system's overall hegemonic design" (1992, 313). "Multivocality" refers to the presence of multiple viewpoints or representations, some of which appear to challenge the dominant ideology of the text. One could argue that in order to be popular with its female readers, the *Atlantic* had at least to give passing attention to the realities of many upper-class women's lives, even if those realities countered the tenets of naturalization.

Outside the pages of the *Atlantic*, well-to-do and middle-class women were, to a degree, challenging gender norms that restricted women's access to the public realm. They were involved not only in clubs but also in the suffrage and temperance movements and various socialist and reform organizations. To justify their actions, these activists "based their political action on the notions of the moral superiority of women and an expansive woman's sphere" (Baker 1994, 91). "Social homemaking," as it has been termed, refers to women's entrance into the public sphere in their roles as mothers and homemakers in an effort to shape the policies and institutions that affected their abilities to make a better home for their families (Matthaei 1982, 173). Despite the limitations of "social homemaking" (Epstein 1981), the public involvement that it engendered allowed women to cultivate a unique women's public culture. Women developed bonds on the basis of their common values and experiences as middle-class women and they formed networks on the basis of their common desire to uplift the public world. These communities represented a "separatist political strategy," also called "female institution building," and "helped sustain women's participation in both social reform and political activism" during the late nineteenth and early twentieth centuries (Freedman 1979, 513, 514).

A year following the well-publicized July 1894 constitutional convention in New York in which upper-class pro- and antisuffragists argued their respective views, an *Atlantic* article echoed the tenets of social homemaking and gave credence to middle- and upper-class women's public-sphere activities. In "A Woman's Luncheon," which appeared in 1895, a conversation took place among wealthy women seated around a lunch table. Their talk loosely reflected the debates taking place between pro- and antisuffragists outside the pages of the *Atlantic*. Teresa, identified as an "ardent believer in and worker for the cause of the New Womanhood," was virtually the lone voice for women's equality. She overtly criticized the artificiality of the cult of True Womanhood as a "very complicated and insincere formula" that has regulated "woman's whole habit of thought and expression" (194).

The article reassured readers, however, that the New Woman is not "one-sided," in other words, self-centered. Teresa explained that women were "raising the general average of truth, cleanliness, and purity day by day" (196). Put differently, the New Woman was still a True Woman; she was simply extending her domestic duties to the larger world we call home. Teresa explained that the New Woman was a result of "social evolution" and that "a great natural force is working through the New Womanhood, and if any of us refuse to acknowledge it, it is because mankind has always refused to acknowledge the miracle which takes place before its eyes" (200, 201). According to this view, women's changing roles were inevitable; they happened naturally, miraculously.

Absent from this view are the experiences of discrimination against women in the abolition movement and the monotonous life of household duties, which were two of the motivating factors in middle- and upper-class women's push for suffrage in the mid- and late 1800s (Flexner 1959, 71–73). Stung by exclusion from full participation in an 1840 World Anti-Slavery Convention in London, Lucretia Mott and Elizabeth Cady Stanton planned the Seneca Falls Convention of 1848, where the Declaration of Sentiments outlined demands for women's social and civil rights. In addition, abuse and abandonment by drunken husbands opened many women's eyes to what Epstein calls "the politics of domesticity" and prompted some to join the temperance fight (1981). In short, it was not mere spontaneity nor the miracles of evolution that spurred women's public-sphere participation, but rather lived experiences of discrimination and abuse. "A Woman's Luncheon" effectively evaded an extra-discursive reality—including political disenfranchisement, abuse, not to mention deplorable work conditions and starvation wages for those who had to work outside the home—faced by women that often gave rise to their public protests.

In the *Atlantic* article, Teresa's critical stance regarding women's assigned position in society was further undermined by the overall flow of the conversation. Discussion of fashion and who married whom was woven in and out of talk about the New Woman. Even Teresa was ambivalent, admitting that a "woman should use all her talents," which included good looks and admirable fashion (198). While dining on croquettes, pâté, and petites timbales, Teresa attempted to convince her wealthy sisters of the virtues of becoming a New Woman. By involving themselves in various causes, Teresa explained, women could discover a higher purpose. She could discover her Self, no less.

Although a break from the traditional Victorian mold, Teresa's sentiments remained within a dominant framework that did not fundamentally disrupt the status quo. Like upper- and middle-class activists of the day, Teresa made women's involvement in the public realm acceptable by associating it with traditional "feminine" attributes and roles. Thus, Teresa's New Woman represented an updated variation of the True Woman. The story of Teresa and her well-to-do friends provided a way for the *Atlantic* to discuss the rudiments of feminism while remaining within the bounds of propriety. The New Woman was still proper and, what was perhaps most important, her concerns were decidedly upper class. She did not broach the topics of factory work or domestic labor—issues that may challenge the stability of industrial capitalism, which was burgeoning during these years and financially underpinned these women's class. The New Woman engaged herself as a moral being in the public sphere, addressing herself to issues "characteristic" of her sex, rather than calling attention to material or class disparities.

Kind women, mean-spirited women, and New Women dotted the pages of the *Atlantic* in the mid–1890s. These images fit into the prevailing cult of True Womanhood circulating widely in popular as well as medical, scientific, and political discourses through the turn of the century. The rhetoric of the True Woman was directly connected to the needs of industrial capitalism. The sexual division of labor prescribed by this ideology shifted responsibility for the care and reproduction of workers onto the family, at whose center stood the wife and mother. Images of women within the *Atlantic* reinforce this rhetoric through portrayals of women who were naturally suited to domesticity and purity.

Since women's labors beyond the hearth were irreconcilable with True Womanhood, working women were virtually unknown in the *Atlantic Monthly* in the mid-1890s. Yet in the world beyond the *Atlantic*, women made up a substantial percentage of the labor force (20 percent by 1900),[7] and they served a very specific purpose within the capitalist system. In particular, women were viewed as an important source of unskilled, cheap labor at a time when skilled jobs (dominated by male workers) were becoming increasing obsolescent as a result of technological advances. In most jobs, women earned less than the government-determined minimum subsistence level and they were more likely to be employed in seasonal trades where layoffs were the norm (Tentler 1979, 17–21).

Though greatly in need of workplace organization, a majority of female workers were not unionized in the mid–1890s (Foner 1979, 266, 267). Yet it was during this decade that the American Federation of Labor (AFL), headed by Samuel Gompers, and its membership of skilled white male workers rose to prominence. Though union membership declined during the depression of 1893–94, the unrest and impoverished circumstances of workers as a class remained a social issue of importance. In the *Atlantic*'s world, however, class as an issue remained largely unacknowledged, as labor issues lurked between stories of kings and literary figures.

Evading the Working Class

In 1893, the labor activist and social democrat Eugene V. Debs formed the American Railway Union. The next year, one of the most well known labor confrontations, the Pullman Strike, halted railway transportation and sparked violence on the part of federal troops in Chicago. Yet the working class was virtually nonexistent in the pages of the *Atlantic Monthly* in the years 1894–95. This absence is remarkable given the significance of wage laborers *as a group* during this time period. Hundreds of thousands of workers belonged to labor organizations and staged numerous strikes throughout the 1880s and 1890s. Further, many of these mass actions took place in the Northeast, where the *Atlantic Monthly* was based. Silence on the part of the *Atlantic Monthly* was itself an ideological response that reinforced the naturalness and immutability of industrial capitalist–labor relations—no need to recognize what is always already before us. What limited coverage of labor that was to be found in the *Atlantic* focused primarily on railway workers.

A few articles that appeared in 1894–95 demonstrated sympathy toward the plight of labor. In the beginning of the article "The Railway

War," printed in 1894, Henry Fletcher noted that "little has been done to insure the just treatment of [railway] employees" (534). And in describing the Pullman strike, he admitted the existence of the powerful combination of the Pullman company, the railroads, the courts, and the police, which conspired against the protesting strikers. Another author openly asserted that the worker had a right to the "whole net value created by his labor" and that it was right for workers to "persist in the more difficult task of directing their own production" (Ludlow 1895, 387, 388).

This type of support for labor organizing is quite remarkable for the time period and the magazine, but the critical edge is in part undermined by rhetorical frames that implied a natural order. The author of "The Railway War" advocated the just treatment of railway workers on grounds having little to do with class solidarity. According to Fletcher, treating workers fairly would prevent the inevitable bloodshed that would ensue if employers continued to play the heavy hand with organized labor. Fletcher established a false dichotomy in which the choices were no strike *or* "violence, bloodshed, and fire" (Fletcher 1894, 537). Such a dichotomy framed strikers as irrational, mindless mobs bent on complete destruction. "Taunts lead to blows; the taste of violence is maddening, like the taste of blood; a riot flames up and runs before the gale of passion" (537). Fletcher discredited collective action by associating it with disorder and exhorted capitalists to grant concessions to workers in order to stave off crises. The article's perspective on mass confrontation as "social chaos" reflected prevailing fears of an out-of-control laboring class (see Ewen 1996).

Throughout the teens, *Atlantic* articles continued to apply norms of propriety (self-control, reason, stability) to situations involving anger, poverty, and dire material circumstances, which required not only discursive but also physical confrontation. Such responses were wholly rhetorical, that is, they were situated discourses motivated by dominant interests. In these examples, "civility and decorum serve as masks for the preservation of injustice . . . [and] become the instrumentalities of power for those who 'have'" (Scott and Smith 1969, 8).

In the *Atlantic*, readers glimpsed the struggles of labor from time to time among the predominance of poetry, book reviews, and treatises. The *Atlantic*'s neglect of labor issues is perhaps not surprising, as it is in keeping with the magazine's general oversight of social and political issues during these years. The absence is significant, however, insofar as it reflects the evasive banality described above. One way to reinforce the status quo is by simply not acknowledging challenges to the system. A later section will demonstrate how the *Atlantic* devoted much more attention to the struggles of the working class in the teens, when organized labor represented a greater threat to the continuation of industrial capitalism as well as to the nation's ability to unify its citizens around the causes of World War I.

1902-1904: The *Atlantic* Acknowledges

Labor unrest continued through the early twentieth century, with women workers at the center of hundreds of strikes and walkouts. The American Federation of Labor (AFL) grew in strength among skilled workers, and at this time two other major labor organizations sprang into existence. In 1903, the Women's Trade Union League (WTUL) was formed in order to assist wage-earning women in organizing themselves and in combating sexism in the workplace. The Industrial Workers of the World (IWW) formed in 1904 with the intent of organizing unskilled workers and immigrants excluded by the AFL.

Depressions in 1894 and again in 1904 hit almost all sectors of society and contributed to a general increase in awareness of the struggles of labor. Also at this time, Progressive Era reformers, largely middle- and upper-class individuals, formed organizations, agencies, and settlement homes designed to confront the shortcomings of the system and ameliorate hardships endured by the poor. Beginning in 1902-1903, the *Atlantic* discussed some of these reform efforts, providing readers information on the activities of individuals of similar class position and a perspective that contrasted with the naturalization framings that continued to assert the permanency of the system.[8] Still, the limitations of these seemingly more transgressive articles must be noted. First, controversy exists over just how broad-minded the Progressive Era was.[9] Kolko (1963), who refers to this era as the "triumph of conservatism," argues that "major economic interests" controlled political regulation rather than the other way around (3). Sklar demonstrates how the Progressive Era "corresponded with the period that constituted the first phase in the corporate reconstruction of American capitalism" (1988, 33). In short, these scholars have pointed out that Progressive Era legislation was more help than hindrance to big business operations. Thus, the *Atlantic*'s reform-minded articles can be viewed as texts that did not rhetorically challenge, but rather preserved, their readers' upper-class privilege by purporting to speak for the welfare of a "general public" while in fact equating those public interests with those of big business.

Further, although the *Atlantic* departed somewhat from its naturalizing frame in various debates on labor, housing, and union activity in this period, discussions of women and even woman suffrage continued to uphold the image of the naturally domestic and moral woman. Despite the remarkable presence of millions of women who organized themselves and led strikes—often with the financial assistance of upper-class men and women—this group was largely absent from the pages of the *Atlantic Monthly*, an absence that continued through the next period. In portrayals of women, the naturally domestic woman remained true to her calling.

Reconciling True Womanhood and Woman Suffrage

Mary Harris Jones was a labor activist who was so well known for her militancy and bravery in fighting for the rights of workers across the country that she became known as Mother Jones. In 1903, at a time when Jones was leading a group of child laborers from Pennsylvania to New York to publicize their plight, the pages of the *Atlantic Monthly* were offering images of women as pure and moral beings who were naturally suited for domestic duties.

The few *Atlantic* articles that acknowledged the issue of women in the workplace were subtly crafted through the frame of naturalization. Jocelyn Lewis, in "An Educated Wage-Earner," related her experience in a factory among other wage-earning women (1903). Throughout the article, Lewis distinguished herself as an "educated" wage earner in contrast to her coworkers, whom she referred to as "units" within "the proletariat," "the multitude," or the "wage-earning masses." The article's tone and word choice created a "second persona" (Black 1970) or implied auditor that embodied the upper-class values of privacy and restraint. Readers were encouraged to identify with social distinction and the propriety and order resulting from class differences rigidly imposed.

Lewis explained that she "needed ready money every week for living expenses" and thus decided to try factory work (387). She began her account with commentary on her shopmates' "rough," "boisterous," and "unmannerly" conversations (387). When workers got together they formed a "mob" in which they were "as destitute of the attributes of individual men, as brainless and heartless and usable as fists and feet" (388). The description of workers as susceptible to mindless mob actions was characteristic of *Atlantic* articles on the subject of workers. *Atlantic* writers often reflected the sentiments of growing numbers of reformers and theorists, who were concerned with the revolt of the "masses" sparked by Enlightenment principles of democracy and played out in the Paris Commune of 1870 (see Ewen 1996, 65, 66). The writings of social psychologists and scientists such as Gustave Le Bon and Gabriel Tarde influenced thinking on the issue and encouraged the application of social-scientific ideas to control of the crowd. In *Atlantic* articles, labor, depicted as an amorphous, unthinking mass, was associated with chaos. The alternative to chaos—order—could be found only through the detached, private individual. The conclusion of "An Educated Wage-Earner" summed up the author's position: the "wage-earning masses . . . ha[ve] reverted to pre-Christian ideas and methods in consequence of the social decree that no sort of personal merit, no degree of intelligence, no acquired culture, no refinement of manners, shall receive social recognition, but only the possession of money or material things that money will buy" (392).

In contrast to this perspective, many wage-earning women viewed their experiences on the shop floor as empowering and supportive. The historian Annelise Orleck explains how working women's political identities were shaped through their interactions with fellow workers, many of them socialists (1995). It was their common experiences of exploitation and their growing consciousness of themselves as a unified group that inspired these women to revolt time after time throughout the first two decades of the twentieth century. Pauline Newman, a socialist and labor agitator who worked in one of the worst garment factories of all, the Triangle Shirtwaist Factory, described the girls' situation this way: "We . . . knew nothing about the economics of . . . industry or for that matter about economics in general. All we knew was the bitter fact that, after working seventy and eighty hours in a seven day week, we did not earn enough to keep body and soul together" (quoted in Orleck 1995, 33–34). Furthermore, workers knew from firsthand experience that confronting bosses as individuals was seldom, if ever, successful. The WTUL expressed this concern in a flyer depicting a young female worker standing before a man, presumably her boss, seated behind a desk. The flier read: "Dealing with the individual. Is this an even Bargain?" ("Dealing with the Individual," n.d.).

Yet "An Educated Wage-Earner" framed worker solidarity as an undesirable, if not unnatural, state of being. The writer relied on individualist values such as refinement and self-control in order to portray labor organizing and solidarity as ineffective, chaotic, and hence, unnatural. Hartz's observations regarding American liberalism demonstrates how the *Atlantic*'s reliance on individualism corresponds to its ideology of naturalization (1955). Since liberal individualism has always been a cornerstone in American culture, the rhetoric surrounding it contains a "matter-of-fact quality" that places it beyond question (7). The *Atlantic* framings that naturalized the system or discredited group action deflected potential criticisms of capitalism, suggesting that human intervention was useless (or dangerous) in the face of a force that, like the weather, is uncontrollable and natural.

The *Atlantic* readily engaged the debate surrounding women's suffrage, in contrast to its stance on the issue of women in the workplace. This makes sense, given the large numbers of upper-class women who were involved in the suffrage movement at this time. Whether pro- or antisuffrage, both points of view were presented in the *Atlantic* within the norms of the cult of True Womanhood, which asserted that women were naturally domestic, submissive, pious, and pure. Thus, writers were drawing on the language of suffragists themselves, who by the early 1900s were relying more heavily on arguments that called up women's moral superiority in order to justify votes for women (Kraditor 1965).

In "Why Women Do Not Wish the Suffrage," written in 1903, Lyman Abbott employed nature metaphors in order to demonstrate that certain historically constructed relations or institutions were inevitable and contributed to a "natural" social order. He likened the family to an acorn in order to demonstrate its necessary role in giving rise to and maintaining a functioning society. "Open an acorn: in it we find the oak in all its parts,—root, trunk, branches. Look into the home: in it we shall find the state, the church, the army, the industrial organization" (Abbott, 289). Abbott went on to explain that sex differences were the basis of familial arrangements and were, by extension, as natural as the acorn. The different functions of the sexes were "essential to the life of the organism," i.e., society.

Arguing against woman suffrage through a frame of naturalization provided a way for Abbott to place opposing viewpoints out of consideration. As he stated, sexual differences "inhere in the temperament; [they are] inbred in the very fibre of the soul" (290). Characteristic of the naturalizing rhetoric found throughout the *Atlantic*, the author justified the status quo by establishing a dichotomy that provided an unsavory alternative to the existing order: "Some masculine women there are; some feminine men there are. These are the monstrosities of Nature . . . grotesque variations from and violations of the natural order. . . . This distinction between the sexes . . . is universal and perpetual. . . . Should society ever forget it, it would forget the most fundamental fact in the social order . . . " (291). Throughout the article, the argument for natural sex differences remained unequivocal, leaving the reader with no choice but to accept the premise or risk transgressing the "instinct of humanity" (291).

Abbott's tranquil vision of the family stands as a popular forerunner to the Cleaver family (*Leave It to Beaver*) of the 1950s and the Huxtables (*The Cosby Show*) of the 1980s. Like the images of the Cleavers and Huxtables, Abbott's depiction stood in stark contrast to the realities faced by families beyond the pages of the *Atlantic*. At the time this article was written, thousands of women could not afford the luxury of remaining "true" to their "natural" domestic role. The wages of immigrant women and girls who labored in mills and factories and of black women who worked in the fields and as domestic servants were often the only source of income in families where the husband died, became disabled, or unemployed (see Matthaei 1982, 245–255).

Even members of Abbott's target audience did not confine themselves to the "law of Nature." Indeed, it was largely middle- and upper-class women who launched the suffrage movement and worked tirelessly for over seventy years in order to win political enfranchisement. Similarly, middle- and upper-class allies alike assisted female wage earners in forming working girls' organizations and union locals to demand safer working conditions and fair pay. Moreover, in the first decades of the twentieth century, middle- and upper-class women themselves entered the paid labor force to supplement their husbands' incomes in order to meet rising standards of living in an increasingly commodified culture. With the development of the department store and the corporate office, middle-class women joined their wage-earning working-class sisters in the labor force, working as clerks, secretaries, and stenographers.

The rhetoric of naturalization was forceful because it presented its case unequivocally, but when applied consistently there was no way for the rhetoric to account for exceptions to the rule. Consequently, *Atlantic* articles employing the naturalization frame were often strained in attempts to acknowledge glaring inconsistencies with the constructed image. This was certainly the case for Abbott, who did not completely ignore the reality impinging on his rhetorical vision. In the last paragraph of his article, Abbott tentatively acknowledged women's labor activities: "Necessity, born of an imperfect industrial system, may drive a few thousand women into battle with Nature in bread-winning vocations . . . but the great body of American women are true to themselves, to the nature God has given them" (296). With an air of gentility, the author reduced the horrors of capitalism to imperfections, thus reinforcing the perception of the stability of the status quo. Furthermore, he downplayed women's influence in the economic sphere—only "a few thousand women" were involved—and framed women's public protests as virtually hopeless—"a battle against Nature." Yet a system that resulted in widespread poverty, disease, and physical disability appeared to many wage earners as more than merely "imperfect." Hundreds of thousands of workers—male and female—expressed their anger at workplace exploitation and demonstrated the success of direct confrontation in their battles not against nature but against the people who controlled their ability to feed and clothe their families.

To fully acknowledge the difficulties faced daily by thousands of poor families living in slums and tenements in large cities across the country represented too great a challenge to the *Atlantic*'s demand for decorum. As a writer, Abbott assumed a voice of propriety, assuring readers of women's natural, and thus perpetual, domesticity. Tied to the code of decorum was a suppression of the body and bodily functions—that realm which humans are always striving to control, yet cannot.[10] Portrayals of the "domestic" woman controlled the female body by simply ignoring its presence in public and work environments. Wage- earning women, striking women, and union women were simply not present in *Atlantic* articles because they represent *laboring bodies*, bodies existing outside the controlled environment of the home.

A materialist view of language provides an incisive explanation of Abbott's narrative as it encourages a contextualization of the discourses under examination. A rhetoric of familialism and the corresponding naturalization of sexual differences arose at a specific time period and justified a specific familial arrangement that in turn enabled the operation of a particular mode of production, industrial capitalism.[11] Popular and political discourses portrayed the family as the source of love and support, where all needs, emotional and material, could and should be met. Further, the rhetoric of True Womanhood represented women as naturally suited to fulfilling these needs. Acceptance of these dominant ideologies relieved the state of the financial costs of providing adequate childcare, healthcare, and other forms of support that ensured the welfare of its citizens. Furthermore, the sentimental cloak that surrounded work within the family mystified this type of labor, making it a moral duty rather than a job that deserved economic compensation like any other form of work.

Abbott's article appeared at a time when women and men (some from the upper classes) were actively challenging this system, through the WTUL, the Consumers' League, and various women's clubs. In his article, Abbott assumed rhetorical agency and in effect "took over" their protesting voices. He implied that he spoke for all women and explained to his audience (which presumably included some upper-class suffragists) "why women do not wish the suffrage." He persuaded by creating a vision of sexual relations that invalidated political challenges and enforced a "natural" order that was, in fact, consonant with the status quo.

In the early 1900s, around the time of Abbott's article, mainstream suffragists and temperance activists were relying on notions of women's "innate" qualities to explain why women *do* wish the suffrage. Characteristic of such arguments was the rhetoric of Frances Willard, leader of the Women's Christian Temperance Union (WCTU), who stated that the group's goal was "to make the whole world more homelike" (Buhle 1981, 65; see Campbell 1989, 121–132).

Though an overarching frame provided the contours for discussion of controversial topics, *Atlantic Monthly* articles at times provided perspectives considered to be quite radical for the period. An article appearing in the magazine in 1902 drew on the sentiments of Willard and other middle-class activists to support the vote for women. Though similarly grounded in the dictates of True Womanhood, "What is the Real Emancipation of Woman?" (Salter) provided a stark contrast to Abbott's article and demonstrated the ideological variability in popular magazines.

Salter began his article establishing woman's "essential humanity" and hence her right to be free from servitude: "That women . . . are coming to realize that they are members of humanity, that they have the essential human rights and duties, that they are not simply an appendage to mankind . . . is one of the most encouraging signs of the times" (Salter, 29). The author advocated "economic independence" for women and favorably cited *Women and Economics,* by Charlotte Perkins Gilman, a well-known socialist and feminist who argued vociferously for women's rights through the first decades of the twentieth century. The amalgam of voices in this article demonstrates the ways that popular and vernacular discourses influenced one another ("vernacular culture" is defined as the values, beliefs, activities, and lifestyles of subordinate groups). Popular writers were influenced by voices of protest outside the pages of magazines, and women of the labor and suffrage movements often embodied popular norms and values as part of their campaigns (see Enstad 1999; Finnegan 1999).

Salter's ideas provided an opening through which *Atlantic* readers could gain a broader perspective on gender roles. Readers ostensibly could seize upon the vision provided in the article and, putting it together with information from other sources, incorporate it into their own arguments for sexual equality. The popular-culture scholar Barry Brummett describes this process as constructing a "mosaic" from discursive "bits" in order to understand social issues (1991). Despite Salter's introduction of a broader perspective, it is still important to consider how his ideas were tempered by tacit assumptions of women's natural attributes. Salter's arguments for women's economic independence framed work as freedom from household drudgery, freedom to do "something worthwhile" outside the home. And though he emphasized the common humanity of the sexes, Salter fell back on True Womanhood in assuring readers of women's contributions to public welfare: "Perhaps her very sympathies, her very innate motherliness, will make her keen to find out . . . a way that will alleviate the sorrows of the world. Ah, if we could join a woman's heart, a woman's faith, a woman's patience, a woman's sweet reasonableness, to the cause of social transformation, what added force . . . that cause might have!" (31).

Examining Salter's article in the broader context of suffrage struggles in the early 1900s points up significant parallels. At the time of Salter's article, though suffragists of all stripes were employing a variety of arguments in order to win the vote, they were turning increasingly to arguments of expediency, based on women's innate characteristics, as opposed to an earlier emphasis on arguments of justice, based on the natural rights of all humans (Kraditor 1965). By 1910, suffragists "were as likely to argue that women deserved the vote *because* of their sex . . .

as to argue that women deserved the vote *despite* their sex" (Cott 1987, 29). Expediency took the form of self-protection arguments, and mainstream suffragists began to include the concerns of wage-earning women, who, it was argued, needed the vote in order to protect themselves in the workplace (Kraditor 1965, 55). As their struggles wore on, however, some suffragists turned to racist and classist arguments in order to make the case for their getting the vote. They argued that giving the vote to white literate women could counteract the influence of the "undesirable part of the electorate"–immigrants, blacks, and workers (Kraditor 1965, 53).

While magazine writers and mainstream suffragists were advocating votes for women based on arguments of expediency, wage-earning women were also advancing arguments for woman suffrage that variously aligned with and diverged from those of their more well-off counterparts. Wage earners often relied on the notion of True Womanhood in order to point up the benefits of granting women the vote. Yet because their own life experiences often belied the credibility of True Womanhood and its inherent assumption of privilege—an implication that all women could afford to remain sheltered from the workaday world—wage-earning women often crafted an argument based more on pragmatics than on woman's purity. Throughout her career as a labor activist, Leonora O'Reilly supported suffrage in varying degrees and often used the suffrage platform to point out fundamental differences in the experiences of working- and middle-class women. O'Reilly was a member of the Equality League of Self-Supporting Women, a group of wage-earning and more well-to-do activists that included among its members Florence Kelley and Charlotte Perkins Gilman (the socialist feminist quoted in Salter's *Atlantic Monthly* article). O'Reilly also headed the Wage Earners' Suffrage League, whose membership was made up solely of working-class women. Though O'Reilly supported woman suffrage, she often spoke of its limitations. In an address given in the early teens,[12] O'Reilly put the matter to her audience this way:

> [T]he working women are asked why they do not join the movement for universal suffrage. . . . Now, when you put that question, they look at you with that look that speaks volumes. . . . They may answer you as yet, Politics do not seem to concern themselves with the industrial conditions. See our brother workers—they vote, and most of the time they but serve as bait to catch the politician['] s office for him. No, there must be something wrong industrially, as well as politically. . . . You see, while politicians are fooling the people, it may be that hunger is teaching them (n.d., "From 1848–1911").

Time and again workers such as O'Reilly emphasized the more pressing need for economic democracy and framed the vote as one tool among others that could assist women in achieving workplace justice.

Wage-earning women were often quick to offer a more realistic assessment of women's work outside the home than middle-class or nonworking women's, thus highlighting the hypocrisies of True Womanhood. For women who labored out of necessity, economic freedom meant the "freedom" to earn slave wages, to work fifty to sixty hours a week, and to be subject to workplace disease and hazards. Rose Schneiderman, a cap maker, explained in a 1915 article, "The Woman Movement and the Working Woman," in *Life and Labor*: "The working woman . . . has always had full liberty to work; indeed, from her is demanded the hardest and most exacting kind of toil. Work to her spells no gateway to freedom."

Early–1900s *Atlantic* articles broached the controversial issue of women's political equality but remained largely silent on the issue of women in the workplace—despite the fact that wage-earning women and girls constituted an increasing percentage of factory and office workers in the early 1900s, and were often supported by well-to-do women through suffrage and labor organizations. The *Atlantic*'s accounts of labor were projected through the frame of naturalization, which relied on the stabilizing effects of decorum and self-control. Images of the wage-earning woman called forth the laboring body—put another way, the domesticated woman out of control. The code of decorum demanded suppression of the body, especially woman's body, which represented irrationality, emotion, and, by association, disruption of the status quo. Labor, in the pages of the *Atlantic*, was a strictly masculine enterprise in the early twentieth century.

Progressive Reform's Challenge to Naturalization

By 1903, industrial capitalism had been hit with challenges on numerous fronts. Political movements such as Edward Bellamy's Nationalism and the Socialist and Populist parties were formed as alternatives to the status quo, and economic slumps and depressions were regular occurrences. Further, technological advances such as the refinement of the sewing machine led to speedups and a general deterioration in workers' conditions (Orleck 1995, 33). For millions of workers during this period, industrial capitalism was not perceived as an "inevitable" system to be left unchallenged. Even before the great women's strike of 1909—the Uprising of 30,000—women workers organized and staged the largest rent strike that New York City had ever seen. The *Atlantic* responded to the increasing labor unrest and Progressive reform spirit by alternating articles that employed a naturalizing frame with others that at least tacitly acknowledged the rights of workers and the need for improved wages and housing. In short, the *Atlantic*'s frame of naturalization began to bend under the weight of substantial upheavals outside the constructed world of propriety.

Articles by prominent reformers and activists such as Vida Scudder, Booker T. Washington, and W. E. B. Du Bois appeared in the *Atlantic* in the early 1900s. Discussions supporting municipal reform and the organization of labor were interspersed between articles such as "Absalom's Wreath" and "Wordsworth's Secret." The appearance of these voices suggests quite a bold move on the part of *Atlantic* editors, who continued to adjust content to the events beyond the magazine's pages. Magazine popularity depends on the ability to "speak to people's experiences," to acknowledge the "real world" as lived by readers day to day—even when that reality is "radical." Yet, as this book seeks to demonstrate, popular rhetorical framings such as naturalization, universalization, and domestication placed limits on what was said about oppression and resistance and provided an oftentimes startling contrast to voices of protest beyond the magazine's pages.

In 1902, a series by a Progressive reformer, Vida Scudder, departed from the *Atlantic*'s naturalization frame and thus serves to illustrate how ideological framings often operated in conjunction with one another. In the *Atlantic*, when naturalization gave way to contextual pressures universalization took up the slack. Characteristic of Progressive Era reformers of the early twentieth century, Scudder framed her *Atlantic* articles with a rhetoric of universalization. As the next chapter elaborates, universalization frames social disparity and transformation in terms of ideals such as morals, values. Similar to naturalization, universalization avoids issues of materiality, —dirty and dangerous factories, disease, tenement housing, scant wages, labor/capital disparities. But whereas naturalization accomplishes this through an emphasis on inevitability (struggle against material institutions is not necessary since the social hierarchy results from natural causes), universalization focuses on ideals (struggle against material institutions is not necessary since common values are sufficient to overcome disparities).

Vida Scudder was a well-known Christian Socialist involved in the settlement house movement who devoted her entire life to social welfare and was often quite critical of the deleterious effects of industrial capitalism on the working class. Her views in the *Atlantic* reflected the concerns of many of the upper classes who were increasingly exposed to the widespread poverty and labor unrest associated with urban growth. Scudder's 1902 articles described a nation in crisis: "The world clamors for Brotherhood and finds it not" (1902c, 348); "We grieve, finding among ourselves extremes of poverty and luxury" (1902a, 638). Scudder held out the possibility of social harmony achieved through the "transforming force" or "socializing impulse" of democracy (1902c, 349, 353). She explained: "Slowly the democratic idea pervades life at every point, and transfigures the abiding, normal activities of men into a new likeness" (349).

Scudder's accounts of democracy and society emphasized ideals—morals, spirit, character, values. Class disparity was characterized as differences in feelings as opposed to differences in wages, housing, healthcare, and education. Social problems stemmed from spiritual crises; it is not, for instance, starvation wages "that holds our producing class in isolation" but "bitterness" (1902c, 354). In order to be a democracy, a nation "must possess spiritual unity. . . . Grant such a common life, in which thought, desire, emotion, circulate freely, and material inequalities and disasters will matter little" (1902a, 639). Likewise, for Scudder the solution lay not in class struggle but in "the invincible power of a high conception [that] can put to flight the evil phantoms of timidity, distrust, distaste, and create fellowship unhampered. In the familiar interchange of thought and feeling that results, the common life we seek is born at last" (1902c, 352).

The solutions to social ills propagated by Progressive activists such as Scudder often had as their aim the Americanization of the wave of immigrants settling in the United States in the early 1900s. In particular, reformers increasingly viewed formal education as an effective means to instill "acceptable" social norms (discipline, respect of privacy, individualism, punctuality). Scudder's June 1902 installment explained how democracy could be achieved through education. The article, speaking from a position of privileged benevolence, discussed the type of education that should be offered to the laboring masses. Rather than "offering the people what they like—cheap music, vulgar chromos, and so on . . . [w]e have to discover . . . the common ground, which assuredly exists in every province, where educated and uneducated can alike rejoice to wander" (1902b, 820, 821).

A rhetoric of universalization was common among Progressive Era reformers, who as members of the middle class dealt in cultural capital, ideas rather than things. In their positions as teachers, therapists, office managers, and writers, middle-class individuals served as moral liaisons between the bourgeoisie and the working classes. Their calls for change reflected their own ambivalent position within industrial capitalism, in which they benefited from the system of wage labor but often struggled to make ends meet themselves. A rhetorical strategy emphasizing social unity and promoting values, ideas, and education as the way to transcend social disparities was consistent with their middle-class role as cultural facilitator and arbiter between the upper and working classes. The rhetoric of universalization offered a challenge to the rhetorically constructed intransigence of capitalist relations as presented through naturalization. Yet the emphasis on character and attitude diverted attention away from material issues—laboring bodies that experienced exhaustion, hunger, heat, and cold as a result of factories, sweatshops, owners, and landlords. In short, within a framework of democracy-as-spirit, the materiality of social ills went unrecognized, and hence unchallenged. Where naturalization disciplined the body out of existence, universalization idealized human experience. In either case, the laboring body was ignored or remained invisible.

The visions of more well-to-do reformers often clashed with those of wage-earning women who experienced firsthand the effects of a society marked not simply by bitterness but by very real material disparities that affected not only their spirits but their bodies. Members of the working class desired education, leisure time, vacations, and trips to the theater. As women of the 1912 Lawrence, Massachusetts, textile strike proclaimed, "[W]e want bread and roses too." But, as many workers noted, a decent homelife was inconceivable as long as wages and hours in the workplace remained unbearable. As such, workers most often spotlighted the factory floor or assembly line as the front from which to fight their battle. In contrast to Scudder's vision in the *Atlantic*, a more democratic society was shaped by actions involving laboring bodies, men and women who engaged in strikes and walkouts. Improvements in physical conditions rather than spiritual condition was a sine qua non in the achievement of democracy.

Still, the views of Scudder and other activists appearing in the *Atlantic* represented gaps in the rhetorical frame of naturalization that otherwise continued to define the magazine's ethos. For example, in 1903, in "A Great Municipal Reform," Burton J. Hendrick considered the issue of tenement housing in New York City and, rather than present current conditions as natural or inevitable, recognized the need for change. As in the Scudder series, however, the diagnosis of and proposed solution for the problem were brushed with a Progressive Era morality that allowed for change but that remained within the prescribed bounds of propriety associated with naturalization.

From the perspective of many middle- and upper-class reformers, bettering the lives of those less fortunate involved a component of moral uplift, to which was tethered a host of upper-class values, including cleanliness, privacy, and social harmony. In "A Great Municipal Reform," the image of the tenement became a synecdoche for all of the city's evils, which, according to Hendrick, ranged from runaway greed to moral degradation. In short, tenement life represented a transgression of values and norms deemed "appropriate" and necessary for rising up the social ranks. Chief among those values was individualism. Collective living arrangements, it was asserted, stymied individual personal growth and represented a breeding ground for various anarchist and socialist thought.[13] Hendrick's assessment of the tenement problem reflected these middle-class concerns and echoed the ethnocentrism of much Progressive Era rhetoric:

> This herding of more than 2,500,000 people in a conglomeration of poorly constructed and poorly ventilated rooms naturally has a most important bearing upon the physical and moral character of the metropolitan population.... The apartment and tenement mode of life ... is a deplorable evil.... [It's results] appear ... most offensively ... in the Jewish, the Italian, and the negro quarters. The effects, physical and moral, of crowding a single family ... usually reinforced by two or three more in the shape of "boarders," in an apartment comprising from two to four rooms ... can be readily imagined (668).

As in the Scudder series, universalization, or the emphasis on common values or morals, provided a way for the *Atlantic* to address pressing social issues that surely confronted the lives of its upper-class readers. Yet the emphasis on personal character localized the source and solution to issues of poverty and suffering in the individual. The author cited communal living conditions as the source of social disintegration while leaving systemic discriminations rooted in the growth of industrial and, later, corporate capitalism out of the discussion entirely.

Universalization became, in effect, the *Atlantic*'s response to events outside its pages and lent a controlled flexibility to the frame of naturalization. *Atlantic* accounts of the "less than perfect" capitalist system insinuated that if social change was in order, there were "proper" ways to achieve it. Here, naturalization, even when it gave way to a Progressive Era reform spirit, prescribed the bounds of social change and the terms upon which change could be achieved. Indeed, tinkering with the system under the guidance of morality and character improvement did not disrupt, but rather could be demonstrated to *reinforce*, the status quo.

Ask many immigrant and poor working families in the early 1900s to paint a picture of life in the tenements and it would very likely have differed markedly from the Progressives' view. Though often dirty, crowded, and lacking air and light, as discussed in the *Atlantic* article, the tenements were a central location for the formation and sustenance of communal ties and collective efforts central for survival for many of the working class. "Women utilized the proximity of neighbors, friends, and kin to mutual advantage, socializing a variety of domestic tasks and customizing Old World principles of mutuality and collectivity. . . . Even the time-honored custom of swapping household items became formalized as women sought to stretch scarce resources" (Cameron 1991, 60), including sharing household duties and childcare. Furthermore, "[T]he local centers of female activity—grocery stores, streets, stoops, bath houses, kitchens—also enhanced women's concepts of material rights and sustained efforts to negotiate and agitate for economic justice" (Cameron 1985, 47).[14] The communal ethos of tenement living carried over to strikes and walkouts, where coordinated efforts were required to sustain the action. The Chicago branch of the Women's Trade Union League used "existing networks" as a point of departure and drew on the collective sentiments already present in neighborhoods in their efforts to unionize women and involve them in labor struggles (Hyman 1985).

In the early 1900s, the Progressive reform spirit pervaded the *Atlantic* in articles about the suffering wrought from an "imperfect industrial system." The meanings these articles held for readers were shaped in part through their juxtaposition with others that continued to emphasize the inevitability of the system. One month after the Scudder series, an *Atlantic* article, "Commercialization," by Edward Atkinson, stood as a direct response to Scudder's calls for spiritual transformation (1903). The author relied on a rhetoric of naturalization to justify commercialism and directly confronted and undermined the arguments of those, such as Scudder, who may be shifting their sympathies toward labor. Atkinson asks, "What is this commercialism which is so often held up to present scorn as if the pursuit of wealth had not been the motive of action in former days?" (517).

This article illustrated how naturalization, as an "innocent speech," first justified social disparities, then placed the status quo beyond criticism. Naturalization justified by effacing human intervention, involvement, or influence ("I can't help it"), then rendered change impossible by emphasizing nature's permanence. The author's portrayal of society made social transformation (even of the spiritual kind) otiose. Society is a "great organism" in which "men" must be "true to their functions" (517). And, "since the mental endowments of men vary and are unequal, it follows . . . that inequality and progress must be reconciled, as they are by the facts of life." In a final move to place the system beyond criticism and thus change, Atkinson elaborates on "two fundamental rules of action" pertaining to labor "which are based on human nature" (518). Social disparities are natural and thus must be accepted as inevitable.

Some *Atlantic* accounts (Gray 1903; Lloyd 1902; Winston 1902), were not wholly unsympathetic toward trade unions and the need for labor organization. "The union exists for the purpose of increasing or at least maintaining wages. Few would deny their right to do this if they can," asserted Henry Demarest Lloyd, the author of a "A Quarter Century of Strikes" (1902, 662). A book review appearing in April 1903, "'The Social Unrest,'" favorably discussed a book of that title that condemned the "intolerable competition among capitalists," which led to "temptation on the part of capital to oppress and crush the individual workman" (Gray 569). The reviewer defended workers who were capable of "agitation and political action" and were "able to voice their fear and resentment at an economic inequality and injustice" (570).

Yet even as *Atlantic* articles increasingly recognized labor as an organized entity, framings remained constrained by the bounds of propriety and self-control ordained by a natural order. These early-twentieth-century portrayals hinted at what later became a common way to portray labor: as the promoter of values in support of liberal capitalism. Unions were framed as a necessary counterpart, even helpmate to, employers. Granting workers the right to organize, Lloyd further asserted that trade unions alongside employers were necessary to confront the "uncontrollability of capital" (1902).

Other *Atlantic* writers justified labor unions to their readers by associating them with norms and values such as individualism, self-control, opportunity through hard work, and consumption, values that actually sustained the existing order.[15] Minimum-wage systems proposed by trade unions actually promoted competition and "facilitate[d] the process by which men pass upward or downward to their proper places," explained one writer in December 1902 (Winston 795). In his review of *The Social Unrest*, John Gray explained how unions represented the sane alternative to socialism: "[T]he choice appears to lie between permitting the unions to develop . . . or seeing the state driven into socialistic experiments for which we are ill prepared" (1903, 572). The author went on to reassure his audience that unions were beginning to give up their "regrettable resort[s] to foolish boycotts and reckless sympathetic strikes." They are turning more and more to "legal and peaceful methods" in order to achieve a "minimum and progressive standard of living, and a reasonable opportunity in life for themselves and their children" (571). Thus, the *Atlantic* was able to broach potentially controversial issues by framing them in a manner that tempered the flames of divisiveness. Even when discussing issues of labor, the genteel reading experience crafted by the *Atlantic* was preserved by a picture of social order maintained through well-mannered union tactics.

Indeed, some labor organizations (the AFL and, to an extent, the WTUL), in their attempts to appeal to a broad audience, linked their cause to traditional mainstream images and values such as progress, consumption, female domesticity, and morality. Still, voices of protest both within and outside the AFL and WTUL maintained the importance of distinguishing themselves and their worldview as *oppositional*, in other words, not reconcilable within a capitalist picture. Insofar as they believed that justice was attainable only by a massive overhaul of the system, these groups shaped a message with a sharp critical edge, one that would call attention to the brutality of the system and the stark differences between upper- and working-class values and material conditions.

In her speeches, the labor activist Leonora O'Reilly referred to the "exploitation of the workers by the idlers" and the "sacrifice of the workers for the luxury of loafers" (1911c). Laborers must "work . . . to eliminate all those who do not pay their way, for they are the parasites that absorb the fruits of those who labor" (n.d., "To be used in every lecture"). Perhaps best known for their confrontational tactics and vituperative language, the IWW used songs to arouse worker enthusiasm and create solidarity: "Workers of the world awaken! / Break your chains, demand your rights. / All the wealth you make is taken / By exploiting parasites" (quoted in Cole 1978, 235). In short, for many labor activists, pointing out differences, not similarities, between themselves and their audiences was a key persuasive tool. The strictures of decorum and propriety had no place in many labor protests.

Furthermore, boycotts and sympathetic strikes were hardly "regrettable" or "foolish," as they were characterized by writers like Gray and Lloyd, but were a deliberate part of the workers' overall plan to successfully win fair wages. The tactics of mill workers in Lawrence, Massachusetts, provide a good example. To sustain their 1912 strike, women boycotted unsympathetic stores, and "any that refused credit or food found red scab signs on their front doors" (Cameron 1985, 50). From fourth-story windows they taunted scabs and poured scalding water on neighbors headed to work. All in all, 30,000 workers representing forty different nationalities coordinated efforts in households, stores, and picket lines in order to bring mill owners to their knees in hopes of reversing wage cuts enacted in January 1912.

Recognition of labor and reform efforts, though not frequent, dotted the pages of the *Atlantic* into the twentieth century and represented some of the earliest attempts on the part of mass-circulation magazines to control voices of protest by acknowledging and absorbing them into a hegemonic frame. Stepping down from its lofty position of letters, the *Atlantic* sought a way to manage upper-class concerns arising from labor unrest and economic instability. Into the second decade of the twentieth century, the *Atlantic* provided space for critical voices but responded to these critical openings with accounts that reaffirmed the natural state of existing work and gender relations.

1909–1917: Offering Reform and Justifying the Status Quo

As the twentieth century progressed, working-class and upper-class women alike were active in various public realms. Assisted by the WTUL and the IWW, working-class women organized their own union locals, held meetings, led male and female workers in walkouts and strikes, and spoke on their own behalf as workers and as women. Moreover, wage earners were often joined by middle- and upper-class allies who assisted on the picket lines and frequently spoke publicly for women's economic and political equality. In particular, organized labor challenged capitalism in a series of strikes that took place between 1909 and 1916. From these struggles, workers won gains in the workplace and passed laws in favor of workers' rights. In short, women were defying gender norms as never before and industrial capitalism was losing its credibility on a number of fronts.

During a period of mass labor uprisings, the *Atlantic* continued to provide articles advocating social betterment, thus recognizing the very real concerns of its readership, many of whom were involved in political and cultural reform circles.[16] But the more broad-minded articles were frequently undermined by the magazine's overall "flow" (Williams 1975), or the juxtaposition of these accounts with others in the same or following issues that continued to naturalize industrial relations and thus place them beyond criticism. Williams discusses flow as applied to television, but the concept can also be applied to magazines. When examining the ideology of a particular magazine, it is often useful to consider the reading experience in terms of how the tone, images, and content of articles throughout an entire issue and immediately following issues relate to each other and direct potential reception. Despite the appearance of an unconnected or multifaceted presentation of ideas, the *Atlantic* was unified through a persuasive strategy of naturalization that guided the flow of various articles and established the limits of what could be said within one article.

"Feministic Agitation" and the Threat to True Womanhood

Into the teens, the *Atlantic Monthly* continued to increase its attention to women's struggles for equality through various fiction and nonfiction stories. Some of these accounts were imbued with the progressive tone hinted at in the magazine's pages in the early 1900s. In fact, "The English Working-Woman and the Franchise," by Edith Abbott, which appeared in September 1908, provided a radical account of the perseverance and organizing capabilities of working-class women in England. Unlike other

Atlantic articles, Abbott's account viewed the vote from a working-class perspective and provided testimonies from working women.

Abbott's article exemplifies how popular texts often responded to and were influenced by the voices of marginalized groups, or vernacular rhetorics. Further, Abbott's framing illustrates the complexities involved in examining cultural texts. Magazines, not to mention television shows, newspapers, and popular novels, rarely embody a monolithic world-view. Rather, a rich amalgam of values, perspectives, and ways of being and living is often presented within one narrative, as well as by competing stories and images. Though specific boundaries delimit what can and cannot be spoken, within these boundaries is some flexibility, and Williams's conceptualization of the dynamic nature of cultural texts is insightful (1977). According to Williams, dominant practices react to emergent elements through "incorporation." At the same time, "[N]o dominant culture ever in reality includes or exhausts all human practice, human energy, and human intention" (125). Further, as many cultural scholars have pointed out, reading and viewing are not passive processes of consumption but often result in raised awareness or improved self-esteem (Brummett 1991; Fiske 1987; Radway 1984). For example, Fiske explores images of female sexuality and power in soap operas, noting that women's experiences and perspectives "are given a high valuation . . . [which] can serve as a source of self-esteem for the fans and as an assertion of women's values against the place assigned to them in patriarchy" (1987, 182).

With its radical view of women and work, "The English Working-Woman and the Franchise" likely provoked debate among husbands and wives, and perhaps increased women's awareness of their own position in society. Yet in any examination of popular culture texts, one must consider the workings of a narrative as it is embedded in a wider rhetorical and material context. *Atlantic* articles demonstrate how ideological framings and magazine flow demarcate the perimeters of what can be said and how. Furthermore, in addition to narratives and images present, gaps and silences persuade and shape understandings. How do readers, viewers, and social critics fill the gaps and bridge the textual discontinuities? The daily realities of women activists outside the magazines' pages, their voices of anger, and their demands for justice belie the silences and stand at the farthest remove from the confines of propriety and decorum.

Though many *Atlantic* articles responded to the swelling of public protests beyond its pages, the contours of such portrayals excluded the voices and concerns of wage-earning women, many of whom were receiving widespread support and financial assistance from their more well-to-do sisters. Abbott's article remained the sole exception with its description of an active group of wage-earning suffragists who demonstrated among themselves a "new solidarity . . . which has grown out of a new consciousness of their own needs and which brings with it a new sense of their own power" (346). In general, however, the image of the militant wage-earning woman placed too great a strain on the code of decorum mandated by a rhetoric of naturalization. Still, naturalization proved a versatile strategy as it was employed in articles both for and against women's equality.

Arguments against gender equality invoked warnings of what transgressing the norms of womanhood would do to the family and to society. Naturalization operated in these accounts by reifying existing gender norms and divisions, implying "that what has been true always and everywhere is innate to human nature, and so cannot be changed" (Eagleton 1991, 59).[17] Agitation for gender equality represented no less than a challenge to the natural order. *Atlantic* writers placed no limits on what disasters might occur when such challenges erupted.

"Woman has a different nature, a different purpose," Harriet Anderson, the writer of "Woman," explained in August 1912. As "a prototype of Mother Nature, a symbol of divine creativeness," woman is "incomplete without motherhood" (180, 182). According to the author, "feministic agitation" was at odds with the natural duties of women as mothers and thus put "the whole fabric of our world . . . in danger": "We have the criminal spectacle of a woman's not achieving her purpose for fear she will not be 'happy.' She selfishly commits inverted murder by not allowing the race to be born that should come to flower" (180). Another author, Molly Eliot Seawell, equally alarmed at the chaos that might ensue, concluded unequivocally that "woman suffrage [is] an unmixed evil" (1910, 303). If women get the vote, Seawell deplored, "No lawyer or financier living would undertake to prophesy the result, except stupendous loss to women and a cataclysmal confusion and destruction of values" (294). She placed her hope that the natural order would be retained in "basic principles opposed to woman suffrage," explaining, "A basic principle works with the merciless mechanism of a natural law, like gravitation, and is indeed a natural law. . . . Civilization cannot be destroyed by legislative enactment. It may be grievously injured . . . but the basic and natural law will always . . . rise above the statute law and civilization will maintain itself at all costs" (290).

Naturalization secured women's relegation to the home by making her "natural" duties of domesticity and motherhood the very foundation of civilization and social order. The trope of familialism prevalent in present-day political and popular discourses had its roots in the early-twentieth-century rhetoric of naturalization, which attempted to contain women's demands for equality by naturalizing her roles in the home.[18] Lorin F. Deland, the author of "The Change in the Feminine Ideal,"

which appeared in 1910, established rapport with her readers by acknowledging their feelings and speaking clearly and openly to their own
experiences. She directly named the "prevailing discontent among
women" and noted the achievements of women in government, business, and education. Once a common ground was established, Deland
explained that women's growing sense of "individualism" was a "menace to family life" and thus represented no less than a threat to civilization itself. She reasoned: "Civilization, in other words a highly differenti-
ated idea of property, is like a pyramid standing on an apex that rests on
the permanence of marriage. Any one who tampers with the stability of
that base, tampers with civilization" (296).[19]

Other writings more pointedly addressed motherhood in all its glo-
ries—often with a subtext that highlighted the racist undertones of
"motherhood" invoked during these years. The "sanctity of motherhood" was a rhetorical front for politicians and reformers who feared
"race suicide" from increased immigration and declining birth rates
among American-born middle-class families. The "motherhood" implied
in these messages was that of white women of relative privilege who met
the criteria of True Womanhood. Ellen Key extolled motherhood as being
"as tremendous an elemental power, a natural force" as the sun and the
sea (1912, 562). Woman, she said, "is the one who, through the serenity
and wisdom of her own nature is dew and sunshine to growing souls,"
(1913, 51). Central to Key's message was the "importance of motherliness
to the race": "Motherliness must be cultivated by the acquisition of the
principles of heredity, of race-hygiene, child-hygiene, child-psychology"
(1912, 569). Like her counterpart the True Woman, the "True Mother" was
race- and class-bound, achievable only by those who did not rely on a
woman's income to feed the family: "The socially pernicious, racially
wasteful and soul-withering consequences of the working of mothers
outside the home must cease" (1913, 50). These and other *Atlantic* articles
relied on persuasion through naturalization to place all alternatives out
of reach. Mother-in-the-Home could not be replaced any more than "the
heart in an organism [can] be replaced by a pumping engine" (Key 1913,
51). Cooperative childcare disrupted a child's "progress of growth" and
"is as fruitless as to put plants in the ground blossom downward and
roots in the air" (54).

The *Atlantic*'s sentimental depictions of family and motherhood appeared on the heels of the 1912 textile strike in Lawrence, Massachusetts,
in which thousands of female workers and housewives participated. Images and exhortations regarding mother's permanence in the home stood
in stark contrast to the living conditions in Lawrence, where entire families had to work in order to survive. While an *Atlantic* author bemoaned
cooperative childcare, parents in Lawrence organized for their children

to be sent to the homes of sympathetic socialists in New York and other cities so that the children would be safer and so that parents could more effectively participate in the strike. In the *Atlantic*, naturalization operated as an "innocent speech" (Barthes), justifying one version of "motherhood" by comparing it to something as natural and obvious as "the heart in an organism."

Fiction appearing in the early teens further reinforced the concept of the natural duties of women (Comer 1911; Gilmore 1914; Humphrey 1912; Kemper 1915; Leupp 1911). Mothering qualities revealed themselves early in a young girl's life (Gilmore 1914) and remained long after a woman passed away, as was the case in "The Lady of the Garden," whose "nature . . . must give itself in some fostering love and care" even six months after she died (Humphrey 1912, 526). Other stories expressed dismay at changing gender roles and expectations. What happened to the "old-fashioned Lady?" asked the author of "The Vanishing Lady" (Comer 1911, 722). Though the article appeared in late 1911, its description of the "Lady" echoed a mid-nineteenth-century etiquette book:

> She was dauntless and sweet, that old-fashioned Lady; witty but tender; as notable a housewife as a hostess; full of gentle concern for others, with a mind ever at leisure for their affairs, and a heart whose sympathy was instantaneous in their service. She stimulated and she soothed. Fine, complicated, and interesting as the old lace and finely wrought gold she delighted to wear, she was a very precious piece of porcelain. The brilliant, soft daguerreotype that has preserved her early likeness for us did not idealize her beyond her just due. Perhaps the intimate secret of her influence was the impression she gave of one whose heart is fixed, one whom the world can no longer harm (723).

In "The Problem of Priscilla," a married couple worried over the effects that a college education would have on their daughter's potential as a wife and mother (Leupp 1911). The author concluded that although Priscilla may not choose the road of matrimony so desired by her parents, mother and father can rest assured that her newly acquired intelligence will not hinder her homemaking and motherly abilities, should she choose that route.

Many *Atlantic Monthly* articles held particular significance in light of the United States' growing involvement in World War I. With the advent of the war, the government relied on popular media to recruit women as munitions workers, streetcar conductors, telephone operators, and government office workers. Most of these positions were filled by women who were already in the paid workforce (Foner 1980, 26; see also Greenwald 1980). Newspapers and magazines promoted images of "war mothers," who enthusiastically sewed uniforms, tended victory gardens, and gave public support to sons and husbands. The *Atlantic* gave its "mothers in the home" an appropriate way to support the war effort by recruiting them as "mothers of the state." *Atlantic* writers elaborated women's roles quite frankly: "The State imperatively needs a birth-rate. It must have citizens. Mothers bear and rear citizens; hence mothers should be paid for the service" (Nock 1914, 159); "Mothers should be considered the servants of the State" (Key 1916, 841). Just at the moment when thousands of women were discovering opportunities in skilled and higher-paying jobs vacated by men gone off to war, one author asserted that "[h]er [woman's] ability to bear and educate her children and build a home is so handicapped by her leaving her home to procure a livelihood that the only way to solve the problem would be to consider her motherhood a state service" (Key 1916, 842).

The image of woman as a "national object of protection" reinforced the depiction of men risking their lives overseas in order to protect women and children from "the Hun." "Do the American women who prate about the wrong done to womanhood by war ever reflect that it is for wife and child, as well as for home and country, that men are bound to die?" asked one writer in 1915 (Repplier, 581).

In the prewar and early war years, in the *Atlantic* no one perspective was revealed as uniformly dominant regarding women's rights and roles. Between 1909 and 1917, many articles openly advocated women's suffrage as well as other social and economic rights.[20] This ideological variability is in fact a facet of the magazine's hegemonic workings. Early-twentieth-century magazines such as the *Atlantic* "incorporated" (Williams 1977) evolving gender and work relations and often contained "utopian" visions (Jameson 1979/80) that offered readers optimistic accounts of how life might be better. These textual elements were consent-seeking devices. By acknowledging and giving voice to readers' needs and concerns, these mechanisms attracted reader attention and established common ground. Once given voice, the needs and concerns were then "managed" or "repressed" in terms that legitimated the status quo (Jameson 1979/80).

For example, as in the early 1900s, the *Atlantic* continued to draw on the political arguments of mainstream and wage-earning suffragists who were relying on presumed "natural" female characteristics to demonstrate the benefits of granting women the vote. *Atlantic* writers benefited from association with political voices gaining public credibility at this time, and they were able to do so without transgressing the bounds of naturalization which permeated the magazine. One writer, Mary Johnston, in "The Women's War," explained the Woman Movement to her readers in this way:

The Woman Movement did not begin to-day, or last night, or yesterday, or the day before yesterday. It began an uncertain number of millions of years ago. It began when first a primitive, asexual organism slipped almost unawares into a sexual method of reproduction. It began when the union of two cells, hitherto undifferentiated, gave way to the union of two cells gradually, very, very gradually" (1910, 561).

Framing the Woman Movement as natural evolution reassured the reader who may have been threatened by women's protests by explaining that this social phenomenon was really nothing new; rather, it had existed since the beginning of time and was a natural part of the progression of civilization. In this view, primitive, asexual organisms operating "unawares" replaced self-aware and active protesters, including educated and well-to-do women such as Harriet Stanton Blatch and the millionaire heiress Mrs. O. H. P. Belmont, among others who paraded, picketed the White House, and organized trolley tours in their struggles for the vote (Flexner 1959, 254–257).

Echoing the arguments of suffragists beyond the pages of the magazine, *Atlantic* writers also relied on the "natural" differences between the sexes to argue that women's influence in the public sphere was a necessary complement to men's. "[D]istinctions of sex exist—naturally," explained Johnston in "The Woman's War," "they play an enormous part in life. But the sexes are but the two arms of Life, and Life is ambidextrous. And unless the hands work together, the potter will have an ill-shaped vessel" (1910, 565). Similarly, the writer Ellis Meredith explained that though men's interests lie in national politics, the interests of enfranchised women "begin[] at home" with concerns for the water supply, clean streets, and child welfare (1908, 197).

In much the same way, the National American Woman Suffrage Association activist Anna Cadogan Etz implicitly called up women's superior morality by referring to the existing state of affairs in various public institutions: "Since the powers that work for good—the churches, the schools and most other reform bodies—are composed largely of women; and since the powers that work for harm—the saloon, the gambling places and most outgrowths of commercial greed—are managed by men, how could society be otherwise than benefited by granting suffrage to women?" (1910).

Wage earners also on occasion advanced arguments premised on women's natural traits, though their work in factories and foundries made their position as "true women" more problematic. The working-class activist Leonora O'Reilly painted a picture of the state of chaos and corruption in politics. The remedy, according to her 1911 article "Looking over the Fields" in the *American Suffragette*, was to introduce the influence of women: "If politics to-day is the product of intelligence let women go to work politically to see what an infusion of human sympathy and mother instinct can do in managing the affairs of the State and nation. . . . Men have accepted every wrong way; they have rejected every right way. It is for woman to reverse this kind of intelligence and to instill into government some of her innate honesty" (1911b, 7–8).

A side-by side comparison of popular and vernacular sources points up the oftentimes quite similar portrayals of woman suffrage arguments. Yet it would be premature at best to draw an optimistic conclusion regarding popular magazines' roles in women's struggles for economic and political equality. As is argued in this book, one must also consider the broader historical context in which the text is situated, as well as intertextual influences and the ways that liberatory portrayals are negated, silenced, or trivialized within one article.

Early-twentieth-century portrayals of suffragists, feminists, and working-class activists represented the forerunners of contemporary popular portrayals of women's struggles for equality. Present-day persuasive strategies were born in magazines such as the *Atlantic Monthly* and *McClure's*, which acknowledged women's protests and then rewrote them as struggles that fit within the parameters of the magazine's overarching frame. Naturalization reinforced propriety during a period of upheaval, universalization created consensus in a context of gender and work divisions, and domestication quelled dissent in the midst of hundreds of strikes and walkouts. In addition, silences and gaps in narratives of struggle played an important role in the negation of feminism, making it essential to turn to the voices of women themselves as part of the study of women's struggles in the early twentieth century.

As upper- and middle-class women sustained their push for the vote into the second decade of the twentieth century, textual "leaks" in the magazine's overarching frame became more frequent. Between visions of "motherliness" and the romanticized family, *Atlantic* readers heard arguments that challenged, and in some cases debunked, the naturalness of womanly traits. As the media scholar Todd Gitlin has put it, the *Atlantic* had to "remain sensitive to currents of interest in the population, including the yank and haul and insistence of popular movements" (1979, 263). A 1914 article by Samuel McChord pointedly upended the "naturalness" of True Womanhood, proclaiming that "many women are becoming conscious of what some women have always felt, that some of the limitations which have been accepted as natural are in reality only conventional, and so can be removed" (541). Such challenges to social norms were tamed by the writer's calm, deliberative tone, which placed the issue within the bounds of propriety that underwrote the overarching frame. Who could argue with the writer's eloquent entreaty: "It would be a counsel of perfection to ask any one to meditate on Votes for Women with the same detachment with which one might meditate on the Passage of Time, the Beauties of Nature, or the Vanity of Human Greatness" (539).

Articles acknowledged, and at times defended, women's right to earn wages outside the home, though the issue of necessity and financial want were not a part of such arguments. "Some degree of economic independence is necessary to intelligent thinking and orderly living," argued Earl Barnes in August 1912 (262). A year later, an author by the name of W. L George elaborated on "Feminist Intentions," one of which was to grant women in their roles as housekeepers a proportion of their husband's income. George quoted one such feminist, Mrs. M. H. Wood, as saying that "she hopes to do away with 'pocket-searching' while the man is asleep" (1913, 729). Accounts noted the occupations and activities increasingly considered "acceptable" for middle- and upper-class women. "College-bred" women were suited to the book trade (Barnes 1915), while "women surgeons, women nurses, women orderlies" supported the war with a "brave punctilio" (West 1916, 3). Women were escaping boredom by making their marriages a "profession" and "planning their own lives as men plan theirs" (Woodbridge 1915, 637).

The *Atlantic* provided readers a variety of viewpoints on "the general topic of woman's intelligence" through a debate that appeared in the magazine between 1915 and 1916. With cool detachment, W. L. George in "Notes on the Intelligence of Woman" tried to "arrive at the greatest possible frequency of truth" regarding intellectual differences between the sexes (George 1915). From a study of sixty-five women, George concluded that women were more emotional and less logical than men. "Naturally, where there is a question of love, feminine logic reaches the zenith of topsy-turveydom," (725); and when it comes to economy and expenditure, "[W]oman is still something of a savage" (1916, 100). The author conceded, however, that women's inferiority was "temporary" and stemmed from lack of education and various other "local influences," though the reader is left wondering to what extent George really believes that women's intellect can be altered. Those offended by such broad generalizations found support in an article that appeared two months later, which directly responded to "Notes on the Intelligence of Woman." In "Woman and Religion," Bernard Iddings Bell asserted that women were just as intelligent as men, often "very much better equipped mentally than is the average man" (1916, 380). Further, "It is not at all true, as thoughtless people sometimes assume, that woman has a spiritual sensitiveness which man does not possess, that she is by nature more fitted for religion than he is" (380).

In a prestigious popular magazine such as the *Atlantic*, the appearance of articles discussing and often supporting women in nontraditional roles was significant, for it further legitimated upper-class women's entrance into the public sphere. Female readers could find visions of themselves as something other than mother or wife. However, of equal importance was the glaring lack of accounts of wage-earning women who worked out of necessity, not boredom, and who were exploited not only as women but as workers, as immigrants, and as women of color. The strategies of present-day television shows can be seen in the *Atlantic,* where "[c]onsent is managed by absorption as well as by exclusion" (Gitlin 1979, 263). Liberatory accounts of changing gender roles were tempered by associating women's new opportunities with a comportment becoming of a "lady." The bounds of decorum delimited what constituted the "female laborer," thus excising the harsh reality that offended the sensibilities of natural womanhood, which was a constant undercurrent in the magazine.

It can be said that early-twentieth-century accounts of gender and labor represent some of the earliest attempts on the part of popular texts to manage and co-opt social movements. Mass-circulation magazines such as the *Atlantic Monthly*, *McClure's* and *Comfort* pioneered the way for contemporary cultural products that acknowledge and absorb oppositional movements in forms compatible with dominant ideology.

Between 1909 and 1917, *Atlantic* articles both for and against women's suffrage were framed by a rhetoric of naturalization. This persuasive strategy was not monolithic, but contained leaks that responded to female readers' protests outside the magazine's pages. The popular responses, however, were well contained remaining overwhelmingly silent on the experiences of female wage earners. The combination "mother and career" was not broached by this magazine, a circumstance that points up the need to maintain a consistent narrative of homebound mother.

Such complexities were left to the pages of mail-order magazines. They had to perform a more intricate rhetorical dance, for they addressed a target audience whose role as mother was at odds with the demand for her unskilled labor in factories and laundries. Well into the teens, when women made up nearly 20 percent of the paid labor force, portrayals of labor in the *Atlantic* were limited to the male experience.

Reconstituting the Individual Moral Man

As workers and labor organizations gained widespread attention in the teens from Congress, courtrooms, reformers, and the mainstream press, the *Atlantic Monthly* gradually devoted more space to issues surrounding the working class, a group with which many of its readers had little first-hand experience. Articles reflected the ambivalence of business owners, who often feared the power of trusts and corporate competition as much as they feared the strength of labor (see Ohmann 1996, 54–55). The shifting frame that started to emerge in reform-spirited articles of the early 1900s continued throughout the teens as the rhetoric of naturalization frequently gave way to that of universalization. Rather than contain unrest by presenting the economic system as inevitable, articles often focused on seemingly transcendent values that, when applied universally, appeared to be a cure for labor's ills. Wherever naturalization was unable to absorb and recast voices of dissent as a popular hegemonic strategy, universalization assumed predominance. "Naturalizing has an obvious link with universalizing, since what is felt to be universal is often thought to be natural" (Eagleton 1991, 59). Consequently, universalization was able to provide a response to contextual pressures that naturalization was unable to justify or preserve as inevitable.

More specifically, issues surrounding labor and unions were defined through association and negation. In this the magazines made use of ideographs, McGee's term for words and slogans that embody a culture's ideological commitments (1980). McGee suggests typographically highlighting what he calls ideographs with the symbols < >. Articles associated labor with the mob—chaotic, out-of-control—and placed "labor organization" in contradistinction to the ideographs <individualism>, <efficiency>, and <progress>, which were made to appear axiomatic, essential to an American way of being and acting. Often, the immigrant or socialist was made to personify the "mob" and provided an identifiable scapegoat. Ideographs operate much like a frame of naturalization, for they hold themselves above scrutiny. They encourage a "logical commitment just as one is taught to think that '186,000 miles per second' is an accurate empirical description of the speed of light even though few can work the experiments or do the mathematics to prove it" (McGee 1980, 7). In their "function as guides, warrants, reasons, or excuses for behavior and belief" (6), ideographs encourage a "Well, of course!" response that makes further inspection of the issue an apparent waste of time. In the *Atlantic*, ideographs played a "preservationist" role, allowing the magazine to address controversial issues in a manner that reinforced the existing economic system.

Between 1909 and 1916, *Atlantic* articles decried "Our Lost Individuality" (Knox 1909), bemoaned the lack of "Americanism" (Repplier 1916), and often laid the blame for such transgressions at the feet of labor. Such themes took shape amidst and responded to upper-class concerns regarding increased immigration, constant labor unrest, and industrial instability. Articles painted a picture of striking workers as "mobs" with "inflammable temperaments." They had a "dull mentality," in contrast to police and employers, who were "wise," "bold and firm," (Deland 1912,

695, 696). "Everywhere and always, strange as it may seem, labor stands for monopoly, violence, and coercion, and against personal independence," an author warned (Fay 1912, 769). A frequent *Atlantic* contributor, James O. Fagan, took a more ambivalent position in his four-part series "The Industrial Dilemma: Labor and the Railroads (1909a, 1909b, 1909c, 1909d). Debating the pros and cons of railroad labor organization, Fagan assumed a stance of objective bystander or spokesperson for the pubic welfare. When considering the fairness of various labor tactics used by railroad unions, Fagan gently reminded readers to keep at the forefront their "ideas of personal liberty and the first principles of American civilization" (1909b, 329).

Atlantic writings on labor often revolved around the immigrant who represented the antithesis of a natural order. In response to Old World traditions and customs that often threatened the stability of industrial capitalism, *Atlantic* writers forged an "American" identity through ideographs such as <efficiency>, <progress>, and <individualism>, which embodied values supportive of the economic status quo. For instance, <individualism> connoted privacy and restraint, while <efficiency> and <progress> stood for upward mobility. All of these were essential to the operation of a system that relied on alienation, separation, and profit based on surplus labor.

In an article appearing just months after thousands of Lawrence, Massachusetts, textile strikers coordinated efforts to resist a wage cut, the writer W. Jett Lauck lamented that the "responsible . . . American wage-earner is rapidly disappearing" and is being replaced by immigrants who are "tractable and subservient" (Lauck 1912b, 694). Articles accused immigrants of a "low standard of living" (1912b, 694), one "lower even than the pauper labor of Europe" (Deland 1912, 697). Most inexcusable, according to these authors, were the collective living arrangements typical of many immigrants. "They collect in such compact masses as to make it impossible to assimilate them" (Deland 1912, 698), and they regularly took in boarders in order to cut the rent (Lauck 1912b, 694). Such practices ran counter to a "normal family life" typified by "independent family-living arrangements" (Lauck 1912a, 712).

In the mid-teens, as hundreds of Socialist candidates were elected to local governmental posts, *Atlantic* articles relied on the ideograph <individualism> to attack socialism as a system that ran counter to "American" ideals. "Private opinion in America is individualistic to the core," explained Fagan (1911b, 581). Pointing out the unfeasibility of socialism in another article, he asserted: "[I]t must be remembered that this is a country whose every chapter of growth, progress, and prosperity is an unbroken narrative of the individual effort of its citizens" (1911a, 26). Two articles in the May 1911 *Atlantic* provided readers with contrasting viewpoints. While it may be carried out either by "rash" revolutionaries or with the "prudence" of the Fabians, socialism is a movement that cannot be stopped, as it "seems likely to break suddenly, some day, into avalanches and floods," one writer philosophized (Larned, 579). Fagan's response to socialism was not as sympathetic: "Contrary to popular anticipation, individualism in America . . . seems now to be taking on a new lease of life" (580). Through repeated reference to <individualism> and <progress>, Fagan conveyed a sense of urgency and sought to reaffirm free enterprise as a natural and thus unquestionable state of being. "[I]ndividualism as a working force in the natural evolution of society is bound to reassume its intrinsic importance. . . . Individualism is the leaven in human society that dignifies labor" (582).

As explained in the opening pages of this chapter, naturalization is a justificatory rhetoric. As a persuasive strategy, naturalization justified certain social arrangements by framing them as immutable—always in existence, already like that—and thus beyond critique. Though the frame bent in response to labor protests, it never completely gave way, but rather worked in conjunction with universalization. In articles discussing labor-versus-capital disputes, naturalization justified industrial capitalism by concealing the agency behind certain behaviors or practices, thus short-circuiting any attempt to scrutinize the ideograph.

The author of "Socialism and Human Efficiency" placed the "intrinsic importance" of individualism beyond question, proclaiming that the "capitalistic idea is born with every human creature" (Fagan 1911b). "Friction" is, no less, a part of human nature. "Humanly speaking, the principle spreads itself out into all manner of life-giving, life-energizing undertakings. All life seems to have some kind of a frictional outset. At this point the competitive system of the universe begins its career" (588). Here and in other articles, naturalization effectively halted arguments against capitalism in their tracks (Deland 1912; Holt 1908; Laughlin 1913). Reform ideas and philanthropic projects popular among some of the upper classes were framed as hare-brained ideas doomed to fail. How can one possibly go against "life-giving" principles?

According to Holt, owners, bosses, and stockholders were not behind corporate competition any more than they controlled plant and animal life (1908). Rather, competition was a hidden force basic to life itself. Covering all bases, Holt maintained that "[c]ompetition is certainly not an invention of the devil, unless the whole order of nature is the invention of the devil: all educated people know that competition was ingrained in nature long before there was merchandizing, or manufacturing . . . or savages . . . or fishes, or gastropods, or amoebas" (1908, 518). When competition ceases, life and industry as we know it come to an end: "With competition everywhere else, the idea of wiping it out of industry must, at best, be a counsel of perfection, and at worst the idea of making industry cease" (519).

Other writers relied on "immutable economic laws" (Deland 1912), and "natural monopolies" (Laughlin 1913) to justify working conditions and wages that were otherwise difficult to accept. While acknowledging the extremely low wages of the Lawrence, Massachusetts, textile workers, one writer fell back on the "twenty centuries of a certain relationship between capital and labor" in order to demonstrate the impossibility of meeting the strikers' demands. "So long as economic laws govern all our industries to the extent they do to-day, it is asking much of Lawrence to demand that she should go beyond all precedents and inaugurate a new order" (Deland 1912, 699). In similar spirit, an October 1913 installment affirmed "natural monopolies," which were "based on the admitted inequality of mankind; [and are] the *inevitable* expression of superiority in the field of open competition" (Laughlin, 448, emphasis added). Union attempts to control wage rates and the supply of labor through the closed shop represented "an 'artificial monopoly,' not based on any natural causes" (447). Naturalization established choices clearly: accept the natural—i.e., inevitable—order *or* force artificiality and accept the dire consequences. Fagan put the matter plainly with this question: Is it "better, healthier, and wiser that a given community should be constituted of about nine hundred and fifty strenuous individuals, battling in all the ups and downs of a competitive system of progress, or of one thousand listless creatures, dreamily satisfied and inevitably headed towards extinction?" (1911b, 590).

Naturalization was further reinforced by a tone of detachment, objectivity, and impartiality by means of which writers implied that "everyone from Adam to the Chief Druid has shared their opinions" (Eagleton 1991, 58). By claiming to present "just the facts," the *Atlantic* placed its portrayals of events beyond question. Like nature, facts "just are." Once discovered, they are immutable. This detached and reflective stance had the further effect of reinstilling propriety and repose in a context of mass protest and openly expressed anger at worker conditions. The seemingly rash behaviors of workers contrasted with the "reason" of *Atlantic* writers, who sought to "clear up a confusion resulting from too much statement and too little reflection" (Deland 1912, 694). Lorin Deland assured her audience she would avoid "the dangerous use of sentiment in place of reasoning" (Deland 1912, 700), while another engaged "insight, . . . experience, . . . breadth of view . . . capacity for fairness and impartial examination" in his account of labor and capital (Laughlin 1913, 445). Another account relied on a "convincing array of facts found in certain public documents" (Fay 762). Finally, lauding a previous *Atlantic* article on the decline of individualism in America, James Fagan asserted that "[w]ithout exaggeration of any kind, the process by means of which every form of American individualism has been fully uprooted and scattered to the winds, was carefully described and scientifically accounted for" (1911b, 580).

The *Atlantic*'s reliance on objectivity was rooted in journalistic conventions dating back to the 1830s and the development of the penny press. In contrast to the partisan papers of the early 1800s, the penny newspapers saw themselves as the providers of "facts," unbiased and free of party influences. Still, objectivity was more than a journalistic convention; it served a specific rhetorical purpose within the early-twentieth-century context. To assert "objectivity" is to lay claim to neutrality, to announce oneself nonideological and presumably beyond critique. Objectivity is an "invisible frame" (Schiller 1981, 2) that promotes a specific worldview even as it denies such promotion. Put differently, objectivity masquerades as nonideological even as it presents a defense of the status quo (Reese 1990, 395).

Though *Atlantic* writers went to lengths to assert detachment in presenting "just the facts," Kenneth Burke reminds the critic that any reflection of reality is necessarily a selection of facets of reality, "and to this extent it must function also as a *deflection* of reality" (1966, 45). Absent from many *Atlantic* accounts were the very real conditions faced by workers across the country, which were the reason for the workers' actions and emotions. Like many other factory jobs during this period, the textile mills in Lawrence, Massachusetts, were known for their deplorable conditions. Entire families were required to work just to survive. Foremen and overseers sexually harassed women, slapped petty fines on workers, and refused to pay overtime (Foner 1979, 426–428). Malnutrition and disease were commonplace—36 out of 100 of all workers in the mills died by the age of twenty-five (Zinn 1980, 327).

Philip Foner, a labor historian, offers a view of the situation facing Lawrence textile workers to contrast with the *Atlantic* portrayal: "Suddenly, all the years of suffering from lack of food, miserable housing, inadequate clothing, poor health, and the tyranny of the foremen came to a head and erupted in an outburst of rage against the machines, the symbols of the bosses' repression" (1979, 429). Not "inflammable temperaments," but justified anger directed at identifiable persons supported labor protests such as this one. Through words and actions, workers contested the American identity developed in the *Atlantic*. As *Atlantic* articles upheld <individualism>, workers were swiftly learning the meaning of the phrase, "an injury to one is an injury to all." Only through solidarity demonstrated in walkouts and strikes could workers hope to achieve even the smallest of gains. <Efficiency>, far from being a part of American character, was described by one wage earner as "slick means of getting the best of Organized Labor" (O'Reilly 1915, 35).

Atlantic articles often conveyed a sense of disbelief regarding behaviors of immigrants and workers that appeared to so blatantly transgress putatively commonsense notions of decency and propriety. Yet a "coherence and unity" supported workers' actions that appeared on the face to be disorderly and at times, senseless (Cameron 1985). By moving in groups, women in the Lawrence, Massachusetts, strike protected each other and avoided arrest: "By creating chaotic scenes and constant noises they hoped to confuse officers and camouflage the identity of individual attackers" (51).

The portrayal of women workers in the *Atlantic* was characterized not only by framing but also by rhetorical silences, or strategic omissions. Though women and girls stood at the center of hundreds of strikes and walkouts throughout the teens, in the pages of the *Atlantic* labor was strictly a masculine enterprise. Leafleting, organizing, confronting, defying—all of these activities lay well outside the limits of True Womanhood, a concept supposedly rooted in women's natural traits and abilities. It is not surprising, then, that actions upending or contradicting True Womanhood would be most fully suppressed, concealed, or ignored. Even when the *Atlantic*'s naturalizing frame was bent by Progressive Era influences, such persuasive silences delineated the parameters within which narratives and images of social conflict must remain. The media critics Paul F. Lazarsfeld and Robert K. Merton remark on the function of gaps and omissions in contemporary media accounts: "To the extent that the media . . . have an influence upon their audiences, it has stemmed not only from what is said but, more significantly, from what is not said. For these media not only continue to affirm the *status quo* but, in the same measure, they fail to raise essential questions about the structure of society" (1948, 107). Much like the *Atlantic*, *McClure's*, and popular mail-order magazines of the early twentieth century, contemporary magazines negotiate portrayals of "working women" through rhetorical silences. These parallels will be elaborated in Chapter 5.

Reform issues were not totally ignored by *Atlantic* writers, who after all answered to a readership that by and large benefited from Progressive Era legislation. Historians have noted how reform through legislation has actually saved capitalism by enabling individuals to function more smoothly within the system (Hall et al. 1978, 181–217; Piven and Cloward 1971; Zinn 1990, 118–136). For example, in the first two decades of the twentieth century, Progressive Era legislation became the political means by which big business could control labor unrest. Businessmen such as J. P. Morgan and John D. Rockefeller invited and in fact depended on government intervention.[21] Similarly, New Deal legislation gave "just enough to the lower classes (a layer of public housing, a minimum of social security) to create an aura of good will . . . [and] to get the traditional social mechanism moving again" (Zinn 1990, 119). Thus, interspersed between disparaging accounts of labor and immigrant lifestyles were *Atlantic* articles supporting reform and the rights of workers to organize. These portrayals spoke to the experiences of readers who were themselves involved in reform efforts and provided a way for the magazine to control and reframe voices of opposition outside its pages.

Unions, some writers demonstrated, advanced the cause of the business owner by keeping workers in line and teaching appropriate work behaviors. "The value of unionism," one author explained, "has ever consisted in the emphasis it has placed on the dignity of the individual" (Lincoln 1909, 474). And in his series on the railroads, Fagan (1909a, 1909b, 1909c, 1909d) defended railroad unions as a viable way to reach the uncontrollable minority who put the riding public in danger through negligent work practices. Fagan explained: "The center of influence upon the personality of the men has passed, to a very great extent, into the hands of the Union. This is the power behind the men at the present day, that can be exerted in a variety of ways in the interests of efficiency" (1909c, 552). An article by William Cunningham, "Brotherhoods and Efficiency," appearing in the same year, agreed with Fagan's observations. Cunningham explained how the two concepts of brotherhood and efficiency go hand in hand (1909). Railroad unions promoted discipline and loyalty among workers and even facilitated the bargaining process in a way favorable to employers. In short, these *Atlantic* articles put readers' fears to rest by confining labor protests within a frame that did not disrupt the status quo.

Indeed, it was the case that many unions promoted discipline and efficiency in the workplace as these *Atlantic* articles described. In particular, AFL-affiliated unions were known for conservatism in labor/capital bargaining and many union locals adhered to the AFL's racist and sexist policies. Yet the significance of the *Atlantic* accounts lies in what is not mentioned. *Atlantic* writers upheld the virtues of propriety and decency through silence—by avoiding the mention of apparently unnatural or "inappropriate" behaviors. The omission of references to female labor activists and wage-earning women's experience was wholly rhetorical, preserving the sexual division of labor and denying the possibility of cross-class identification between upper-class readers and wage-earning women.

Participating in the wider discussion of reform among politicians, ministers, and muckrakers, *Atlantic* writers also addressed themselves to issues such as worker's compensation, city housing, and widespread poverty. Much like the sympathetic accounts of labor, articles addressing the "shortcomings" of the system reassured readers that reform measures would secure a smoother operation of business affairs. Poverty was described as "economic insufficiency" (Hollander 1912, 493). "Its presence implies maladjustment. . . . Its disappearance is a fair inference from the course of economic progress, and its ultimate passing may be hastened by wise social policy," explained the same writer in October 1912. Another writer supported worker compensation for job-related injuries citing the "immense value of measures which contribute to the social peace" (Lewis 1909, 63). Employers must learn the "economic profit of saving life and limb" (65). A patriotic fervor permeated other articles in which writers detailed the benefits of recent legislation on food, public health, and housing. "The men and the women who aim at a social betterment in both the getting and the spending of fortunes are the advanceguard of the soldiers of the coming change," wrote one author (Martin 1908, 297). "Behind them . . . there are marching philanthropists, doctors, lawyers, business men, and legislators . . . followed by the swelling army of privates who are ready sturdily to walk along the road to the land of promise . . . " (297). In her support for "sanitary regulations" in the tenements, a writer called up "the golden dreams of the immigrant [who turns] for freedom and help to our shore, to that great 'Melting Pot'" (Godfrey 1910, 549). And another writer referred to "American hospitality" in her appeal to clean up the "wretched conditions" in which immigrants live (Kellor 1916, 59).

Between 1908 and 1917, *Atlantic* articles advocated everything from "lunch-rooms, baths, [and] clean and well-ventilated shops" (Martin 1908, 290) to municipal water service and individual baths in tenements (Godfrey 1910) to food purification laws (Godfrey 1909). The Christian Socialist and frequent *Atlantic* contributor Vida Scudder contributed two articles garnering upper-class sympathy for the working classes. Such issues pushed the boundaries of the magazine's overarching frame of naturalization. But the reform-minded articles' emphasis on values and morals contained voices of protest within a metaphysical realm and bypassed a discussion of material underpinnings that may have disrupted the presumed naturalness of the present system.

Like her 1902 article, Scudder's later contributions were undergirded by an ideology of universalization; they offered the reader a blend of "mysticism" and "economic determinism," described democracy as an "inevitable" force, and emphasized the role of religion in effacing class hostilities (1910, 1911). Her 1911 article explained class consciousness as a movement inspired not so much by the needs of fair wages, housing, and working conditions as by "a passion of good-will for all men" (328). Scudder's article provided an ironic contrast to events occurring outside the *Atlantic*'s pages. In March 1911, as thousands of laborers expressed outrage at the owner negligence and corporate greed that had resulted in the deadly Triangle Shirtwaist factory fire, Scudder's article affirmed the "enlightened energy . . . high impulses . . . [and] rich devotions" of the "governing classes" with whom the dispossessed must join hands.

Other *Atlantic* articles expressed concern for the "poor immigrant" with varying degrees of condescending benevolence. The rhetoric of Progressive Era reformers embodied middle-class values regarding living conditions and work and spending habits. Legislation and lessons on "appropriate" ways of life were viewed by reformers as tools to uplift the working-class masses (see Connelly 1980; Cameron 1991; Horowitz 1985; Ohmann 1996). Echoing these sentiments, a 1910 article on city housing relied on repeated images of "cleanliness" and "privacy" to persuade readers of the necessity of individual tubs in tenements (Godfrey 1910). The author's somewhat ironic attempt to create reader identification points up the patronizing air of much Progressive Era reform. Lamenting that many tenement dwellers have to carry water from the first floor up to their apartments, the writer encouraged the reader to "imagine shopping without an elevator, and then think of the weariness of those long flights to tired women and little children" (553).

Other portrayals offered more pointed critiques of the system. In 1916, "Lo, The Poor Immigrant!" described the system that contributed to tenement conditions and served as a startling contrast to earlier *Atlantic* portrayals, which blamed immigrants for their own conditions (Kellor). The writer cited "inadequate housing and . . . insanitary conditions" (61) and a "system of heartless exploitation and of neglect" (62) as the cause of labor unrest. The following year, an article explained the practices of the IWW through similar observations (Parker 1917). American syndicalism is "stamped by the lowest, most miserable labor conditions and outlook which American industrialism produces" (656), and must be seen as a "byproduct of the neglected childhood of industrial America" (654). Finally, "A Message to the Middle Class" (Deming 1914) offered wholesale criticism of American patriotism, religion, the mainstream press and higher education for obscuring the realities faced by the working class and immigrants.

The *Atlantic*'s naturalization frame fluctuated in response to extra-discursive events and to the perceived concerns and experiences of its readers. Such equivocality reflected the varied perspectives of many in the upper classes who variously promoted reform while justifying the basic soundness of the system. For example, *Atlantic* articles that supported the rights of labor or criticized capitalism (in however limited a manner) frequently appeared in the same issue with an article that reacted against the Progressive reform mentality, or such an article followed in the next issue. In four instances articles persuading through naturalization directly followed those with a more Progressive Era tone; and in three instances, reform-minded articles and naturalizing articles

appeared in the same month. For example, Deland's unsympathetic account of Lawrence, Massachusetts, textile workers appeared one month
following an article advocating the "closed shop" for workers (Mussey
1912). And one month after an article supporting "Social Reconstruction
Today" (Martin 1908), a writer justified inequities arising from competition by means of a comparison between Standard Oil and amoebas who
compete for the "best places" in the pond (Holt 1908). Such flexibility
played a part in the magazine's popularity and, most important, represented the hegemonic workings of the text.

Viewed in isolation, the *Atlantic's* more progressive articles represented "emergent" discourses emphasizing "new meanings and values"
(Williams 1977), textual "leakages" that pushed the constraints of the
dominant hegemonic mode (Gitlin 1979), or utopian visions that held up
a different and better way of life (Jameson 1979/80). Readers possibly
seized upon and exploited these popular discourses for their own ends,
for example, to achieve woman suffrage or more economic opportunities
for women. Yet to more fully grasp the interpretation of these articles,
one must examine them as they were produced and circulated within the
larger rhetorical and material contexts, as this chapter has attempted to
do. For readers of popular magazines, pictures of working-class and immigrant life were also shaped by the flow of articles, which was characterized by juxtapositions of transgressive portrayals with others that reaffirmed gender, class, and race inequalities. Further, within a single text a
hegemonic frame (naturalization, universalization, domestication) managed voices of protest in terms that did not threaten existing gender,
class, and race relations. In Chapter 4, which examines the protest
rhetoric of women, attention is called to extra-discursive influences that
in part shaped women's own definitions of themselves as workers, mothers, wives, and activists. Comparing popular and vernacular rhetorics
points to the extent to which workers seized upon popular ideologies but
also highlights how workers defined themselves in contradistinction to
popular portrayals.

Early-twentieth-century magazines represented some of the first attempts to negotiate the limits within which voices of protest may be portrayed. Examining popular periodicals such as the *Atlantic Monthly*, *Mc-
Clure's*, and various mail-order magazines directs scholars to the origins
of hegemonic strategies that have been elaborated by contemporary popular-culture scholars. The persuasive strategies employed by these magazines "negotiated and managed" alternative perspectives "in order to
override" them (Gitlin 1979, 264). Furthermore, "The hegemonic system
is not cut-and-dried, not definitive. It has continually to be reproduced,
continually superimposed. . . . To put it another way: major social conflicts are transported *into* the cultural system, where the hegemonic

process frames them, form and content both, into compatibility with dominant systems of meaning" (264). Indeed, as Gitlin and others remind, hegemony is not a static or monolithic process. Its very success depends on its flexibility in response to changes in the broader historical context. Yet in addition to flexibility, this study of protest and popular culture points to the resilience of hegemonic strategies. Despite important changes over the past century in the economic and cultural contexts such as the predominance of information-based workplaces, a more deeply entrenched consumer ethos, and the growth of communication technologies, this study of protest and popular culture points to important parallels between early and late-twentieth-century hegemonic strategies that permeate popular texts and perpetuate gender, class, and race divisions.

Conclusion

Around the mid-1890s, when the *Atlantic* was on the brink of shutdown, Walter Hines Page recognized the need for the *Atlantic* to step outside its narrowly constructed world of fine arts, letters, and figures. Between 1894 and 1917, under Page's and later Bliss Perry's editorship, the *Atlantic* increased its recognition of the struggles of labor as well as women's fight for political and social equality. But by making use of an ideological frame of naturalization, the *Atlantic* was able to present these timely issues in a timeless manner. The *Atlantic* constructed a world for its readers that justified class privilege and perpetuated the genteel character of the magazine. Despite the presence of reform-oriented articles, industrial capitalism, a sexual division of labor, and the values of individualism, progress, and efficiency were continuously presented as essential to a natural order, unquestionable and impossible to change.

Between 1902 and 1917, the naturalizing frame began to give way in articles that recognized the need and ability to alter the "imperfect system." In this way, the *Atlantic* responded to upper-class readers who may have been sympathetic to or actively involved with labor struggles. Even when taken all together they appeared to express multiple points of view, *Atlantic* articles were constrained by an overarching frame of naturalization that mystified the historical constructedness of various political and economic systems, justified unequal relations, and diffused challenges to material disparities by placing them in a metaphysical realm. This is not to deny the possibility that some *Atlantic* readers came away with a more sympathetic viewpoint regarding women's right to vote or labor's struggles for fair wages. The premise of this study, however, is that interpretations of popular texts are shaped and constrained by a host of contextual factors. As will be elaborated in Chapter 4, visions of women and work were not limited to the parameters of popular texts, but found expression in the lives of wage-earning women who formed their own images and definitions, shaped in part by their firsthand experiences in factories and tenements.

While the *Atlantic* maintained a world of propriety for its upper-class readers, muckraking magazines—the subject of the next chapter—exposed middle-class readers to the underbelly of American capitalism, including the plight of wage-earning women and girls. Given their readers' ambiguous place within industrial and corporate capitalism, how did muckraking journalists confront issues of labor unrest, women, and work? How were middle-class individuals living and working around the early 1900s encouraged to understand their place—and women's place—in industrial capitalism?

Notes

1. For example, in 1908 articles on women's suffrage and industrial organization appeared in between "The Playwright and Playgoers" and "Honest Literary Criticism."

2. See Breen and Rottman 1995, Calvert 1982, Joyce 1995, and Wright 1989a for overviews of the "class debate."

3. In "The Second Persona," Edwin Black explains how texts rhetorically create or imply a specific type of reader through various "stylistic tokens." In rhetorical texts, he argues, "we can find enticements not simply to believe something, but to *be* something" (1970, 119).

4. Much debate has surrounded the role of the middle classes and their interests within a capitalist system. Particularly during moments of historical crises, history has shown that the middle classes are more likely than the upper classes to identify with working-class struggles, owing to their own experiences of subordination within the capitalist system. In general, however—as history has demonstrated—the middle classes are more likely to side with the needs of capitalism, from which they, like the upper classes, benefit in numerous ways. As Wright (1989b) explains, this is what makes capitalism a hegemonic system: "It is able to effectively tie the class interests of various subaltern classes, in this case the middle classes, to the interests of the capitalist class" (203).

5. According to a critic writing in the magazine *Dial*, the *Atlantic Monthly* stood "more distinctly for culture than any other American magazine" (quoted in Mott 1957, 4:44).

6. For discussions of the late-Victorian reading experience, see Lears 1981; Schneirov 1994; and Wilson 1983.

7. Foner 1979, 257.

8. Gray 1903; Hendrick 1903; Scudder 1902c.

9. Scholars offer differing perspectives on what exactly constituted the "Progressive Era." In this project, I use the term to refer to the period roughly between 1894 and 1920 when various individuals—largely educated, white, middle and

upper class—focused on the need for government regulation of and intervention in the economic and political spheres. These individuals included journalists, settlement workers, labor and suffrage activists, politicians, and even capitalists. The motives behind such efforts varied. Politicians such as Woodrow Wilson jumped on the Progressive bandwagon to promote their political careers. And Gould points out that some reformers' efforts were motivated by racism and a desire to return to a preindustrial homogenous white America. See Gould 1974; Kolko 1963; Sklar 1988.

10. See the Introduction, page 22, for a definition of "decorum."

11. See Stephanie Coontz 1988 for a history of family life over the past three hundred years. Coontz views the family "as a culture's way of coordinating personal reproduction with social reproduction—as the socially sanctioned place where male and female reproductive activities condition and are conditioned by the other activities into which human beings enter as they perpetuate a particular kind of society" (1–2).

12. The nature of archival work makes determination of historical details somewhat difficult at times, particularly when the research involves the lives and voices of those most obscured by dominant accounts of history. According to the O'Reilly Papers (archived at the Schlesinger Library, Radcliffe Institute for Advanced Study, Harvard University), the speech was likely given at the Pennsylvania Woman Suffrage Association fourth annual convention in November 1911.

13. See Ohmann 1996 for elaboration of the "evolution of home design" and its importance in the formation of a "professional managerial class" (138–149).

14. See Coontz 1988, 200–204; Boydston 1994; and Stansell 1994 for more on the activities and relationships common within working-class communities.

15. This rhetorical tactic was used more frequently into the teens as the working class showed increased solidarity, particularly in communities where the entire population worked for and hence was exploited by one or two employers, for example, in Lawrence, Massachusetts. Other articles that equate labor unions with individualism include Winston 1902 and Cunningham 1909.

16. Deming 1914; Godfrey 1910; Hollander 1912; Kellor 1916; Lewis 1909; Martin 1908; Tucker 1913.

17. Though I use the terms "reify" and "reification" to describe how naturalization persuades, this is not to imply that the ideology is monolithic or static. As this book demonstrates, cultural artifacts contain a combination of "dominant," "residual," and "emergent" discourses (Williams 1977). Further, as manifestations of cultural hegemony, persuasive strategies such as naturalization (as well as universalization and domestication elaborated in the following chapters) are never all-encompassing or complete, but rather are carried out through an ongoing process of negotiation and consent.

18. See Cloud 1998b for an analysis of contemporary discourses that rely on the notion of "family values" in order to offer a "utopian return to a mythic familial ideal" while "scapegoat[ing] private families—especially those headed by single parents, racial minorities, and the poor—for structural social problems" (388).

19. Of course, a society's particular familial formation does serve as a means by which the state exerts control over individuals. To that extent, the ideal family within society does represent "order." However, what this *Atlantic* account ig-

nores is that the particular formation of the family is never natural or enduring. Rather, the shape of the family and its role in civilization has changed substantially over time, according to the needs of society. See Coontz 1988.

20. Barnes 1912a, 1912b, 1915; Bell 1916; Crothers 1914; Johnston 1910; Meredith 1908; West 1916; Woodbridge 1915.

21. See Piven and Cloward (1971), who demonstrate how welfare relief is expanded or contracted in order to regulate the behaviors of the poor.

2

Helping Our Sisters Out:
Middle-Class Reformers in
the Muckraking Movement

Early-1970s television programming was characterized by a "shift to 'relevance,'" which the media scholar Todd Gitlin describes as a change from "cornball comedy to expressions—however ambiguous—of liberal ideas" (1979, 206). Not only contemporary television shows but newspapers, magazines, and popular music have increasingly acknowledged the struggles of various marginalized and previously silenced groups. Prime-time television portrays blue-collar families (*Roseanne*), gay and lesbian lifestyles (*Wil and Grace*, *Ellen*), and single motherhood (*Murphy Brown*, *Grace Under Fire*); from radios sound the voices of disenfranchised black youth through rap and hip-hop; magazines promote "grrrl power"; and Hollywood makes millions off "chick flicks" that portray women who defy patriarchal institutions and rely on their own female networks in order to make it in the male-dominated world.

Such recognition is due in part to the highly segmented nature of late-twentieth-century popular media. With cable and satellite technologies, the growth of the Internet, and even changes in the magazine trade, media industries are increasingly well equipped to target specific niches or segmented markets.

A related and more fundamental reason for such recognition has to do with the corporate bottom line. Portending to "speak to" the needs and even discontent of blacks, single women, gays, lesbians, blue-collar families, etc., media industries have broadened their audience share and circulation and have thus widened the consumer base. Of interest to social critics then is often not what issues make the news but rather how such issues are framed.

Scholars have noted how the experiences and struggles of disenfranchised groups are framed by a liberal capitalist ethos in which successes and failures are portrayed as the result of individual merit or shortcomings (Cloud 1996; Dow 1996; Gray 1994). Mainstream media accounts of feminism, from TV sitcoms to news accounts, explain women's achievements as being due solely to their own hard work and individual character. Such a frame assumes a freely acting agent unmitigated by structural discriminations (Dow 1996). Feminists who make the headlines and subsequently become the "legitimate" voices of feminism are most often those who reinforce a "larger cultural narrative" that "celebrates individual choice and accountability, and minimizes cultural constraints on personal identity and choice" (Wood 1996, 172; see also McDermott 1995). Similarly, television portrayals of blacks are characterized by the "primacy of individual efforts over collective possibilities, the centrality of individual values, morality, and initiative, and a benign (if not invisible) social structure" (Gray 1994, 179). Popular biographies that narrate the life of Oprah Winfrey exemplify this frame as they construct a story that negates the collective nature of black oppression and struggle and reinterprets "Oprah's" experiences as a typical rag-to-riches story in which one overcomes poverty through individual efforts (Cloud 1996).

   In short, popular media acknowledge social struggles but place them squarely within the parameters of liberal capitalism through decontextualization and personalization. Systemic discriminations that constrain and delimit social behaviors are ignored as women, blacks, and other disenfranchised groups are shown to rise to the top solely on the basis of individual merit. Feminism is no longer a collective struggle for broadreaching social transformation but rather a lifestyle decision, an "attitude" that women can "wear," or the "freedom" to choose "to be seen as sexual object because it suits [a woman's] liberated interests" (Goldman, Heath, and Smith 1991, 336, 338; see also Ebert 1996; Ehrenreich 1981). By framing the issues in this way, media industries can acknowledge voices of discontent so as to broaden their consumer base while mitigating potential counterhegemonic side effects.

   The shift to "social relevance" can be traced to the magazine industry of the early 1900s. Ten-cent monthlies such as *McClure's*, *Muncey's*, and *Cosmopolitan* carved a niche for themselves by targeting a market previously excluded by the more expensive and elite literary magazines such as the *Atlantic Monthly* and *Harper's*. Considered more down-to-earth and accessible, these magazines addressed the struggles and concerns of "everyday people" and, for a few years, offered exposés revealing how big business and local politics often cheated the "average citizen." *McClure's* magazine, considered one of the most successful of the ten-cent monthlies, also contained articles on and openly supported woman suffrage, feminism, birth control, and divorce during a period when these topics were controversial, even taboo. This chapter explores *McClure's* magazine in order to trace the modern origins of popular framings of social movements. More specifically, this chapter argues that *McClure's* magazine laid the groundwork for the ways that contemporary popular media portray issues of social relevance and struggles for social change.

Popularizing Social Movements:
The Rhetoric of Universalization in *McClure's* Magazine

Media studies of popular portrayals of the women's movement have focused primarily on contemporary texts such as newspapers and television programs from the 1960s forward.[1] Yet representations of the women's movement can be found as early as the teens, when magazines responded, often quite favorably, to organizations and "movements" struggling on women's behalf. For example, *McClure's* magazine, one of the most well known muckraking magazines of the early twentieth century, frequently discussed the activities of the "Feminist Movement" and in 1912 installed "A New Department for Women," to provide further focus and framing for the issues surrounding gender equality. From its inception in 1893, *McClure's* immersed itself in the current scene, embroiling its readers in the grit and grind of business and politics and presenting to them the people who made their mark on everyday life. One writer said of *McClure's* in 1893, "It throbs with actuality from beginning to end" (quoted in Mott 1957, 4:596).

Known for investigative reporting on economic exploitation and political graft, muckraking magazines provide a way to further explore questions regarding social reform efforts such as the women's movement and the media that portrayed them. Between 1894 and 1917, when tens of thousands of women of all social and economic backgrounds were publicly demanding political and workplace equality, how did *McClure's* respond? More generally, how did a popular magazine frame the struggles of women whose needs, concerns, and demands often differed depending on class, race, and ethnicity?

This chapter explores these questions through an analysis of portrayals of women and labor in *McClure's* magazine. Through an ideology of universalization, *McClure's* presented the values and interests that were specific to a time, place, or group as those of all of humanity (Eagleton 1991, 56). During the peak years of *McClure's* popularity, society was marked by heavy class distinctions and social unrest. Between 1894 and 1917, *McClure's* acknowledged this reality and presented numerous pieces on the plight of labor and women's struggles for equality. Through universalization, *McClure's* encouraged the reader to dig deeply to discover the commonalities among people rather than the differences and conflicts separating them. Thus, though examples of discriminations were uncovered, *McClure's* elided the material conditions shaping these inequalities. Universalization blurred class disparities as it focused on human qualities, character, and values that seemingly apply to everyone.

McClure's targeted a middle-class audience. The term "middle class" has been used to refer to a variety of social and economic groups (see Breen and Rottman 1995; Calvert 1982; Joyce 1995; Wright 1989a). In this project "middle class" refers to individuals who neither owned the means of production nor were directly involved in the production of goods. Rather, they dealt with words, ideas, and records in order to facilitate, administer, or improve upon the present means of production. Writers, teachers, reformers, administrators, and managers made up this "new middle class" (Deacon 1989) or "professional managerial class" (Ohmann 1996), a group who manipulated cultural capital and mediated between the upper and working classes by serving as go-betweens, liaison, or arbiters. As a consensus-building rhetoric, universalization was a persuasive strategy tailored to this in-between position. Universalization emphasized human commonalities by focusing on values and ideals that seemingly transcend material differences. There was no analysis of entrenched systems and institutions that divided or distinguished groups from one another, as articles demonstrated how attitude and sound American values could lift one out of the most dire of circumstances. Indeed, the very act of accommodating and giving space to voices of dissent enabled *McClure's* to reframe such voices in terms that reinforced the current industrial system. Readers learned that, though life was difficult for many of the wage-earning classes, collective transformation of material systems was unnecessary, as good character and firm values were sufficient to overcome adversity.

To understand the intentions and worldviews underlying *McClure's* stories, we must have a background on the muckraking practices that were common in this and other magazines of the time, in addition to the writers who composed these critical exposés.

McClure's: The Magazine "Synonymous with Muckraking"[2]

S. S. McClure, an astute businessman and part owner of a business syndicate, launched *McClure's* magazine in 1893. McClure knew that a large untapped audience existed for magazines that were cheap and more down-to-earth than the prestigious *Atlantic Monthly*, *Harper's*, and *Century*, which were geared to the upper classes. *McClure's* began at fifteen cents an issue, but after one of its principal competitors, *Muncey's* magazine, lowered its price to ten cents, *McClure's* followed suit.

Beginning around the mid-1890s, advertising became an important source of revenue for magazine publishers. Of the three most popular ten-cent monthlies—*Muncey's, McClure's,* and *Cosmopolitan*—*McClure's* carried the most pages of advertising. According to *Printer's Ink,* in the period 1895–99 *McClure's* had more advertising than any other magazine in the world (Mott 1957, 4:597). In the December 1895 issue alone, *McClure's* carried 150 pages of advertising. The growth and importance of advertising directly shaped the magazine publisher's job. As the magazine historian Theodore Peterson points out, "No longer was he [the magazine publisher] interested in the reader just as a reader; he became interested in the reader as a consumer of the advertiser's goods and services" (1956, 26). The magazine thus became first and foremost a carrier of advertisements.

Two departments of the magazine that contributed to *McClure's* popularity in the early years were "Human Documents" and "Real Conversations." These columns offered up-close and personal biographies on various personalities and contributed to the persuasive workings of universalization. As Ohmann explains, the purpose of these biographies was "not to heroize a mortal, but to humanize a hero" (242). Biographical pieces cultivated an intimate relationship as readers learned how famous people were really quite like themselves. Investigative reports of workers and immigrants relied on a similar biographical approach in order to bridge the distance between middle-class reader and wage-earning woman.

Muckraking refers to the popular journalism that uncovered corruption and graft permeating politics and big business around the turn of the century. The muckraking journalism of *McClure's* can be viewed in light of the magazine's editorial voice and also within the larger context of Progressive Era reformism of which it was a part. *McClure's* and other popular monthlies set out to distinguish themselves from more prestigious magazines, such as the *Atlantic Monthly,* which they viewed as impersonal and detached from the affairs of "the people" (Ohmann 1996, 33). A focus on the everyday issues and problems faced by its readers led, however indirectly, to the muckraking practices that prevailed between 1902 and 1911. Muckraking is said to have begun with Ida Tarbell's series on Standard Oil, which appeared in *McClure's* over a period of two years beginning in 1902. Tarbell's original intent in writing about Standard Oil was to explain to readers "the achievements of business in production and efficient distribution" (Wood 1971, 132). However, "What had started out to be a study of a great business became, by virtue of the facts uncovered, an exposé of big business as sometimes practiced" which included fraud, violence, and bribery (Wood 1971, 132). Thus began muckraking, however accidentally.

Muckraking went hand in glove with a Progressive Era "reform spirit," which was motivated by a certain optimism toward American society, according to which despite the ill effects of runaway capitalism, the system was basically good (Gould 1974; Mowry 1963; Regier 1957). Progressive Era reformism was distinctly moral in tone (Caine 1974; Filler 1939; McCraw 1974; Mowry 1963), and was marked more by "group hope" than "group fear" (Mowry 1963, 55). Its underlying premises were that disparities in wealth were caused by "crooks," and class disputes were the result of both "greedy labor" and "selfish businessmen." Good men with good character were the cure for cleaning up politics. The progressive mentality, according to Mowry, "was imbued with a burning ethical strain which at times approached a missionary desire to create a heaven on earth. It had in it intense feelings of moral superiority over both elements of society above and below it economically" (1963, 54, 55).

This emphasis on morality mystified the economic relations behind the corruption and obscured the distinctly middle-class values that underpinned progressive reformism. The writings of various household and factory inspectors during the early 1900s provide a good example of the inability of progressive reformers to overcome their own class biases. Though they attempted to correct old notions of poverty that blamed the individual for his or her poverty, their findings still operated within a frame that emphasized "bourgeois values of hard work, respectability, and self-restraint" (Horowitz 1985, 50). Progressives emphasized legislative and other changes that altered but did not disrupt capitalism. Corporate corruption was exposed and trusts were busted, but the system went on as usual, with only a few changes. In fact, some scholars have demonstrated the extent to which the Progressive Era was not "progressive" at all, but rather quite soundly conservative (Kolko 1963; Sklar 1988).

Muckraking journalism can also be understood as part of the "broader Progressive drive to found political reform on 'facts'" (Schudson 1978, 71). In the late nineteenth and early twentieth centuries, federal and state bureaus were springing up to investigate factory and tenement ills, and muckraking reporters saw their role as presenting a "realistic" view of society. Yet conveying the "facts" was only part of the job: muckrakers were also eager to stir indignation and celebrate reform. *McClure's* primary muckrakers, Tarbell, Lincoln Steffens, and Ray Stannard Baker, made their stories "dramatic and damning" (Wood 1971, 135). *McClure's* muckrakers criticized the labor boss, exposed corruption in St. Louis politics, decried "The Shame of Minneapolis" (Steffens 1903), and uncovered the organized crime of labor unions. Yet an underlying tone of optimism—faith in human goodness and national progress—pervaded the magazine throughout its muckraking years. Ohmann explains that muckraking criticisms "coexisted with celebration" of industrial capitalism's achievements, the American nation, and scientific advances, at least in the early years of the movement (1996, 279). And so, side by side with

Tarbell's condemnation of Standard Oil and Baker's criticism of the labor boss, readers find an accolade to the inventor of wireless telegraphy, a tribute to Louis Pasteur, and an editorial call to "Patriotism" (see Ohmann 1996, 273–278). The purpose of muckraking was not wholesale condemnation but rather to point out the few "bad apples." The solution to ills uncovered was to "replac[e] evil men with good citizens" (Kolko 1963, 161).

Above all else, muckraking was good for the bottom line. As Mott notes, McClure "was no single-minded reformer. He was primarily a magazine-maker. . . . His chief motivation was practical rather than ethical" (1957, 4:597, 598). McClure was aware of the prestige that muckraking stories brought to his magazine. Interestingly, muckraking attracted advertisement from businesses that wanted to associate themselves with *McClure's* reputation for honesty, not only profit from its high circulation (Wood 1971, 135). Ironically, muckraking helped big business. And when muckraking no longer turned a profit for magazine publishers, it was no longer pursued. Mott (1957) explains that the need for large amounts of capital to fill the demands of mass publishing contributed to the decline of muckraking. Another factor in the demise of muckraking was the United States' increasing involvement in World War I and a concomitant conservative social climate, which quelled the voices of discontent.[3]

In making his editorial decisions, McClure explained to one of his writers, "I go most by myself, for if I like a thing, then I know that millions will like it. My mind and my taste are so common that I'm the best editor" (quoted in Mott 1957, 4: 594). Interestingly, McClure's statement itself is an example of the universalizing strategy that prevailed in *McClure's* magazine from 1894–1917. McClure hinted at the affinity between himself and his millions of readers. In an analogous fashion, throughout the magazine *McClure's* emphasized "common human experiences" in order to portray the working class and owners as "just like us." The effect of universalization was an eliding of class differences stemming from fundamental structures and systems.

Universalization:
Human-Interest Stories as a Rhetorical Frame

Terry Eagleton explains universalization as an "eternalizing" ideology whereby "[v]alues and interests which are in fact specific to a certain place and time are projected as the values and interests of all humanity" (1991, 56). In *McClure's*, common values and interests such as thrift, hard work, and good citizenship were presented as what held people together. Through individual profiles and human interest stories, the magazine demonstrated how these values played out in the lives of "real people" and held up a model worker or citizen against which readers could compare themselves or their neighbors. This chapter argues that universalization was a situated discourse responding to specific events in a historical context.

This frame can be linked to the broader role of narrative in societies. Halttunen explains that "from the mid-eighteenth through the mid-twentieth century, Western societies have evinced an extraordinary need for narrative, whose cultural function has been to assign meaning to the chaos of human experience largely by defining its shape in time through attention to plot" (1993, 79). More specifically, *McClure's* narratives paralleled the conventions of literary realism popular at the time. Indeed, many of the popular novelists of the late nineteenth and early twentieth centuries—Theodore Dreiser, Jack London, Stephen Crane—were also newspaper and magazine writers (Schudson 1978, 73). This chapter examines *McClure's* universalization frame from a rhetorical perspective, asking why this frame was employed for a specific audience, what were the underlying motives and assumptions, whose interests were promoted or obscured, and what effects the frame may have had on understandings of women, work, and social change.

It is important to note that universalizing is a rhetorical strategy employed by subordinate groups as well. In their attempts at social transformation, social movements often present their visions and values as being in the best interests of the whole. However, a comparison of mass-mediated and vernacular discourses demonstrates how not all values and interests are equally liberating. We can refer to a material reality outside our rhetoric in order to make judgments as to what visions are the most sound and the most fair. These issues are explored more fully in Chapter 4, which compares the persuasive strategies employed by wage-earning women with those found in the popular rhetoric of *McClure's*.

McClure's relied on biographical formats and investigative reports to draw out the common values held by employer and employee alike. In *McClure's*, universalization operated in part through metonymy, a process by which complex issues surrounding women, work, labor disputes, and living conditions were simplified into images more easily understood by readers. For example, in an attempt to shed light on the deplorable work and living conditions faced by millions of female industrial workers during the early twentieth century, *McClure's* profiled the lives of select wage-earning women. In his study of popular texts, Brummett expresses optimism regarding the abilities of popular texts to metonymize complex issues into "images with which the public can *identify*" (1991, 181). More specifically, readers and viewers may construct a "mosaic" from "bits" of information in various popular media sources in order to symbolize, and presumably better understand, complex social issues. Brummett explores how the "complexities of race relations in Milwaukee [were] metonymized in public discourse" by examining popular-media images surrounding two house fires in a black community in September and October 1987 (1991, 172–195). He explains: "[T]he close proximity of the houses, and the long-term economic problems of both sets of victims, allowed the two fires to become a metonymy for the problems of Black Milwaukeeans in general" (178–179). While Brummett acknowledges that metonyms do not always foster reader identification (182), his conclusions hold out the potentials of metonymized mosaics to create personalization, encourage individual action and attitude change, and lead to legislative reform (188).

Applying Brummett's insights on metonymy and mosaics to *McClure's* magazine may lead to a favorable conclusion regarding the magazine's ability to create identification between a middle-class readership and the plight of the working poor. One might explore how *McClure's* readers may have constructed a mosaic from fiction and nonfiction accounts in *McClure's* (and other media) in order to better understand the experiences of wage-earning women. Indeed, the frame of universalization with its emphasis on transcendent values and ideals lends itself to reader identification. Some scholars are quite optimistic regarding the transformative potentials of muckraking magazines such as *McClure's*. Wood concludes that *McClure's* had great influence over public opinion and that some of the magazine's exposés led to "reform, to legislative action and to improvement in politics and the conduct of business" (1971, 135). Similarly, Regier credits a long list of reforms in the business, legislative, and political realms to the muckrakers, whose efforts resulted in over fifteen reform laws, including mothers' pension acts and the eight-hour laws for women. "The whole tone of business in the United States was raised because of the persistent exposures of corruption and injustice" (1957, 201).

Putting aside for the moment the possibility that widespread protests of thousands of workers year after year throughout the early twentieth century prompted business and political officials to grudgingly alter workplace policies, let us focus on the transformative potentials of popular texts such as those of the muckrakers. Other scholars are less optimistic regarding the roles of popular texts in initiating reform (Budd, Entman, Steinman 1990; Ebert 1996; Gitlin 1979; Williamson 1986). In their study of the portrayal of race and mugging in the British press, Hall et al. note how biographical pieces obscure complexities. "[A]t the point where further analysis threatens to go beyond the boundaries of a dominant ideological field, the 'image' [of the ghetto or new slum] is evoked to foreclose the problem" (1978, 118). Hall explains how the connections between family, school, and work are "displaced into . . . biographical pieces." "Rather than trace the complex links between the deteriorated physical environment, patterns of cultural organisation and individual acts of crime, the inference is that a derelict and neglected house or street infects the inhabitants with a kind of moral pollution" (115). Christopher Wilson expresses similar skepticism in his analysis of muckraking magazines, asserting that they "mired the reader in spectatorship" (1983). Rather than promote a particular political stance, muckraking became a "matter of style, a literary strategy rooted in the often vacuous process of stimulating and unveiling for its own sake" (62). And according to Ohmann, muckraking journalism did not represent "a questioning of deep social structures or an act of resistance to the gathering of corporate and state power" so much "as a cry of 'foul play' against familiar kinds of infractions" (1996, 282).

This chapter examines and continues to raise questions regarding the double-edged nature of popular stories pertaining to social injustice and transformation. As was the case with the *Atlantic Monthly*, *McClure's* articles did not represent monolithic hegemonic exhortations but rather contained textual leakages that readers may seize upon to support their own efforts at social change. The overarching frame of universalization made room for voices of dissent through fiction and nonfiction that painted a less-than-rosy picture of life in early-twentieth-century America. And the associated progressive impulse represented a "utopian" element (Jameson 1979/80) with which readers could identify. Yet these voices were managed and contained through a frame that emphasized consensus achieved through common ideals, thus short-circuiting a contextualization or analysis of underlying structures that created material disparity. Much like the naturalization of the *Atlantic Monthly*, universalizing in *McClure's* diverted attention from historical conditions and the ways in which these material circumstances affected individuals differently.

McClure's writers positioned themselves as spokespersons for "public welfare," and often fostered identification on both sides of the political and economic aisles. *McClure's* writers did not refrain from dispensing equal doses of criticism and praise to employer and employee. At times workers were portrayed as being just as corrupt and greedy as the individuals for whom they worked. "Capital and Labor Hunt Together," warned Ray Stannard Baker in 1903. Conversely, *McClure's* articles often depicted employers as being just as hard working and goodhearted as workers but overwhelmed by a system in which they had little control. They are "doing the best they can under the circumstances," two writers explained of employers in the laundry business (Clark and Wyatt 1911). "Pressure of extra work in the hotels [laundries] is produced, not by ill-willed persons who are consciously oppressive . . . but simply by the un-regulated conditions of the laundries" (412).

Nondominant viewpoints regarding women's political and economic rights emerged most notably in articles detailing the plight of working-class women and girls and in a "Department for Women," which discussed the burgeoning feminist and suffrage movements. A series appearing in 1910–11 informed readers of the deplorable conditions faced by women in skilled and unskilled factory positions (Clark and Wyatt 1910a, 1910b, 1910c, 1911). Accounts detailing minimal wages, lack of decent clothing and healthy diet, long hours, layoffs, speedups with no breaks, and harassment from foremen created a critical aperture that may have allowed for a more systemic critique of the industrial system.

Yet universalization's persuasive power lies in its ability to control such textual openings. Harsh realities and class disparities were given space so that common values and ideals could be provided as the antidote.

For example, in a series on female wage earners, readers learned how these workers transcended their material situation through cultural activities, positive demeanor, and education. In an article on the shirtwaist workers in New York City, the authors explained, "Nearly all the Russian shirtwaist-makers visit the theater and attend clubs and night classes, whatever their wage or their hours of labor" (Clark and Wyatt 1910b, 79).[4] And in the profile of Getta Bursova, "an attractive Russian girl," the reader learns of Getta's enduring character. In spite of her layoff, "She was eager for knowledge, and through all her busy weeks had paid 10 cents dues to a self-education society" (78). Within this frame, collective confrontation of entrenched material systems became obsolete as workers were shown to transcend material circumstances by accumulating cultural capital.

Still other articles relied on universalization in order to promote the qualities of good American citizenship. Such portrayals often amounted to immigrant bashing, as in "Toilers of the Tenements" which appeared in 1910 (Sergeant). In this article, the reader met a number of Italian families who did "home work"—labor outside of factories done chiefly by women and children. Little sympathy was built for these impoverished families. Rather, the emphasis was on the immigrant's responsibilities and their "new status in society," which they "fail to recognize" when they arrive in the United States. Pictures accompanying the article depicted entire families seated around kitchen tables making artificial flowers and silk pompons, children with blank stares on their faces. Both text and photos created the image of the dirty, disease-spreading immigrant family and became a forum for the author to speak for the "welfare of the public." Horowitz's observations of Progressive Era investigations shed light on *McClure's* accounts. "At the heart of the Progressive standard of living investigations was the attempt, by force of law and public opinion, to make informed citizens and 'thoughtless employers' realize that poverty undermined the general welfare" (1985, 58). Universalization's emphasis on common values enabled *McClure's* writers to speak for a general "public" by eliding material issues that gave rise to class differences and that problematized the notion of a unified "public opinion."

McClure's responded to voices of protest through universalization, a strategy that elided material discriminations through an emphasis on values and ideals. This persuasive strategy may have encouraged reader identification with working-class women and immigrant families who were struggling to make ends meet during this period. Accounts focused on the good character of workers and the abilities of the downtrodden to pick themselves up by the bootstraps through upbeat attitude, thrift, and hard work. But universalizing particular values and morals veiled the ways the ideals existed in support of a specific socioeconomic system— liberal capitalism. Hard work, perseverance, positive attitude, and individual responsibility were characteristics necessary to the smooth functioning of an industrial system that depended on punctuality, discipline, and rigid separation of work and leisure. Put differently, emphasizing values and ideals as the engines of human behavior and social change obscured the roles of material systems and institutions in shaping human experience. Furthermore, the frame's focus on personal character ignored systematic class discrimination and thus the collective nature of both the problem and potential solutions. The protest rhetoric of wage-earning women and girls provides a contrast to *McClure's* portrayals and indicates the limits of popular biographical pieces that sever the connections between social values and historical conditions.

Muckraking had yet to sow its seeds in the pages of *McClure's* in the mid–1890s. During these years, the magazine upheld the decency of workers and owners alike and maintained the dignity of True Womanhood much like its more prestigious distant cousin, the *Atlantic Monthly*.

1894–1895: Universalization and Harmonious Relations

The depression of 1893–95 hit all sectors of U.S. society hard. Business owners shut down their shops and factories closed, leaving three fifths of the total labor force unemployed and trade unions barely able to survive (Foner 1979, 235). The effects of the economic slump hit women workers harder than male workers. As the labor historian Meredith Tax points out, "Industrial cycles and employer persecution affected both sexes but affected them unevenly, because of women's more insecure place in the work force and the fact that much of their value to the employer depended on their remaining marginal" (1980, 92). Male workers who viewed women workers as competition for scarce employment also played a role in women's marginal status in the workplace.[5] It was in part due to these hard times that middle-class individuals became more aware of the struggles of labor. The labor historian Philip Foner points out that the 1893 depression brought working-class women and middle-class suffragists close together; workers realized the importance of the vote in order to alter working conditions, and suffragists' consciousness was raised regarding the plight of working women. In addition, both groups were well aware of the benefits that a cross-class alliance would bring to their own cause (1979, 237).

Though union membership was adversely affected by the depression, widespread unemployment and the struggle to make ends meet generally sharpened workers' awareness of the ways they were exploited by the system. Upper-class fears of widespread revolt were reflected in the reaction by authorities to a public statement by the anarchist and labor activist Emma Goldman. When Goldman told a group of unemployed men gathered in Union Square in New York City that "'it was their sacred right' to take bread if they were starving," she was sentenced to one year in the Blackwell Island prison in New York (Foner 1979, 235).

During a time of economic austerity and growing class awareness among workers and some middle-class reformers, *McClure's* provided readers with a vision of harmony in which hard work and generosity applied equally to employers and employees. Cleveland Moffett, the author of "Life and Work in the Powder Mills," described the owners of a particular mill, the du Ponts, as having "fierce courage," "inflexible justice" and as enjoying the "absolute worship of three hundred workmen" (1895, 4). In this depiction, the du Ponts worked side by side with their employees, both parties stood on equal ground. In "The Mistress of the Foundry," Mrs. Sterns, the wife of an iron foundry's owner, represented a mother-figure to the workers who adored her (Joslyn 1894). Worker and owner expressed a mutual concern and devotion to one another. One night when strikers were burning down the houses of various factory owners, Mrs. Sterns's workers, particularly "Big Luke," fervently protected their "mother." "You've been good to us, we'll take care of you," Big Luke reassures Mrs. Stern (269).

The world beyond these happy factory depictions stood in stark contrast to the popular portrayals. Particularly during the mid- to late 1800s, the lines between owner and worker were more clearly drawn than ever before. Railroads were laid and bridges suspended by the labor of tens of thousands of immigrants who were paid one or two dollars a day while the pocketbooks of business magnates were lined with millions. Rich, family-owned corporations had the government, the courts, and in some cases the military on their side in profit-making schemes, while workers had to draw on their own meager resources to establish funds to give to widows and orphans of men killed while on the job. In the face of such glaring disparities, workers did not stand idly by, but halted production hundreds of times *each year* in the 1880s and 1890s, and were often met by corporate-instigated police beatings and federal troop intervention. As Howard Zinn writes in *A People's History of the United States*, "[I]n industry after industry . . . shrewd, efficient businessmen [were] building empires, choking out competition, maintaining high prices, keeping wages low, using government subsidies" (1980, 251).

When women's entrance in social, political, and economic realms became more acceptable and common in the extra-discursive world, their presence increased dramatically in the pages of *McClure's*, just as they did in the *Atlantic Monthly*. In the magazine's early years, images and stories about women, though not prevalent, displayed a somewhat surprising degree of variability. *McClure's*, negotiating the dictates of True Womanhood with more nuance than the mid–1890s *Atlantic*, tailored images to a middle-class audience whose very real material circumstances often stymied women's abilities to remain domestic and submissive. Articles and poems reinforcing the "natural" traits of womanhood remained an undercurrent around and over which other portrayals pushed the boundaries of acceptable gender norms. A poem in the June 1893 issue recounted for readers each attribute becoming of a woman: "The rose is such a lady / So stately, fresh, and sweet . . . / So dignified and fine . . . / So courteous, pure, and fair" (Hall, 82). Two years later, "My Jenny" provided an equally delicate if not more down-to-earth, portrayal of woman: "My Jenny hasn't a penny—/But that matters not to me: / She has two fine eyes, /As soft as the skies, /And deep as the tranquil sea. / There's nothing of art / In her true-blue heart; /She's just like a morn in May . . . " (McCann 1895, 90).

Women who were sweet as a rose and tranquil as the sea were also able to manage careers as factory owners, businesspersons, writers, and actresses. In mid–1890s *McClure's*, images of publicly active women were reserved for women of means. The implication was that wealthy women did not *have* to labor outside of the home (or their labor was temporary), thus it presented less of a threat to her womanhood. It appears that for *McClure's* writers, the verdict was still out on how such traits and behaviors would square with the demands of True Womanhood. In some accounts, women were quite capable of managing careers while maintaining womanly delicacy, whereas in others, women paid a dear price for overstepping their bounds.

The intimacies of the actress Ellen Terry were recounted in an 1894 article, accompanied by photos, in the magazine's "Human Documents" department: Ellen Terry "has wonderful courage, indomitable will" (McKenna 1894, 460). She was well read in her profession, took part in her own costuming, and dabbled in photography and cycling. However, these accomplishments did not take away from her womanly attributes. Readers were reminded that the actress was a "delicate woman, . . . with a rare magnetic sympathy . . . [and] captivating tenderness," and she was "an admirable housekeeper" to boot. Similarly, a rendering of Mrs. Gladstone, the "mistress of Hawarden Castle," in the village of Hawarden, detailed her accomplishments in the public realm. Extending her intellectual and monetary resources to assist the poor, Mrs. Gladstone founded Newport Market Refuge, Free Convalescent Home, and an orphanage, Hawarden. Though an active participant in the public sphere, Mrs. Gladstone did not range too far from home: she was a "true and careful mother who would not give over her duties to another, even to the best of nurses" (Burnett 1893, 237).

In its 1896 issue, *McClure's* carried two articles by the well-known writer Elizabeth Stuart Phelps. Phelps detailed her experiences as a student at Abbot Academy in Andover, Massachusetts, and described her successes as a writer with contributions to such magazines as *Harper's*, the *Atlantic Monthly*, and *Century* (1896a). Phelps's second installment recounted the writing of one of her most famous pieces, "The Gates Ajar" (1896b). The writer explained her experiences of frustration as a relatively privileged young woman with ambitions that conflicted with gender expectations and she detailed a sort of political awakening as she witnessed an industrial accident while on a visit to the mill town of Lawrence during her years at Abbot.

These stories were insightful both as missives about the upper classes and as messages about women. They provided a middle-class audience with images of a benevolent upper class that, despite its wealth, still held a genuine work ethic. Wealthy individuals were portrayed as being in touch with the realities of their world. In this way, these articles reflected the universalizing strategy discussed above. *McClure's* created a world in which people, regardless of their material position, held similar values and interests. By fostering reader identification with the upper classes, these stories functioned hegemonically by encouraging middle-class readers (who were also frequently exploited by industrial capitalism and the growing consumer society) to strive to enter the ranks of the wealthy.

As stories that centered on female figures, these articles employed the rhetoric of True Womanhood that naturalizes women's abilities and attributes. Given this rhetoric's prevalence in society during this time period, it is not surprising to find the True Woman in popular texts targeting different audiences. Thus, in a variety of forms, the True Woman could be found in the *Atlantic Monthly*, *McClure's*, and mail-order magazines, discussed in the next chapter. But in contrast to the *Atlantic*, *McClure's* offers images of women such as Mrs. Gladstone and Ellen Terry,

who could be successful workers and still maintain their womanly attributes. These images corresponded to the reality of many middle-class
women, who involved themselves in the public realm as activists or in
order to supplement their husband's income. Yet the stories reminded
the female reader of her most "enduring" qualities.

During the same years, these more progressive images were interspersed with other articles warning women of what would befall them if
they forsook their domestic duties. For one woman, enduring love and
marriage slipped away because of her ambition for greater things. After
years of unhappiness, the protagonist, Eleanor, realized her mistake and
won back the lost love. Marriage made her life whole once and for all
(Moulton 1894). In another article, women's desire for education became
the reactionary target. In "Nervousness: The National Disease of America," Dr. Mitchell warned that females were prone to the "school fiend,"
i.e., education, which "wilts" the "flower of American womanhood" before it has a chance to bloom (Wakefield 1894, 306). Again, the message
was directed toward middle-class women who at this time were breaking
into the public realm both as activists and as income generators. The
message in this article encouraged a sedentary lifestyle as well as upward mobility for the female reader. The author wrote, "If the mass of
American women led the life of the Four Hundred [a popular term for
the top echelon of New York society], specialists in nervous diseases
would find their occupation gone" (306).

An 1894 work of fiction by Robert Barr provided a more ambiguous
image of a woman which allowed for a number of interpretations. "The
Revolt of the _____" relayed a story of a husband and wife whose gender
attributes were completely reversed.[6] The wife was business-smart, assertive, and commanding. She was described as having "decided features" and dressing "almost like a man. . . . Her brown hair was cut short
and parted at the side" (170). In contrast, her husband was weak around
his wife and dependent on her decisions and her money. In short, the
wife, Mrs. Maddax, defied all prescriptions of True Womanhood. To this
extent, she provided a liberatory image for *McClure's* female readers who
experienced the confines of domesticity and submissiveness. Many popular-culture scholars celebrate ambiguous images such as that of Mrs.
Maddax, which pose a challenge to traditional gender norms and practices. Indeed, this story—and others that appear in later years covering
controversial issues such as birth control and divorce—provided readers
with alternative visions. Particularly for female readers, these portrayals
raised awareness and offered possibilities of what gender relations *could*
be like. John Fiske, in his contemporary study of female viewers of soap
operas, notes how women create their own meanings out of a popular

text's "semiotic excess" that "legitimate feminine values and thus produce self-esteem for the women who live by them" (1987, 197)

"The Revolt of the _____" granted to women a measure of liberation, but reminded them of the price to be paid. The story made clear that Mrs. Maddax did not make a good mother. Her business duties caused her to neglect her children; and though she was well aware of this fact, she appeared not to care. Like much contemporary rhetoric, the story invoked motherhood in all its sanctity in order to rein women back into the home.

While we can acknowledge the complexity of any popular story or television show, the limitations of liberating potentials must also be explored. Female readers and viewers may choose to overlook or disregard a certain text's reinforcements of traditional gender norms (in *McClure's*, natural motherhood; in a soap opera, female submission to male power), but they are nonetheless surrounded by ample political, legal, and other popular rhetorics that exhort them to abide by certain prescribed behaviors. Perhaps more important, however, women past and present are disciplined not only textually, but materially—in workplaces and homes. Regardless of the increase in progressive images of women in recent years, the fact remains that women are still paid less than their male counterparts for the same work; women represent two thirds of all poor adults; and nearly 80 percent of working women remain locked in low-paying sex-typed jobs such as secretaries or sales clerks and are still held primarily responsible for domestic duties and child rearing (Faludi 1991, xiii). Textual liberation does not always translate into improved material living conditions.

The images of women in *McClure's* were more multifaceted than those in the *Atlantic* and represented an attempt on the part of writers and editors to speak to the reality of their readers while at the same time attempting to control perceived threats to the status quo such as women's demands for autonomy, education, and careers. While women were being encouraged to remain true to their "natural" duties, increasingly around the early 1900s, middle-class women were working outside the home in order to raise their family's standard of living. In addition, owing to their own precarious economic position, middle-class individuals were more likely than those of the upper class to identify with and join the struggles of the working class. Thus, in these as well as later years, women were often portrayed in *McClure's* in a variety of liberating roles. Yet the varied images of women in *McClure's* were accompanied by stern warnings against "too much liberation." Always present was a reinforcement of the sexual division of labor, which was central to an economic system that *McClure's* magazine, as a business and profit-making institution, relied upon.

1902–1903: Universalizing Through Ideals

In the early twentieth century, most wage-earning women remained unorganized and subject to extreme discrimination and exploitation. In
1900, a report by the federal Industrial Commission noted that in many
instances women workers did not earn enough to survive.[7]

Despite the dedication and militancy that women workers demonstrated over years of strikes and union activity in the late 1800s,[8] they
continued to face hostility from the largest organizer of workers, the
American Federation of Labor (AFL). Samuel Gompers led the AFL for
over twenty years, and by 1920 the organization represented 80 percent
of all organized workers. The organization was founded on the principles of craft unionism, which emphasized workers in skilled trades.
Thus, the very policies that guided the AFL effectively barred women
from union participation. First of all, the craft union approach of the AFL
was not conducive to the organization of women workers, who occupied
largely unskilled positions. In many cases, union constitutions specified
outright that women were not allowed to join. In a more roundabout
manner women's attempts to join locals were thwarted by excessively
high dues, entrance exams, and required apprenticeships, from which
they were excluded (Foner 1979, 250). And finally, when female workers
formed their own locals and applied for a charter from the AFL, they
were either turned down or simply ignored. The AFL's exclusion of
women from unions hurt both male and female workers. As long as
women workers remained unorganized, employers could continue to
hire them at lower wages and undercut wages of the industry as a whole
(Tax 1980, 105, 106). Female workers were "abused by employers who
valued [them] primarily for their 'cheap labor,'" and they were "isolated
by male workers who were afraid their wages and their jobs would fall
victim to the competition" (Kessler-Harris 1975, 100).

Increasingly, these workers turned to middle-class reformers who
themselves had become frustrated at the difficulty of improving labor
conditions through the settlement house movement and the Consumers'
League. The year 1903 marks an important point, for in that year middle-
class reformers and working-class women joined to form the Women's
Trade Union League (WTUL), whose primary goal was organizing
women into unions. During this time, when the needs of working-class
women received increasing attention from middle-class reformers, *Mc-
Clure's* magazine refrained from broaching issues concerning wage-earning women. When it came to labor outside the home, *McClure's* remained
focused on male-dominated unions. But through works of fiction, writers
hinted at women's struggles for political and educational equality, which
were acquiring increasing prominence outside the magazine's pages.

With varying degrees of subtlety stories recognized the growing presence of women in the public realm and often addressed women's ambitions for something more than True Womanhood offered. The adventures
of a young schoolgirl, Emmy Lou, were related in two stories appearing
in 1902 (Martin). In the May 1902 issue, readers experienced Emmy Lou's
initiation into grammar school, where she learned, among other things,
how to associate properly with boys her age. The July 1902 installment
finds a more confident Emmy Lou studying zoology in high school and
composing poetry. Other stories used the context of a romance to address
women's desires for equality. In "A Strenuous Courtship," Margery justified her marriage to a less-than-wealthy character from Colorado, ex-
claiming, "Forgive me, auntie, it is not so awful with us Colorado people;
there the women have an equal right with men" (Fowler 1903, 27). A year
later, a romance between a well-to-do European prince and a down-
home Kansas woman imparted the importance of earning one's keep,
whether male or female. Mary Daley forewent matrimony with Prince
Roseleaf until the prince could support Mary on his own earned income.
Mary explained the situation to the prince's father, "I've simply got to go
back to Kansas to teach . . . I'll go to work and so will he [the prince]. It's
best for both of us" (Michelson 1904, 350).

Other stories offered a less encouraging portrayal of the possibilities
for women that lay beyond the doorstep. A 1902 article, "Mrs. Shanklin's
Ambitions," might be more aptly entitled, "Mrs. Shanklin's Failed Ambitions," for it related one mother's futile attempts to educate and marry
off her daughter (Young). Defying the wishes of her husband, Mrs.
Shanklin enrolled her daughter in Penangton Academy, only to find that
schooling made her daughter nervous and ill. "The Committee on Matrimony," appearing one year later, related one man's attempts to win the
hand of his love, Phyllis. Following advice she had received from her
friend in the "woman movement," Phyllis resisted immediate acceptance
of Robert's marriage proposal. Robert discredited Phyllis's friend, describing her as a part of the "ultra-anti-masculine wing of the woman
movement" (Cameron 1903, 663). He continued by invoking the sanctity
of that most defining of all womanly duties, motherhood. According to
Robert, Phyllis's friend "doesn't seem to have soul-depth enough to realize that that puny, spindle-legged boy of hers needs more of her attention
than her clubs and classes" (663). Phyllis remained strong throughout
most of the article and defended her beliefs against Robert's attacks, but
in the last paragraphs she deferred and accepted Robert's proposal.

Despite the reality that by 1900 millions of women were participating
in the labor force and moreover that many of these women had organized their own union locals in the face of hostility from bosses as well as
fellow male workers, the pages of *McClure's* were devoid of any recogni-

tion of this group. As is the case with the *Atlantic Monthly*, women who labored outside the home represented a contravention of True Womanhood, and most popular discourses could not envision a female figure that did not fit into that mold.

In early 1900s *McClure's*, labor was portrayed as a male domain. Through universalization, class disparities were flattened as writers established the opinions of the "general public" and elicited reader identification with "model" workers who embodied American ideals. *McClure's* articles created a second persona through verbal cues that encouraged the reader to assume the outlook and attitude of "moral arbiter." The rhetorical devices of universalization and audience-as-arbiter were compatible with the positions of *McClure's* middle-class writers and readers. As individuals who dealt in cultural capital—*ideas*—the reform-minded among this class served as moral liaisons between the upper and working classes. In this role, the middle classes served as a legitimating voice for the upper classes and as the "legitimate" voice for the working class, identifying and expressing workers' needs and concerns to legislators, factory owners, and the workers themselves. In *McClure's*, disparities and issues that divided were continually bridged through reference to the all-encompassing invented concept of "general welfare." Like the naturalization of the *Atlantic Monthly*, universalization diffused and contained dissent, but accomplished this through consensus building rather than justification giving.

In portrayals of labor and capital, *McClure's* articles overrode systemic discriminations arising from the different positions a person occupied within industrial capitalism. In this way, class as a point of discrimination was elided; instead, ideals were spotlighted as that which divided or brought a people together. In 1903–4, the popular muckraker Ray Stannard Baker contributed articles on the growing power of unions. In these accounts, labor and capital competed against each other on an even playing field. Capital and labor were equally greedy, "crush[ing] independent competition" at the expense of the "defenseless, unorganized public" (Baker 1903b, 451, 452). An article one year later offered little distinction between employee and employer: "A union is no longer a mere strike mob, clamoring for more to eat. It is learning *business*. It has gone to school to Wall Street. . . . The union is a cold business proposition. . . . The object of this new business union . . . was . . . like that of our trusts and employers' associations: It sought to control the market" (1904a). Elsewhere, parallels were drawn between the methods of unions and employer associations. The "strike, under the name of 'lockout,' is equally the chief weapon of the Employers' Association, and it is as fair for the one as for the other" (1904b, 284). Similarly, Baker explained that the "germ which causes the monopolistic trust among employers is responsible for the 'closed shop' among labor unions. And the argument of unionism is exactly the argument of the trust: 'If we can get a complete monopoly, we can take what profits (wages) we will" (1904a, 367).

In the *McClure's* accounts, the "general public" stood between capital and labor and were made to suffer at the hands of these two groups. The teamster gained wage increases, owners "fattened their bank accounts . . . and the defenseless, unorganized public paid the bill" (Baker 1903b, 452). Appealing to his readers as "general public citizens," Baker asked: "[I]s there any doubt that the income of organized labor and the profits of organized capital have gone up enormously, while the man-on-a-salary and most of the great middle class, paying much more for the necessaries of life, have had no adequate increase in earnings?" (1903b, 463). Even the labor leader John Mitchell, who in "The Coal Strike" explained a 1902 strike of coal miners in Pennsylvania, asserted, "The final judge of all social contests, whether wars or strikes, is the public" (1902, 220). "Public opinion," Mitchell, the president of the United Mine Workers, reassured, gathered "on the side of justice" (220).

Only by eliding systemic material discriminations was Baker's one-to-one comparison of labor and capital possible. Universalization provided a way for writers to broach salient social issues surrounding labor-capital relations without opening the Pandora's box of an analysis of the influences of industrial capitalism on those relations. As portrayed in *McClure's*, labor and capital were equally greedy and the real victim was the "general public," which stood for the common interests of all. Universalization *decontextualized* the situation in order to preclude a discussion of an industrial system that placed control of necessary resources in the hands of the few while the majority were forced to sell their labor in order to survive. It did this by means of flattening class differences and interjecting the neutral public bystander. A discussion of the actual industrial system—contextualization—would call attention to the different interests of workers and owners and would make direct comparisons problematic. Grounding the motives of labor and capital within this material context would disable universalization's attempts to "speak for" a public or to assert an "all-ness" to the picture it frames.

Personalization, the focus on individual action and individual merit, was another device used to sidestep meaningful analysis. By means of personalization, writers could demonstrate support for labor while maintaining control over its more radical elements. As mentioned earlier in the chapter, universalization often relied on metonymy, a rhetorical strategy that reduces complex social issues to simple images with which the public could identify. Put differently, metonymy encouraged personalization of issues that may be distant from a reader's immediate experiences. For example, *McClure's* readers were invited to identify with labor through portrayals of model labor leaders and workers who embodied values that seemingly transcended time and place. Writers invoked the ethos of Horatio Alger in order to demonstrate how character overcame obstacles. Readers became familiar with workers such as David Dick and James Winstone. Dick, a coal miner, "had come to this country without money, and had been able to save enough to purchase himself a good home of his own. He was a member of the Scotch Presbyterian Church . . ." etc. (Baker 1903a, 324). Likewise, Winstone arrived in Pennsylvania "without money [and] was able, working as a common miner and supporting a family, to save enough in fourteen years to make him the possessor of two fine homes and everything paid for" (330–331). "Masters of Their Craft," which appeared in April 1903, described how workers performed their labors with "spirit" and "inspiration" (Kirk). The writer interviewed conductors and newspaper copy-cutters, focusing on the men's character—their ability to remain calm and cheerful in stressful jobs. Readers learned of content workers who passed up promotions just to remain in their current positions. "I'd rather run a cablecar than eat," remarked one worker (365).

Other accounts highlighted the ideal labor leader—responsible, disciplined, and deferent to big business. Lincoln Steffens contributed a profile of John Mitchell of the United Mine Workers. Mitchell was described as "patient and reasonable," his voice of sanity calming the "passions and ignorance" of the rank-and-file miners. Personalizing Mitchell and focusing on his character, Lincoln let readers know that Mitchell was not so different from many familiar business figures: "[H]e would put himself in a position to sell mining labor just as Mr. Rockefeller would sell oil, Mr. Havemeyer sugar" (1902, 355). The following month, an article extolled "What Organized Labor Has Learned" (Easley 1902). According to this account, the revitalization of organized labor was the result of "improved leadership and responsibility to the membership . . . [and] the improvement in the character of the unions, their broadening policies, the conservatism of their leaders, which have made possible the inauguration of joint conferences and agreements with employers based on mutual concessions" (483). Such portrayals were further reinforced by a fiction work that told of hardworking "Roaring Dick" Darrell, the teamster who "worked like a demon" and kept the men he headed in line (White 1903, 395).

Focusing on character personalized social issues and precluded an analysis of systemic discriminations that required more than an upbeat attitude to alter. In his studies of contemporary popular texts, Barry Brummett acknowledges the "paradoxes of personalization" and the potential for an awareness of "underlying causes" of social issues to become lost through the process of reader identification (1991, 172–195). According to Brummett we can counteract such paradoxes by developing a heightened awareness of how we assemble "mosaics" from popular texts, "that include positions for others and for ourselves" (191). Brummett suggests metonymizing "more strategically . . . with more awareness" (193).

However one proceeds with caution, Brummett's emphasis remains on popular texts and focuses on textual constructions of oneself and of others as "like me or unlike me."

Yet one need not rely solely on the images of popular texts to understand the experiences of subordinate groups and dominant group implication in their oppression. The words of workers themselves—shaped by lived, not textually constructed, experiences—often provide a very different picture.

Mary Harris (Mother) Jones and other female labor activists were often at odds with leaders such as John Mitchell, who operated in the interests of white, male, skilled workers.[9] Though Mother Jones was also a central organizer of coal miners, her contributions were not a part of the landscape of labor in *McClure's*. Her confrontational tactics and involvement with the wives of coal miners lay beyond the bounds established by *McClure's* ideological frame. In coal-mining communities such as the ones described in *McClure's*, Mother Jones convinced striking male coal miners to stay at home with the children while Jones led the wives, banging pots and pans, to the mines to keep scabs away. In countless strikes, "Mother Jones was able to utilize the element of surprise by having the miners' wives step out of their traditional roles as housewives. They were thus able to cause the company gunmen and strikebreakers to panic by surprising and confusing them" (Foner 1979, 282). In *McClure's*, universalization established the boundaries of acceptable labor leadership: the "responsible leader" and happy-go-lucky followers who worked with "spirit" and "inspiration" provided figures on which writers could paint seemingly transcendent values and characteristics. Jones's confrontational tactics lay well beyond these boundaries.

Though *McClure's* accounts of labor in the early 1900s focused exclusively on the male worker, child labor was the subject of two accounts (Nichols 1903; Poole 1903). Ernest Poole's article decried the menace of child street peddlers who gave in to the "cheap pleasures" of the city and eventually became society's "most illiterate . . . most dishonest . . . most impure" citizens (1903, 48). "Children of the Coal Shadow," an account by Francis Nichols of young coal miners, generated a bit more sympathy; yet the author's opening statement undermined any critical potential: "It is not my purpose to attempt an explanation of this chronic unhappiness" experienced by coal-mining families. Rather, "I only wish to call attention to the atmosphere and life into which a child of the coal shadow is born" (1903, 435). Nichols's stance typifies the muckraking journalist's tendency to "stimulat[e] and unveil[] for its own sake" (Wilson 1983, 62). The magazine's framing ideology of universalization precluded a contextualization of coal miners' hardships which would have gone beyond "calling attention to" conditions—to exploring underlying reasons for these conditions.

Outside the pages of *McClure's*, as the first decade of the 1900s progressed, wage-earning women became increasingly organized, in part owing to the assistance of the WTUL, which continued to provide financial assistance and cultivate leadership skills in the working-class women under its wing. In the teens, *McClure's* openly responded to the growing presence of organized women workers and suffragists by providing readers stories and images that were often quite supportive of women's political and sexual equality. These narratives surrounding women's rights were complex and must be examined carefully in order to understand the multiple implications of such progressive, and sometimes controversial, texts.

1909–1917: Universalization and Mainstreaming

Six years after its formation, the WTUL became a nationally recognized labor organization when it assisted garment workers in the Uprising of 30,000. Yet organizations between working-class and middle-class women were not without conflict, and the WTUL provides a good example of the successes as well as difficulties faced by cross-class organizations during this period. In particular, the middle-class allies of the WTUL conceptualized work much differently than their wage-earning sisters. For the more well-off, work was a way to escape the confines of domesticity; work was liberation. Wage-earning women, by contrast, knew the harsh realities of work outside the home from their own daily experiences in factories, mills, and shops. They also learned from firsthand experience the importance of class struggle and the necessity of solidarity with men of their class.

The middle-class allies for whom material necessity was a less pressing issue most often ignored class consciousness and instead focused on education and cultural uplift. For example, Jane Addams, WTUL vice-president and the well-known founder of the Chicago settlement house Hull House, believed that an independent worker movement was unnecessary (Tax 1980, 107). WTUL allies often spoke on behalf of, as opposed to speaking *with*, working-class women, and so were unaware of or downright ignored the needs of those they were attempting to assist. Thus, the WTUL ultimately became a vehicle through which middle-class values such as harmony, disciplined leadership, and upward mobility could be instilled (see Dye 1980; Tax 1980). Put differently, the motivations of the allies and the working-class women differed substantially.[10] Middle-class allies sought to train the promising few to be "respected" labor leaders—accepted by politicians, wealthy philanthropists, and middle-class Americans. Working-class activists saw very little benefit in acculturation and refined manners and instead sought to "ris[e] *with* their class not *from* it" (Tax 1980, 111).[11]

During the years 1909–14, when the WTUL and other Progressive organizations were improving upon the system primarily through legislative reform, *McClure's* was a popular forum through which many of the same Progressive Era beliefs and values were transmitted. Indeed, the voices of many well-known middle-class activists of the WTUL and other women's movement activists such as Jane Addams, Sue Ainslie Clark, and Inez Milholland were heard in *McClure's* during these years.

The period 1909–17 offers the widest diversity of female images in *McClure's*. Between 1910 and 1911, the struggles of working women received extensive coverage, and in 1913 *McClure's* launched "A New Department for Women," which guaranteed regular space to issues surrounding suffragism and the feminist movement.

As one of the most widely read ten-cent monthlies of the early twentieth century, *McClure's* pioneered the way that popular texts manage and produce social movements for mass consumption. The decontextualizing and personalizing elements of universalization provided the requisite mechanisms for *McClure's* to popularize feminism and smooth the movement's more radical edges.

Describing and Moralizing the Struggles of Working-Class Women

While the *Atlantic* remained aloof, avoiding the dirt and grind that marked thousands of wage-earning women's daily lives, *McClure's* contained investigative reports detailing deplorable conditions endured by women in factories and tenements. Works of fiction with a down-to-earth appeal interspersed between these exposés provided further ideological support for women's struggles for equality. In these narratives, writers often made pioneer women central protagonists, thus providing an unthreatening pretext for women's bold and daring actions. The rugged western frontier seemingly elicited such defiant behaviors in these heroines. The significance of the narratives lies in the subtle recognition of female desires and struggles for equality beyond the pages of the magazine.

"Mrs. Piper's Limit," by George McCulloch, appearing in August 1909, portrayed a Mother Jones–like figure who saved the day by thwarting a group of scoundrels who attempted to rob a wagon. Mrs. Piper defended herself and her fellow passengers by "lunging toward" the robber and "wrest[ing] the six-shooter from his hand and lamm[ing] him over the head with it" (McCulloch 435). Ensuring the robber's demise, Mrs. Piper grabbed him by the shirt-collar and exclaimed, "'[Y]ou skin out o' here, and skin durned hard,' and she kicked the seat of his jumpers a couple of times and gave him a shove into the underbrush" (435).

A few months later, "Pioneer Goes Suffragette" related the bravery of two Idaho women, Birdie and Flora, determined to cast their votes despite the misgivings of their husbands (Green 1909). When the couples arrived in town on Election Day, the women endured taunts from mobs in the streets. The day was saved, however, by the famous "New York Blondes," a troupe of burlesque dancers that happened to be in the western town on this day. As Birdie and Flora were harassed, the New York Blonde Maude Montmorency stepped up and placed a .38 revolver "into unpleasant proximity with [a male harasser's] square jaw" (682). The story concluded with "Miss Montmorency and ten burlesque ladies of sturdy statue as marshals" of a parade of two hundred women who cast their ballots. The story's impressive conclusion foreshadowed the more militant suffrage parades to become common in the mid-teens: "With eyes alight, and revolver poised for action, Maude Montmorency pushed two men out of her path. Her staff, carrying umbrellas, pick-axes, and brooms hastily collected from odd corners of the hotel, menaced the enemy and warned them to stand aside" (682). In other stories, women abandoned abusive husbands and sought solidarity with female friends (Hay 1910; Roberts 1910). These narratives gave female readers strong female figures to identify with and in many ways confirmed these readers' own experiences of struggle against a male-dominated culture.

Readers were informed of the real-life experiences of wage-earning women through a number of articles written in the muckraking style of the early 1900s. In 1910 and 1911, *McClure's* carried a series written by Sue Ainslie Clark and Edith Wyatt documenting the lives of working-class women and girls in a variety of trades.[12] These articles enlightened a middle-class audience to the extremely low wages and the harsh living and working conditions endured by wage-earning women each day. An article focusing on unskilled workers told of an employer who "was very lax about payment, and sometimes cheated [the female employee] out of small amounts" (1910c, 202). Workers were subject to "uncertain and seasonal employment, small exploitations, monotony in occupation, and fatigue from speeding" (204). Shirtwaist workers labored from 8 A.M. until as late as 8 or 9 P.M. during the busy months, and the slack season brought little or no work and, of course, no wages (1910b). Laundry workers "risk[ed] mutilation from unguarded mangles" and were often subjected to contaminated water and "verminous and unhealthful" dressing rooms (1911, 402).

The Clark and Wyatt series relied on profiles of individual working women and girls to discuss the conditions these workers faced. Readers became familiar with "Natalya Urusova, a Russian Jewish Shirtwaist-Maker," "Irena K., a Sixteen-Year-Old Operative Who Supported Four People on $9 a Week," "Marta Neumann, a Homesick Austrian Worker," "Mrs. Hallett, Earning $6 a Week After Working Sixteen Years," in addition to many others. The profile format provided a way to personalize the workers, to put a human face on the "working masses," fostering reader identification. *McClure's* readers learned that these young women—though they dressed in old clothes and lived in crowded tenements—held many of the same desires and aspirations as did they. Betty Lukin, introduced in "The Shirtwaist Makers and Their Strike," attended the theater and various clubs. She displayed "[s]uch an eager hunger for complete change of scene and thought, such a desire for beauty and romance" (1910b, 79). Similarly, Getta Bursova was "eager for knowledge, and through all her busy weeks had paid 10 cents dues to a self-education society" (78). The article on unskilled and seasonal workers explained how Sarina Bashkitseff escaped her world by reading Shakespeare. Sarina's "fate might be expressed in Whitman's words, 'Henceforth I ask not good fortune, I myself am good fortune.'" Whatever Sarina's circumstances, "[F]ew persons in the world could ever be in a position to pity her" (1910c, 202).

In keeping with its muckraking mission, *McClure's* revealed various social ills. Still, the magazine required a rhetorical strategy that would allow such exposures yet stopped short of wholesale criticism of the socioeconomic system in which the magazine enterprise—its writers, publishers, advertisers, and target audience—were invested. And not least important, the magazine must approach such controversial issues without threatening audience identification with the subject matter. The frame of universalization allowed space for acknowledging social imperfections but contained counterhegemonic tendencies by eliding the systemic and materially rooted nature of problems and potential solutions surrounding wage-earning women's poverty.

The individual profile format rhetorically served this overarching frame in two ways. First, profiles invited reader identification with working girls and women by focusing on values that seemingly crossed class boundaries and character that called forth a common humanity. At the same time, however, the profile as a format *individuated* wage-earning women's circumstances; profiles appeared on the page as separate accountings. Thus readers were encouraged to understand the situations of Irena K., Marta Neumann, and Natalya Urusova in isolation from their position in a broad and deeply entrenched economic system that relied on class exploitation. Biographical pieces enhanced the hegemonic effectiveness of universalization by obscuring systematic discrimination and dispersing it among seemingly isolated cases. And in each case, cheerful attitudes and education were demonstrated as the glue that held society together.

In *McClure's* portrayals, "forces," "initiative," and positive attitudes lift these workers out of their material circumstances. The article containing the profile of Getta Bursova mentioned that she had just been laid off. "In spite of this defeat in her fortunes, her presence had a lovely brightness and initiative, and her inexpensive dress had a certain daintiness" (1910b, 78). "The Story of Betty Lukin," in the same article, conveyed a similar tone of transcendence. Despite little income left over after lodging, food, and payments to support her family, Betty responded "with the tacit simplicity of that common mortal responsibility which is heroic" that it was "'all in a day's work,'" (79). The report on the misfortunes of shirtwaist makers such as Betty Lukin and Getta Bursova concluded on this upbeat note: "Wonderful it is to know that in that world today unseen, unheard, are forces like those of that ghetto girl who, in the meanest quarter of New York, on stinted food, in scanty clothes, drained with faint health and overwork, could yet walk through her life, giving away half of her wage by day to some one else, [and] enjoying the theater at night" (86).

Mentions of trips to the opera and club memberships had the additional function of depicting workers as upwardly mobile; meanwhile, the specific activities that enlivened working-class leisure time were not described. Rather than shed light on the specific needs, concerns, and actions of working-class women as a group, biographical pieces highlighted how individual women made do by cultivating their own inner resources.[13]

A textual "leakage" in the magazine's frame appearing in the account of shirtwaist makers demonstrated the degree to which hegemonic ideologies give or bend in order to accommodate dissenting behaviors and avoid a total disconnection from the reality they purport to reflect. The story of shirtwaist makers, while profiling individual workers, also provided space for the firsthand testimony of one worker, Natalya Urusova, who detailed the infamous Uprising of 30,000 (1910b). Urusova's account exerted pressure on the magazine's ideological frame by giving voice to the thousands of workers who knew that cheerfulness was not sufficient to get one through the slack season. Urusova explained how she and the other shirtwaist makers rose together in solidarity from their machines and exited the factory by the front door. She related the police brutality endured by strikers and her own arrest on false charges.

But closure was brought to the confrontational event through universalization, and the dissenting voices were contained. The article concluded with a reaffirmation of the ideals that overcome material injustice: "Wonderful to know that, after her very bones had been broken by the violence of a thug of an employer, one of these girls could still speak for perfect fairness for him with an instinct for justice truly large and thrilling. Such women as that ennoble life and give to the world a richer and altered conception of justice—a justice of imagination and the heart" (86).

Universalization provided the rhetorical strategy to promote an idealist stance toward the conditions faced by early-twentieth-century wage earners. "Idealism . . . [refers] to the tendency to overemphasize consciousness, speech, and text as the determinants of [social] change" (Cloud 1994, 145). *McClure's* promoted education, values, and personal character as the vehicles for transcending material want. In the process, the magazine's exposés obscured the historical and material underpinnings of a society's values and cultural narratives.

In many respects, universalization can be viewed as a rhetorical mainstay of American culture. As in early-twentieth-century *McClure's*, stories abound in contemporary popular media detailing how individuals overcome harsh economic conditions by adhering to "universal" human values that in fact support a specific sociopolitical system—liberal capitalism. In particular, positive attitude, perseverance, and individual responsibility are shown as the staples of success throughout popular culture texts, including movies, magazines, and, most recently, television and radio talk shows.

Still, hegemony is an ongoing process of negotiation—a rhetorical give-and-take in which social disparity and dissent are at times given space and then renamed or reframed so as to be made to fit within the parameters of a dominant worldview. Further, no ideological frame can completely contain all counterhegemonic pressures. *McClure's* middle-class readers learned of the deplorable conditions existing behind locked factory doors. Through the firsthand testimony of Natalya Urusova, they glimpsed the necessity of solidarity in working-class struggles. And though these accounts did not delve deeper into the workings of the economic system that perpetuated material need, readers may have been motivated to join the local chapter of the WTUL or buy the union label. Yet from face-to-face contact with wage earners, middle-class women may have heard a story of working-class solidarity that upended *McClure's* universalization frame. Wage-earning women provided a frame of their own to explain their circumstances, a framing based on their daily experiences as garment workers, cigar makers, waitresses, etc. They emphasized themselves as laboring agents and highlighted solidarity as their vehicle for social transformation. And as Chapter 4 further elaborates, these activists employed not only words but extra-discursive tactics such as walkouts and pickets that further called attention to their roles as producers of society's wealth.

As the Clark and Wyatt series noted, wage-earning women desired more out of life than work and sleep; they struggled for "bread and roses too." But the testimonies of wage earners themselves paint a less optimistic picture of idealistic possibilities than the accounts in *McClure's*. Rather, many indicated the extent to which worklife permeated all areas of their lives, thus preventing any semblance of a life beyond home to work and back again. As Pauline Newman, organizer for the International Ladies' Garment Workers' Union, explained of wage-earning women, they led "a life which is mere existence, that is all. . . . They live on five-cent breakfast, ten-cent lunch and a twenty-cent dinner; live in a dingy room . . . wear clothes of cheap material . . . " (1914, 313).

Despite their difficult living and working conditions, wage-earning women did not remain passive. Time after time, in speeches, writings, and testimonies, working-class activists emphasized the need for unions and the benefits of unionizing as the answer to their situation. Most were unable to enjoy Shakespeare and the theater until conditions in their workplace were altered. "Women Must Organize!" wrote Louisa Mittelstadt, a member of the Beer Bottlers' Union Local 169 (1914). "Co-operation among the working girls is an absolute necessity," proclaimed Pauline Newman (1914, 312). Sarah Smith, a laundry worker in New York City, explained, "We formed a union at last, and we're striking for a shorter day and better conditions. God knows we've endured it quite a long while" (Dreier 1912, 69). Broom makers, glove and corset workers, department store waitresses, stockyard workers, cigar makers, hotel "maids," and countless other workers testified to their dedication to solidarity and their successes in winning workplace gains through organization: Hotel maids "realize what organization can do for them and are willing to work with all their might" (Levi 1918, 75); cigar workers were prepared to "fight to the finish" against employers (Smith 1918, 93); stockyard women "will stick in the face of great hardships and make greater sacrifices than men could dream of" (Sullivan 1918, 102). A strike of waitresses was so "effective at drawing customers away from the restaurant and attracting attention to the reasons why" that employers were forced to settle and workers won wage increases ("Department Store Waitresses," 141). In strike after strike, women and girls demonstrated the effectiveness of class solidarity and the need for confrontation in the workplace in order to materially alter, rather than metaphysically transcend, deplorable conditions.[14]

In addition to the Clark and Wyatt series on wage-earning women, *McClure's* pursued its muckraking impulses in a number of articles touching on life in the tenements, the dangers of factory fires, the white slave trade, whereby young women were lured into prostitution, and the struggles of coal miners. "Heroes of the Cherry Mine" eulogized those who died in a fire at a mine in Cherry, Illinois (Wyatt 1910). Widowed mothers and fatherless infants were the focal points of the story that elicited reader identification and sympathy. Photos depicted mothers holding infants and families gathered around kitchen tables without a father. Portraits were accompanied by text that told of the heroes who risked their own lives in order to save their coworkers.

Similarly, text and photos both served to describe the lives of tenement dwellers, though in a manner showing less sympathy than toward coal-mining families. One article relied on the profile format to describe the home work engaged in by entire families in order to survive. Readers learned of the Rapallos, a mother and her five children who made artificial flowers; the Misettos, a "depressed middle-aged mother," a "toothless grandmother," and three girls whose work was fabricating "cheap violets"; and the Callabrosos, a family of "eight untidy, slant-eyed children," a "melancholy mother," and a father who sewed trousers (Sergeant 1910).

Like the Clark and Wyatt series, all of these accounts offered description with no contextualization. The focus remained—however sympathetic—on a few individuals or families. The accounts thus became a way to localize problems, most often onto immigrants, and to propose individualized solutions, e.g., heroic fortitude, a tidier tenement. The locus of the problem was seen to be the immigrant who had failed to learn appropriate American values concerning hard work, cleanliness, and privacy. Workers in the Cherry mine were "foreign-born. . . . Some of them are inexperienced and do not take proper precautions either for their own safety or for the safety of others" (Wyatt 1910, 492). "Invading immigrants," "timid-and utterly ignorant," occupied packed tenements that "reeked of stale cooking." A "tuberculosis suspect" rolled cigarette wrappers while "hot and dirty fingers" worked on trousers that lay on the "greasy floor of the kitchen" (Sergeant 1910). Even the cause of tragic fires that often tore through these crowded apartments was localized onto the dwellers, who were careless with matches, dried clothes too close to the stove, or practiced dangerous religious customs, e.g., lighting candles on Yom Kippur (McFarlane 1911). In these accounts, universalization, the promotion of seemingly transcendent values and ideals, worked through negative identification. The importance of such values was conveyed through narratives that showed the consequences of deviating from them. Completely absent from these accounts was an analysis of the role of an economic system that relied on maximum production

with minimal workplace protections, and allowed a home-working network that exploited workers in the most extreme ways in the total absence of any workplace regulations.

From November 1911 to March 1912, *McClure's* carried a series of articles by the well-known Progressive Era activist Jane Addams in which
she explored the issue of commercialized vice. Each installment recounted the hardships of wage-earning women and their families and
the dangers that arose when these workers became involved in prostitution. Consistent with *McClure's* universalizing frame, Addams's articles
discussed the issues by means of profiles of individual girls and women,
which afforded opportunities to advance arguments for proper morals
and values.

The December 1911 article opened by acknowledging the extremely
low factory wages and the need for many girls to seek employment elsewhere in order to make ends meet. Addams mentioned the "economic
pressure grinding down upon the working-girl at the very age when she
most wistfully desires to be taken care of" (232). Describing the conditions faced by millions of young girls, the author explained, "In addition
to the monotony of work and the long hours, the small wages these girls
receive have no relation to the standard of living which they are endeav-
oring to maintain" (232). Addams related conversations with working-
class girls who explained the economic basis of their prostitution. Of
thirty-four girls interviewed, Addams explained that twenty-two entered
prostitution "from a desire to fulfill family obligations such as would be
accepted by any conscientious girl" (233).

Thus, the article opened a space for a "working-class voice," but like
the Clark and Wyatt articles, the majority of the Addams series relied on
profiles of individual girls in order to convey to readers the nature and
extent of prostitution. Although the relationship between low wages and
prostitution emerged at various points in the series, morality was the
overarching theme that threaded these stories together. The metonymic
images of young girls and immigrant families focused on prostitution as
either an individual moral breakdown or the collapse of family morals.

For example, young girls were described as having "fallen from grace"
or having given in to a "natural love of pleasure," a "reckless adventure,"
or an "unsatisfied love for finery" (1911b; 1912b). The December article
described the temptations facing the typical department store girl who
worked amidst "a bewildering mass of delicate and beautiful fabrics,
jewelry, and household decorations such as women covet" (234). Her
daily contact with shoppers may lead the young worker to "believe that
the chief concern of life is fashionable clothing. Her interest and ambition
almost inevitably become thoroughly worldly, and from the very fact
that she is employed downtown she obtains an exaggerated idea of the

luxury of the illicit life all about her" (235). Hotel chambermaids were also considered to be particularly vulnerable to moral traps, as explained in a profile in the February 1912 issue, "The Story of a Pretty Chambermaid and Her Reckless Adventure." As the story goes, the young worker "finally consented to accompany a young man to Seattle, both because she wanted to travel and because she was discouraged in her attempts to 'be good'" (472). The profile explained that after the tryst, the girl was "under the glamour of the life of idleness she had been leading [and thus] had gone voluntarily into a disreputable house" (472).

When not pictured as the result of an individual moral lapse, prostitution often was tied to the families from which these girls came. In these instances, the Addams series became a forum for what today is called "family values" rhetoric, a moralizing discourse that upholds a "mythical familial ideal" while scapegoating "private families—especially those headed by single parents, racial minorities, and the poor—for structural social problems" (Cloud 1998b, 388). Describing the experiences of a typical immigrant girl, one story explained the cynical attitude that often developed from overwork, long hours, and lack of leisure. But as the profile continued, the family became the source of such cynicism. Quoting from records of the Juvenile Protective Association of Chicago, the profile explained that many of the young girls they dealt with "come from families in which there has been a lack of warm affection and the poor substitute of parental tyranny" (1911b, 236). A similar story explained an Italian girl's transgressions as stemming from the "over-restraint" and "lack of understanding" of her father (1911b, 237).

Often, the remiss parent or lax family atmosphere was connected to the neighborhoods in which such families dwelled. One *McClure's* article described the breakdown of modesty arising from "the overcrowding of tenement-house life" (1912a, 342). The same article profiled "The Promiscuous Households of the Poor and Their Influence on Young Children," recounting the narrow escape of two sisters (1912a, 340–341). Their mother, a widow, worked all day and was thus unaware that her girls were visiting a neighbor who let them "powder and paint" their faces and "try on long dresses" (1912a, 341). When the mother learned of the girls' temptations, she immediately moved out of the "disreputable neighborhood." Another story told of the plight of black children who are "shut out from legitimate recreation [and thus] are all the more tempted by the careless luxurious life of a vicious neighborhood" (1912a, 341).

McClure's portrayals of prostitution and the magazine's muckraking journalism were part of the larger Progressive Era attempt to reinstill morals into business and government and to "clean up" urban neighborhoods that housed the nation's working poor. Investigations conducted by middle-class reformers of the period often decried the lack of privacy and the crowded living arrangements in urban tenements (Cameron 1991, 60; Horowitz 1985; see Henry 1913). Such conditions, it was believed, sowed the seeds of depravity. The underlying theme in Progressive writings on prostitution was moral control (Connelly 1980, 38). In *McClure's*, metonymic images bypassed the complexities of industrial capitalism and instead focused on personal or familial character flaws.

Again, the workers themselves give a slightly different view of prostitution and life in immigrant neighborhoods. Wage earners' reasons for entering prostitution were often multilayered, but most often it was to satisfy hunger, not a "love of finery" (Rosen 1982, 145–161). And in contrast to the tone of some *McClure's* profiles, crowded life in the tenement often provided the familial and communal networks necessary for survival in a new country.

In front of judges, factory investigating commissions, and to their fellow comrades, working-class women and girls who worked as prostitutes testified to the material basis of their occupation. If they raised the issue of morality, it was often to demonstrate its hypocritical application. In "Low Wages and Vice—Are They Related?" in the April 1913 issue of *Life and Labor*, the official organ of the Women's Trade Union League, women working at a brothel in Chicago all "asserted that [their] downfall had come from having insufficient wages to live honestly" (Mason and Franklin 1913). A typical worker, "R.A.," had earned three dollars a week in a St. Louis paper factory since she was sixteen. "When she was 20 she could not earn enough to assist her parents and took the shadowy life. She told the commission she would willingly return to her former life if she could earn $12 a week" (110). At a rally of wage earners at Cooper Union a year earlier, Clara Lemlich, a shirtwaist maker and working-class organizer, pointed to society's double standards for the sexes. She asserted:

> There are two moralities, one for men and one for women. Have you noticed when a man comes across a fallen woman what he does to take the burden off her back? Does he claim that he is responsible or acknowledge at least that men are responsible? . . . No, he takes advantage of her if possible. If she becomes a woman of the streets and is arrested, the judge fines her and the woman who has no other means of getting money has to go out and sell herself again in order to pay the court (quoted in Orleck 1995, 103).

Lemlich and others highlighted the interconnections between gender discrimination and class exploitation. As working women, these individuals were forced to transgress prescribed gender roles in order to survive. And as female workers, they were not granted the protection of social norms that deemed certain behaviors acceptable for men but unspeakable for women.

Fanny Kavanaugh, an outspoken working-class activist, worked on the Illinois Woman's Alliance police committee reporting abuses against prostitutes in courts and jails. Her incriminating investigations called widespread attention to the plight of prostitutes and made the issue a central one for the labor movement. Quoted in the *Chicago Times*, Kavanaugh observed: "[T]he public should remember that [women's] terrible economic conditions, tending ever to lower women's wages, even to the starvation point, drive women and young girls rendered desperate by destitution . . . into a life of shame" (Tax 1980, 71). In addition to explicating the economic basis of prostitution, Kavanaugh detailed the network of profit and exploitation that extended from police to bail bondsmen and judges. Women in working-class neighborhoods were rounded up and jailed as prostitutes on no evidence and were released only after paying a fee to the bailer and judge (Tax 1980, 70). Through firsthand witnessing and testimonials, Kavanaugh and the Alliance laid bare issues surrounding prostitution not captured within the *McClure's* metonymies.

In addition to the economic basis of prostitution, the work of the Alliance called attention to the contradictions of industrial capitalism, a system that relied on women as a cheap source labor while also depending on a sexual division of labor that upheld the home as "woman's place." The actions of Illinois police signify how the very status of "wage earner" marked women as a class that could be exploited not only as workers but as women who could not afford the luxury of adhering to traditional gender norms of domesticity and submissiveness and thus forfeited the protections that the norms called for.

As the *McClure's* series noted, domestic workers—isolated and often with little or no time off—were particularly vulnerable to the sexual advances of the male head of household. Rather than rely on ladies' reform organizations or charities to confront this situation, Jane Street, a domestic worker from Denver, organized fellow domestic workers for better wages and working conditions (Tax 1980, 134–138). In particular, Street and her sisters fought the employment "sharks" who controlled access to available jobs and amounted to little more than contractors for the white slave trade. The newly formed local of domestic workers developed a job listing and agreed to demand the same price when responding to jobs.

The *McClure's* series found the causes of prostitution in the individual girl, her family, or their neighborhood. This reduction was further underscored by the moral overtones of the pieces in *McClure's*, which emphasized individual character—either character flaws or special abilities to overcome "temptations." Indeed, it is precisely this focus on the character of an individual as representative of a common humanity that encouraged middle-class readers to identify with the individuals in the stories and thus mediated readers' reception of the issues at hand. As we have seen, identification through universalization came at a price: there was no further exploration of the ways that material systems shaped, influenced, and benefited from certain values in the first place.

Universalization and Feminism

Through the teens, *McClure's* openly discussed the suffrage and feminist movements in addition to other women's concerns such as birth control and divorce. Given the time period, some accounts were quite radical, demonstrating the give-and-take process between cultural hegemony and the social forces that it attempts to contain. Universalization came into play most prominently in the framing of feminism as discussed in the "Department for Women."

Where the *Atlantic* decorously broached woman suffrage as the means for purifying politics, *McClure's* unceremoniously delved into the issue through firsthand accounts written by militant suffragists from Great Britain. In her article "Woman's War: A Defense of Militant Suffrage," the English suffragist Elizabeth Robins justified the confrontational and at times violent tactics employed by suffragists in England (1913). Photos accompanying the text depicted well-known suffragists such as Alice Paul and Christabel Pankhurst being arrested and also showed the hammers the protesters hid in socks and "Dorothy bags," which they used to smash windows during protests. Further support for these activists' cause was garnered in an article appearing a few months later written by the suffragist Sylvia Pankhurst (1913). Pankhurst described her ordeal in prison, which included being forcibly fed, for having thrown a rock through a store window during a rally for women's suffrage. These two articles provided a textual opening, however narrow, for outspoken activists to present their own accounts of dissent; further, these narratives challenged the magazine's constructed world of universal values and cheerful cooperation.

Three years later, the magazine broached the subjects of birth control and divorce through a series of articles penned by Anna Steese Richardson. Framed as "human documents," the articles were firsthand testimonies told to Richardson, who then imparted them to *McClure's* readers. In this way readers were granted a glimpse into the lives of women who struggle against a sexist legal system. The protagonists in these accounts suffered social sanctions because their relationships were not aligned with the norms of the traditional nuclear family. The articles served as a forum through which the legal system's double standards could be debunked. "Am I My Husband's Keeper?" provided a defense of birth control and concluded with words of fortitude expressed by the central character: "I mean to organize the fight against the unjust law which makes it impossible for a wife and mother to protect herself against excessive child-bearing. When repeated child-bearing becomes a menace to her life or her health . . . then she has a right to knowledge concerning birth control" (1916b, 87).

In the following month's installment, "A Man in Her Life," a woman imparted to Richardson the stigma that she had endured for divorcing her first husband, who was abusive. She openly criticized social norms that required women to sacrifice their own needs and desires for their children and husbands. The woman told Richardson, "I made my first mistake when I decided that duty to my children and my family demanded that I live with John [her husband] even though our relations meant spiritual and physical degradation for me. No woman should pay that price for her children or relatives" (1916c, 52). In the same tone, the October 1916 issue in "Outside the Law: As Told by the Woman in the Case," gave voice to a woman who was ostracized for having an affair with a married man while her lover got off scot-free. The "modern woman . . . learns that while society banishes her permanently, irrevocably, it never gives up hope of redeeming the man by setting his feet in the straight and narrow path of matrimony" (1916e, 29). Even by contemporary standards, these women's insights were quite transgressive. Their perspectives pushed the boundaries of universalization at a time when women beyond the magazine's pages were voicing their own discontent with legal and political restrictions.

Given the social and legal sanctions against both divorce and birth control, *McClure's* can be credited with discussing these two issues in a relatively supportive light. The articles were controlled, however, through a subtext reinforcing traditional gender norms. Birth control was acceptable because motherhood (and hence womanhood) had already been secured. The protagonist had given birth to three children, but would risk her life if she became pregnant again. Thus, she needed birth control, lest she "force temptation" upon her husband to seek sexual relations elsewhere—in other words, birth control became a matter of preserving morality. In the following month's serial, though the stigmatized woman was allowed to criticize cultural norms, what she lamented most of all was that she had no "man in her life." And the protagonist who, through her affair, lived "outside the law" eventually married her lover, which brought her back within the norms of the regulated social realm.

In 1913, when *McClure's* introduced its "Department for Women," the editors explained the new feature to readers this way: "No movement of this century is more significant or more deep-rooted than the movement to readjust the social position of women. . . . This movement in its largest general aspects is termed feminism; in its immediate political aspects, suffrage. *McClure's* recognizes fully the impressiveness and vitality of this development. It proposes to treat of it in a sensible, straightforward manner. To do so, this department is established."

Inez Milholland, whom the magazine one year earlier had dubbed "spokesman for suffrage in America," became the writer for the "Department for Women." In choosing Milholland as the "spokesman" for women's suffrage, *McClure's* made quite a radical gesture in the way of women's rights. Milholland was a socialist and radical suffrage leader who was known for her involvement in the National Woman's Party and the Equality League of Self-Supporting Women.

The Equality League of Self-Supporting Women was formed in 1907 by Harriet Stanton Blatch, the daughter of Elizabeth Cady Stanton, in an attempt to unify women around the issue of work rather than the ideal of domesticity. The organization was a combination of workers like the well-known Leonora O'Reilly and Rose Schneiderman and professionals, including lawyers, writers, doctors, and social welfare and government workers. In the Equality League, Blatch, Milholland, and other upper- and working-class suffragists, brought new life and more aggressive tactics to the suffrage struggle which had been dominated up to that time by the conservative National American Woman Suffrage Association and their "tea-party style of organizing" (Tax 1980, 170; see DuBois 1994, Flexner 1959, 250–54).

Like her reformist contemporaries Jane Addams, Sue Ainslie Clark, and Edith Wyatt, Milholland worked closely with wage-earning women and devoted her life to fighting both class and gender discriminations. Despite good intentions, conflicts between middle and wage-earning activists often arose out of women's differing views on work and the vote. Middle-class activists often framed work as the fulfillment of psychological needs rather than as a necessity for survival. As Dye explains, "Because they idealized work and equated it with economic and emotional self-sufficiency, many allies [middle and upper-class activists] never seemed to come to terms with the fact that most women were not independent laborers but part of a family economic unit in which work did not usually connote independent economic status" (1975a, 31). Views on suffrage also differed. Middle- and upper-class professionals saw the vote as a way to increase their power in government positions, whereas wage-earning women viewed the vote as a tool for achieving workplace improvements that would allow them to live humane lives. Of interest here is the ways such conflicts were portrayed or elided in popular magazines and the ways decisions were made as to whose perspectives were held up as the voice of suffrage.

The magazine's overarching hegemonic strategy placed limits on what could be said in the "Department for Women" and played a role in what was left out of the picture. The mere presence of the department validated many of the struggles of women for equal rights in a mass-mediated form. From an economic viewpoint, the new department indicated a recognition on the part of *McClure's* of a large and increasingly vocal audience of consumers that required more direct targeting. The task of the "Department for Women" was to reach this target audience without offending other readers or hindering the ability to attract advertising dollars. How was this accomplished?

In 1913, Milholland cowrote an article detailing the activities of the Fourth Annual Convention of the American Woman Suffrage Association (Irwin and Milholland 1913). Here and in other Milholland writings, universalization provided an appealing framing for support of woman's political and cultural equality. The authors asserted that contemporary women "seem[] capable of organizing and working together only under the stimulus of a great *ideal*, and that ideal is morality, which is the home" (251, emphasis added). The vote provided the vehicle through which women could become more effective "house-cleaners of the nation" (251). According to the writings in the "Department for Women," women organized around ideals and morals rather than material interests. Further, as the announcement introducing the "Department for Women" noted, suffrage constituted the primary point of struggle for the feminist movement. Yet during this time period there were numerous women's political organizations for suffrage and other aims from which the magazine could have chosen for emphasis or elaboration. Omitted from the picture painted by the "Department for Women" were the thousands of women and girls who organized around material interests and who viewed the vote as one among many tools to be deployed in order to achieve the larger goal of workplace equality.

In their article Milholland and Irwin mentioned Leonora O'Reilly, a well-known working-class activist who played a central role in the Uprising of 30,000 and who was also a member of the Equality League. O'Reilly, who was present at the convention, was described as "gaunt and Irish and pale with the burden of her destiny" (248). O'Reilly's provocative testimony revealing the hypocrisy behind the concept of "sacred motherhood" stood in stark contrast to the voices of more mainstream suffragists such as Dr. Anna Howard Shaw and Carrie Chapman Catt, which filled up most of the article. Appealing to their middle-class audience, for whom woman suffrage may still be an unacceptable notion, the authors reassured: "'Women's place is in the home' to-day as much as yesterday. But she is bringing the home to the place where it belongs— into contact with the nation" (251).

The Milholland and Irwin article embodied the argument of expediency increasingly employed by mainstream suffragists into the teens (Kraditor 1965). Arguments of expediency can be described as a "whatever works" strategy (see Kraditor 1965, 45). Rather than rely solely on natural rights arguments, suffragists started linking "woman suffrage to reform [because it] seemed to be the best way to secure support for their principal goal: the vote" (Kraditor 1965, 45, 46). To justify votes for women, suffragists relied on traditional gender norms and expectations (such as in the Milholland article), but also turned to racist and classist arguments in an effort to make their case (Kraditor 1965, 53; see also DuBois 1994; Davis 1981; Tax 1980).[15] In the context of a popular magazine such as *McClure's*, Milholland's expedient approach fit within the parameters of the magazine's rhetorical frame and it was in concordance with the values of a mainstream middle-class audience. Given *McClure's* muckraking, which made readers painfully aware of the graft in local and state politics, what reader could dispute the benefits of a woman's touch in the public realm? Given the need to satisfy reader expectations and to elicit advertising revenues, it may not come as a surprise that *McClure's* highlighted middle-class suffragists' expedient arguments. Of interest are the ways that the *McClure's* balanced controversy and concordance and, more generally, what role mainstream portrayals such as those in popular magazines played in a larger public discussion regarding women, work, and social change. Though the voices of wage-earning women were a substantial part of the public debate, in the pages of *McClure's* their presence was largely absent.

Future installments of the "Department for Women" more pointedly disputed dominant ideas regarding male-female relationships, the family, and marriage. Milholland questioned the norms and institutions that supported a pure and submissive True Woman. "There is no use in blinking [at] the fact that we can not liberate woman without ultimately finding ourselves facing radical changes in her relations with man as regards the two vital matters of property and sex" (1913a, 188). The March 1913 issue touched on economic changes in the lives of women and challenged the earlier assertion that "woman's place is in the home." Milholland explained that as many domestic tasks such as canning, spinning, and sewing have moved to factories, women have followed. To "order [women] 'back to the home' is . . . nonsense" (211). Milholland criticized the "parasites" who live off of their husbands' incomes and lauded the efforts of those who have engaged in an "alliance with that great army of workingwomen" (212). Other articles in the "Department for Women" advocated minimum wages for workers (1913b) and supported "the growth of economic opportunity for the individual woman" so that she can "resist the idea of merely 'marrying for a living'" (1913c, 192).

Milholland's series challenged gender norms and envisioned a new future for the sexes that some may have found unnerving: "Those unthinking ones who expect the old submission and silence from the free woman of to-day and to-morrow are certainly in for some exceedingly rude shocks" (1913a, 185). Yet the conceptualization of feminism in these *McClure's* articles remained well within the bounds of universalization, a persuasive strategy that allowed acknowledgment so as to contain voices of dissent. Through selection and repression, the articles highlighted cultural norms and sexual relations while eliding material interests and workplace relations. Though each article briefly mentioned the concerns of wage-earning women and the involvement of "well-kept women" in working-class organizations such as the WTUL, the emphasis remained on women's "age-old subjugation to man" (1913b, 212). Similarly, Milholland noted that "this pressure toward a constantly growing freedom and power on the part of the sex means that . . . the institutions most certain to be touched and changed . . . are the home, and marriage itself" (1913a, 185). Conflicting concerns among wage-earning and middle-class women were absent in these portrayals, in which women were seen to work "all in harmony with the new spirit that is pressing woman to extend in every direction the new freedom and power of a sex that is on the eve of liberation" (1913b, 212).

McClure's "Department for Women" framed sexual relations as the basis of women's oppression and promoted political equality and changes in the home as remedies. Equality in the home was certainly an issue of importance to many if not most women in all classes; in addition, however, women of color and working-class women voiced particular concerns regarding their position in the workplace and were also concerned about the "age-old subjugation" to the boss, even as they struggled against domination by their husbands. The "Department for Women" provided a forum for universalizing middle-class interests as those of all women.

Furthermore, viewing women's struggles through the window of universalization allowed a more optimistic outlook on women's position. Class conflict and the hypocrisies of True Womanhood laid bare in factories and laundries could be rhetorically swept under a rug of values and ideals that were deemed universal. Eliding the experiences of wage-earning women, *McClure's* could proclaim that a "New Era of Woman Is Here" (Milholland 1913b, 219). Milholland's April 1913 installment concluded that "there is reason to believe that the present swift growth of liberty for woman means ultimately a new freedom for her in every department of life—above all, in the deepest of all relationships" (1913c, 192).

Indeed, Milholland was writing during a time when norms regarding sexual relations were rapidly changing. The True Woman was replaced

by the New Woman with her short hair, loose clothing, and assertive attitude. Yet the material reality of millions of women's lives during this period told a different story. Just one year prior to Milholland's writings, on
March 25, 1911, a fire at the Triangle Shirtwaist factory claimed the lives
of 146 girls and women, many of whom were the sole providers for their
families. The factory's dangerous working conditions and poor building
construction, including inadequate fire escapes and obstructed exits, contributed to the horror of this event. Many of the women and girls jumped
to their deaths on the sidewalks of Washington Place below as horrified
bystanders looked on helplessly, making public for the first time the extreme exploitation and intolerable working conditions in the shirtwaist
trade. Thus, Milholland's announcement of a new era stands in embar-
rassing contrast with the lives of millions of women who continued to
work ten-hour days for scant wages in dangerous surroundings, only to
come home to fulfill the domestic duties still expected of them.

Ideological support for Milholland's "Department for Women" came
in subsequent articles that detailed how women were able to "have it all"
(Hale 1915; Richardson 1916a, 1916d). These accounts further explained
feminism to *McClure's* readers and softened the movement's more radical
edges. In "What Women Want," Beatrice Forbes-Robertson Hale asserted
that women wanted "love, children, and work" and feminism simply
provided the enabling mechanism (1915). Like previous *McClure's* accounts of the women's movement, the feminist manifesto "What Women
Want" garnered reader acceptance of this relatively new term "feminism" by aligning it with widely held social values such as individualism
and upward mobility. Feminism was really "humanism," according to
Hale: "Once women stand beside men in education, freedom and responsibility, both can go forward together" (Hale 1915, 18).

Perhaps most appealing to readers who may have been uneasy about
feminism was the association of this movement with a more healthy family life. Feminism encouraged "mutual respect and companionship" and
led to women's becoming better mothers. "The age of Feminism is also
called the age of the child, for a free and enlightened womanhood implies a noble and conscious motherhood" (Hale 1915, 19). Families would
become stronger through an "enlightened motherhood," as well as
through increased leisure and consumption, which the author similarly
associated with feminism. Wives will earn income "so that the children
may have better surroundings" (19). Husbands will no longer get caught
up in the rat race of business life, but will spend more time with their
wives, who are presumably their equals.

Photos of specific women accompanying the text conveyed to readers
that feminism enabled women to have it all without upending "business
as usual." These pictures assured readers that though women could now

"bring home the bacon, [and] fry it up in a pan," she would still "never, never, never let you forget you're a man. . . ." The middle- and upper-class women shown in the photos embodied liberal individualism, individual freedom, and opportunity to reach one's potential. A subtitle under a photo of Margaret Illington says, "Emotional actress, wife, home-lover." On another page, a picture of Mrs. Norman de R. Whitehouse, "Society leader, ardent suffrage worker," was positioned beside a picture of Mrs. Leonard M. Thomas, "Whom Hellue called the most beautiful American" (19).

As is still the case in many present-day popular-media accounts, in this article liberal feminism came to stand for the entire women's movement.[16] Rooted in the ideas of the Enlightenment, liberal feminism is itself a manifestation of universalization with the feminist theory's emphasis on the mental over the physical, and on the enduring principles of reason and rationality. Liberal feminism relies heavily on education as the means to an equal society, the theory being that when women are granted the same tools of reason held by men they will transcend the socially constructed inferior qualities associated with femininity such as frailty, dependence, and excessive emotion, and will be more equipped to develop the mind and compete with each other and with men on an equal basis in the public sphere (Bryson 1992, 17–27, 159–163).

Scattered throughout the history of feminist thought,[17] the ideas of liberal feminism detach concepts such as equality, reason, and human nature from a specific historical context. As such, the material underpinnings of a society's values, norms, and practices—for example, capitalist production and its reliance on the nuclear family—are obscured within liberal thinking, and thus the systematic ways that women have been and are discriminated as a sex are not given consideration (Bryson 1992, 164–176).

Though Hale's article offered appealing visions of gender relations and family life, they promoted a view of human agency as being unconstrained or uninfluenced by material structures and institutions. The voices of wage earners, though absent in this *McClure's* article, provided a contrasting viewpoint that highlighted the structures that at times constrain working-class women's actions and potentials. Many working women were quick to point out that a fulfilling home and family relations and decent leisure time were directly related to—indeed dependent on—workplace structures and relations that regulated their wages, hours, and physical safety (Newman 1914; Rudnitzky 1912; Whitehead 1914). Work did not spell freedom and wages were necessary for much more than creating "better surroundings" for children—they were essential for putting food on the table and paying the rent.

As with most feminist thinkers past and present, one cannot easily reduce the ideas of *McClure's* writers such as Jane Addams, Inez Milholland, Edith Wyatt, and Sue Ainslie Clark to one form of feminism. Most variously advocated liberal or radical feminist solutions to the "Woman Question," and while radical feminism more readily addressed the collective dimension of women's oppression particularly in relation to men, neither strain of feminism broached issues of class conflict or the specific roles that women play in an industrial capitalist society. Then as now, women's unpaid domestic labors were essential in the reproduction of labor, and the thousands of immigrant, black, and poor women were considered a steady pool of cheap labor for the growing number of unskilled and "pink-collar" jobs.

Through descriptions of factory life, accounts of suffrage struggles, and feminism, *McClure's* created a specific subject position for female readers, a position that defined their experiences, goals, needs, and desires. The subject-woman identified and described by Clark and Wyatt, Addams, and Milholland clearly pushed the boundaries of traditional True Womanhood. These and similar contemporary popular portrayals encouraged female readers to broaden their perspectives on themselves, other women, and women's place in society more generally. Addressing suffragism and feminism allowed *McClure's* to, in effect, "keep up with the times" (and thus lure readers); universalization represented a historically situated rhetorical choice through which these "isms" could be acknowledged, then absorbed back into the mainstream. By omitting stories of class struggle and work-related exploitation, the most critical voices for justice were muzzled. In their stead, *McClure's* provided a picture of feminism that could be most readily subsumed within the prevailing socioeconomic system. This ideological process was further supported through works of fiction that shaped and neutralized the effect of feminism. This process is called "recuperation."

Recuperating Feminism

Universalizing women's struggles for equality in *McClure's* magazine was a two-part process that involved acknowledgment and containment. The "Department for Women" introduced readers to the ideas of feminism and woman suffrage, emphasizing the movements' influences on sexual relations and cultural norms. Such challenges to established institutions such as home and marriage did not remain free to rhetorically roam the landscape of early-twentieth-century popular culture. Rather, they were tethered to dominant gender norms and practices through the process of recuperation, the "ideological effort that goes into negating and defusing challenges to the historically dominant meaning of gender" (Barrett 1980, 111).

Fiction and nonfiction works appearing between 1915 and 1916 undermined articles advocating birth control, divorce, and feminism by means of storylines that reinforced images of women as dependent helpmates and redirected them back to the home sphere. A two-part fiction work called "Woman Stuff" that appeared in 1915 and 1916 was about how such "stuff" as women's emotions continually got in the way of the relationship between Andy Benson and Corinna (Gatlin). Corinna was jealous and manipulative while her lover Andy chalked it up to the behaviors of a "typical" woman. "She refused to understand a man's responsibilities, was utterly unreasonable, was guided primarily by her emotions—more woman stuff! But her faults, somehow, made her only the dearer" (Gatlin 1916, 65).

Other stories portrayed ambitious, attractive, financially well-off, talented, or otherwise assertive women from whose lives, despite their accomplishments, something was missing. Through a tragic experience or an adventure gone awry, the protagonist realized that the home front provided the true source of happiness. In "The Gayest Woman in Marchmont," Julietta Carson unwittingly learned a lesson regarding the sanctity of her home, husband, and children from a local "notorious" woman who shared with Julietta the events that had led to her downfall into prostitution (Kerr 1916). Julietta's previous disdain for the woman turned to sympathy as she learned that the woman had been forced to sell herself in order to support her two children after her husband's death. As Julietta listened to the sad story, she began to regret a recent argument with her husband in which she defied his wishes to get rid of a "conspicuous" rose-colored dress that she had recently purchased. Upon hearing the woman's narrative, Julietta "fled from the story she had heard and the pitiful wreck of womanhood who had told it," home to Lonny and her children. As Julietta arrived at home, she fell into Lonny's arms and proclaimed, "'Lonny . . . hold me tight! Don't ever let me go. Suppose it had been I—suppose it had been I—and—oh, Lonny . . . dearest, tell me you love me—and that you'll take care of me—and then come upstairs with me—I want to burn that rose-colored dress'" (54).

A similar lesson reinforcing woman's place at the hearth was imparted in "Home, Mother and the Cabaret" (Irwin 1916). Susie Mackintyre, down-home country girl, learned the real value of homelife only when she strayed too far on an adventure in New York City. Wishing to "say something that would teach girls how it was better to stick by the old home farm, to grow up with the daisied and clean fields—and their mothers," Susie wrote a song praising the security of "home-sweet-home" (14). The song became a big hit in the cabarets of New York, having been transformed into a snazzy rag tune. Upon hearing her song thus co-opted, Susie's opinion of the artificiality of city life was confirmed and she returned once and for all to the farm. In "The Honey Bee: The Story of a Woman in Revolt," by Sam Merwin, another *McClure's* heroine, Hilda, reconsidered her life upon the death of her lover (1915a, 1915b). Finally feeling freed from the constraints of tending to her ill paramour, Hilda renewed contact with her mother so that the two could "build a home together—a home and fresh interests" (1915b, 42).

The protagonists in *McClure's* fiction belied the portrayals of women who decried legal double standards and social sanctions endured by females because of their sex. These stories provided a way to recuperate the counterhegemonic ideological strains of articles appearing in contemporary issues. The subtext spoke a warning to females who would attempt to make something more of their lives than home and husband. Corinna's superficiality stigmatized and trivialized issues surrounding birth control and divorce as "woman stuff"; the protection of Mother on the farm subsumed struggles for self-sufficiency and workplace equality; and the burning of the rose-colored dress made the suppression of women's self-definition a fait accompli.

Not only fiction but also nonfiction articles reinforced the image of women as domestic creatures or objects of the male gaze. "Safeguarding American Motherhood" (Richardson 1915), which appeared one month prior to the feminist manifesto, "What Women Want," relied on notions of "expertise" and "science" to portray homemaking as a vocation for women. This article, in conjunction with the previously mentioned fiction stories that focused on domesticity hold particular significance in the context of the United States' growing involvement in World War I. As in the *Atlantic Monthly*, *McClure's* "recruited" female readers as mothers and homemakers in order to rhetorically create a supportive home front during the war. In March 1916, "The Fashionable Figure" served as a reminder that women were not only for mothering (Gould). The article recounted women's attempts to keep up with fashion fads that come and go. Sounding quite like modern-day fashion magazines such as *Cosmopolitan* and *Vogue*, this article explained the fashion maneuvers of the "real woman": "[S]he is adaptable and plucky. She knows what she wants and she goes after it. She knows, too, all the tricks of the trade, so that many things that can't really be will seem to be. Besides, she knows that the foundation of any particular figure is the corset, and she selects that with the utmost care" (Gould, 32).

Between 1910 and 1916, images of women and women's struggles for equality in *McClure's* were multifaceted and complex. The introduction of the "Department for Women" represented the magazine's effort to appeal to an audience whose needs and concerns ran counter to traditional gender norms. As Entman notes, however, "[E]xclusion of interpretations by frames is as significant to outcomes as inclusion" (1993, 54). *McClure's* universalization frame provided a rhetorical strategy for acknowledging voices of dissent while absorbing them into mainstream discourse on gender and work relations. Acknowledgment and containment were accomplished through the ideological strategy of universalization, which made values and ideals salient while obscuring the influences of extradiscursive structures and systems that shaped, and at times benefited from, various social values and norms. *McClure's* magazine pioneered the strategy used by contemporary popular media texts that recognize social issues such as racism, sexism, and antiwar sentiments within rhetorical frames that do not fundamentally disrupt the socioeconomic system.

Conclusion

McClure's magazine gained widespread popularity for its muckraking journalism, exposés that revealed the conniving and corruption in politics and big business without, however, directly undermining or attacking the status quo. The magazine's target audience was the middle classes, a group who neither owned the means of production nor produced goods for consumption but rather, comprising administrators, managers, writers, and reformers, occupied an in-between position. Its role was to arbitrate and facilitate the relations between capitalists and workers. *McClure's* magazine addressed the unique concerns of this class, whose members benefited in many ways from the economic system but whose position was precarious during times of social uncertainty and economic upheaval. In the early 1900s, the magazine explored labor organization, labor/capital disputes, and the travails of immigrants and tenement housing. In the teens, well-known middle-class reformers such as Sue Ainslie Clark, Jane Addams, and Inez Milholland gave voice to the political and economic struggles of women. It remains debatable whether or not these exposés impacted the legal and political spheres in any meaningful way. Still, one should not underestimate the oftentimes radical edge of *McClure's* articles and the potential consciousness-raising affect on its readers. Of significance is how *McClure's* honed a strategy for discussing contentious and potentially divisive issues while rhetorically maintaining social consensus.

Universalization aptly served the magazine's self-definition and goals as it provided a frame for unveiling or acknowledging sex discrimination, political corruption, and workplace sufferings while suppressing alternatives that suggested class conflict or systemic discrimination. Human interest profiles, with their structural tendency to decontextualize and personalize, provided a format through which universalization operated. Biographical accounts of individual workers and families glossed over the historical and socioeconomic circumstances that had an impact on their situation. Furthermore, biographical profiles, by focusing on individuals' successes and failures, left unexamined the collective nature of discrimination and the need for communal confrontation. In this way, *McClure's* could talk about the greed of labor bosses, unscrupulous owners, or oppressive sexual norms without fundamentally disrupting the socioeconomic status quo.

Universalization provided a persuasive strategy by which a popular, relatively accessible magazine could address the Progressive Era concerns of its middle-class audience while offering a view that did not tear at the underlying fabric of liberal capitalism. The articles in *McClure's* provide a way to explore some of the earliest attempts to recognize and negotiate the voices of social movements in mainstream media. Particularly from 1910 to 1916, *McClure's* articles supported woman suffrage and feminism and broached controversial issues such as workplace exploitation, prostitution, divorce, and birth control, thus lending female readers insight on how they were oppressed as women.

Equally important, however, is what was left out of the picture. Working-class women and girls knew all too well the central influence of the industrial system on their workplace conditions and on opportunities for education and leisure. Stories and speeches recount again and again how women displayed spirit and fortitude not only in order to get by at the machine but primarily in order to confront and alter workplace conditions. And through extra-discursive tactics such as walkouts, women and girls highlighted a society marked by class distinction and they shaped themselves as laboring agents capable of radical change within this society.

Yet working women's consciousness did not develop in a vacuum. Their rhetorical strategies and identities were shaped in part by the ideas of the middle-class reformers who worked with them, as well as by popular discourses targeting them. Cheap serials and mail-order magazines were forms of popular culture that the working-class enjoyed. How the stories and articles in these magazines constructed working-class identity, especially that of working-class women, and how these popular discourses represent, explain, and/or justify to workers their experiences in a class segregated society is the subject of the next chapter.

Notes

1. The Spring 1995 issue of *Signs: Journal of Women in Culture and Society* had a "Forum on Feminism and the Media" with articles detailing "the complex relationships between the contemporary feminist movement and the commercial media" (Farrell, 642; see Johnson, Kozol, McDermott, and Rhode). For other studies

of press treatment of the women's movement of the 1960s and 1970s, see Morris 1973 and Epstein 1978.

2. Wood 1971, 130.

3. See Schneirov 1994, 245–263 for further analysis of the decline of muckraking.

4. Sue Ainslie Clark was a well-known middle-class reformer and an active member of the Boston Women's Trade Union League. The appearance of articles by Clark and other middle-class reformers such as Jane Addams in *McClure's* magazine points to the ways that vernacular rhetoric both shaped and was shaped by popular discourse. Though the two spheres overlap, each can be studied as reflecting distinct motives, interests, and ideological strategies.

5. The hostility that female laborers faced from male coworkers will be detailed subsequently. Much of this antagonism was fueled by Samuel Gompers and other leaders in the American Federation of Labor (AFL).

6. The dash in the title stands for a woman who does not look or act "like a Woman." Interestingly, the author is unable to come up with a word for such a being.

7. See Foner 1979, 256–269, for a description of conditions faced by wage-earning women at the turn of the century.

8. During the late 1800s, women's labor activism was often linked with the Knights of Labor, "the largest and most encompassing labor organization of the century" (Levine 1983, 324). Unlike the American Federation of Labor, the Knights of Labor extended membership to women and unskilled labor.

9. Though Jones worked for a number of years with Mitchell organizing and assisting coal miners, she eventually parted ways with the leader as a result of his cozying up to big business leaders such as J. P. Morgan and John D. Rockefeller.

10. Of course, the beliefs and values held by various members of the WTUL did not always neatly break along class lines. Certainly there were allies who believed in the necessity of a specifically working-class struggle and who emphasized industrial training. Conversely, some working-class women did adopt the values and strategies of the middle-class reformers, and some, such as Rose Schneiderman, eventually held government positions and repudiated their socialist beliefs.

11. Tax (1980) attributes this phrase to the Socialist and labor activist Eugene V. Debs.

12. Both writers were middle-class reformers. Clark was the president of the Boston WTUL during the Lawrence, Massachusetts, strike in 1912. She was a vocal supporter of the rights of unskilled laborers.

13. This is not to say that wage-earning women did not desire education or enjoy various cultural events such as the opera and museum trips. The experiences of wage-earning women in the WTUL provide a good example of the complexities surrounding issues of material and cultural transformation. Within the WTUL, wage-earning women were often confronted with conflicts between their own knowledge of solidarity and struggle, and their desire for comforts offered by ascent into the middle class and their need for approval from the middle-class reformers who provided crucial financial assistance. Thus, wage-earning women themselves experienced the contradictions inherent in universalized values and perspectives. I will elaborate on this issue in Chapter 4.

14. Chapter 4 elaborates further on the countless strikes and walkouts that proved successful for thousands of workers in the early twentieth century. Primary sources documenting these and other strikes can be found in *Life and Labor,* the organ of the WTUL, available through interlibrary loan service, and "The papers of the Women's Trade Union League and Its Principal Leaders," available on microfilm from the Schlesinger Library, Radcliffe Institute, Harvard University. The Rose Schneiderman Papers and Leonora O'Reilly Papers are part of this collection. A few of the more provocative secondary sources include Cobble 1991; Foner 1979; Orleck 1995; Tax 1980.

15. Elite suffragists saw the vote as a way for women of the upper classes to increase their influence on government. In their arguments, they reassured politicians and other wealthy women that votes for women would serve as an antidote to the growing power of the "ignorant" masses (DuBois 1994). The two principal suffrage advocates Elizabeth Cady Stanton and Susan B. Anthony retaliated against Republican leaders who did not grant women the vote at the same time that black men received it by shifting their support to openly racist Democratic politicians and they made overtly racist arguments in an attempt to woo southern opinion in favor of their cause (see Davis 1981; Tax 1980).

16. See Dow 1996, 51–54, for the ways that liberal feminism came to dominate the mass media in the 1970s.

17. See Bryson 1992 for a detailed analysis of the development of liberal feminist ideas from Mary Wollstonecraft in the late 1700s to Elizabeth Cady Stanton and John Stuart Mill in the mid–1800s to Second Wave feminists of the 1960s. Wollstonecraft, Stanton and others did not always espouse a purely liberal feminist line. Yet liberal ideas were a part of or underpinned the ideas of many feminists from the 1700s to the present.

3

Domesticating Dissent:
Replacing Collective Protest with
Homelife and Self-improvement

The early twentieth century saw the introduction of so-called mail-order magazines, cheaply made, inexpensive magazines that became increasingly popular among the working classes. In contrast to more upscale magazine such as the *Atlantic Monthly*, these magazines were filled with advertisements for the products of companies that sold by the direct-mail method. *The People's Home Journal* was one of the most popular of these periodicals; in the opening pages of its December 1910 issue, the magazine explained its fundamental goal: "to produce a journal of popular literature for the masses as distinguished from the classes" ("*The People's Home Journal* for 1911," 2). Where literary magazines such as the *Atlantic Monthly* emphasized their refined and exclusive content and muckraking magazines like *McClure's* thrived on the realities of everyday life, mail-order magazines frequently emphasized their widespread appeal and usefulness around the home for the less well-off.

During these years, working-class family life was marked by a continual negotiation between social expectations and material necessity. Prevailing gender norms dictated that women be domestic, submissive, pious, and pure (Welter 1966), but the reality of working-class lives necessitated the transgression of such traditional sex roles. Wives and daughters entered factories and sweatshops in order to generate income needed for survival. In their positions as workers, women and girls could not be protected or sheltered, but rather ran heavy machinery side by side with male coworkers and were necessarily exposed to the "impure" and secular world of work and public affairs. In appealing to their target readership, how did mail-order magazines reconcile the daily tensions and contradictions faced by wage earners? More broadly, how did popular narratives frame the hardships and daily concerns of those who

experienced extreme economic exploitation and political marginalization? And how did these images and narratives change over time as the
most exploited members of society increasingly rose up against social injustices?

Working-class individuals and families did not have a great deal of
time or money to devote to leisure activities, but they did enjoy a variety
of activities, including nickelodeons, movies, and amusement parks, in
addition to noncommercialized activities such as sidewalk and street
games, trips to the park, and social clubs (Enstad 1999; Piess 1986). One
of the most popular type of commercialized media among working-class
women was the mail-order journal. These magazines were notably
cheap, were edited for a less-educated audience, and often contained se-
rialized works of fiction. This chapter explores how three popular mail-
order magazines—*Comfort*, *Home Life*, and *The People's Home Journal*
(PHJ)—approached working-class concerns through a rhetoric of domestication, a frame that encouraged readers to focus on personal space—
home or inner self—as places to transform in order to live a more fulfilling life. These magazines recognized the hardships inherent in limited
budgets and arduous workdays, but they advised readers to regenerate
themselves through attitude adjustments, a romantic relationship, or by
lending a helping hand to someone more needy than they rather than by
protest or political action.[1]

Through fiction and nonfiction as well as advertisements and advice
columns, the tensions between "True Womanhood" and working-class
reality were reconciled through images of the "Practical True Woman," a
figure crafted by means of three rhetorical devices: appeals to tradition,
recognition, and negation. The Practical True Woman embodied the conflicting demands of industrial capitalism and thus depicted for readers a
way to resolve the tensions between gender norms and material need.
Moreover, the image played into the hands of an emerging economic system that benefited from women's cheap labor even as it continued to discipline women to tend to home and husband.

In essence, the ideology of domestication was a rhetoric that effectively circumscribed working-class readers' political and economic experiences by privatizing them. Through stories, advice columns, and regular features, this rhetorical framing taught readers to cope *within* their
present environment by making adjustments to self, home, and personal
relationships.

Like the universalization frame found in *McClure's* and the naturalization frame used by the *Atlantic Monthly*, the domestication frame obscured systemic origins of social problems and negated the need for collective action in the struggle for justice. Where naturalization
accomplished this through an emphasis on inevitability and universal-

ization accomplished this through an emphasis on ideals, domestication focused on personal spaces. This rhetorical maneuver was particularly suited to a target audience whose members were openly and publicly demonstrating for economic and political change during the magazines' peak years of popularity.

In many respects, the type of advice promulgated by these popular mail-order magazines is a forerunner of today's self-help advice found in books, magazines, and television shows. Like contemporary therapeutic discourses, the magazines' ideology of domestication shifted social critique of broad-based institutions and systems—industrial capitalism, factory labor, consumerism, and sexual division of labor—onto personal spaces.[2] The need for collective and publicly expressed demands was eclipsed. Dissent was brought home and domesticated along with the individuals who would potentially engage themselves in public protest. The system remained intact as readers were encouraged to bring a smile to someone's face and to relish the "gold mine of the mind" ("The Picture Before Us," 1913b, 5).

Popular mail-order magazines' hegemonic overtones and the strategies through which popular texts personalized problems that were social and systemic in nature are central to understanding the complex role that cultural artifacts play in the formation of class consciousness. In her study of popular culture and working-class women's lives, Enstad comes to quite an optimistic conclusion regarding the relationship between wage earners and popular-culture practices (1999). According to Enstad, "Working women formed subjectivities as ladies by using the fiction and fashion commodities available to them" (13). Further, "When working women went on strike, they utilized the subjectivities and languages they developed through popular culture practices to claim formal political status" (13). In contrast to Enstad's conclusion, the analysis in this and the following chapter points to *lived* (as opposed to *read* or *viewed*) experiences as that which motivated women to join together in struggle for humane working and living conditions.

The low prices of monthly mail-order magazines—usually around twenty-five cents a year—made them readily available to a working-class audience with little disposable income for leisure activities. "Working class" here refers to those who must sell their labor in order to live. Particularly around the early 1900s, the working class was composed of the millions of factory and sweatshop workers, miners, and servants who worked for owners who made large profits off of the backs of their employees. This class was ethnically and racially diverse and included immigrants from Russia, Eastern and Western European countries, and China. As the most exploited class within industrial capitalism, members of the working class had the most to gain from Progressive Era reforms, as well as from their own efforts to transform their conditions. As such, their voices of dissent and struggles for social transformation represented a constant threat to those who had a stake in the status quo.

Negotiators of Consent:
Publishers of Mail-Order Journals for the Working Class

Little historical research has been done on the publishers of cheap mail-order journals and newspapers in the early 1900s, though *Comfort*, *Home Life*, and *The People's Home Journal* were extremely popular and had some of the widest circulations of any magazines of this time. In 1905, *Comfort* was one of two magazines claiming (by sworn statement) a circulation over one million (Mott 1957, 4:16). And *Home Life* and *The People's Home Journal* each claimed 900,000 readers by 1910. All three magazines were produced by well-established publishing houses that held multiple interests in magazine, book, and newspaper enterprises. *Comfort*, considered to be the most important of mail-order journals, was published by Gannett and Morse and was edited by W. H. Gannett. *Home Life* was published by Balch Publishing Co. and later by *Home Life* Publishing Co. *The People's Home Journal* was published by F. M. Lupton Publishers. F. M. Lupton was owner of a printing and binding company and part owner of a typesetting company. He is perhaps most remembered for the cheap popular books he published under the Leisure Hour Library series (Stern 1980, 215–219). It is notable that beginning in June 1916, the editor of one of the magazines, *Home Life*, was a well-known middle-class activist, Josephine Conger-Kaneko, a socialist journalist who for some time wrote a regular column for the socialist newspaper *Appeal to Reason*. Conger-Kaneko's embrace of Christian socialism shaped her views on women and labor, and the influence of her more radical edge can be seen in the pages of *Home Life* during this time.

The content of the magazines provides many indications that the target audience was working-class families, and particularly working-class women. *Comfort* presented its June 1903 issue as a "woman's number. . . . [As] we figure that ninety per cent of our readers are women it is only fair that ninety per cent of the matter in *Comfort* should appeal to women." Romance stories, a genre popular among female audiences, were a regular feature of all three magazines. These narratives told of how happy couples made do on love alone. In addition, editorials and poems often quite explicitly exhorted readers to find happiness in meager circumstances (Carpenter 1911; Mortimer 1909; Dolson 1914; Cooper 1914; Chapman 1913b; "The Picture Before Us," 1912a, 1912b, 1912c, 1913b, 1914e, 1914f). The content of regular magazine columns gave evidence of the desire to appeal to female readers. *Comfort* ran "The *Comfort*

Sisters' Corner," a column devoted to answering questions pertaining to household and family matters. A March 1910 letter gave an idea of the typical reader. Mrs. Willie Sanderson wrote, "We are poor and have to make every cent go as far as it will. My husband works in a sawmill and has only one hand." (7). Other columns of interest to female readers included "The Pretty Girls' Club" (*Comfort*); "Talks With Girls" (*Comfort*); "Mother's Circle" (*PHJ*); and "The Care of the Children" (*PHJ*).

The wide appeal of these magazines was due in part to their extremely low yearly subscription prices—between 1894 and 1920, from twenty-five to fifty cents a year. Even compared to the "ten-cent monthlies" such as *McClure's*, this was a remarkably low price. Consequently, the publishers relied almost entirely on money received from advertisers, and so it is not surprising that editors were particularly tied to the interests and tastes of the businesses who advertised in their pages. Thus, although the growth of advertising supported and enabled the spread of popular magazines to previously unreached audiences, it curtailed editorial independence and greatly narrowed the boundaries of acceptable magazine content.[3]

Further, the advertisements in these magazines became a medium for transmitting a "therapeutic" ethos (Lears 1983) that further bolstered the ideology of domestication. In the early 1900s, advertising agencies consulted psychologists, who helped them shape "therapeutic advertising," a "method of social control—a way to arouse consumer demand by associating products with imaginary states of well-being" (Lears 1983, 19). Ads answered to readers' desires for life betterment by touting individual purchases of specific products directed toward home or self-improvement, displacing worker organization and mass confrontation as means to life betterment. Thus, advertisements— necessary in order for these cheap magazines to survive—affected the content of the magazine and became another site from which domestication could operate.

In addition to negotiating between their audience and their monetary sources, magazine editors and writers had interests unique to their own position as the middle class. As previous pages have explained, the middle classes occupied an ambivalent position within capitalist society, for their interests did not lie clearly with those of either the upper or the working classes. Though they too struggled to make ends meet and keep up with the ever-growing consumption orientation of society, they also benefited from the labor of the millions who made clothing, processed food, and manufactured appliances in factories and sweatshops in the early twentieth century.

Thus, the perspectives offered in these magazines' works of both fiction and nonfiction were complex and often ambivalent. Writers and editors acknowledged the realities of their readers' lives—the rising cost of living, labor strikes, desires such as for a dream home. But the remedies were seen to be found in the private, not the public, sphere, specifically, the contradiction between gender norms and material want was reconciled through the "Practical True Woman," an image that resided within, and further reinforced, the ideology of domestication framing the texts. More specifically, domestication discouraged readers from understanding the public nature of their difficulties and the need for collective action in working toward a solution. The interests of advertisers, editors, writers, and publishers necessitated a domestication of dissent, even as material disparities and difficulties were acknowledged.

Popular Framings of Working-Class Life: An Overview

Ideology of Domestication

The ideology of domestication privatized problems and issues that were public in origin, thus obscuring the social nature of work relations and the family. This rhetorical frame transformed political issues of power, exploitation, and material resources into personal issues by locating the source and solution of various hardships in one's home or one's inner self. Such understandings elided the need for public and collective action. The domestication frame can also be understood as a manifestation of a "therapeutic discourse." Cloud's definition of late-twentieth-century therapeutic discourses reveals a similar dynamic as that of domestication: "Therapy subverts potential opposition to the social order by blaming sufferers for their own sociopolitical victimization (predominantly, in our society, under capitalism and in systems of racial and gender oppression) and by encouraging people to adjust to life as it is rather than to attempt to change the structure of society" (1998a, 10). Like therapeutic discourses, an ideology of domesticity was a gendered discourse frequently, but not always, targeting women. It is not surprising, then, that from time to time the magazines examined in this chapter provided special issues claiming to be of particular interest to their female readers. Likewise, these magazines contained far more stories and images of women than either the *Atlantic Monthly* or *McClure's*, indicating a desire to appeal to a female audience.

As discussed, popular early-twentieth-century magazines such as the *Atlantic Monthly* and *McClure's* were not monolithic in presenting hegemonic ideas but rather contained textual leakages through which the experiences of various disenfranchised groups were acknowledged. In the case of magazines targeting the working class, an audience who had the most to gain from social transformation, recognizing dissent or social antagonism required a particularly delicate rhetorical procedure. The task was to speak to the experiences of readers so as to maintain audience attention while keeping "alternative" perspectives in check. As such, the rhetoric framing the messages in these mail-order magazines is complex and in many respects represents an amalgam of naturalization, universalization, and domestication.

Like the *Atlantic Monthly* and *McClure's*, mail-order magazines acknowledged the fears and anxieties experienced by their target audience. Indeed, it is precisely through acknowledgment of these concerns that they can then be contained through the ideological workings of the text. As with inoculation, the disease is introduced so that it can then be controlled (Jameson 1979/80). The three magazines examined in this chapter frequently acknowledged everyday difficulties faced by wage earners in the early 1900s to which, once they had been recognized, the stories offered a personalized resolution. Visions of happy homes and romantic relationships were shown to overcome the difficulties previously acknowledged. The magazines translated readers' desires for control over work relations and economic stability into desire for domestic control.[4] In this way, potential dissent was literally domesticated.

Certainly, fulfilling personal relationships are desired by all individuals, and for many of the working class, the home did indeed represent an arena of freedom from the mechanization and discipline of the factory. However, the images and narratives that created the "ideal" family have historically played a specific role in the maintenance of the primary features of the dominant society: class privilege and the sexual division of labor. Historians have documented the changing role of the family in response to various changes in a society's economic structure (Barrett and McIntosh 1982; Coontz 1988; Zaretsky 1973). In particular, industrial capitalism and the subsequent removal of production from the family necessitated a different function for the newly privatized family and shaped women's domestic roles in specific ways. The family became sentimentalized and commercialized (Coontz 1992) and its maintenance depended on women's roles as caretakers, homemakers, and consumers.

In feudal or precapitalist arrangements, the home was often the seat of economic production. In contrast to this, in the capitalist arrangement the home became associated with love, intimacy, and personal development; it became a source of emotional and physical renewal for the next day's labor in the fragmented and impersonal world of factory production.[5] Consumption became an integral function of the family and a part of women's duties as homemakers. Thus, familial structure evolved to fit the needs of the changing socioeconomic system. As part of this development, discourses creating the sentimentalized family and "True Woman" emerged to support and justify the changing role of the family and of women within it as homemakers and consumers.

Thus, the ideology of domestication played a hegemonic role in the reproduction of both class and gender relations. By severing the private family from its connections to the socioeconomic system, this discourse encouraged individuals to identify their problems in personalized terms and to seek personal adjustments to problems requiring massive economic and political transformation (see Cloud 1998a).

Strategies for Domesticating Dissent

Consistent with the intimacy implied in a rhetoric of domestication, these magazines spoke to their readers in a personal tone, in effect creating a personal relationship between the reader and magazine. Works of fiction were frequently told in the first person, as though the reader were being let in on a piece of advice or a secret. More broadly, the entire magazine, including its regular columns and editorial pages, conveyed a feeling of intimacy. *Comfort's* regular features included "Chats with Aunt Minerva," "Told Around the Stove," and "Talks with Girls," conducted by Cousin Marion. *Home Life's* editorial page was titled, "A Few Words with Father" beginning around 1914. In such ways the magazines made readers feel a part of a "magazine family." This personal relationship between editor-cum-father and reader is strikingly similar to that of therapist and patient and was further reinforced in advice columns on home and relationship cultivation that told readers how to set a pretty table, and how to spread a little sunshine wherever you go.

A primary goal of the rhetoric of domestication was to resolve the contradictions faced by workers in industrial capitalism. This was accomplished through interlocking story lines and complex images imparting dual messages that often appeared to be at odds with one another. Romance stories discouraging material gain ran side-by-side with pull-yourself-up-by-the-bootstraps narratives that legitimated capitalist wealth and promoted upward mobility. The image of a Practical True Woman recognized women's roles as workers in the paid labor force even as it reinforced her natural abilities to mother and maintain the home. Fiction relating tales of worker uprisings appeared along with a regular column, "The Sunshine Society," which encouraged readers to "scatter smiles" in order to improve their lives. Despite the seemingly odd mixture within their pages, mail-order magazines threaded these images together with a rhetoric of domestication that resolved contradictions for readers in favor of personalized solutions.

The Practical True Woman.   The Practical True Woman represented a class-specific form of the notion of True Womanhood that permeated legal, political, and popular discourses through the early twentieth cen-

tury. The multiple roles expected of wage-earning women and the contradictions they faced between gender norms and material want necessitated a more complex rendering of their experiences.

First, the image of the Practical True Woman was tethered to naturalization, a discourse of *tradition* that established the enduring traits of
womanhood and provided the backdrop against which other rhetorical
strategies could be painted. Second, the daily experiences of wage-earning women as participants in the labor force were acknowledged through
recognition. Like many of the revealing muckraking accounts in *McClure's*
magazine, this facet of the Practical True Woman acknowledged the
evolving roles and relationships of early-twentieth-century women and
can be viewed as an "emergent" discourse (Williams 1977). Finally,
through *negation*, certain aspects of working-class women's experiences
were silenced—specifically, their experiences as activists, picketers, and
labor organizers. Negation domesticated women through omission. By
making no mention of the very real presence of women in strikes, walkouts, and parades in the real world outside the magazines' pages, these
texts reinforced women's roles in exclusively domestic terms. Tradition,
recognition, and negation worked together to craft a class-specific image
that could speak to its readers' experiences while confining their concerns and struggles to the domestic realm.

The Sunshine Society. Work-related situations and wage-earning
women are the subjects of stories in mail-order magazines from the
mid–1890s onward, but not until the teens did *Comfort, Home Life,* and
The People's Home Journal begin to acknowledge or discuss worker unrest
more specifically. As spontaneous and general strikes became more widespread and workers continued to organize and demand a fair share of the
wealth they created, popular magazines targeting this group responded
through stories and articles that encouraged readers to cope and adjust
within the current system.

Notably, in July 1911 *The People's Home Journal* established the Sunshine
Society, a club with local branches whose activities were published
monthly in a column, "Some Sunshine Work." The editor of the magazine subtly acknowledged the strikes and demonstrations common during these years in his explanation of "the Sunshine Movement" as "a
silent force as compared with the many organizations of elaborate purpose and varied aim so often exploited. The object of the Sunshine Society is to distribute through unselfish agency in homes everywhere as
much sunshine as possible" ("The Sunshine Society is Yours," 2).

The workings of the Sunshine Society provide an example of the ways
that dissent was domesticated in these magazines. Images of "movements" based on idealistic strategies (spreading sunshine) and privatized

goals (happy homes) stand in for the very real materially motivated, collective actions occurring outside these pages. At the same time, from the mid–1890s until around 1908, worker uprisings received little if any attention from the magazines' writers and editors. During these years, female readers faced contradictory images and messages concerning their roles as homemakers and wage earners. Collective action and protest in real life, "sunshine" activities in the magazines. Moreover, time and again both female and male readers were reminded through fiction stories that money would not bring them happiness.

1894–1903: Managing Contradictions

Through the turn of the century, everyday life for working-class families was characterized by the struggle for survival. Family members relied on each other and on their communities to get by. Young girls were frequently sent out at an early age to work in factories or department stores in order to supplement the family income, while mothers stayed home either doing "home work" or taking in boarders.[6]

The experience of the working class was fraught with contradictions. Material necessity frequently forced working-class women to violate prevailing gender norms. Adding insult to injury, working-class families were bombarded with messages to consume more even as they struggled to feed and clothe their children. These contradictions began to manifest themselves more sharply between 1894 and 1903, and were reconciled for readers in *Comfort* and *The People's Home Journal*.

The Practical True Woman: Reconciling Norms and Realities

In striking contrast to the early–1900s *Atlantic Monthly*, which portrayed a world virtually devoid of female figures except for queens and princesses, both *Comfort* and *The People's Home Journal* offered numerous images of women in a variety of roles. Given the gendered nature of the overarching rhetorical frame this may not come as a surprise. Yet, the complexity and multifaceted nature of these images is notable. As early as 1895, *Comfort* and *The People's Home Journal* offered accounts of women as newspaper workers, club activists, shopkeepers, and train engineers. "Women and Newspapers," an article in *Comfort*'s December 1895 issue, advised women on how they could break into the newspaper business (King). The author encouraged her readers to be adventuresome and creative, and to take initiative. A regular *Comfort* column initiated around 1903 imparted advice on "How Women May Earn Money" (Smith). The feature also printed letters from readers "who are already making money for themselves and who are willing to describe their methods and plans for the benefit of less fortunate sisters."

Fiction works encouraged identification with protagonists who were clever, brave, and defiant. In 1895, "Taken into Partnership" in *The People's Home Journal* described the adventures of a young woman who worked at a millinery shop (Augusta). Juliet Wayne successfully works side by side with the male proprietor and demonstrates courage by outwitting a burglar who breaks into the shop. In "A Woman's Way, " the heroine Kate Bradley redefines herself through her defiance and strength (Boyce 1896). Much to her mother's dismay, Kate cares more about pleasing herself than about any marriage prospects. She gets her face and hair messed up while engaging in one of her favorite pastimes, breaking in horses. "I've taught that colt something. . . . He's thrown me three times, and this morning he rubbed me up against the fence. . . . But I'm his master now, and he knows it" (2). Kate demonstrates similar self-assurance in her dealings with John and Emil, the two men who battle to win her hand. In "Engineer Nettie," readers might also identify with Nettie, a woman who learned to conduct a train and eventually applied her skills in order to save her lover's life (Pike 1902). Realizing her lover's train is about to crash head-on into another locomotive, Nettie takes charge of the nearby idle No. 76 and gives her uncle orders as they chase after the train headed for doom. "The engine swirled and swayed from side to side till Nettie could hardly keep her seat with both feet braced against the boiler head. . . . The cab was full of smoke and half-burnt cinders and the heat from blazing furnace scorched their clothes; but still Nettie drove recklessly ahead" (3). Nettie and her assistant-uncle reach the train in the nick of time and save the day.

On the one hand, mail-order magazines openly recognized the work-related experiences of their female readers. Articles and columns took into account women's roles as income contributors and stories featured protagonists who defied domesticity and submissiveness as they ran locomotives and apprehended burglars. On the other hand, these articles were interspersed between others that reminded readers of their duties as homemakers, mothers, and sex objects. To the left of the 1903 article on how women may earn money was an advertisement reminding women of the importance of a perfect body: "Your Bust Developed Six Inches Free." Further down, the reader was encouraged to send away for a "catalogue of all the latest, best and cheapest jewelry, cutlery, novelties, fancy goods, Christmas and birthday presents." This page disciplined women to be consumers and objects for the male gaze, even as it acknowledged them as contributors to the family income.

A similar juxtaposition in *Comfort*'s July 1903 issue revealed the ways working-class women were faced with the contradictions inherent in the cult of True Womanhood. "The Beauty Patch and Its Meaning" set the standards for female attractiveness and held up various "society" women as role models for the audience to strive toward (3). Just as Queen Alexandra, Miss Roosevelt, and Miss Leiter had taken to applying the beauty patch "to enhance the brilliancy of the complexion or the sparkles of the eye," so too should *Comfort* readers consider this tactic when attempting to attract the attentions of men.

First and foremost, however, the Practical True Woman as her image was crafted in these magazines was practical. Thus, a few pages after learning how to follow the beauty trends of their more well-to-do sisters, *Comfort* readers were instructed by Christine Terhune Herrick on "How to Make Work Easy": "It is a woman's duty to make her work as easy as possible" (12). This could be accomplished through a host of "labor-saving appliances" and kitchen arrangements that "make . . . toil lighter without doing it any less well" (12). Nor were female readers to forget their duties as mothers, as the December 1903 *Comfort* reminded. The lyrics to the song "None Can Take a Mother's Place" extolled the purity of "mother love" (Douglas, 13).

Articles on beauty patches and mother love might just as easily be found in *McClure's* or the *Atlantic Monthly* (see Flynt 1899; Gould 1916). The appearance of these articles in mail-order magazines is significant for the ways they tempered and controlled other accounts that acknowledged women's moxie and independence outside the home. The narrative of the Practical True Woman recognized readers' day-to-day lives as income providers—to do otherwise would not make good rhetorical or economic sense. From the magazine's standpoint, writers had to speak to their audiences' experiences in order to maintain readership. At the broader socioeconomic level, acknowledging women as laborers was an economic imperative. Particularly in early-twentieth-century industrial capitalism, women and girls represented a large and cheap pool of labor to fill unskilled and pink-collar, or clerical, jobs. Grounding the Practical True Woman in the tradition of True Womanhood assured that realities could be recognized while gender norms could remain in force.

The complexity surrounding images of women in these popular texts reflects the very real contradictions that wage-earning women faced in a society in which material circumstances necessitated that they push the boundaries of "acceptable" behavior. In her study of working women's consciousness in the early twentieth century, Eisenstein explains that "despite the degree to which women accepted the . . . dominant ideas about what was an appropriate and desirable life for a woman to lead— working women of the period recognized the necessity to work and fought for the right to do so. . . . In the process, they began to develop a rudimentary critique of the social and structural assumptions underlying the socially desired female life pattern" (1983, 33). Their critiques of dominant society and the ways in which they rebelled against the images and narratives in these magazines is the subject of the next chapter.

Redirecting Dissent

The labor historian Philip Foner notes that around the turn of the nineteenth century, "Evidence presented before the Industrial Commission proved conclusively that unions benefited workers" (1979, 266). A previous chapter detailed the benefits that workers gained—for example, in the Uprising of 30,000—from organizing and demonstrating for higher wages, shorter hours, and safer working conditions. In the pages of *Comfort* and *The People's Home Journal*, however, fiction and nonfiction articles conveyed one of two variations on a theme that undermined material struggle and staved off discontent. One common story line related the "lifestyles of the rich and famous." These articles bore a message of upward mobility and held out the possibility of material well-being without spelling out how that could be accomplished. A second theme, "love, luck, and pluck," provided a partial answer. In these stories love was always deemed more important than financial security, yet often, through luck (a fortune bequeathed by a long lost relative) or pluck (savvy or determination), economic stability was secured while the purity of love was kept intact. Both themes individuated material well-being and conspicuously avoided the possibility of cooperation or community struggle in attempts at social transformation to improve material well-being for a large segment of society.

Through advertisements and articles, *Comfort* and *People's Home Journal* readers were told how they could get their share of the American pie. Amidst the columns of ads for products ranging from "Genuine Confederate Money" to "Cures for Epilepsy," the January 1895 issue of *The People's Home Journal* carried a "pseudo" article, "Finding Fortunes." Much like contemporary advertisements that disguise themselves as scientific accounts or fact-revealing studies, "Finding Fortunes" provided the testimonies of various individuals—"Can hardly believe my own eyes," "A lucky investment I assure you"—who gained fortunes selling "Oxien and Oxien Plasters" (13). To learn more about how to become an Oxien salesperson in their local area, readers were encouraged to send away for the "Free Lucky Investment Booklet" by mailing twenty-seven cents to the manufacturers.

Numerous stories in *Comfort* depicted lifestyles for readers to emulate and aspire to. A 1903 article elaborated on "The Tableware of the White House" (Fawcett), and a regular column "Men, Women and Things" (Davis) portrayed the successes of justices, generals, lawyers, and marchionesses. The January 1902 issue pictured William Loeb, President Theodore Roosevelt's private secretary, who "has won his way to what has grown to be an important position through merit and ability," and Mrs. Edwin Gould, a "young matron of four years' standing who has already proved that neither social success nor the prestige of the Gould millions can divert her from serious pursuits" (Davis, 8).

In January 1902, two articles appeared explaining the generosity and goodwill of the millionaires Andrew Carnegie, Mrs. Leland Stanford, and Phillip Armour. "Forty Million Dollars For Education" tells of the money donated by Carnegie and Stanford for higher education. The author concluded that these donors "will go down to posterity to be praised and glorified for all future time" (17). Absent from this portrayal of the philanthropists were the shrewd business dealings of wealthy capitalists such as Andrew Carnegie who, with their mergers and combinations, ensured high profits for themselves, low wages for their workers, and no competition (Zinn 1980, 247–289). Zinn also provides a different perspective on the donations that these individuals made to educational institutions: "The rich, giving part of their enormous earnings in this way, became known as philanthropists. These educational institutions did not encourage dissent; they trained the middlemen in the American system . . . those who would be paid to keep the system going, to be loyal buffers against trouble" (256, 57). "Forty Million Dollars For Education" encouraged reader loyalty to the individuals and the institutions that effectively kept readers in their place of subordination (1902, 17). Most readers who learned of Andrew Carnegie's generous donations to higher education would never have access to these places of learning; moreover, they were part of a class of workers who suffered directly at the hands of Carnegie (and others) and their big businesses and monopolies.

"Great American Givers" provided a typical pull-yourself-up-by-the-bootstraps story of Phillip Armour, the meat-packing tycoon (1902). The article at one and the same time painted Armour as an average "self-made" man who overcame a "series of hard knocks" and as a "Merchant King" of America and the whole world. (6). On one hand, the readers learned, Armour was really quite an ordinary person who is "up with the sun," eats "bread and milk" for lunch and is in bed again by nine p.m. On the other hand, "His private benefactions are untold . . . [He is a] true King of men dispensing wisely the wealth of nations that has flowed at his feet" (6). Reverence was shown for Armour's accomplishments but they were not placed too far beyond the reach of the average reader, who was encouraged to place him- or herself in the context of Armour's success story. Portraying Armour's wealth as that of a self-made man individuated success and obscured the workings of a broad-based system from which a few benefited by exploiting the many.

Four years later, Upton Sinclair's *The Jungle* would provide a startling contrast to this portrait of the meat-packing magnate.[7] In his well-known exposé of the meat-packing industry, Sinclair told of the squalid conditions in which workers lived and worked. Through a fictional character, Jurgis, Sinclair offered a more accurate account and explained the dehumanization typical of factory life: "They [the owners] had got the best out of him—they had worn him out, with their speeding-up and their carelessness, and now they had thrown him away! . . . The vast majority [of unemployed workers] were simply the worn-out parts of the great merciless packing machine; they had toiled there, and kept up with the pace, some of them for ten or twenty years, until finally the time had come when they could not keep up with it any more" (149, 150).

It seems likely that at least a few readers of *Comfort* would recognize the contradictions between their own work experiences and those pictured in the articles. Yet the images of comfort and success are appealing, and between reading articles such as "Great American Givers" and "Forty Million Dollars For Education" readers could peruse advertisements on how they too could win fortune and prestige. To the right of "Great American Givers" was an ad that asked the reader, "Are you in line for promotion?" and went on to provide information about how the reader could climb the capitalist ladder by taking various correspondence courses.

There was also an implicit contradiction between promises that all could get rich easily and admonitions to be satisfied with little in life. Even as articles and ads conveyed a frenzy of offers promising "free," "you can win," "buy now," "we pay you $10 for 1¢," advice columns and stories advised readers to hold out for the afterlife or rely on love to carry them through the rough times. Henry Ward Beecher's 1895 advice column implored readers to "be patient. . . . Steady, patient industry is both the surest and the safest way [to earn a fortune]" (8). In other magazine articles of the early 1900s, love was the glue that held working families together. A story in the March 1894 *People's Home Journal* related how one couple exchanged vows of love while buried in a coal mine awaiting rescuers. The gallant Mr. Maples replied to his lover, "What is death, darling, if we are loved by our beloved and know we shall die with our love?" (Bennett, 3). In another coal-mining story written by "Hero Strong," the narrator expressed his love for Katie, his wife-to-be: "We loved and trusted each other perfectly, and when there is love enough a dollar can be made to go a great way" (1903, 14). Other stories informed readers of the misery to be had if one did not follow the path of love. Miss Wealthy Leighton, having married an affluent man at her sister's behest, lived a miserable existence with the man, who was cruel and bitter and who eventually abandoned her (Townsend 1895). Another story in the same issue of *The People's Home Journal* provided a comparison between two sisters that made the path to happiness clear for readers. Lenore, described as having "a wealth of raven hair . . . the very embodiment of pride and beauty, yet a beauty all of this earth," openly acknowledged that she wished a life of ease and repudiated her sister's sermons about earthly suffering and happiness in the afterlife (Fleming 1895, 5). The "fair, frail, and spiritual" Rose led an honest life, believing that her reward would come later. The sisters' fates provided the story's moral. Lenore ends up in a madhouse, a "gibbering idiot," and Rose, "purified by affliction . . . goes through the world doing good, blessed and loved by all, with her eyes on that far-off Garden, where she yet hopes to rest—Heaven" (5).

A variation on these love stories was a story line that, where love holds strong, fortune may fall upon the lovers through luck. These stories played an important role by holding out to readers the *possibility* of material wealth achieved not by labor organizing but by chance. They provided the ideological carrot that encouraged the working-class reader to carry on in her or his daily toils while not giving in to complete despair or, more important, turning to labor unions for material betterment. The story "Ruby" in the June 1894 issue of *The People's Home Journal* exemplified this story line, which appeared in this magazine on three different occasions (Jones).

Ruby, an eighteen-year-old orphan who lives with her aunt, is bequeathed a fortune by her late grandfather, St. Aubyn. The only stipulation, according to the will, is that Ruby "wed for her husband one Richard Russel, son of the Countess of Lindenwold" by her twenty-second birthday (1). In spite of the fortune, Ruby repeatedly states that she will not marry Russel. One day Ruby is rescued from a brutal rain storm by a gentleman, Clifford Heath. Mr. Heath expresses his love for Ruby and proposes to her: "Can you give up all, friends and title and wealth, and be content with my love? . . . Even though I am of humble birth and dependent on my own exertions?" asks Clifford. Ruby replies with a resounding affirmative and willingly foregoes her fortune by accepting Clifford's proposal. In the end Ruby is rewarded for choosing the path of love. As it turns out, Clifford Heath was really Richard Russel all along, so disguised in order to win Ruby's love through consent rather than by force of her grandfather's will. "Ruby" is truly an *All's Well That End's Well* story offering an unadulterated union between love and wealth. "The Lady of Leigh" (Austin 1903) and "The Heiress of Heathcourt" (Strong 1895) provide almost identical story lines in subsequent issues of *The People's Home Journal*.

Still other stories related the successes of individuals as a result of their pluck or determination. Flossie Fields is a spirited young woman who is forced to make her own way as a domestic after her mother's death

(Comfort 1902). Flossie works hard, resists various temptations of the big city, and eventually wins the hand of a wealthy artist, Geoffrey Marchlands. A similar story, "The Lost Mine," told of the trials and tribulations of Arthur, a poor farm boy who sets off into the wilderness to find fortune in a hidden coal mine (Marshall 1902). Not only does Arthur find the mine and reap the wealth for his family, he discovers the value in his father's teachings on spirituality. As he picks away at a mountainside, Arthur's mind turns to his "poor old father and mother—of their simple, unquestioning faith." He recalls how his father "used to ask for heavenly guidance and instruction" and soon Arthur begins to do the same (17). By the story's conclusion, Arthur has brought affluence to his family while keeping family norms intact.

Through fiction and nonfiction accounts as well as advertisements and advice columns, *Comfort* and *The People's Home Journal* addressed the contradictions experienced by wage-earning readers in early-twentieth-century capitalist society. Articles variously encouraged the audience to plod along in their current position and also to strive for capitalist success. Both messages reinforced and supported the economic status quo. The factory system relied upon the endless labors of workers; so visions of earthly toil leading to a happy afterlife represented an effort to prevent anyone from halting the Machine. Fiction stories portrayed individuals who willingly accepted poverty in order to have "true love," yet who, by luck or determination, ended up with both love and wealth. At the same time, however, the system that churned out an increasing amount of products required an increasing number of consumers. Thus, the working-class as well as middle- and upper-class individuals were inundated with messages to work their way up the capitalist ladder, to earn more income, and to buy, buy, buy. Articles profiled the lives of the rich and famous as a way to legitimize individual wealth while advertisements conveyed to readers how they could become just like those depicted. In many respects, these themes align with the universalization rhetoric of *McClure's*, which emphasized the power of ideals in surmounting material hardship. Yet there is a subtle difference; in *Comfort* and *The People's Home Journal*, these story lines carry a distinct domesticating tone which redirected dissent and collective struggle into the private realm. The image of the Practical True Woman further reinforced this frame as it recognized the necessity of a woman's paid labors but reassured that her nurturance and purity would still be present to uphold the home. In short, domestication provided a class-specific frame that showed visions of domestic bliss and inner tranquillity to an audience most of whose members toiled six days in the factory, went without medical care or proper diet, and increasingly turned to labor organizing and confrontational tactics in order to improve their lives.

From the mid-1890s through the turn of the century, the stories and articles in *Comfort* and *The People's Home Journal* revolved around these themes with little variation. Into the teens, as the labor movement carried some of its most notable and far-reaching strikes, mail-order magazines placed even greater emphasis on coping and self-monitoring, explicitly directing readers to discipline their bodies and behaviors. Though strikes, walkouts, collective bargaining, and union meetings were part of the experience of their target audience, *Comfort*, *Home Life*, and *The People's Home Journal* suggested quite different measures for achieving well-being. As many of the working class were participating in or at least witnessing firsthand the benefits of solidarity, these popular magazines proffered personal contentedness and coping in a hegemonic move to manage dissent.

1909–1917: Managing Class Unrest

In 1909, the Uprising of 30,000 was the inspiration for a series of large-scale strikes over the ensuing years that called attention to the exploitations of the factory system and spread worker enthusiasm from city to city throughout the Northeast. Between 1909 and 1917, workers repeatedly held mass meetings, staged factory walkouts, and petitioned for fair workplace conditions (see Photo 3.1). Industrial Workers of the world (IWW) leaders such as Elizabeth Gurley Flynn rallied workers such as those of the Patterson textile mills who toiled in the most degrading of conditions (see Photo 3.2). Thousands of cloak, garment, and corset makers and white-goods workers among others brought entire trades to a halt as they walked out en masse and successfully won new wage scales, sanitary conditions, reduced workweeks, pay for overtime, and union recognition for some (Foner 1979, 346–373).

As workers demonstrated the successes of solidarity as never before, *Comfort*, *Home Life*, and *The People's Home Journal* devoted increasing space to redirecting dissent to home and personal life. As in the early 1900s, romance stories, poems, and editorials continued to implore readers to find contentedness in interpersonal relationships, and stories and advice columns further sharpened the contours of the Practical True Woman through the strategies of tradition, recognition, and negation. In July 1911 *The People's Home Journal* initiated the Sunshine Society, a department designed to "inspire your better self and give gladness to many of the human family" ("The Sunshine Society Is Yours"). Ideological support for domestication of worker unrest could be found in the editorial pages of *The People's Home Journal*, where readers were often given advice on how to improve their tone of voice and scatter smiles in order to improve their lot.

PHOTO 3.1   Arrested striking shirtwaist workers on the stage at Carnegie Hall during a mass meeting in 1909. International Ladies' Garment Workers' Union Archives, Kheel Center, Cornell University, Ithaca, New York.

PHOTO 3.2   The labor activist Elizabeth Gurley Flynn speaking at the Patterson, New Jersey, textile workers' strike, 1912. Sophia Smith Collection, Smith College, Northampton, Massachusetts.

"Love or Money"

Editorials in all three magazines often clearly acknowledged the hardships faced by their readers. Though living conditions may be sparse and incomes limited, readers were encouraged to see the good in their present conditions. In *Home Life's* "A Few Minutes with Father," the editor noted, "We are all equally rich in time. We may have to hustle like Sam Hill while [Mr. Rockefeller] sits at a table clipping coupons but when you come to think of it, that isn't very interesting work and the sun will go down on him at the same time it does on us. . . . We can be just as gracious and kind to others in each twenty-four hours as any plutocrat living" (Jan. 1916). A few months later the editor encouraged readers to take inspiration from their forefathers, who lived simple lives and had "clean hearts." In a similar spirit, the editor of *The People's Home Journal* prompted readers to see the significance in a penny: "A penny may seem to you a very insignificant thing. But it is the small seed from which fortune springs. . . . Treat that little disc of copper—one cent—with the respect that a fortune seed deserves" ("The Picture Before Us," 1914c).

Readers of *The People's Home Journal* could take heart in reassuring poems, while *Home Life* ran a four-part series imparting to readers how to deal with "Problems of Life." "God's Word is a cheque to be cashed in at the bank," counseled the Rev. J. Wilbur Chapman, who penned the series from August to November 1913. In September 1913, Chapman reminded readers, "Your trial, your burden, your sorrow will sweeten your temper, strengthen your soul, build up your character" (9). Poems in *The People's Home Journal* betrayed a similar theme. One need only scan the poem titles for an idea of the central message: "Contentment" (Cooper 1914), "The Simple Life" (Dolson 1914), "Little Things" (Davies 1915), "The Price of Life" (Patterson 1915). "Contentment" gave readers a peace of mind to strive towards: "Nope, I haven't got much money, jest enough for a bed an' / board, / But I'm richer, Jim, in lots of ways than you will ever see . . . " (Cooper 1914). "Little Things" and "The Price of Life" acknowledged strife but provided the personalized solution. "Little Things" (Davies 1915) trilled: "To smile at someone in the clutch / Of black despair, and greet / A lonely heart—it isn't much / But oh, it makes life sweet!" The author of "The Price of Life" (Patterson 1915) bravely asserted: "Yet gladly do we take our griefs and joys / The cares that crowd existence, and its strife, / Because they are the price we pay for life." "The Simple Life" was even more purposeful in redirecting attention away from collectivized solutions: "No rush for wealth in crowded mart— / No threat from banded labor's arm— / To hear, from far, the world's great heart; / Yet know its throbbings cannot harm" (Dolson 1914). If poems were not persuasion enough, the editor exhorted on the October 1913 editorial page: "It is only when we go beyond that which is given us for the day . . . when we are not content to bear the evils of the day, but harass ourselves with anticipations of those the future may bring . . . it is only then that outraged nature takes revenge for the neglect of her laws, and sanitariums and lunatic asylums are filled with the victims of ill-regulated lives" ("The Picture Before Us," 1913c, 5).

Beyond the pages of mail-order magazines, however, workers were fortifying their character through labor organizations. In contravention of the advice provided in *The People's Home Journal* and *Home Life*, workers did not always gladly accept grief nor were they content to settle for a smile while in the clutch of black despair. They joined unions by the thousands and picketed for shorter hours and decent wages. Between September 1909 and September 1913 over 60,000 women joined trade unions of New York City's garment industry. In the first months of 1913 alone, 7,000 to 25,000 white-goods workers, waist- and dressmakers, and wrapper, kimono, and house-dress workers walked out of factories in New York City, and the strike fever spread to workers in Boston. In the January 1913 strike of white-goods workers, young picketers sang the "Song of the White Goods Workers": "We're getting beaten by policemen, / With their heavy clubs of hickory, / But we'll fight as hard as we can / To win 'Strong Union Victory'" (Foner 1979, 370). Time and again workers testified to the importance of the union: "You know if we had to go back [to work] without the union I would die;" "I eat two meals a day and wear my clothes until they fall off me, but I wouldn't be a scab" (quoted in Foner 1979, 370, 371).

Ignoring the passion to organize, mail-order magazines buttressed their editorial advice and poetry with stories much like those of the early 1900s in which the pursuit of love transcended all material difficulty. Protagonists proclaimed their love for one another and made material sacrifices in order to sanctify their relationships. "John is poor, but he is richer than any Worth that ever lived! Richer in mind, richer in heart, richer in gentleness and true manliness. He is far, far richer than you Joshua Worth, though you are the millionaire, and he the beggar!" declared Norah in the 1911 *Comfort* story, "Love or Money" (Carpenter, 32). *The People's Home Journal* ran two stories the same year with a related theme. In these narratives, the poor but pure-hearted protagonists win love *and* money by the story's end. In "Jenny," Colonel Murray gave up his plantation and home in order to keep custody of his granddaughter, Jenny (Gordon 1911). But by twist of fate, a court of law grants the plantation back to Murray and he is able to live out his years in comfort with Jenny. Similarly, two poor cousins desperately in need of two thousand dollars in order to repair the beloved old house in which they were raised are brought together by a fire which destroys the house (Mortimer 1911). The tragedy winds up benefiting the two, who eventually express their love for each other, receive two thousand dollars from the Safety Insurance Company, and are able to restore the house and live happily ever after.

Though romance stories were common in *Home Life*, *The People's Home Journal*, and *Comfort*, these magazines did not confine women to the image of mistress, wife, or lover. The Practical True Woman was a class-specific image that recognized women in a variety of occupations even as it reinforced the magazines' ideology of domestication. The counterhegemonic elements of the Practical True Woman were controlled by *tradition* and *negation*, the tradition strategy grounding women's activities in the ethos of "true womanhood" and the negation strategy silencing women's roles as activists.

The Practical True Woman: Silencing Dissent

Tradition. As in the *Atlantic Monthly* and *McClure's*, images of women in *Comfort, Home Life,* and *The People's Home Journal* revolved around domestic duties traditionally expected of women. But mail-order magazines targeting the working classes more directly addressed the obstacles faced by women who had to balance "womanly" duties and qualities with the practice of household economy. Editorials, regular columns, and articles suggested short cuts and "useful hints" for making do on limited budgets (Booth 1909; Squire 1912; "The City Housewife," 1910; "Useful Hints," 1911). In February 1910, *Comfort* advertised its March issue as a tool for "improving, repairing, renovating, beautifying and making the home and all its contents and surroundings more comfortable, attractive and healthful with the least expenditure of money" (2). Elsewhere readers were given hints on how to "economize[] in every part of the home" ("Useful Hints," 23). On one March 1911 page of *Comfort* the conflicting concerns and expectations of wage-earning women came to a head as the article imparted advice on thriftiness—"Never spend your money before you get it"—while a neighboring advertisement told readers how to buy a piano on credit.

Home Life similarly addressed the issue of limited budgets in a June 1912 article "Woman's Problem, The Housekeeping Money" (Squire). The article was accompanied by the initiation of a contest in which readers could win ten dollars for submitting the best advice on household concerns. Addressing the reality of scarce resources, these magazines opened a space for critique of working-class living conditions. Yet the strategy of tradition cut short a deeper analysis of domestic difficulties by intimating that women were naturally equipped to transcend these shortcomings. *Comfort's* March 1911 editorial page framed the issue this way: "However small and humble the abode or slender the family resources, woman's knack under the impelling force of wifely and motherly love can find a way to make it truly homelike, cozy and attractive if she has the ideals characteristic of her sex" ("A Few Words by the Editor," 3). Similarly *Home Life* introduced its magazine's contest for household advice by asserting that "the success of the home depends as much or more on what [the housewife] does with her housekeeping money, and the return she gets for it, as it does upon the amount of the family income" (Squire 1912, 9).

Women's homemaking roles were celebrated for smoothing the harsh edges of wage-earning life, while motherliness was praised for its soothing effects. The poem "Mother's Face" told of the difficult and lonely adventure of a grown child who left home to travel the world (Johnson 1915). Upon returning the narrator was reassured by the appearance of

Mother: "Will the dear scenes welcome me back again, / Is it home, my home, just the same as then? / But the wide door creaks, and a face I see, / Ah, my mother's face—It is home to me!" (28). Editorials in *The People's Home Journal* explained how destitution and dire circumstances were overcome by Mother's presence ("The Picture Before Us," 1912c, 1914g, 1915a). The August 1912 "Picture Before Us," asserted: "If you travel through the stifling alleys where crowded tenements cut the field of the sky into pitiful squares and patches, you will see the splendor of mother faces lighting up the dim aisles along which humanity frets and surges. The radiance of them as they lean above the half-starved babies at their breast makes sunshine in the most darksome spots" (3). Regular columns in *The People's Home Journal* further reinforced women's natural mothering abilities. "The Care of the Children" provided advice for mothers while "Our Mother's Circle" provided a forum for readers to express their own opinions on child rearing.

While *The People's Home Journal* columns and editorials imparted advice and shared ideas, fiction stories offered an imaginary world of wives and mothers who could fulfill their duties without the constraints of wage-earning existence. In "The Wife," Kate Walters devoted herself full time to her husband and provided the inspiration he needed to be successful in his business: "All that matters to me is that I shall be your mate, that I shall create a home for you, no matter where" (Goodwin 1915, 8). Likewise, in "The Shared Mother" Kathie Lee's mother extends her love and nurturance to the other young people in the apartment building who live in the city without their mothers (Boylan 1913). According to Kathie, it is not bread that these individuals lack, but "mother-love."

In light of the predominance of cultural norms demanding a domestic and submissive woman, wage-earning women often did identify themselves in terms consonant with a cult of domesticity. Yet they expressed a "negotiated response" (Eisenstein 1983) in which they simultaneously upheld traditional gender norms while struggling for the right to fair treatment and equal opportunity as workers. In testimonies and speeches, wage earners called attention to the hypocrisies of True Womanhood and the realities of working-class life that made adherence to cultural norms impractical, if not impossible. Indeed, in order to ring true with their readers, mail-order magazines needed to acknowledge the experiences of women in the workplace, which they did through the strategy of recognition.

Recognition.   While tradition recognized the unique hardships faced by wage-earning women as homemakers, recognition accounted for women's activities outside of the home. The image of the Practical True Woman, comprising elements of tradition and recognition, exemplified the dynamic nature of cultural products, the "complex interrelations between movements and tendencies both within and beyond a specific and effective dominance" (Williams 1977, 121). New relations, roles, and values emerge in cultural products in opposition to dominant culture, yet are often reframed so as to be incorporated back into the dominant mode.

Fiction and regularly featured columns in *Comfort*, *The People's Home Journal*, and *Home Life* provided a way to explore the interplay between these two strategies and the ways that mail-order magazines reconciled dominant norms with working-class realities. Throughout the 1910s, works of fiction developed female characters who displayed strength, independence, and bravery.[8] In *Comfort*, young heroines defied orders and risked death in order to save individuals from house fires (Marlborough 1909) and to stave off hold-ups (Brown 1910). In "How Amy Handled the Bandits," Amy and one of the male passengers work together to steer the traveling coach away from armed bandits (Brown 1910). Amy takes the initiative and gives orders to her partner: "[Y]ou stay here and wait for their [the bandits'] return. I'll ride one of their horses and overtake the stage." Her helpmate gladly defers: "All right, young lady; you are my superior officer. If I had your brains I'd have been a General in the Phillipines [*sic*] instead of a Captain" (17).

Other narratives depicted women who set out to make it in the big city, often meeting with great success. In "Penniless and Alone in the Capitol City," Nelly Harris, wearing a shabby dress and boots with holes, determines to succeed: "She *would* not return and own to the neighbors that she had failed. She *must* stay here and conquer" (Boteler-Sanders 1912, 7). And conquer she does as Nelly lands a job in a senator's office and goes to school to cultivate her musical talents. Other heroines succeeded as magazine writers (Higginson 1910), cashiers (Giebler 1912), artists (Simmons 1913), senators (Hoerle 1915), and professors (Chase 1912). "One Fearsome Lady" related the experiences of Helen Burton, "the only woman senator in the United States" (Hoerle 1915). Men feared Miss Burton, who was a "woman of action, [a] woman of brilliant language and clear reasoning" (19). Allyn Locke in "The New Woman and the Old Man" similarly had traits more often seen in her masculine counterparts (Chase 1912). With a "tall strong figure and an easy stride," Locke was a professor who befriended a homeless man and related to him her beliefs as a feminist. "Woman, nowadays, is not dependent, not even economically. . . . I hold that in this modern world a woman is just as capable as a man, and just as well able to meet every requirement" (9).

Advertisements and feature columns provided ideological support for fiction that acknowledged women as income generators and workers. Both *Comfort* and *The People's Home Journal* regularly carried an ad headlined "A Woman Can Earn $5000 a Year," which explained that she could do so by making dresses in her home. And *The People's Home Journal* ran a regular column, "How Women May Earn Money." *Home Life* carried a series in 1912 and 1916 informing girls how to get employment in the city. The March 1912 installment of "The Girl Who Comes to the City" provided advice for readers interested in stenography (Ransome). To be successful, the young stenographer must be ambitious: "[S]he has no time for the office boy's jokes. . . . She is bending every energy to make herself necessary to her employer" (11). Further, the writer advised, the stenographer "will have no one to shield her . . . from the results of any folly she may commit, therefore she must learn to rely entirely upon herself" (11). In the July 1916 issue, "Girls in the City" gave advice pertaining to living arrangements, job applications, and proper work attire (Greaves); the October issue provided information on "lines of work . . . which are not only pleasant . . . but which pay well for the bright, proficient worker" (Brown, 15).

Of particular significance was the August 1916 "Girls in the City," written by Agnes Johnson, a boot and shoe worker and a member of the Women's Trade Union League. Written from the perspective of one who experienced factory labor directly, this article differed dramatically from other accounts of labor in the mail-order magazines and provided rhetorical leverage from which to expose and overturn the more conservative elements of the Practical True Women. Johnson provided an explicit critique of the capitalist system in order to persuade readers of the need for organization. Working girls, she explained, were "cogs in a wheel," "part of a vast machine that must be kept going at all hazards. . . . And girls very quickly become unfit cogs under many of the conditions that are imposed upon them in city industries. It is for this reason, to save their very lives, that many girls have organized themselves into unions to demand better working conditions" (8).

Undermining editorials and poems that encouraged readers to rest easy in the nurturing environs of home and Mother, Johnson accentuated the importance of unionization: "In the organized trades the girls have much better opportunities for gaining their rights and needs than in the unorganized trades. . . . When a whole body of girls working together ask for certain rights the management will pay attention. . . . So the 'union girl' has become quite a factor, and great advances have been made in factory conditions through the girls banding together for the mutual interests" (8). Johnson's account, though it appeared in a context of other discourses both within and outside the magazine that reinforced women as mothers, wives, and homemakers, was shaped by firsthand experiences and thus provided readers with a compelling critique of the capitalist system that fell outside the magazine's hegemonic rhetorical frame. In contrast to the personalizing effect of domesticity, Johnson highlighted the structural nature of women's exploitation and encouraged a collective solution to women's workplace toils.

As these stories were circulating among wage-earning readers in the early 1900s, working-class women were also receiving increased attention from the Socialist party. In 1908, the Second International officially addressed the issue of women's status within the party and concluded by forming the Woman's National Committee to work to organize women. The committee was quite successful in recruiting women to the Socialist party and distributed thousands of pamphlets to working women on issues such as suffrage, sex relations, and alcoholism. The party also initiated the first International Woman's Day in 1909, a day of rallies and demonstrations across the country focusing primarily on the issue of women's suffrage (Tax 1980, 188).

Mail-order magazines such as *Comfort, Home Life,* and *The People's Home Journal* competed for women's attention by crafting a nuanced image that recognized the conflicting expectations of working-class women. They acknowledged the realities of a working-class woman's experience without radically challenging dominant norms and behaviors. The Practical True Woman provided a site on which tradition and recognition could play off of one another, at once legitimating the new or novel while reconciling them in terms of the dominant mode. The strategy of recognition represented an emergent discourse whereby new experiences that did not align with the traditional sexual division of labor could be explored. Tradition acted as a tether, redirecting oppositional ideas and behaviors back into the dominant mode. For instance, readers learned that Miss Burton, the first woman senator, was actually quite unhappy because men avoided her owing to their fear of "her learning and her quick tongue" (Hoerle 1915, 19). By story's end, Miss Burton receives a marriage proposal and reassurance from her new fiancé that she is just as feminine as the next woman. Miss Burton asks, "'Then I'm really not such a terribly fearsome lady as I'm pictured to be?'" Her fiancé replies: "'Terrible, dearest? You're the sweetest—'" (22). Indeed, the marriage proposal provided the staple denouement in the narratives of artists (Simmons 1913), cashiers (Giebler 1912), and office workers (Boteler-Sanders 1912), while Mindy Evans, in "Full Many a Flower," forwent an education and career as a magazine writer in Boston in order to tend to her mother in the country (Higginson 1910). Similarly, the March 1912 issue of "The Girl Who Comes to the City," which advised readers on how to become a stenographer, concluded with this: "Remember, when you are looking for a vocation, that you can only stay in the business world for a limited number of years, while you can stay in a home as long as life shall last. Go into the business world if you must, but stay in your home if you can" (Ransome, 30).

The Practical True Woman was a class-specific image crafted to recognize working-class realities while reconciling contradictions in terms consonant with dominant class and gender relations. It was an image constructed in part through omission or negation, in that the narrative of the Practical True Woman acknowledged and even supported women's experiences in the paid labor force but remained silent on their experiences as activists.

Negation. Though she wound up tending home and husband in the end, the Practical True Woman still represented a substantial challenge to traditional gender norms. *Comfort, Home Life,* and *The People's Home Journal* carried stories of women who gave orders to men, saved men's lives, and had "masculine" attributes. In the pages of the mail-order magazines that constructed the image of the Practical True Woman, female characters might defy men in interpersonal spaces, but conspicuously absent were women's agitations and transgressions in public spaces such as the workplace. Though strikes and walkouts were a regular part of the industrial landscape during the first decades of the twentieth century, labor organization and collective confrontation were acknowledged minimally in all three magazines. This absence, or negation, rounded out the picture of the Practical True Woman by denying or silencing women's roles as labor activists. Female labor agitators represented a "third persona," a group "whose presence, though relevant to what is said, is negated through silence" (Wander 1984, 210). This textual omission sent a deliberate message to readers, informing them what behaviors should be avoided (209). Mail-order magazines counteracted women's participation in strikes and walkouts by rhetorically denying readers this option. Negation acted in conjunction with tradition to neutralize the subversive effects of recognition.

On a few occasions, *Comfort's* editorial page spoke to worker indignation ("A Few Words by the Editor," 1909, 1910, 1912). The March 1910 issue recognized the "pinch of poverty" and the workers' "daily grind of building up profits for King Coal, King Steel and King Iron," and castigated congressmen who "play[] politics and mak[e] nice speeches to beguile voters" ("A Few Words by the Editor," 3). In January 1911, *Comfort* ran a curious article signed by the magazine's publisher, W. H. Gannett. Entitled "Strike!," the one-page piece of advice aroused reader attention with its repeated use of the word no doubt on the lips of thousands of readers during this period. "Strike! But don't quit work; get busy and do something to make the world better and happier" was the advice imparted. Among other things, readers were encouraged to "abolish[] dishonesty in high places" and to "[m]ake the best of things and be happy."

Such advice exemplifies the persuasive hegemonic force of domestication prevalent in all three magazines. Domestication was a strategy particularly suited to a working-class audience as it acknowledged readers' limited budgets and frustrations with "King Coal" and unscrupulous politicians, but replaced collective confrontations, which were proving so successful in the actual lives of their target audience, with personalized solutions. In the world of mail-order magazines, workers' anger and energies were rechanneled to private spaces—the home, the inner self— leaving deeply entrenched discriminatory systems intact.

The People's Home Journal ran two short stories of workplace unrest in mills and mines. Both stories encouraged identification with workers who toiled beneath the eye of unscrupulous employers. In "Yansen: A Story of the Mines," Yansen, a mine worker, attempts to arouse class consciousness in his fellow workers: "Do you think he [the boss] cares, him or his lady? Bah! they do not look at us. They step out of their fine coach, step into their fine carriage, and mud flies in our faces! Off they go to their grand house on the hill, and we go back to our cabins to sleep so we can rise in the morning and go to work for them" (French 1912, 6). This story and "The Kimberly Mills" acknowledged the injustices of class privilege and the anger so frequently felt by mill workers and miners. Yet in both stories it is not a successful strike that wins the workers their due. The transformative effects of collective confrontation—and the pivotal roles of women therein—remain unmentioned. Instead, worker loyalty to the boss is reaffirmed. In fact, in "The Kimberly Mills," the owner's privilege is legitimated and sealed in the concluding paragraphs in which a "crowd of happy operatives eating their plentiful dinners in the mill yards" all agree that the owner is "the best master that ever was, and his wife is as good as the queen, as she always was" (Strong 1910, 15).

While fictional laborers and owners made amends in the pages of magazines, real workers were proving the necessity of direct confrontation rather than reconciliation with owners who controlled their workplaces, homes, and neighborhood stores. Women played central roles in the success of these strikes by setting up soup kitchens, boycotting unsympathetic establishments, providing childcare, and circulating fliers. In *The People's Home Journal*, however, savvy and militancy on the part of thousands of wage-earning women were negated as the Practical True Woman's know-how was confined to her own home. What went untold were the ways that women applied their traditional roles as wives, mothers, and homemakers to a workplace and community context. For example, striking families in Lawrence, Massachusetts, established cooperative living arrangements and shared childcare and household utensils

(Cameron 1985, 1991). These communal organizations "provid[ed] an additional female space where women shared information and collective grievances" (Cameron 1991, 60).

Of the three mail-order magazines, *Home Life* most readily addressed the activism of women through editorials and articles. Particularly in the mid-teens, the magazine's editorial page, "Let Us Read the News Together," offered accounts of women's boycotts and peace and suffrage efforts, and on one occasion even supported birth control for women (1916a, 1916b, 1917a, 1917b). The few more extended accounts of women's rights activities focused on those of middle- and upper-class women, most typically women's clubs and suffrage (Adams 1916; Brush 1912; Redd 1917). "The Woman's Party Convention," appearing in August 1916, detailed the activities of the National Woman's Party (Adams). This group, composed primarily of middle- and upper-class women, was one of the more radical suffrage organizations of the teens; many of its members were also involved as socialists. The article created a favorable image of women protesting for the vote, describing them as "dauntless" and determined to have their demands heard.

Thus, *Home Life* offered select bits of information on women's activism, which made it appear to represent the whole story. In fact, this selectivity disguised what was omitted. While readers were encouraged to identify with middle-class organizations and arguments for the vote, information on wage-earning women's struggles was suppressed. For instance, "The Woman's Party Convention" generated respect for wealthy activists such as Mrs. O. H. P. Belmont while eliding the problematic relationship between activists such as Belmont and the magazine's target readers as a group. Belmont was the wife of the heir to the New York subway system. Like other middle- and upper-class activists, her involvement with working-class women during this period was full of conflict stemming from the very different worlds from which these women came. More specifically, Belmont was unable to understand the importance of class solidarity, and she often used women's labor uprisings as occasions to promote woman suffrage while turning a blind eye to women's unique needs as workers. In the *Home Life* article, the voices of Belmont and other well-to-do suffragists come to stand in for—and suppress—wage-earning women's demand for equality.

As the next chapter details, wage-earning women generally viewed the vote as a tool for workplace improvement, and many of them included critiques of class as well as male privilege in their arguments for the vote. The socialist and IWW member Elizabeth Gurley Flynn viewed the vote skeptically and avoided alliances with middle- and upper-class women. She supported the right of women to vote but believed that "the vote was useless for revolutionary purposes, the agitation around it was divisive, and workers had more important things to do" (Tax 1980, 179). On a few occasions, socialist and wage-earning women joined efforts with the mainstream suffrage movement such as in 1909, when socialists participated with the National American Woman Suffrage Association (NAWSA) in an enormous petition drive as part of the first International Woman's Day celebration. Though some efforts were successful, the alliance between socialist and upper-class suffragists was tenuous at best. Attacks and counterattacks were frequent as upper-class suffragists tried to discredit socialist women and downplay their efforts; while socialists saw their upper-class sisters as snobby and out of touch.

Not always at home in more mainstream suffrage affiliations of the NAWSA, wage earners often formed their own worker-centered organizations. One such group, the Wage Earners' Suffrage League, advanced what Leonora O'Reilly called "straight labor suffrage talk" and passed out flyers at a large 1912 meeting rallying wage earners around the vote (Tax 1980, 173). The flyer read in part: "Why are you paid less than a man? Why do you work in a fire-trap? Why are your hours so long? . . . Why does the cost of living go up while wages go down? . . . BECAUSE YOU ARE A WOMAN AND HAVE NO VOTE. VOTES MAKE THE LAW. VOTES ENFORCE THE LAW. THE LAW CONTROLS CONDITIONS. WOMEN WHO WANT BETTER CONDITIONS MUST VOTE" (quoted in Tax 1980, 173, 74).

In *Home Life*, the issue of suffrage could be reconciled in nonconfrontational terms through association with "cultured" or "refined" activists such as Belmont. But the strikes and walkouts of working women and girls posed a significant problem for symbolic negotiation. The first decades of the twentieth century have been documented as a remarkable moment in the history of social change as wage-earning women and girls defied norms to make their demands public and demonstrate their organizing and speaking abilities—often without the support of their fellow male workers (see Dye 1980; Foner 1979; Milkman 1985; Orleck 1995; Tax 1980). To describe or even acknowledge a particular group or activity grants a degree of validity. In omitting any images or narratives of significant events that directly affected their target readership, these popular magazines avoided legitimizing events that challenged not only symbolic oppression but material exploitation.

In these magazines, the option to be demanding, confrontational, and defiant in a public manner was rhetorically taken away from female readers so as to maintain a coherent frame of domestication, at the center of which stood the domestic woman. Here it is important to recall the hegemonic role that discourses surrounding the sentimental and private family played in maintaining a class-segregated society. In the working-class family, a woman's place as mother, wife, and nurturer played an important role both materially and ideologically. For industrial capitalism, the working-class family facilitated the reproduction and maintenance of workers necessary for the growing factory output and expansion during this period. In their prescribed role as homemakers, women cooked meals, cared for children, and often took in boarders or home work to supplement the family income. Ideologically, the visions of domestic comfort and home as a safe haven represented the utopian element that made these popular magazines so persuasive to their readers. Certainly the home did represent for many workers a space of autonomy and dignity, but the discourse of domestication operated to sustain class privilege and women's subordination by encouraging readers to focus on, control, and critique personal spaces and individual actions while ignoring the social basis of and public influences on these private areas. Self-involvement replaced social criticism and public protest.

The Practical True Woman was not only a mother, wife, and homemaker but also an income provider and successful workplace compatriot. This multifaceted and complex figure provided an appropriate hegemonic response to working-class concerns that fit well with the needs of early-twentieth-century capitalism for an essential source of cheap labor to fill the scores of unskilled factory and office jobs that were burgeoning as a result of technological advances. Female strength, independence, and endurance as depicted in *Comfort, Home Life,* and *The People's Home Journal* were worker attributes that ensured continued factory production with minimal need for monitoring or oversight on the part of owners. Further, the silence of women's labor militancy and organization can be viewed as part of the rhetorical effort to instill a capitalist mind-set regarding workplace norms such as punctuality, conformity, and worker competition.

The strikes and walkouts of thousands of workers during the first decades of the twentieth century were extra-discursive actions that to a degree altered existing work and gender relations. The ideology of domestication and its Practical True Woman allowed the magazines to provide their own framings and solutions to working-class problems and relations. Demonstrations such as the Uprising of 30,000 defied symbolic reconciliation because they represented the workers' own answers to material disparities. The most effective way for publications to symbolically negotiate the material confrontations of the system was simply to ignore them or to provide alternative means of coping. In addition to the narrative of the Practical True Woman, *Comfort, Home Life,* and *The People's Home Journal* exhorted readers to seek happiness and security in a comfortable home or a strong personal character.

Sunshine and Self-improvement

By 1909, the Industrial Workers of the World had gained a reputation around the world for their militancy, persistence, and success in organizing workers. When the IWW came to a town to help in a strike or to circulate information to workers, the local authorities and factory owners took notice—and often reacted violently. Throughout the teens, the Wobblies' message of worker empowerment was making its way across the United States. Syndicalism, as it was known, advocated shop-floor organization and a general industry-wide strike in which workers would bring down the economic system by halting production. "The workers are more powerful with their hands in their pockets than all the property of the capitalists," said the IWW organizer Joseph Ettor (Zinn 1980, 324).

As the IWW's message of solidarity reached ever greater and greater numbers of factory, mill, and mine workers, popular journals that targeted these individuals were advocating a turn inward, to homelife and self-improvement. In order to resonate with their readers, however, these magazines acknowledged the everyday experiences of hardship and toil faced by their wage-earning readers in their work environment. As Jameson explains, mass-mediated texts are not "empty distraction or 'mere' false consciousness" (1979/80, 141). Rather, popular texts such as early twentieth century mail-order magazines introduced readers' fears and anxieties so that they could then be managed and controlled. Once the "pinch of poverty" and the oppression of "King Coal and King Steel" were recognized, mail-order magazines offered their own solutions. As precursors to contemporary society's self-help books, these popular magazines taught readers how to cope within their present situation by discovering "gold in the smile" ("The Picture Before Us," 1913b), and maintaining a positive attitude. Framing solutions to hardships in this manner personalized the readers' difficulties and posited private solutions to problems requiring collective and public action.

The purpose of *The People's Home Journal*'s "New Department of Human Interest" called the Sunshine Society, introduced in July 1922, was to "make life bigger, brighter, better for others. . . . Its aim is Usefulness; Good Cheer; Good Will" ("The Sunshine Society Is Yours," 2). The department's introductory article explained the history and mission of the Sunshine Society and solicited readers to form their own branches of the society. Subsequent issues of *The People's Home Journal* published a column called "Notes and Reports by Branch Presidents" so that readers could remain abreast of the society's good deeds.

Sunshine Society columns acknowledged readers' difficulties. "Those who have to endure an existence of gloom have a burden to bear which cannot be measured," noted the November 1911 column ("Sunshine and Shut-ins"). Other issues recognized "lives that need real cheer, real help and genuine uplift" ("Our Sunshine Society," 1911), and persons who are in "want or in loneliness" ("Sunshine Work Now!" 1911). Speaking directly to readers' sympathies, the August 1911 column, "Our Sunshine Society," asserted, "You will find it wherever you look—there never was yet a neighborhood where human suffering and loneliness did not exist." Yet the rhetoric was unceasingly optimistic and made inviting references to "Humanity," "hopefulness" and "brotherhood and sisterhood" in a manner quite reminiscent of the rhetoric of the labor movement.

The Sunshine Society spoke to readers' experiences of suffering and want but replaced activities of the labor movement with a movement all its own: "The Sunshine movement is a silent force as compared with the many organizations of elaborate purpose and varied aim so often exploited," notes the July 1911 column, "The Sunshine Society is Yours, " implicitly alluding to the labor organizations across the nation that were apparently creating quite a noise. According to "Sunshine Work Now!," the way to "lift yourself up permanently" was to reach out to others, to "get your heart so interested in the welfare of Others that you are one with the big heart of Humanity" (1). The November 1911 column "Sunshine and Shut-ins," encouraged readers to "Dispel a little worry, somewhere; take a little faith, somewhere. Smile into someone's face. And give them something to smile about." Elsewhere readers were urged to give "a new thought, a kindly visit, a book, a picture, a flower" in order to brighten someone's day ("Our Sunshine Society"). But perhaps most important, readers were encouraged to start their own Sunshine branches: "Establish a Branch that will have for the object of its existence the brightening of the lives that need brightening right where you are" ("Our Sunshine Society"). Readers learned of the specific activities of different branches in subsequent issues. The Chelsea Branch reported in the November 1912 issue the assistance to a "widow with young children" and the donations of clothing and food to the needy ("Universal Sunshine Society," 36); the Summit, New Jersey, branch reported the following "Good Cheer Work" in the September 1913 *People's Home Journal*: "[A]t Christmas six dinners were provided for needy families . . . clothing and $10.00 to Maine family" ("Universal Sunshine Society," 30).

The Sunshine Society epitomized what Jameson refers to as the utopian potential in mass-culture texts. In its regular columns, the society offered appealing visions of community and solidarity much like that offered by the labor movement. It is through these utopian visions that the ideology of the text operated: "[T]he works of mass culture cannot be ideological without at one and the same time being implicitly or explicitly Utopian as well: they cannot manipulate unless they offer some genuine shred of content as a fantasy bribe to the public about to be so manipulated" (1979/80, 144). Acknowledging readers' desires for community and for the betterment of living conditions, the Sunshine Society offered them a "fantasy bribe" and also provided a textual opening from which readers could launch a critique of the conditions thus described. Paradoxically, it was precisely in giving voice to readers' "fundamental hopes and fantasies" (Jameson 1979/80, 144) that the magazine was able to offer a solution aligned with the ideology of domestication. As readers of the November 1911 issue were told: "The man, woman or child who has lived any part of Life has had unfortunate experiences. To everybody their own suffering is keen, is real. There isn't any way to forget its keenness and to dispel its reality half so good, half so quick, as the way of kindness—the Sunshine path" ("Sunshine and Shut-ins," 2). The Sunshine Society neutralized social critique and public protest by defining life improvement in terms of communal coping—"scattering smiles"—as opposed to communal transformation— organizing a demonstration. Consolation replaced collective action and social critique was never given voice as readers were encouraged to make the best of their given lot.

The Sunshine Society appeared in *The People's Home Journal* at a time in history when millions of poor and immigrant Americans continued to labor each day in dangerous factory conditions. Notably, the Sunshine Society first appeared in the same year as the horrific fire at the Triangle Shirtwaist factory in which 146 girls and women died, trapped in an inferno as a result of unscrupulous owners' neglect for elementary safety measures such as fire escapes and unlocked doors. In large cities such as New York and Chicago tens of thousands of families dwelled in tenements where disease was rampant and poor diets were the norm. In these neighborhoods, communal networks based on Old World traditions were a defining characteristic and enabled these families to survive and live fulfilling lives in a new environment.

Spreading smiles and doing good deeds for neighbors were ways to survive within difficult living conditions. But there is a difference between survival *within* current conditions and struggle for *transformation of* conditions. The individuals and families who lived in big city tenements and worked in factories also strove for alteration of their conditions. They frequently put their communal connections and family ties to work toward political ends such as boycotting stores and circulating petitions.[9] And they knew firsthand the necessity of directing their anger outward to the institutions and individuals they viewed as exploitative. Popular texts such as *The People's Home Journal* redirected anger and public demands through the domestication of dissent. In contrast to *McClure's*, which relied on an idealistic strategy of universalization, the editors of *The People's Home Journal*, *Comfort*, and *Home Life* recognized the materiality of work and home conditions, but then closed the potential for public outcry against such conditions by advancing personal salves as a solution.

The personalized philosophy of the Sunshine Society was supported by articles and editorials in *The People's Home Journal* and *Home Life*, whose tone became increasingly admonitory throughout the teens, as the magazines' target audiences were turning more frequently to collective confrontation. More specifically, readers were called upon to attend to their homes or their personal dispositions in order to achieve happiness. Adjustments to one's domestic space or one's inner self were the only acceptable response, not potential adjustments to one's position in work or political spheres.

In some cases, the magazines encouraged readers to view the home as the site from which all happiness and well-being stemmed, ignoring that the quality of one's homelife depended upon one's economic and political position (Armstrong 1909; "Our Home Ideals" 1915; "The Picture Before Us," 1912a, 1914a, 1914e; Thompson 1916). According to one editorial, the home was "more than the whole great factory, more than the biggest bank where you work, more than the capital where laws are made to protect man's dwelling; more than the cathedral where man is taught how to live" ("The Picture Before Us," 1912a). Other commentaries lauded the "here-to-stay" qualities of wage-earning communities while denouncing the superficial atmosphere of upscale neighborhoods. "By comparison of values per square foot, how poor a place is the proud avenue where mere fashion rules and where real neighbors there are none!" ("The Picture Before Us," 1914e). Two months later, an editorial provided a similar lesson through the story of the "Mr. Newly Riches" family who "failed to bring along their homely treasures" when they moved to their fine home ("The Picture Before Us," 1914f).

Recognizing that some readers may not own their own house, *People's Home Journal* articles encouraged readers to visualize and plan the perfect abode ("The Picture Before Us," 1914a; "Our Home Ideals" 1915). The April 1915 issue engaged readers in a "discussion" based on the question "What is your conception of the ideal home?" and printed reader responses in an article titled "Our Home Ideals." Another article explained to readers how to decorate their homes so as to lessen "the discomforts of [the] home" (Armstrong 1909, 20). "Discordant colors" or a "crowded pattern" should be avoided because they may make "life exceedingly wearisome and living very irksome" (20). Here the home decor became another salve for a difficult day at the factory.

Other editorials provided another mechanism by which to redirect readers' energies inward and away from social institutions by focusing more pointedly on individual self-improvement. Between March 1912 and September 1914, *The People's Home Journal* editorial page, "The Picture Before Us," counseled readers on everything from tone of voice to countenance. Editorials imparted the transformative effects of personal behaviors. Cheerful facial expressions help make the world a better place (1914d), while "[t]ones that befit affection furnish a house more than pictures" (1913a). The smile was of equal effect: "If you smile into your mirror, it smiles back; and it is the same with the world. As soon as the world finds out that you have a pleasant smile, it will bring you many a pleasant story, many a happy circumstance" (1913b).

In an ironic terminological twist, the February and April 1914 issues applied business metaphors in their advice to readers. The February page encouraged readers to "take stock" of their lives:

"Taking stock" is just as necessary for the individual as for the corporation. We should stop at least once a year to determine what purposes have helped us, what endeavors have figured out a spiritual profit, what lines of conduct have perhaps slackened our hold upon the better things. . . . That man, whatever his work, who is not getting on as he should, needs to take an inventory. It may show him that his stock of enthusiasm and energy has not been kept up, that the shelves of his mind and heart are crowded with "shoddy," which the world does not want and will not buy (5).

In April readers learned, "Income is not wages and salary alone. It is interest on capital, on 'securities.' The only safe securities are personality, the personal force, the gold mine of the mind" (5). Through metaphor, the editorials transferred control over stock, capital, and income from the public realm to the private. The commentaries encouraged readers to apply capitalist concepts to their own lives rather than challenge the underlying basis of such notions.

Throughout the teens, *Comfort*, *Home Life*, and *The People's Home Journal* moralized to readers, gave helpful hints on how to get by, and disciplined readers to be happy and content. Through the magazines' frame of domestication, survival was emphasized at the expense of struggle. In editorials, stories, and regular columns, personal upkeep replaced public outcry as the remedy for inequities. Particularly into the teens, as large-scale strikes continued to break out and the ideas of the IWW, the Socialist Party, and the Women's Trade Union League spread from city to city, these popular journals domesticated the arguments, as well as the very bodies, of those who would potentially join together in their attempts to get a square deal.

Conclusion

As cheap mail-order journals, *Comfort*, *Home Life*, and *The People's Home Journal* provided entertainment for working-class families who had little

disposable income for leisure activities. Serial romance stories kept readers captivated and advice columns provided indispensable hints on how
to make ends meet with limited income and resources. This chapter has
detailed how, as magazines targeted readers who had the most to gain
from public protest and social reform, these texts employed an ideology
of domestication in order to frame change in terms of personal, not social, transformation. Dissent was defanged as readers were shown that a
love relationship or a smile could alter the conditions of their lives for the
better.

The ideology of domestication was a gendered discourse insofar as
women have traditionally been held to be the natural keepers of the
home. Thus, many articles and stories in these magazines featured female characters and spoke directly to female readers. In contrast to the
Atlantic Monthly and *McClure's*, however, mail-order magazines held up
the image of a "Practical True Woman." The Practical True Woman was a
multifaceted figure crafted by means of three rhetorical strategies: tradition, recognition, and negation. First, the Practical True Woman fit the
traditional mold of mother and homemaker. Yet she was also an income
generator and possessed qualities appropriate in a workplace setting
such as independence and courage. These magazines recognized
women's public-sphere roles and the real-life circumstances facing wage-
earning families who relied on the incomes of wives and daughters to
survive, but did not encourage them to make the public sphere the locus
of their efforts to improve their lives. Through negation, women's experiences as labor activists were made invisible. Negation rhetorically denied
the option to be demanding and confrontational in a manner that challenged economic relations. The Practical True Woman provided a site on
which the contradictions faced by wage-earning families could be negotiated and reconciled in terms consonant with the needs of capitalism.

Domestication's emphasis on the inner self and personal space persisted throughout the early 1900s, revealing itself through a variety of
themes. Stories alternately demonstrated how love transcended material
want, while advertisements and profiles of wealthy capitalists promoted
a money-oriented consumer ethos. Beginning around 1912, magazine editorials and regular columns such as those dealing with the Sunshine Society recognized worker unrest, unhappiness, and discomfort, but provided a personalized cure to such ills in place of the collective responses
in the form of strikes and walkouts occurring outside the magazines'
pages. Articles encouraged readers to transform their home spaces and,
in the final hegemonic move, attempted to micromanage attitude and
tone of voice.

These magazines were not overt disciplinary texts, however. Like the
New Age and self-help rhetoric of contemporary society, these discourses

were appealing to readers in identifiable ways. Acknowledging difficulty explicitly lets readers know that their pain is understood, there are people who sympathize. Also, visions of love relationships and happy homes are appealing insofar as they fulfill basic human needs for companionship and protection from the elements. The ideology of domestication provided a class-specific frame that acknowledged and responded to readers' realities as wage earners while leaving the systems and institutions that contributed to workplace injustices intact. In other words, the collective action that time and again had proved necessary and successful in altering public arenas—the factory, the market, the business monopoly, the political system—was undermined, when it came to questioning the workings of labor and capital, by popular images and narratives calling on readers to turn inward for self- and home maintenance.

No doubt working-class readers were influenced by the dominant ideologies circulating during this period, such as those in *Comfort, Home Life,* and *The People's Home Journal.* Nevertheless, in speeches, testimonies, and through organizational involvement, wage-earning women offered their own views of working-class life and shaped their own identities as workers, wives, mothers, and activists. Furthermore, women exercised agency in resisting the objective institutions and arrangements that perpetuated their second-class status as female wage earners. More specifically, women engaged in strikes and walkouts that forced the hand of factory owners and, in conjunction with confrontational rhetoric, contributed to workplace transformation. Chapter 4 examines the rhetoric of wage-earning women through texts of the Women's Trade Union League, the Industrial Workers of the World, and the labor organ *Life and Labor* to demonstrate the ways that women presented themselves in distinction to their representation in popular-media texts, and to call attention to lessons that remain valuable to workplace struggles today.

Notes

1. I obtained these magazines on microfilm through an interlibrary loan service. In this chapter I examine *Comfort* from 1894 to 1912; *Home Life* from 1912 to 1917; and *The People's Home Journal* from 1894 to 1915. The reason for the difference in the time periods has to do with the availability of each magazine and the ease with which I could borrow them from other libraries.

2. See Cloud 1998a for an in-depth analysis of contemporary therapeutic rhetorics as they are manifested in political, popular, and academic discourses.

3. Mott 1957, 4:364–368; Peterson 1956, 18–39. For a general overview of the political economy of cheap books and magazines, see Stern 1980.

4. By way of comparison to a later situation, see Murphy (1992) for an analysis of Kennedy Administration responses to, and press coverage of the 1961 Freedom Rides. Murphy examines how the government and press domesticated dissent

through four hegemonic strategies: naming, contextualization, legal sanction, and diversion.

5. The changing family and the rise of capitalism is a very complex issue. Numerous arguments have been provided regarding the nature and extent of the relation between familial and social formations, but few scholars would disagree that the family as we know it under industrial capitalism is not a universal formation, but rather differs across time, class, and region, and plays a specific role in social functioning. Barrett and McIntosh detail various perspectives, and conclude, "[I]t is reasonable to argue that the character of production under capitalism exacerbates, if it does not actually create, a split between the domestic and social spheres" (1982, 89).

6. Matthaei explains the "roots of the working girl phenomenon" as due, in part, to working-class families' desires to keep the mother in the home as dictated by the cult of domesticity. Thus, girls were sent into the labor force to supplement the father's income, and oftentimes to pay for her brother's education (1982, 141–156).

7. Sinclair was one of the period's best-known muckrakers. Like many of the writers for *McClure's*, Sinclair exposed the underbelly of the industrial capitalist system. The critique of the muckrakers as set forth in Chapter 2 still stands yet does not preclude the fact that the accounts offered by many muckrakers gave millions of readers a clearer idea of the horrors of the factory system, albeit from a middle-class perspective that often sentimentalized and patronized the working class.

8. Boteler-Sanders 1912; Brown 1910; Brown 1916a, 1916b; Chase 1912; Curtis 1916a, 1916b; "Girls in the City," 1916; Greaves 1916; Hoerle 1915; Johnson 1916; Marlborough 1909; Ransome 1912; Simmons 1913.

9. In June 1912, *Home Life* provided a brief account of similar community protests in the regular column, "Mainly About Men and Women." The column described numerous "Housekeepers' revolts" that had occurred in large cities across the United States in which hundreds of women publicly marched in order to call the mayor's attention to their struggles to beat the rising cost of living.

4

From Sewing Machine to
Solidarity in the Streets

If you smile in your mirror, it smiles back; and it is the same with the world. As soon as the world finds out that you have a pleasant smile, it will bring you many a pleasant story, many a happy circumstance.

"The Picture Before Us,"
The People's Home Journal, August 1913

We all know to-day the day of individual effort is passed. The day of organized effort is here. Here it is and those of us who would accomplish anything in any line, industrial, social, must take advantage of the only powerful force to-day: organization.

Leonora O'Reilly,
speech to shirtwaist makers at Clinton Hall, New York City, June 3, 1904

Popular magazines, since their growth and widespread circulation from the early 1900s, have played an important role in shaping the ways that individuals view themselves and the society in which they live and work. Through visions and narratives of social order, universal human values, and domestic bliss, these popular texts appealed to their target audiences and won financial success in the first decades of the century. Magazines of various types were important sources of information and entertainment for women of the upper, middle, and working classes— but they were not the only such sources for early-twentieth-century women in the suffrage and labor movements. In this chapter we will examine the rhetoric and extra-discursive actions employed by the women themselves in their public attempts to achieve political and economic justice. How did these activists create their own voices amidst the popular texts that allegedly spoke for and reflected their experiences as women? How did their protest rhetoric respond to, differ from, accept, rebel against, and subvert the commercialized images described in the previous chapters? And not least important, how did women engage themselves as laboring agents in their attempts to negotiate and alter objective structures and systems?

Public speeches, pamphlets, and worker testimonies can be examined as texts that competed with popular magazine interpretations of women and work in the early-twentieth-century United States. Though magazines and public speeches often relied on differing conventions and framing devices and were motivated by different concerns, both speeches and popular magazines represented sources of information available to citizens attempting to make sense of rapid industrial growth and changes in work and homelife.

The authors of both types of discourse strove to get their interpretation of events accepted as the accurate, valid version. Still, popular and protest rhetorics did not circulate in discrete spheres, nor did they go uninfluenced by each other. Magazine writers borrowed readily from the arguments of mainstream suffragists and in turn suffragists often relied upon "modern methods of advertising, publicity, mass merchandising, and mass entertainment" in their struggles for political enfranchisement (Finnegan 1999, 2). Given that the target audiences of the two sources of information often overlapped, protest and popular-culture rhetorics warrant comparison in terms of the differences in rhetorical frames, styles, and motivation. Such a comparison is a way of analyzing the different worldviews and interpretations of issues and events made available to a public within a specific historical context and of understanding how subordinate groups formulated their own interpretations of social issues in the face of hegemonic discourses that continued to negotiate the terrain of the public imaginary.

Through a study of the speeches, testimonies, personal papers, and grassroots publications of female activists—many of whom were members of the Women's Trade Union League (WTUL) and the Industrial Workers of the World (IWW)—this chapter demonstrates how working-class women along with upper and middle-class "allies" variously employed a collectivizing rhetoric in voicing their demands for economic justice for workers and political equality for women of all classes.[1]

This chapter also examines how workers demonstrated their collective identity physically through extra-discursive actions, actions and events that exist external to human language (discourse) and involve material institutions and structures ostensibly constituted in culture. Though not language, they can still be considered "persuasion." Humans understand these phenomena *through* discourse—representations, descriptions, framings—but these events and individuals are not *created by* human language. More specifically, activists of the WTUL and IWW engaged in mass pickets, strikes, and walkouts that were material in origin and had material effects. Discourse played a role in these events in motivating women and girls. Meetings were held and pamphlets distributed in order to persuade workers to join with others in standing up for their rights. These labor uprisings held symbolic importance but also constituted a class-based antagonism that was rooted in real relations of exploitation and carried consequences for factory owners which did not hinge on rhetorical influence or compromise. Rather, the collective *absence* of women and girls from factories materially influenced factory owners who relied on their labor to keep the factories running and profits high. Thus, these activists asserted their demands not only verbally but also extra-discursively, by mobilizing their power as the producers of wealth.

For rhetorical scholars interested in social movement and feminist rhetorics, the documents examined in this chapter represent sources that have remained largely untapped. The following analysis of these texts is of particular importance as it challenges the idealist bias in the field of rhetorical studies and expands current understandings of the role of rhetoric in social struggles for change. In particular, wage-earning activists stressed class conflict, including the institutions and manifestations of industrial capitalism—factory life, tenements, rent and food price hikes—and they struggled under a collective identity for the kind of alterations that they could experience in their daily lives as workers and as women. As such, the confrontational and sometimes militant activities of these activists lead us to explore strategies that were often aimed not at audience identification, but at creating group solidarity—physically and rhetorically—against the individuals and institutions viewed as exploitative. Thus, the voices and tactics of wage-earning women and girls point the way to understanding the tensions between social structures that delimit human actions and the ways that groups rhetorically figure themselves within, and struggle against, such material limitations.

Rhetoric and Social Transformation: Expanding Current Studies

Protest rhetoric can be viewed as one aspect of what is more widely referred to as "vernacular culture," or the values, beliefs, activities, and lifestyles of subordinate groups. Recent studies of vernacular cultures have tended to emphasize how marginalized groups "make do" within the constraints of dominant capitalist society, examining activities such as window shopping, parodic performances, or resistant readings (see Brummett and Duncan 1992; Butler 1990; Fiske 1986, 1987, 1989; Radway

1984)—behaviors that are by and large private and individuated. This chapter argues for the necessity of directing attention to the public and collective rhetorics of subordinate groups, namely, protest rhetorics. Further, the story of WTUL and IWW activists underscores the need to address the material structures and relations that have a hand in the nature and outcome of various forms of resistance.

Most scholars of the subject agree that persuasion is a key aspect of social movements. According to Stewart, Smith, and Denton, "[P]ersuasion permeates social movements and is the primary agency available to social movements for satisfying major requirements or functions" (1989, 16). Griffin's 1952 essay represents one of the earliest efforts to delineate the boundaries and bases of social-movement studies. Griffin identifies "pro" and "anti" movements in which the respective goal is to "arouse public opinion" to the "acceptance" or "rejection" of an institution or idea (185). He designates the critic's task as "judg[ing] the effectiveness of the discourse" (187). A similar discourse-centered stance underwrites the work of Scott and Smith, who elaborate the characteristics of "the rhetoric of confrontation" (1969).

Primary works in social-movement studies have also advocated a "functional" approach to the area. Stewart identifies the five functions of social movements as transforming perceptions of history; transforming perceptions of society; prescribing courses of action; mobilizing for action; and sustaining the social movement (1980, 300). Taking a somewhat different tack, Gregg directs scholarly attention to what he describes as the "ego-function" of protest rhetoric (1971). According to Gregg, protest rhetoric operates to form, build, and reaffirm the selfhood of the protesters themselves.

These and other works that make up the tradition of protest-rhetoric studies have in common an emphasis on language, verbal and nonverbal, as the primary tool employed by social dissenters.[2] Other scholars have argued for the need to recognize less traditional forms of protest such as "extraverbal" activities and coercion. Bowers and Ochs define agitation as requiring "more than the normal discursive means of persuasion" (1971, 4). Thus, they explore the persuasiveness of activities such as sit-ins, boycotts, and strikes, which are instrumental and symbolic in nature and can thus be considered rhetorical (43). Likewise, Simons critiques previous social-movement studies, pointing out that "scholars have tended to assume that methods of influence appropriate for drawing room controversies are also effective for social conflicts" (1972, 236). Like Bowers and Ochs, Simons encourages studies of "coercive persuasion," arguing that though these acts "were not always 'nice' . . . in at least some cases and for some receivers, they attracted attention, evoked support from third parties, and convinced targets to reevaluate their attitudes" (237).

Class Differences and Collective Confrontation in Women's Protest Rhetoric

Other scholars have examined the unique persuasive strategies and tactics employed by women as they struggled to justify and gain acceptance not only of their demands but of their public presence as speakers. The works of the Women's Trade Union League historian Nancy Schrom Dye offer detailed analyses of the accomplishments and activities of the WTUL (1975a; 1975b; 1980).[3] In particular, Dye explores the dilemma faced by WTUL activists who tried to make the League both a labor and a feminist organization. Similarly, both Meredith Tax (1980) and Annelise Orleck (1995) explore the tensions between League allies and the wage-earning members, particularly through the experiences of working-class activists such as Leonora O'Reilly, Rose Schneiderman, and Pauline Newman. All three authors provide details regarding the specific historical conditions that influenced the actions and successes of the League. In her study of the WTUL member Margaret Dreier Robins, the historian Elizabeth Anne Payne offers a somewhat more optimistic perspective than the above scholars on the involvement in the League of middle- and upper-class women, called allies (1988). According to Payne, the various social and cultural activities sustained by Robins and other League allies were important in the creation of a female culture that could serve as the unifying force of the League's diverse members.

In the field of rhetoric more specifically, Karlyn Kohrs Campbell's groundbreaking work continues to provide an analytic framework for studies in feminist and woman's movement studies. Her project has been to identify the characteristics and goals of "feminist rhetoric," including turn-of-the-century suffragism and 1960s consciousness-raising. In *Man Cannot Speak for Her*, Campbell provides a detailed analysis of pivotal speeches given by female suffragists, including Elizabeth Cady Stanton, Susan B. Anthony, and Ida B. Wells (1989). She identifies a unique "feminine style" employed by these women in their attempts to overcome the "conflicting demands of the podium" (12). Suffragists' rhetoric, shaped by their experiences as mothers and homemakers, was "personal in tone . . . relying heavily on personal experience, anecdotes, and other examples . . . [and tended] to be structured inductively" (13). Campbell explores these rhetorical characteristics as they are found in women's consciousness-raising in the 1960s (1973). As a rhetoric, consciousness-raising creates sisterhood and "a sense of autonomy," and it "speak[s] to women in terms of private, concrete, individual experience, because women have little, if any, publicly shared experience" (79).

The role of consciousness-raising groups within the feminist movement has received mixed responses. Many point to the potential transformative effects of the process through which women come to see the connections between what appeared to be personal, isolated experiences and a broader male-dominated society. Other scholars "feared that the groups were substituting talk for action and that consciousness-raising functioned more as therapy and self-help than as the basis for social transformation" (Dow 1996, 65). Cloud cautions against the therapeutic tendencies of consciousness-raising, which encourage emphasis on private spaces and personal life at the expense of publicly directed energy and activities that address broad-based systems of exploitation and oppression (1998a). Consciousness-raising avoids the pitfalls of personalization when it "lead[s] to the generation of public political activity and discourse aimed at transforming public structures of power" (105).

In many respects, the rhetoric of the WTUL's middle- and upper-class supporters were characteristic of the consciousness-raising described by Campbell. League allies frequently emphasized bonding on the basis of common female experiences and encouraged self-reliance and leadership for the League's working-class members. Yet cross-class tensions often stymied allies' attempts at universal sisterhood and disrupted the vision of universal feminism presented by middle-class reformers in popular magazines such as *McClure's*. Wage-earning activists frequently expressed frustrations with middle-class allies who attempted to speak on behalf of their "less fortunate" sisters. Though speaking on behalf of others is not by definition always oppressive, "speaking for" wage-earning women—whether through magazine accounts or middle-class reformer leadership—often resulted in ideological appropriation and provided a limited conception of women's roles in industrial society.[4]

Standpoint epistemology provides a useful framework for comparing rhetorical strategies in popular-culture and vernacular accounts and understanding the different perspectives among members of a particular subordinate group. Standpoint theory emphasizes that knowledge is always socially situated and necessarily shaped by one's position (standpoint) within a historical social structure, for example, industrial capitalism (see Harding 1993; Hartsock 1983). Furthermore, it is the perspectives of those at the bottom of a society's hierarchy—those who suffer the most from the given social arrangements—that offer the most critical and therefore most potentially enlightening insights on social beliefs, values, and structures, and consequently, offer the most radical proposals for social change. Standpoint theory points up that not all competing claims to truth, reality, or the social "good" are equally liberating or enlightening. Although *McClure's* writers, middle-class activists, and wage earners all at various times relied on universalization in order to persuade that certain ideas were in the best interests of all and that a certain rendering of events was a "true" account, we can turn to an extra-discursive reality—a reality existing outside of human language—in order to assess the validity of various claims, to judge what constitutes justice, how we are to work toward equity, and when it has been achieved.

From their standpoint as members of the wage-earning class, women and girls developed a politicized sense of their status not only as women but as workers. This is not say that wage-earning women did not employ naturalizing or universalizing strategies commonly used by middle-class activists or magazine writers. Yet their perspectives were rooted in and shaped in part by a material reality that often gave the lie to dominant narratives and prompted wage earners to advance their own claims of reality and social justice. Operating dangerous machinery, working in the hot steam of laundries, working under the constant harassment of foremen fifty to sixty hours a week for scant wages often opened workers' eyes to the contradictions of True Womanhood, the hollowness of ideals that did not address material discrimination, and the futility of individuated forms of struggle. Further, reference to this extra-discursive reality— also marked by malnutrition, exhaustion, and poverty—allowed wage-earning women to "prove" their claims and assert a more accurate version of events and relations in distinction to that proffered in popular magazines. And finally, it was their experiences as individuals occupying a specific position within an extra-discursive reality—namely, as workers in industrial capitalism—that often motivated women to engage in actions that confronted not only oppressive norms and beliefs but the very institutions that controlled their ability to live decent and humane lives.

Protest Rhetoric and Working-Class Experience: Negotiating Between Structure and Struggle

The previous three chapters have examined how popular-culture texts operated hegemonically through various ideological strategies—naturalization, universalization, and domestication—aimed at different audiences. Naturalization portrayed economic and gender relations as inevitable, as always already there, and thus inalterable. Naturalization provided justifications for the status quo and thus reaffirmed a well-to-do audience's position of relative comfort and stability within the system.

Universalization was tailored to the expanding professional middle class, and elicited social consensus through an emphasis on ideals and values that seemingly applied to all and by speaking to interests that allegedly were those of the whole "general public."

The ideology of domestication targeted working-class readers, providing a class-specific response to the presence of large numbers of workers who were striking and walking out of factories across the country. Domestication was an attempt to depoliticize dissent by redirecting working-class anger and energy away from broad-based social institutions and systems toward private spaces such as home and psyche.

Thus, through three different persuasive strategies, mass-circulation magazines supported and helped sustain objective economic structures and defined workers' identities and roles in terms that aligned with those configurations.

The material system that relied on these ideologies also provided fertile ground in which to sow the seeds of discontent. Yet the need for social transformation is not always transparent, and visions of worker solidarity do not spring out of nowhere.[5] A central question becomes: "What sorts of communicative processes enable historical actors to see liberatory possibilities?" (Aune 1994, 13). This chapter explores the conversations, pamphleting, meetings, testimonials, and speech-giving through which women became more aware of the basis of discrimination and the need for struggle to transform their world. Equally important is an examination of the impelling force of women's firsthand experiences in the factory and the tenement and the ways these environments not only delimited but motivated women's actions.

Wage-earning activists held two types of goals, rhetorical and concrete/material, which were interrelated but often required different means to achieve. Rhetorically, women sought to (1) upend the myth of True Womanhood, (2) motivate a struggle among women based on their experiences as workers, and (3) through union organizing, connect women's experiences as mothers, wives, and workers to a broad-based system of discrimination requiring collective confrontation to transform. All three of these rhetorical tasks were motivation-based; they politicized women's experiences and made collective struggle imperative. The success of these rhetorical goals hinged on accomplishing a fourth and perhaps most fundamental goal: creating an audience capable of acting on its own behalf. An audience of young, uneducated, poor working-class women and girls influenced by norms prohibiting public-oriented behavior or characteristics associated with public speaking posed a unique obstacle for the speaker, one that could be transcended in part through specific rhetorical strategies (see Campbell 1973). The testimonies, speeches, and conversations that took place in the workplace and on front stoops were the vehicles through which such rhetorical work could be accomplished.

In addition, working-class women had extra-discursive goals directly related to their experiences as wage earners: (1) higher wages, (2) reduced hours, and (3) safe and clean workplaces, (safeguards on machinery, toilets, rest areas, clean drinking water, ventilation, and fire escapes). Achieving these goals required symbolic communication in order to envision change, call meetings, elicit participation, articulate goals, and plan and agree upon strategies. Yet as the following pages illustrate, workers quickly learned that voicing a grievance, even collectively, often produced little tangible change (e.g., improved wages) unless backed with an action or threat thereof that carried material consequences (e.g., machine stoppage and subsequent loss of revenue). Thus, wage earners (often with the assistance of middle-class allies) did not confine their conversations to front stoops; they made their voices heard in public arenas and combined their critique with extra-discursive tactics.

Popular ideologies reinforced the existing economic structure. The goal in popular magazines such as the *Atlantic Monthly*, *McClure's*, and *Comfort* was to place the status quo beyond challenge, to create consensus, and to replace publicly expressed arguments for social change with private space alterations. In each of these cases, magazine portrayals negated, elided, or tamed a politicized and publicly exercised human agency. (The term "agency," as used here, refers to the ability of humans to act or exert influence on their own behalf—for example, individuals exercise agency when they organize and struggle against oppressive or exploitative systems and institutions.) In contrast, women's protest rhetoric encouraged struggle, in particular, through the formation of a labor-based agency capable of exercising its power as the producer of the world's wealth. Labor-based agency as a means or instrument for social change enabled working-class activists to meet their goals, which were rhetorical but also were rooted in concrete material conditions requiring more than symbolic means to overturn. In the case of wage-earning women, rhetoric was employed to craft an audience capable of speaking on its own behalf and confronting dominant structures. In addition, extra-discursive actions provided a necessary counterpart to rhetorical struggle insofar as they materially affected objective structures (e.g., the factory system) and often played an essential role in the initial formation and exercise of a labor-based agency.

In *Rhetoric and Marxism*, Aune grapples with the "nuclear contradiction of Marxism": the "difficulty in reconciling determination by modes of production and the existence of agents who would struggle against these modes" (1994, 145). How do "subjective agencies" struggle within "objective structures" (Aune 1994, 143); or, more specifically, how do humans confront and change long-standing and broad-reaching systems and institutions that are entrenched but not inalterable? Aune's study raises a question of profound importance to scholars of rhetoric interested in the roles of language in social change: "What alternative institutions, practices, and messages are available to those who wish to reshape class formations within the framework of structural possibilities?" (46). In an attempt to contribute to this conversation, the following pages explore one historical example—women and girls of early-twentieth-century industrial capitalism—in order to illuminate how these activists provided their own self-definitions and engaged their own agency in order to defy and to distinguish themselves from popular ideologies and to overturn oppressive material constraints. But first, to understand the arguments and strategies of early-twentieth-century female labor and suffrage activists, we must have an idea of the historical context in which these women and girls were situated.

Class Differences Among Women and Girls in the Early Twentieth Century

As long as women have worked outside the home, they have agitated for better conditions and fair wages. Beginning in the early to mid–1800s, the infamous Lowell mill girls were active in their own all-female union, the Lowell Female Labor Reform Association. In 1845–46, these workers were an organized group that petitioned and struck for the ten-hour day, testified in front of the Massachusetts legislature, and worked in cooperation with men active in the New England Labor Reform League (Flexner 1959, 55–61).[6] In the 1880s, women wage earners were active in the Knights of Labor, which had been founded in Philadelphia in 1869 and welcomed women and blacks as members. Women members organized their own locals, cultivated leadership skills, and struck side by side with their male coworkers (Levine 1983).

The formation and subsequent growth of the American Federation of Labor in the 1890s represented a major obstacle for women labor activists. Led by Samuel Gompers and viewed by many as an institution of the status quo, the AFL was founded on the principles of craft unionism, which emphasized workers in skilled trades. The organization regularly employed discriminatory practices against immigrant and black men and women and other unskilled workers, whom it saw as threatening the prestige of craft unionism. Numerous accounts have documented the AFL's hostility to women and immigrant workers, who most often occupied unskilled jobs and were most in need of organization.[7] AFL arguments justifying women's exclusion were grounded in traditional beliefs regarding women's roles and abilities as embodied in the cult of True

Womanhood. Women were believed to be "temporary" workers with marriage and homelife as their ultimate goals. Other arguments accused women of not being "serious" workers, despite their demonstrated abilities to organize and participate in strikes. Finally, women workers were scapegoated as the reason for declines in working men's wages; in reality it was owners, deliberately pitting male and female workers against each other and obscuring their common interests as workers, who were the sources and benefactors of wage undercutting.

Previous chapters explored how images of True Womanhood were communicated in popular magazines. Though the contours of this rhetoric had loosened since its emergence in the 1820s, the images and narratives in popular texts revealed the extent to which its dictates still prevailed. As with any hegemonic ideology, the rhetoric's success depended upon its ability to evolve and adjust itself to changes in the historical context. As increasing numbers of women entered the paid workforce, popular-culture images of women captured and reinterpreted this event. The image emerged of a "Practical True Woman"; targeting working-class women, this image negotiated the contradiction between gender norms that excluded working for money outside the home and material need to do exactly that by communicating that women could embody independence and strength without losing their abilities to nurture and tend to the home.

Eisenstein provides an extensive account of the ways that working-class women's identities were affected by the cult of True Womanhood (1983). Despite their experiences as factory workers, women and girls still viewed themselves primarily in terms of their families and sought marriage as a primary goal. Eisenstein maintains that these workers neither passively accepted the dominant ideology of the period nor fully accepted contemporary feminist challenges to that ideology (1983). Rather, they articulated a "negotiated response" in which they struggled for the right to work with fair pay and humane conditions, while still holding on to an ideal of marriage and domesticity as their ultimate and true occupation. At an 1870 labor convention, the Daughters of St. Crispin, a union of female shoemakers, demanded equal pay for equal work but added, "[W]e assure our fellow-citizens that we only desire to so elevate and improve our condition as to better fit us for the discharge of those high social and moral duties which devolve upon every true woman" (Flexner 1959, 140).

Eisenstein's work provides important insights on the complexity of working-class experience, showing the ways that subordinate groups variously accept and reject dominant beliefs and norms that regulate their unequal position in society. The following analysis of working women's protest rhetoric explores how working-class women and middle-class allies at times relied on traditional arguments in their demands for political equality and justice in the workplace. Nevertheless, working-class women were often likely to challenge the ideals of the cult of True Womanhood, because as women of lower socioeconomic status, they experienced first-hand the hypocrisy and class contradiction of this ideal. Furthermore, the image of the True Woman was premised on the experiences of middle-class *white* women, so women of color were twice removed from this con-struction. Sojourner Truth, an abolitionist, suffragist, and former slave, gave the lie to the discourse of True Womanhood in her speech "Ain't I A Woman?": "I have ploughed and planted and gathered into barns, and no man could head me—and ain't I a woman?" (quoted in Flexner 1959, 91). This is not say that wage-earning women did not attempt to lay claim to the status of "ladyhood." Enstad goes so far as to assert that working-class women "actively rejected the class ideologies that excluded women from the privileged label of 'lady'" (1999, 2).

Middle- and upper-class women also widely accepted the norms of True Womanhood, but by the early twentieth century they increasingly employed this ideology to their own ends. During this period, women were entering the public realm at an unprecedented rate. They were ac-tive in the temperance and suffrage movements and were entering col-leges, forming women's clubs, and engaging in various philanthropic en-deavors. In order to justify their breach of the public sphere and their rejection of the idea that their only appropriate sphere was the home, these women applied the rhetoric of True Womanhood to their activities, asserting that they were entering the public sphere in order to purify it.[8]

Increasingly, these activists turned their attentions to the plight of the working poor and immigrant population who worked in the cities' facto-ries and mills. To assist this group, they founded settlement houses in the middle of large urban areas as havens where workers could go for recre-ation, education, or union organizing. Working-class women of the early 1900s were largely unorganized; in New York City, of 350,000 female workers less than 10,000 were unionized (Foner 1979, 266). Despite women's calls for assistance, the AFL paid little attention; thus, working women frequently turned to settlement reformers for help.

In 1903, William English Walling, a resident of University Settlement, founded the Women's Trade Union League with the goal of organizing working women into trade unions and addressing sex discrimination faced by female workers. The organization comprised both workers and middle- and upper-class allies. Its plank demanded "equal pay for equal work, the organization of all workers into trade unions, the eight-hour day, a minimum wage scale, and all the principles embodied in the eco-nomic program of the American Federation of Labor, and the full citizen-ship of women" (quoted in Jacoby 1975, 132). The organization's emphasis changed over the years and differed from branch to branch. The WTUL worked on many levels, its activities including union organization, legislation, and education, and the organization often coordinated its efforts with those of socialists, suffragists, and AFL unionists.

The Women's Trade Union League was founded on a notion of cross-class sisterhood that was reflective of early-twentieth-century feminist thought. The leaders of the League (in the early years most of them were allies) operated on the assumption that all women were oppressed in similar ways, and that women possessed unique feminine qualities that would be beneficial to the public realm. The WTUL historian Nancy Schrom Dye explains: "A conviction that women could relate to one another across class lines in the spirit of sisterhood and an emphasis on the special qualities that women shared linked the league to the larger woman movement" (1980, 46). However, the emphasis on sisterhood often obscured the importance of class as a factor that shaped working women's lives, and contributed to conflicts between the workers and the allies who were trying to help them.

Difficulties aside, the WTUL provided invaluable strike assistance and numerous educational and social opportunities for wage earners particularly between 1909 and 1915. At the height of its organizational success, the WTUL played a central role in the "Uprising of 30,000," the massive strike of shirtwaist makers in 1909–10. Contrary to many public and popular perceptions, this uprising did not arise out of nowhere. To a certain extent, the specific economic conditions of the garment trade during this time period contributed to the prevalence and power of women's strike activities within the garment trade. The labor historian Roger Waldinger describes various changes within the trade in the years between 1900 and 1930 and argues that "the ebb and flow of women's unionism in the garment trades was most closely linked to changes in the social technology of production and in the structure of the industry" (1985, 88). Moving manufacturing from small contractors and home laborers to large factories concentrated labor and made collective action more possible.

Numerous spontaneous strikes occurred between 1906 and 1909, and these were the result not only of workplace conditions but also of the extensive organizing efforts of many young women in the garment trade (see Foner 1979, 324–326; Tax 1980, 205–242). Between 1905 and 1909, Clara Lemlich, a socialist and key figure in the Uprising of 30,000, went from shop to shop organizing workers and encouraging them to strike. Along with her comrades Fannia Cohn, Rose Schneiderman, and Pauline Newman, Lemlich educated fellow factory workers, cultivated a sense of worker agency, and persuaded women workers of the necessity for concerted action. Orleck explains the development among workers of a unique "shop-floor culture" which encouraged them to "feel a sense of belonging to a distinct class of people in the world: workers" (1995, 34). Employees at Weisen and Goldstein's, angered by speedups, walked out of the factory in 1907 with Lemlich in the lead. The following year, workers at the Triangle Shirtwaist Company factory and at Rosen Brothers staged their own spontaneous walkouts (Tax 1980, 212, 213).

Tensions between garment workers and bosses continued to mount and in September 1909, Lemlich led another strike of workers at Leiserson's, which was quickly joined by workers from the Triangle factory. Employers used particularly brutal tactics during this strike, hiring thugs and even prostitutes to intimidate and beat the strikers. Lemlich was arrested seventeen times and suffered six broken ribs. Tax's account of the strike attests to the dedication and militancy of the female strikers: "[W]hile the male workers lost heart and stopped picketing, not wanting to be beaten up[,] [t]he women carried on, suffering assault and arrest day after day" (1980, 214).

After achieving little from negotiating with employers, leaders of the ILGWU decided to call a general strike of the entire shirtwaist trade for November 1909, to demand a union shop, fifty-two hour week, payment every week instead of every two weeks, no more than two hours a day overtime, and an end to requiring the workers to pay for sewing materials and electrical power. Workers enthusiastically volunteered for picket duty (see Photos 4.1 and 4.2), and allies participated on picket lines alongside the workers and garnered publicity of the strike and the girls' inhumane working conditions. The action subsequently became known as the Uprising of 30,000. The WTUL and women from the Socialist Party raised funds needed to sustain the strikers during the winter of 1909–10.

For reasons numerous and complex, the gains achieved by the strikers were limited when they returned to work in February 1910.[9] Despite this less-than-successful ending to a strike that began with such enthusiasm, the uprising was remarkable for many reasons. The workers achieved significant material gains, but "The solidarity the strikers built was its greatest achievement" (Tax 1980, 222). Young girls and women gained experience speaking for themselves and witnessed firsthand what could be achieved through collective action.

This strike served as an inspiration for thousands of workers and led to many other strikes over the next five years. Throughout the teens, the League, along with the IWW and various socialists, assisted in numerous strikes in which wage-earning women substantially improved their work conditions: sixty-hour work weeks (or longer) were reduced to fifty-two; time-and-a-half pay was guaranteed for overtime work; and supplies and power no longer had to be paid for by workers. Further, more women than ever before belonged to a union (63,872 by 1913), thereby improving their position to bargain for economic gains (Foner 1979,

PHOTO 4.1   Striking shirtwaist makers volunteer for picket duty during the Uprising of 30,000 in 1909–10. International Ladies' Garment Workers' Union Archives, Kheel Center, Cornell University, Ithaca, New York.

PHOTO 4.1   Strikers of the Uprising of 30,000 picket for fair and decent hours in 1909–10. International Ladies' Garment Workers' Union Archives, Kheel Center, Cornell University, Ithaca, New York.

324–373). And finally, women who had never before acted or spoken out in a public forum now occupied leadership positions and learned to challenge a system that exploited them both as women and as workers.

From the League's inception, the middle-class founders strove for a cross-class alliance in which working-class women and middle-class allies would participate equally in decision making and leadership. However, the organization was not without class conflicts. Given their quite different daily experiences, working-class women and their middle-class allies often had different perspectives on central issues and advocated different strategies for change. Historical materialism provides an explanatory framework for understanding class differences, as it takes real sensuous activity as the premise for individuals' ideas and conceptions. "Consciousness can never be anything else than conscious existence, and the existence of men [and women] is their actual life-process" (Marx and Engels [1846] 1986, 47). A young girl of sixteen who worked ten hours a day at a garment factory and lived with her extended family in a two-room tenement flat experienced a much different day from the middle-class reformer who spent her hours at the market, at luncheons, or at various recreational and philanthropic meetings. Yet both women were involved side-by-side in various labor and suffrage organizations that fought for women's economic and political rights.

It will be seen that different perspectives often, but not always, fall along class lines. Many of the allies were either ignorant of or refused to accept the importance of class struggle and they saw work not as a necessity but as a form of liberation. As Dye explains, from the reformer's perspective, "[W]ork meant liberation from the confines of proper femininity. This attitude contributed to allies' naiveté concerning the role of work in the lives of female wage-earners" (1975a, 31). For the allies, class struggle and worker solidarity often took a backseat to an emphasis on education and cultural uplifting. Allies spent time and money to provide dances, teas, museum trips, and music lessons for the workers. Leonora O'Reilly, a shirtwaist maker and League activist, was not impressed and, like many other workers, found these activities patronizing and useless. O'Reilly firmly stated, "The work which makes people stand on their own feet is the work that counts—the dignity of labor—teach labor to be self-respecting. Contact with the 'lady' does harm in the long run—gives a wrong standard—No use preaching Christianity until you are ready to live it—Brotherhood of man only possible through brotherhood of labor" (quoted in Tax 1980, 112).[10]

Thus, the real experiences of women occupying a specific place within industrial capitalism ran up against the dominant ideologies of the time and provided a ground upon which poor women and women of color could rearticulate a conceptualization of women and work in society. Ideological stances cannot, however, be reduced to material position; the following pages also analyze those areas where class differences blur and explore the various changing interests and motivations of both the workers and the allies.

In opposing the immutable vision of social relations as provided by the *Atlantic Monthly's* naturalizing framework, wage-earning women and their allies frequently demystified the "inevitable forces" behind capitalist exploitation and unraveled the image of the True Woman through their arguments and their physical actions.

Disrupting a "Natural Order"

The naturalizing frame that prevailed in the *Atlantic Monthly* presented historically situated social relations and systems as natural and therefore immutable or inevitable. Articles justified labor exploitation by framing industrial competition as "uncontrollable" or the "inevitable expression of superiority in the field of open competition" (Laughlin 1913, 448; Lloyd 1902, 658). To disrupt this vision, wage-earning women made frequent use of antithetical language in order to reveal the constructed nature of factory relations and the benefactors behind these exploitative arrangements.

Denaturalizing Capitalism

In contrast to the *Atlantic Monthly*'s portrayal of competition as an "inevitable friction," wage-earning women identified the individuals and institutions that benefited from worker exploitation, thus revealing the human constructedness of workplace arrangements and, by extension, their unnaturalness. Where the *Atlantic*, in effect, personified capitalism and abstracted it from day-to-day relations ("the brutal aggressiveness of capital"), these workers concretized the "forces" by identifying and describing the greed of manufacturers. Leonora O'Reilly, one of the most well known wage-earning members of the WTUL, pointed to the "unholy trinity of Wall Street, Taft, Morgan, and Googenheimer" as the source of worker suffering (1911c, 3). In a talk given to a predominantly middle-class audience in 1913, Rose Schneiderman, a wage earner, explained the home-work system in terms of the benefits accorded the manufacturer. "He saves rent, there is no limitation of hours, no limitation as to the ages, no expense as to machinery, light or heat" (1913, 8).

Official WTUL statements and minutes of a meeting of the strike committee of a 1910 strike of garment workers in Chicago contained statements by a number of workers who detailed the tyranny of the foremen, the tricks played on unknowing workers by supervisors, and the laziness of bosses who stood idly around workers who sewed at frantic rates. Maggie Civic, who worked in a factory on Chicago's South Side, worked from 7 A.M. until 6 P.M. for nine dollars a week. Civic explained how directions for stitching were changed from week to week, though the prices paid to workers remained the same. "We only got 12 cents for making a whole coat, pockets and all," related Civic, "but you could never suit the foreman" ("Meeting of the Strike Committee"). Esther Kier told of how she was hired on as assistant foreman but was paid twelve dollars less than the man whose place she had taken. Such wage undercutting was standard practice in factories and not only saved owners' money but also pitted male and female workers against each other. Kier further related the abuses of the foreman that she endured: "[H]e made me do all his errands for him,—running down stairs to buy his cigars or matches . . . and he said many things to me which no nice girl wants to hear . . . " ("Meeting of the Strike Committee"). Similarly, in the official "Statement on the Strike of the 35,000 Unorganized Garment Workers of Chicago," "Miss G" tells a particularly disturbing story of the foreman, Mr. Gorman, who struck an Italian worker, causing her to have a miscarriage (13).

Such accounts were not aberrations or anomalies but typical experiences expressed time and again by wage-earning women across the nation. Pauline Newman, a close friend and comrade of Schneiderman in the WTUL, interviewed button workers in Muscatine, Iowa, in order to better understand their conditions and assist them in organizing (1911). One woman who had worked all her life as a button worker expressed her frustrations to Newman: "I never thought . . . that our employers would act as mean as they do! Just think of how many years we have worked for them . . . and received almost nothing in return! . . . To get one cent and a half for sewing a gross of buttons on cardboard is mighty little. I remember one week I tried to work as fast as I could, tried not to lose a minute during the day and evening, and at the end of the week I had the magnificent sum of two dollars!" In her account of the Muscatine workers' experience, Newman further explained the vulgar nature of employers' greed. During noontime services where "workers prayed and asked the Lord to help them in their misery, the employer had the buttons weighed, and so in the workers' absence cheated them."

Through the act of speaking their experiences, telling their stories, women heightened their self-awareness and gained a clearer perspective on a system that was not inevitable but rather the result of deliberate and thought-out actions on the part of owners, bosses, and foremen. In addition, through storytelling, wage-earning women demonstrated that their experiences were not isolated and they argued that certain values and social arrangements were in the best interests of all. Thus, they showed that they too could employ a strategy of universalization to gain legitimacy for their viewpoints. As Eagleton points out, "Universalization . . . is not always a speciously rationalizing mechanism. It is indeed ultimately in the interests of all individuals that women should emancipate themselves; and the belief that one's values are finally universal may provide some significant impetus in gaining legitimacy for them" (1991, 57).

In contrast to popular-culture narratives, which relied on universalization to elide the influence of extra-discursive systems and institutions, wage-earning women relied on the same frame to different ends, when they repeatedly invoked the inhumanities of the factory system and drew explicit connections between their suffering and the individuals who perpetuated and benefited from such arrangements. Whereas mass magazines conveyed that social relations and norms were inevitable or readily transcended by values and ideals, wage earners spoke repeatedly of the need for solidarity and of their willingness to physically confront owners who refused to listen. Indeed, the history of social change indicates that systems and institutions are not inalterable, but neither are they transcended merely by adhering to ideals and values. Rather, collective confrontations engaged by thousands of workers throughout the first decades of the twentieth century proved central in winning workplace gains and challenging an unjust economic system.

Leonora O'Reilly's speeches perhaps most poignantly exemplified the use of oppositional language in order to rhetorically deny a vision of capitalist arrangements as somehow natural. Framing the experiences of her wage-earning audience, O'Reilly asserted that workers were exploited for the "idlers," they were "sacrifice[d] . . . for the luxury of loafers" (1911c, 1). She continued by painting a vivid picture of capitalist exploitation and was particularly scathing in assessing the struggles of the Triangle Shirtwaist factory workers. "In that Triangle strike," O'Reilly stated, "the workers were shown by thugs, by women of the street, by the law, by the work house sentence, and by the betrayal of their confidence at last, that while property is sacred, human flesh and blood is the cheapest known quantity on earth" (1911c, 1, 2). And in no uncertain terms, O'Reilly recounted the tragic fire at the Triangle Shirtwaist Factory, identifying the two owners of the factory who refused to provide adequate fire escapes, and pointing to the material motivations behind worker exploitation: "[T]he poor workers of the Triangle Waist Co roasted alive in fire-proof buildings [they are] starved into submission when they strike; beaten back by the strong arm of the law which sides with men like Harris and Blank . . . [and are] maintained by a pitiless plutocracy universally united in a financial agreement to plunder all workers" (1911c, 3). By associating faces and motivations to particular "forces," O'Reilly enabled her audience to see that their circumstances were not inevitable and she provided a target for her audience to transform or overthrow.

Workers not only described the harsh conditions and abusive foremen under which they labored but also directed their attention toward how things could be different. Lifting the veil of naturalization's claim of inevitability, women crafted a picture of themselves as agents capable of changing their circumstances and they struggled successfully for an environment free of discrimination and dire need. Picketing shirtmakers in Philadelphia, arrested under false charges, sang a tune of defiance and established their power as workers: "We are striking for right and justice, / We are striking to win! / The bosses are out to bust us, / But we never shall give in! / If the bosses can make their own shirts, / Let them do—we don't care! / We shall never, never, never go back, / 'Til we get what's fair!" (Burns 1917, 63). Maud McCreery related the worker testimonials given at the Fourth Interstate and Fifth Annual City Conference of Woman Trade Unionists in Chicago in 1918. "Ah, the splendid force of her who told the graphic story of the struggle of the waitresses of her town and their victory over the power that be! . . . I can see her standing with hands clinched in the memory of the struggle, with head high like a spirited colt. No wonder the bosses quailed before her!" wrote McCreery in the November 1918 issue of *Life and Labor*.

The writings and speeches of wage-earning women suggest that their self-image as subjective agent capable of struggling against objective structures arose in part from their firsthand experiences. Time after time, workers explained the consciousness-raising effects of their oppressive conditions. Button workers in Muscatine demanded that their work be weighed fairly. They were promptly locked out by their employers and, as Newman explained, "Only then did they realize their own weakness, and thus formed a union of their craft" (1911). Similarly, many activists described a sort of awakening upon realizing that their material conditions necessitated collective action. Two hat trimmers from New York explained the formation of their union this way: "In October of last year the conditions in the hat trimming trade became so irritating and discouraging that the hat trimmers began to realize that they could no longer protest against or make demands for anything individually. . . . The old hat trimmers began to realize they should do something. We began to organize" ("Report to the Interstate Conference of the National WTUL," 9). Other testimonies reveal the ways that actual participation in union activities and strikes gave rise to a new and heightened consciousness and greater confidence. As two hat trimmers from Danbury, Connecticut, asserted, "If you attend your meetings you soon gain strength" ("Report of Interstate Conference of the National WTUL," 8).

The WTUL organizer Emma Steghagen was called by the striking Journeymen Tailors' Union in Cincinnati to assist female strikers in their August 1913 walkout. Steghagen explained the transformative effect the strike experience had on the female workers. At first, the women had no intention of joining the union, but agreed to assist their male coworkers on the strike line. Steghagen continued, "But when the fight grew hotter, the tactics of the employers more cruel, and when they learned that the firms had all organized to defeat them, they saw the light, and some of them began to think, reasoning that if organization is good for the employer it must also be good for the employed. Then one after another came and signed up to join the union" (1913, 334). Likewise, a strike of steelworkers in Indiana had an "awaken[ing]" effect on the workers' wives, who were initially reticent to support their husbands (Walton, 1919). One woman, arrested for calling a strikebreaker "scab," asserted that before the strike she did not understand or support her husband's involvement in "labor troubles." "Then the strike came. I've been to the meetings every day and I've picketed, too. I'm glad I was arrested. I'm a better woman now" (276). The November 1919 *Life and Labor* article relating the strike proclaimed that the event "has given [the wives] a vision of a possible partnership and comradeship with their husbands. It has created in them a broader understanding of life" (276). These testimonies point to the persuasive force of common material experiences—in conjunction with rhetorical intervention in the form of meetings, pamphleting, and shop-floor conversations—in shaping workers' identities and moving them to speak up for change.

In one respect, *Atlantic* writers were right when they described the "aggressiveness of capital." But in their rhetorical and extraverbal challenges to the system, wage-earning women demonstrated that, though aggressive and out-of-control, capitalist work relations were not immutable or beyond human intervention.

As earlier stated, the protest rhetorics of female activists were not totally separate or distinct from or wholly uninfluenced by other circulating discourses of the period, such as those in popular magazines. Indeed, various dominant beliefs, especially those regarding sex norms and roles, frequently made their way into the strategies, images, and arguments of activists, both wage earners and middle-class allies. Thus the rhetoric of True Womanhood frequently entered their arguments, yet was variously subverted or debunked.

Subverting "True Womanhood"

The WTUL, and more specifically the League's allies, did not so much refute the norms of True Womanhood as they subverted them in order to justify women's economic and political equality. In this the League was strongly influenced by Margaret Dreier Robins, who directed and financed the organization from 1907 to 1922. Robins used "sacred motherhood" as a springboard from which to argue for wage-earning women's rights.

Robins held motherhood, whether literal or "social," to be the common bond uniting women and deployed it as a trope to justify equal pay for equal work and shorter hours.[11] An emblem frequently used on WTUL documents depicted a woman, exhausted and bent over a sewing machine, with a baby at her breast. Motherhood, the WTUL argued, must not be sacrificed at the machine. In her address to the League's third annual convention, in 1911, Robins summed up the League's philosophy, in which motherhood was the motivating force: "Freedom, maternity, education and morality—all the blessed and abiding interests of childhood and home are at issue in this supreme struggle. All women who honor their sex and love their country should unite with us and our working sisters in the struggle for industrial freedom" (quoted in Payne, 117). To the extent that WTUL rhetoric upheld notions of women's unique abilities to purify the public realm, their justifications were similar to some of those offered in *Atlantic* articles that supported women's suffrage, demonstrating the interrelated nature of various discourses in a given period. As previously explained, vernacular rhetorics frequently borrow, subvert, and accept popular-culture ideals and narratives, just as popular discourses frequently co-opt aspects of vernacular cultures.

Working-class women were also greatly influenced by dominant beliefs regarding women's roles and they too referred to women's "innate" abilities and "mother instincts" in their arguments (O'Reilly, 1911b, circa 1914). In her article "Looking over the Field," O'Reilly asserted the influence of women as the remedy for chaos and corruption in politics: "If politics to-day is the product of intelligence let woman go to work politically to see what an infusion of human sympathy and mother instinct can do in managing the affairs of the State and nation. We must cleanse the political quagmires in which we have sunk. Men have accepted every wrong way; they have rejected every right way. It is for woman to reverse this kind of intelligence and to instill into government some of her innate honesty" (1911b, 7, 8). During a period in which a rhetoric of separate spheres and a unique feminine culture were widely accepted, wage-earning women frequently framed their needs and concerns in gendered terms and some formed lasting friendships with middle- and upper-class allies on the basis of their common experiences as women.[12] Equally influential, however, were their experiences as workers, which often led them to articulate arguments that countered the myth of "sacred motherhood."

On April 22, 1912, the Wage Earners' League organized a mass meeting in which activists protested the New York State legislature's failure to pass a resolution for suffrage (Orleck 1995). With sagacity, Mollie Schepps, Clara Lemlich, and Rose Schneiderman articulated a class-based argument to refute the sentimental prose of specific New York senators. Through descriptions of the hardships faced by working-class women and families, they exploded the traditional visions of the family and the sanctity of marriage. These cultural narratives do not apply to us, they argued.

Schneiderman, angered at the way that "femininity" was selectively applied to women of different classes, fired a statement to the senators that brought to light the realities faced daily by working women:

It does not speak well for the intelligence of our Senators to come out with statements about women losing their charm and attractiveness . . . [when] women in the laundries . . . stand thirteen hours or fourteen hours in terrible steam and heat with their hands in hot starch. Surely . . . women won't lose

any more of their beauty and charm by putting a ballot in a ballot box once a
year than they are likely to lose standing in the foundries or laundries all
year round (quoted in Orleck 1995, 104).

Schepps similarly derided the senators' appeals to the sanctity of marriage. Pointing to the absurdity of the politicians' arguments, she remarked, "If long, miserable hours and starvation wages are the only
means men can find to encourage marriage, it is a very poor compliment
to themselves" (quoted in Orleck 1995, 102).

Two years later, wage-earning women were making much the same argument in the context of the forty-ninth annual convention of the National American Woman Suffrage Association in Washington, D.C. Margaret Hinchy, a laundry worker, in response to a New York senator who
referred to "Cornelia and her Jewels" in making the argument that
woman's place was in the home, "gave a few straight tips about the modern Cornelia and her Jewels today sitting in the sweat shops making violets for three cents a gross or running two rows of ribbons in corset cov-
ers and sewing on three buttons for half a cent a corset cover" (Anderson
1914, 12).

As the United States entered World War I, women's growing presence
in munitions plants and other heavy industries gave rise to a spectacle
that even more decidedly undermined notions of womanly purity, submissiveness, and domesticity. Prior to World War I, wage-earning women
were relegated to unskilled, poorly paying jobs on the dubious grounds
that these positions were more fitting for women. In fact, the laundries,
the garment, candy, and cigar factories where millions of women worked
represented some of the most grueling and debased positions. Once
given the opportunity, women repeatedly testified to their preferences
for work in positions previously reserved for men. "Lot easier than doing
washing out," noted one woman who worked in the Ryan Car Company
(Russell 1917, 159). Calling attention to the inconsistent application of
gender norms in the workplace, the November 1919 issue of *Life and Labor* presented three large photographs of women busy at work in factories with hammers, saws, and machines at hand. Under a photo of a
woman operating a large machine, the caption read: "Why Not Women
in the Machine Shop Just as Much as in the Laundry or the Garment Factory?" ("Women Workers and Their Industrial Future," 289).

In a sense, every act of striking, leafleting, organizing, boycotting, and
soapbox speaking was a challenge to the cult of domesticity. As Campbell
points out, when feminists speak publicly for their rights as women, they
are "inevitably radical, because they attack the fundamental values underlying this culture" (1973, 78). Middle-class and wage-earning activists
alike challenged the propriety of True Womanhood not only through

confrontational discourse but through various protest tactics in which they were neither submissive nor domestic. The National Woman's Party (NWP), a suffrage organization with a membership largely of middle-class women, was credited with infusing the suffrage movement with new life through its militant tactics. Throughout 1917, thousands of NWP members—at times assisted by wage earners from the WTUL—picketed the White House for the suffrage cause. The women carried large banners that pointedly attacked President Wilson and called into question the notion of "democracy" in America.[13] On numerous occasions these peaceful picketers were mobbed by onlookers. Ford relates how one picketer, Agnes Morey, was attacked by two soldiers who "jabbed her splintered banner pole between her eyes," while "Grandmother Dora Lewis was knocked about by three youths" (1991, 178). Throughout the month of November 1917, women, most from well-to-do backgrounds, were arrested and imprisoned for persisting in their picketing of the White House. The NWP tactics garnered such publicity precisely because it was largely middle- and upper-class women engaging in such "unwomanly" behaviors. News accounts of the period referred to the picketers as "'crazy women,' 'unwomanly,' and 'shocking'" (Ford 1991, 128).

Similarly, the hypocrisies of True Womanhood came into sharp focus on picket lines in front of factories where wage-earning women endured physical brutality at the hands of corporate thugs and police. Many historians have documented the beatings, harassments, fines, and unjustified jailings of female picketers and strikers, particularly in the teens.[14] The sight of a male police officer beating a wage-earning girl of seventeen while an upper-class sympathizer stood on the same picket line untouched was evidence (particularly to wage-earning women) that the dubious privileges of the True Womanhood were not available to all women, and hence did not constitute an innate quality. It should be noted that middle- and upper-class allies of the WTUL were not blind to such disparities in treatment and were themselves enraged at the police brutality enacted on working women. Though they did not always explicate arguments that would clarify the class nature of these differential treatments, the allies can be credited with closely monitoring police actions and providing thousands of dollars in bail when the picketers were unjustly arrested. Particularly during the Uprising of 30,000, allies called attention to the police brutality as a way to garner sympathy for the working women and girls.[15]

Wage earners often upended the notion of True Womanhood by transforming its locus—the domestic spaces of the kitchen, the tenement stoop, the market—into places for exchanging stories and identifying common experiences and concerns, which then became translated into efforts to organize for change. Denying all notions of feminine purity and propriety, in May 1902, a group of Jewish housewives on New York's Lower East Side protested a rise in the price of kosher meat by entering kosher meat shops and throwing the meat into the streets (Orleck 1995, 28). The very presence of women engaged in public actions such as this one refuted the "naturalness" of the natural order depicted in the *Atlantic*, which relied on notions of the delicate and domestic woman.

Thus, wage-earning women, and to a lesser degree their middle-class sisters, demystified the naturalness of capitalism, identified the individuals who benefited from their suffering, and projected an alternative vision of life with themselves at the center as laboring agents in control of their destiny. Through rhetorical tactics and physical confrontations, women activists politically intervened in dominant hegemonic ideologies and oppressive work relations. One must be careful not to underestimate the influence of True Womanhood and separate-spheres rhetoric on the ways that wage-earning women saw themselves and articulated their arguments for equality. However, wage-earning women were often more likely to employ arguments and engage themselves physically in attempts to unravel the naturalizing narratives and images frequently found in the *Atlantic Monthly*. Furthermore, wage-earning women were keenly aware of the unique concerns among women of their class. So, in contrast to universalizing women's needs, as so often occurred in *McClure's* magazine, they emphasized class conflict and the necessity of solidarity as working-class women.

Revealing Class Differences

The ideology of universalization employed by *McClure's* was an idealizing rhetoric that upheld the power of words, ideas, and commonly held values as ways to alter one's conditions. This frame has much in common with traditional social movement studies that elide the impact of extraverbal phenomena on struggles for change and define "liberation" in terms of image and identity alteration or formation.

A typical story in *McClure's* was "Working Girls' Budgets: The Shirtwaist-Makers and Their Strike." In it, the writers explained how "character" overcame impoverished material conditions. According to the writers, Natalya was a "ghetto girl who, in the meanest quarter of New York, on stinted food, in scanty clothes, drained with faint health and overwork, could yet walk through life, giving away half of her wage by day to some one else, [and] enjoying the theater at night" (Clark and Wyatt 1910b, 86). In addition to emphasizing ideals, *McClure's* smoothed over class conflict and the influences of material institutions through narratives that portrayed workers and owners on equal footing and framed women's concerns exclusively in terms of political and sexual equality. In contrast, wage-earning women such as Leonora O'Reilly were quick to point out the conflicting interests between owner and worker (as well as between allies and working women) in their public protests.

Confronting the "Idlers" Head-on

For working-class activists, pointing the finger at bosses, foremen, and owners who perpetuated their miserable work experiences served two rhetorical purposes. First, putting a face on capitalist forces undermined the justificatory nature of naturalization; the system could no longer plead "innocent" as its workings clearly were not beyond human control. Furthermore, identifying specific individuals enabled workers to highlight salient class differences that could not be bridged by ideals.

The rhetoric of the Industrial Workers of the World perhaps best exemplified how wage-earning activists vilified owners in an effort to highlight fundamental class divisions and in order to build solidarity among themselves. The "parasite metaphor" was a common element of IWW rhetoric as in this passage taken from the IWW publication, *One Union for All Wage Workers:* "Six hundred thousand are maimed, crippled and killed every year in the workshops of the nation, recklessly sacrificed, for no other reason, than to increase the profit of a handful of socially useless capitalists, to give a life of idleness and luxury to their families and cringing hirelings, most of whom never did any work, beneficial to society in all their lives" (Cole 1978, 80, 81). Mary Harris "Mother" Jones explained the principles of the IWW at its founding conference in 1905: "The working class and the employing class have nothing in common. There can be no peace as long as hunger and want are found among millions of working people, and the few, who make up the employing class, have all the good things of life" (Tax 1980, 126).

Though not a self-identified Wobbly—the nickname for members of the IWW—Leonora O'Reilly similarly made use of the parasite metaphor in her own speeches and articles by establishing the common material experiences of working men and women as compared to the "growing money powers" of the "idlers" (1911e). She was committed to the idea that workers "must work further to eliminate all those who do not pay their way, for they are the parasites that absorb the fruits of those who labor" (O'Reilly, "To Be Used in Every Lecture," 3). In an article in *Life and Labor* in 1915, O'Reilly described worker-owner relations decisively: "[W]e know the scientific management, efficiency, safety first,—one and all of them, for what they are worth—slick means of getting the best of organized labor, which while they increase profits for the share holders, leave to the poor wage dupe, but a crumb of the loaf he has made for the army of loafers" ("Miss Ida Tarbell and Woman Suffrage" 35). Thus, though *McClure's* depicted owners and loyal workers toiling side by side, workers witnessed firsthand the benefits wrought by the privileged few at their expense and they targeted these individuals in their protests. Pointing out blatant material disparities, working-class women engaged a fiery, oppositional rhetorical style so as to drive home the relevance of material position to explain human relations.

In testimonies to Progressive reformers and to state legislatures, workers detailed the long hours, low wages, speed-ups, and tyranny of foremen whom they frequently confronted and sometimes defied. During a strike of Chicago garment workers in 1910, WTUL allies listened to the testimonies of working girls and women who expressed the importance of material conditions and formed the beginnings of a critique that pointed to differences based on class and gender privilege. These testimonies contrasted with *McClure's* portrayals, which flattened or elided differences between workers and their bosses. In a typical testimony, "Miss K," a pocket sewer, detailed her difficulties with the foreman. Miss K explained: "The only thing Mr. Richter [the foreman] does is to smoke a cigar and walk around the shop. . . . He counts our work. We are paid so much and are supposed to make our limit every day. If we do not we have a calling down. We call that 'breakfast'—our calling down. If we don't keep up, he keeps at us and calls us bad names and you can imagine how a young lady feels" ("Statement on the Strike of the 35,000," 18).

McClure's often drew one-to-one comparisons between labor and capital to demonstrate how the two were in cahoots against the helpless "public," or were equally rapacious. Workers, however, went to great lengths to emphasize the uneven playing field on which workers and owners fought. O'Reilly infused her rhetoric with a momentum as listeners were made to see the necessity of worker solidarity against a force larger and more powerful than they. "We go to Legislative Hall to plead for mercy, only to meet the Organized Power of the big Industrial interests. We see the political club and the lure of gold used to damn men's souls. We are learning for the first time both to think and then to act" declared O'Reilly in a 1917 article written for the *Union Printer* (O'Reilly 1917). O'Reilly's testimony before the New York State legislature in 1912[16] indicated her frustrations in struggling for a square deal. She asserted to the legislators:

> We go before legislature after legislature to tell our story. Legislatures fail to make laws to help the women who are being speeded up so high in mills and factories from 54 to 72 in stores in New York and 92 hrs in one week in subcellar laundries. . . . [J]ust as soon as our backs are turned, up comes the representative of the Big Interest and says 'Lad, you are dead politically if

you do what these women ask. . . . [W]e get nothing for all our pleading because all the votes are owned. (O'Reilly 1912)

In addition to distinguishing themselves from owners and foremen, wage-earning activists often found it necessary to differentiate themselves from the middle- and upper-class allies who assisted them. Because of their very different daily experiences as women, homemakers, and workers, wage-earning and middle-class women often employed differing rhetorical strategies and emphasized different goals in their efforts for political and economic equality.

Frustrations with Our More Well-to-Do Sisters

When it came to suffrage arguments, middle- and upper-class women—particularly those involved in the early suffrage and temperance movements—put the cult of True Womanhood to work for themselves by justifying their nontraditional activities with a traditional rhetoric of domesticity. They referred to their political activities as "social housekeeping" and they framed the vote as a manner for women to extend their "innate" morality to the public sphere. At times wage-earning women also relied on traditional gender norms in order to justify political equality for women. Yet through their experiences toiling in sweatshops and mills wage-earning women witnessed the duplicity of True Womanhood firsthand and so they often justified woman suffrage on material rather than moral grounds. In New York City in 1912, women marched for suffrage holding signs that read "Women Need Votes to End Sweatshops" (see Photo 4.3).

At times, wage-earning women's unique arguments for the vote were targeted to middle- and upper-class suffragists. In an address to a group of middle-class suffragists given in 1913, Schneiderman pointed to the predominance of daily struggles in the lives of working-class women, "Working nine, ten hours a day and then on their return home attending to their home duties, where is the time for them to take active part in even a suffrage movement?" (11). Working-class women were more interested in how the vote can alter the immediate conditions of their lives, Schneiderman explained. She concluded unequivocally, stating, "Political democracy will not do us much good unless we have industrial democracy; and industrial democracy can only come through intelligent workers participating in the business of which they are a part, and working out the best methods for all" (15).

Similarly, in "The Woman Movement and the Working Woman," an article that appeared in *Life and Labor* two years later, Schneiderman explained the meaning of the vote for working women for whom womanly

PHOTO 4.3   Women march in suffrage parade, New York, May 6, 1912, under a banner reading "Women need votes to end sweatshops." Photo by the Pictorial News Co., 138 West Forty-second Street, New York, New York. Sophia Smith Collection, Smith College, Northampton, Massachusetts.

domesticity had never been a reality. In a tone implying frustration at the need to continually make such clarifications, Schneiderman made plain:

> The working woman, on the other hand, has always had full liberty to work; indeed, from her is demanded the hardest and most exacting kind of toil. Work to her spells no gateway to freedom. Question any working girl and every time she will tell you, "I am tired of going to work every day and coming home just to rest up so as to be fit to go to work again the next day." Work to her is no adventure but a monotonous reality. What she needs is to be released from the bondage of overwork, long hours, insufficient pay and dangerous and unhealthy working conditions (1915).

Like her wage-earning sister, Leonora O'Reilly argued for woman suffrage by painting a vivid picture of the material realities faced by wage earners: "We see as a result of industry as conducted to-day, fatigue, early decline, hacking cough, spineless backs, failing eyesight, loss of teeth, crumbling of bones, tearing of flesh, shattering of nerves by piecework called efficiency in management. . . . In working without the ballot we are deprived of an efficient means to remedy these wretched conditions we find about us" (1917). Influenced by their status not only as women but as workers trapped within the maw of the industrial system, League wage earners such as Schneiderman and O'Reilly more readily upended True Womanhood and framed the vote as a tool to deploy toward gaining workplace justice.

Other issues besides woman suffrage were argued for by wage-earning women in specifically material terms, namely, issues surrounding shorter hours and safer conditions. Schneiderman and Pauline Newman viewed labor legislation as a means to achieve equal standing with working men, who in many states were already guaranteed the eight-hour day (Orleck 1995, 125). In contrast, WTUL pamphlets—whose message presumably was shaped in large by the allies who financed them—justified the forty-eight-hour week by quoting doctors who testified to women's special need to conserve energy in order to "meet the periodical crises of reproduction" ("The Forty-Eight-Hour Week for Women" 1917, 13). Such arguments reflected the League's growing reliance on expediency arguments into the teens as they shifted efforts from organization to legislation (see Dye 1980; Tax 1980). Thus, wage-earning women frequently crafted their own arguments in contrast to those of legislators and even WTUL allies, who continued to emphasize women's biology, innate frailty, and of course her potential for "sacred motherhood."

The role of culture and education in women's organizations was often another point of contention between working women and middle-class activists. The issue of cultural uplift was important to many of the middle- and upper-class allies in the WTUL; indeed, education and recreation were central aspects of Margaret Dreier Robins's program for the League during her years as president. But the dance recitals and tea parties were often received with ambivalence by the League's wage-earning members. On the one hand, workers frequently expressed a desire for more than simply improved wages and hours. They wanted "bread and roses too." Rose Schneiderman in particular looked favorably upon cultural and recreational activities as a way to attract women and girls to trade unionism. In her report to the WTUL around 1909, Schneiderman insisted on making the "labor organization a social as well as economic attraction" (Schneiderman 1908–9, 5). Understandably, vacations to the countryside or trips to the museum were attractive to those who saw little beyond the whir of machines. In *Life and Labor*, the organ of the WTUL, a young worker named Anna Rudnitzky lamented that she had not time, money, nor energy to enjoy all that life had to offer (1912). And Pauline Newman, though she made wages and working hours a priority, maintained that "poverty [should] not deprive us from finding joy and satisfaction in things of the spirit" (quoted in Orleck 1995, 16).

On the other hand, workers were continually frustrated by what they felt was a patronizing attitude on the part of the allies and the inapplicability or uselessness of cultural activities to their lives when they could barely keep a roof over their heads or provide for their families. In a way analogous to the ways they distinguished themselves from their bosses, wage-earning women such as O'Reilly distinguished themselves from the "lady": "The work which makes people stand on their own feet is the work that counts—the dignity of labor. . . . Contact with the 'lady' does harm in the long run—gives a wrong standard—No use preaching Christianity until you are ready to live it" (quoted in Tax 1980, 112).

In 1915, the *McClure's* muckraker Ida Tarbell gave testimony to the Federal Commission on Industrial Relations regarding woman suffrage, to the effect that political enfranchisement would do little to improve women's economic position. Outraged, O'Reilly wrote an open letter to Tarbell which appeared in the February 1915 issue of *Life and Labor*. To emphasize the salience of direct experience and the need for working-class women to speak on their own behalf, O'Reilly used the metaphor of life as a play at which individuals were either "observers" of events or players with vital roles. Miss Tarbell's opinion was shaped by her position as an observer, explained O'Reilly. Had she spoken as a participant, however, she would have provided a much different opinion on votes for women. In this compelling and candid passage, O'Reilly drove home the importance of firsthand experience:

> If Miss Tarbell had lived through one long strike as a conscientious wage earner,—not as an observer in the social laboratory, if for a principle, she had first given up butter for her bread, then the milk for her coffee, then managed to live on two meals a day instead of three, and laugh because it felt so good to be hungry when one knew one was fighting in the cause of labor, if this were not yet enough, and Miss Tarbell was reduced to one meal a day, for the sake of her principle . . . if in this physically weak but spiritually strong condition, Miss Tarbell felt the hand of the law on her shoulder when she tried to keep a thoughtless sister from going in to take her place in the mills, if Miss Tarbell felt an officer's club upon her ribs as she with others were huddled into a hallway to wait for the patrol wagon . . . if Miss Tarbell lived through all this as one of the victims of the whole iniquitous mess,

don't you think she would be for seeing that votes for women, could and would do a great deal, to bring a breath of pure air into the whole body politic? (1915, 34, 35)

O'Reilly's frustrations as expressed in her letter to Tarbell were common among workers in the WTUL and various suffrage organizations. In their associations with workers and in their writings for *McClure's*, middle-class reformers and activists such as Tarbell, Inez Milholland, and Jane Addams relied on universalized ideals in order to bridge the differences between classes. In contrast, wage-earning women highlighted the importance of concrete material conditions and the differences they made in the lives of persons struggling to get by.

In some instances, workers outright rejected allies' efforts at uplift and instead turned to fellow wage earners for support or developed their own ideas regarding the role of culture in wage earners' lives.[17] O'Reilly distinguished between "leisure" and "idleness" (O'Reilly, "To Be Used in Every Lecture," 10). In contrast to idleness, leisure was a necessary counterpart to labor: "Without labor we can have no external wealth nor robust and healthy citizens. Without leisure we can have no internal wealth, which is knowledge, nor healthy and intelligent citizens. . . . [T]he Right to Leisure is as sacred as the Duty to Labor" (10). Asserting their right to leisure, members of the Waitresses' Union Local 240 of Seattle established a recreation home for themselves in 1913. The home served as a central location where the women could relax, recover from illnesses, and further foster their union friendships (Abbott 1914). Rather than culturally lift workers out of their class, the home supported women in their position as workers and reinforced the importance of class solidarity. Similarly, the Ladies' Waist and Dressmakers' Union established Unity House in 1916 as an education and leisure center as part of their "attempt to draw together the membership of the union with ties of greater solidarity and unity" (Poyntz 1917, 96). Juliet Stuart Poyntz, the educational director of the union's Local 2587, explained the class-based nature of Unity House and its place in the lives of workers. The house "developed less as a mere vacation place than as a center of spiritual inspiration. The girls grew to realize that a trade union has a very powerful influence beyond the purely economic field. . . . Devotion to the ideal of trade unionism acquired then strengthened many a Unity girl to continue her struggle as chairman of her shop against an ignorant and deceiving employer" (96). It was not that wage-earning women did not value education, the arts, and recreational activities but rather that their role in working women's lives was different than in the allies' lives, and different from what the allies envisioned for them. Working-class women often rejected cultural activities as means to rise out of their class, and instead formed their own outlets for rest and relaxation where they could strengthen themselves as a working class.

Certainly, as many wage earners were well aware, there were advantages and disadvantages to their associations with middle- and upper-class allies such as those of the WTUL. There was no getting around the need for money in order to sustain important protest activities such as strikes, pamphleting, and holding meetings. In the League most of these crucial funds came from allies. Indeed, the very existence of the League during its tenuous early years can be attributed to the contributions of one ally, Margaret Dreier Robins. At the same time, workers were aware that she who held the purse strings also controlled much of what was said and acted upon by the League, which often ran counter to the experiences and needs of the workers. As Pauline Newman wrote to Schneiderman, "She [Robins] does not give the girls a chance to use their brains, she does not want them to think, but wants them to agree with everything she does. And fortunately they do; they have to; she pays their salaries" (Tax 1980, 116).

Nonetheless, the importance of worker solidarity did not go unrecognized by League allies, in particular Margaret Dreier Robins. In her presidential address to the National WTUL in 1911, Robins asserted, "Persons who suffer in their daily lives the deprivations, injuries or dangers due to non-enforcement of labor laws are the most efficient agencies for inspection and report" (1911d, 279). Similarly, in her speech, "Self-Government in the Work Shop," Robins stressed organizing women into the union shop, where workers could learn "self-government" and the power of "united action" in their struggles for industrial democracy (1912, 110). She continued asserting that the working woman must learn that "her economic problem today is a social one to be controlled by social and collective action" (109).

Allies believed in allowing workers to speak for themselves both through formal meetings and in testimonials. In *Life and Labor*, Robins provided a series of lessons in the series "How To Take Part in Meetings" (1911a, 1911b, 1911c, 1911d, 1911e, 1911f, 1911g). In these studies, Robins explained the rules of parliamentary procedure, including how to preside over meetings. For young girls and women who had never before participated in a meeting and were often intimidated by such gatherings, these lessons imparted valuable information. Further, League allies frequently solicited the testimony of working girls and women in order to learn of their conditions and to gain publicity (and funds) for their cause. Through their stories, workers provided their own conceptualizations of work and liberation that combated those in popular magazines such as *McClure's*, and offered middle- and upper-class women a different perspective on "women's issues." Moreover, these activists—many of them young girls—gained confidence and public-speaking experience, which in turn enhanced their leadership and organizational abilities in strikes and union meetings.

Still, however, some workers saw the limits in such speaking situations, many of which were fundraisers. As Rose Schneiderman once said about the League, "I could understand why working women . . . joined, but I could not believe that men and women who were not wage-earners themselves understood the problems that workers faced" (Dye 1980, 50). When League allies gathered to hear the perspectives of wage earners, it frequently was in relatively formal settings, such as indoor meetings and parlor gatherings, where propriety framed the rules for speaking. As a result, via the situation and the setting the allies often patronized the speakers and obscured the specifically class nature of their demands. During the Uprising of 30,000, a group of wealthy suffragists invited ten striking girls to a fundraiser-lunch at the prestigious Colony Club in New York so that they could tell their stories to a group of rich women. The atmosphere was unavoidably ironic as young girls told of police brutality, dangerous work conditions, and poverty to a group of "bejeweled, befurred, belaced, begowned" women,[18] some of whom were the wives of major industrialists such as J. P. Morgan and O. H. P. Belmont. In light of the wealth of the members of the audience, fundraisers such as these were not too successful in raising money. In her book, *Diary of a Shirtwaist Striker*, Theresa Malkiel, a socialist and working-class activist, observes that in this particular fundraiser, "The women gave us a thousand dollars, but what does this amount to? Not even a quarter piece for each striker" (1910, 133).[19] One contributor to *Life and Labor* expressed her frustrations with one such fundraiser, declaring, "I myself felt that such a meeting was a failure, notwithstanding the tears, because few jeweled fingers opened their rich pocketbooks. Are rich pocketbooks harder to unclasp than poor ones? Could it have been nothing but morbid curiosity that had brought these women together to listen to the struggles and wrongs of those girls?" ("Girls' Stories," 243). Perhaps the overriding motivation in soliciting these testimonies had not to do with the strike but, rather, with gaining support from working-class women for the vote, an issue of importance to many middle- and upper-class women.

The radical potential of these women's stories was often blunted by the decorum of the setting, which itself rested upon the very assumptions of human connectedness and universal values these women and girls were trying to disrupt. Working-class activists like Leonora O'Reilly were quick to point a finger at the monied class when on a soapbox or in a union meeting. Such a tactic would not go over well, however, in the living room of a Vanderbilt or Morgan from whom one was trying to raise money. In the parlors of the wealthy, a speaking environment was created which smoothed over class differences and encouraged a speaker persona that fit dominant notions of propriety. As Melissa Deem notes in her work on the role of decorum in speaking situations, the "very substance of the bourgeois subject is constructed through sanitized modes of address" (1995, 288).

Into the teens, the WTUL, under the influence of allies such as Robins, gradually shifted emphasis from economic organizing and strategizing (strikes, walkouts) to legislation (lobbying for protective laws). The earlier focus on organizational justice was replaced by an emphasis on attaining equal representation through traditional lines of social change such as legislation and state participation. Indeed, many wage-earning members aligned themselves with this shift and eventually held governmental positions.[20] The conflicts within the League did not always fall along class lines, but generally the emphasis on education, legislation, and cultural uplift came from middle-class allies who sought to transform wage-earning members "from working-class activists to female labor leaders who could with comfort take tea on the White House lawn" (Tax 1980, 113).

Reflective of Progressive Era and New Deal politics, the philosophy guiding the League and its activities was one of accommodation in which members learned how to negotiate and compromise within the parameters established by various state apparatuses. The League emphasized "social concord" between contesting political groups, which is defined by the rhetorical scholar Celeste Condit as "the active or passive acceptance of a given social policy or political framework as the best that can be negotiated under the given conditions" (Condit 1994, 210). A "critique of concord," as explained by Condit, entails examining public discourses such as those of the League, the AFL, and various manufacturers for their "plurivocality," or the extent to which competing voices and perspectives were given space. The goal of this critical approach is equal voice and representation of opposing interests.

Communication certainly plays a role in achieving fair wages and safe work conditions. Nevertheless, compromise or "concordance" (see Condit 1994) as exemplified in the WTUL's tactics in later years poses substantial limitations. First, *symbolic* parity—equal representation, grievance rights, "plurivocality"—does not necessarily address *material* disparity. The workshops and lessons sponsored by the League fostered discursive power—speaking up at meetings, honing leadership skills. But, as Cloud has noted, it is important to distinguish between "voice" and "redress" (1999). Certainly, the speaking and leadership skills encouraged by Robins and the League were important for girls and women who historically had been denied the right to speak in public, much less the right to earn a living wage. And, as noted above, the ability to get one's needs and concerns across in a persuasive and forceful manner often resulted in improved material conditions. The point, however, is that equal voice often comes to replace material equality, serving as a form of consolation or reprieve that staves off more fundamental challenges to the system.

Furthermore, what compromise can achieve is limited to the extent that it saves or preserves the dominant system by absorbing various challenges, rhetorical or material, and redirects them to fit within the status quo.[21] The political philosopher Antonio Gramsci referred to this as a "passive revolution": social reforms are instituted through the state with no "active participation of the people. Social reforms which have been demanded by the opposing forces may be carried out, but in such a way as to disorganise these forces and damp down any popular struggles" (Simon 1991, 26). Historically, governmental programs and social agencies have arisen in order to ameliorate severe hardships and simultaneously head off radical challenges to the system. To be sure, many of these programs, particularly those developed in the teens and 1930s, did improve the lives of many. But current statistics on the growing disparities between rich and poor worldwide stand as testament to the fact that governmental compromise in the form of social programs does not fundamentally disrupt a system that allows a few to accumulate massive wealth at the expense of the many.[22] Howard Zinn has argued that these programs can be viewed as just enough "concessions to keep general resentment below the combustible level" (1990, 127).

Nonetheless, a critique of the accommodationist approach must be offered with a dose of caution against sweeping charges. Though we can and should warn against the pitfalls of reformism, we must remember what Gramsci wrote regarding a "war of position," the strategy that requires social groups to engage in the prolonged struggle to establish a working-class hegemony in opposition to the state. Central to this strategy is the building of alliances with those engaged in other democratic struggles, over race, gender, and gay and lesbian rights. The danger arises when alliances based on culture or identity differences are emphasized at the expense of recognizing fundamental similarities upon which to build a coordinated class-based struggle; and when discursive and identity struggles that opt for symbolic change supplant struggle for transformation at a concrete material level.[23] Cultural alliances based on identity—referred to by Lachau and Mouffe as "new social movements"—represent a shift toward micropolitics and are lauded by contemporary cultural theorists who view class-based collective confrontation as irrelevant or ineffective in a "new" era of post-Fordist and information-based production (see Laclau and Mouffe 1985).

An important lesson regarding the nature of social change and the need for collective alliances aimed at material alteration can be gleaned from the experiences of middle- and working-class women, such as those of the League, who struggled for economic and political equality in the early 1900s. Middle- and upper-class activists were often concerned to overturn patriarchal norms that excluded women from political participation and made them less than full persons in the eyes of the law. Wage-earning women—despite also being angered at these norms, which were used to justify their relegation to lower-paying, unskilled jobs—more often remained focused on how to alter their status as workers, which often affected their ability to feed themselves and their families. In many cases, working-class women saw men of their class as comrades or coworkers rather than as enemies, and they learned the importance of sticking together in fights against manufacturers and owners. For that matter, gender norms were crafted and applied selectively and strategically and often changed in response to the needs of the economic system. As the chapter on working-class magazines revealed, wage-earning women were often encouraged to acquire attributes at odds with True Womanhood, e.g., independence and strength, so as to reinforce behaviors that would make them better workers; at the same time they were expected or exhorted to uphold their responsibilities as homemakers and mothers.

Thus, altering hegemonic ideologies or transforming discursive identities does not automatically translate into material betterment. Further, focusing on symbolic alteration obscures the extent to which material systems and institutions rely upon, and help perpetuate, various ideologies in the first place.

As will be elaborated subsequently, wage-earning activists learned from firsthand experience the necessity of transcending race and gender differences in order to form a collective agency capable of forcing the hand of manufacturers who were not impelled to listen when only one spoke up for change. Overcoming differences of gender and race was not simple, straightforward, or always successful, but the countless success stories conveyed by workers themselves testifies to the persuasive force of collective confrontation based on common interests, needs that arise out of day-to-day existence in a world comprising not only symbolic constructions and social norms but factory lines, tenements, and pay envelopes.

The discussion of working-class hegemony vs. new social movements should not downplay the hard work of allies like Robins nor ignore the lessons that wage-earning women learned from League efforts. For many years, Robins's enthusiasm and funding literally held the League together. Furthermore, on a number of occasions and in a variety of contexts, Robins also advanced a philosophy of worker solidarity and emphasized the importance of wage-earning women's acting on their own behalf. Through meetings, workshops, and educational efforts, wage-earning women gained confidence as they learned how to speak for themselves and interact assertively with bosses and other labor leaders. Not least important, through such negotiations these women and girls often won tangible benefits, such as increased wages, shorter hours, and reduced fines.

Yet the views of League allies such as Robins were shaped and necessarily limited by their experiences as middle-class reformers. The WTUL historian Elizabeth Anne Payne draws a clear connection between Robins's upbringing and the approach she brought to the League: "In her perception of herself . . . as a descendant of a long line of socially conscious women, Margaret [Dreier Robins] was bent toward service and reform. The religious perspective, domestic environment, and unconventional education provided for her had the same effect. . . . As a Christian, a citizen, and a woman of means, Margaret came to see her life's task as the fortunate one of redressing social wrongs and realizing the best in human nature" (1988, 14).

Ultimately, Robins's emphasis on traditional liberal values such as self-reliance, citizenship, and uplift taught wage-earning women how to get by within the class- and sex-segregated system, but left these exploitative divisions intact. Compromise occluded the possibility of a fundamental challenge to the relations that were the root cause of labor exploitation in industrial capitalism. In essence, Robins's approach created a protest style that downplayed class conflict and ultimately upheld a liberalist view of social change in which an elite group uplifts the downtrodden and helps them assimilate into dominant society.[24]

Conveying working-class concerns through mass magazines or wealthy parlor settings was not the only alternative for wage-earning activists struggling for economic and political justice. History has demonstrated time and again that less traditional forms of persuasion such as strikes, walkouts, and sit-ins have been the most successful in calling attention to workers' concerns and achieving substantive change that could be directly felt in the lives of workers, for example, a living wage, reduced hours, safe working conditions. Rather than establish common ground with philanthropists and owners, working women often demonstrated their power by employing a sarcastic, fiery, and in-your-face style of speaking and exerted themselves through strikes and pickets. O'Reilly and her fellow wage-earning activists wanted "not patronage, but justice. Not generous distribution of superfluous wealth but righteous restitution of wealth to those who have created it" (O'Reilly "Religion of Labor"). Thus, in an attempt to frame their own argument and prevent their words from being appropriated, many of these activists emphasized collective experience, directing their words *to those who shared this experience*, and engaging their arguments at the site at which these experiences took place.[25]

Common Experience and Collective Agency

Speaking and acting on their own behalf, wage-earning women of the WTUL constructed themselves as laboring agents. Such a concept of speaker agency contrasted with assumptions of human experience implicit in *McClure's* magazine. *McClure's* magazine was characterized by two related rhetorical maneuvers. First, *McClure's* employed a frame of universalization in which material differences, when they were acknowledged, were shown to be overcome by human values and interests assumed to be commonly held by all. Second, to support universalization *McClure's* frequently personalized the lives of workers through metonymic representations that facilitated reader identification, regardless of the vastness of the differences between the reader and the person depicted.

Both of these rhetorical framings elided class conflict and negated the necessity of collective agency. As Chapter 2 elaborated, *McClure's* promulgated a liberal individualist portrayal of work and gender relations in which persons were free to act autonomously, unrestrained by material institutions and systems. If only individuals acted out of the proper values and ideals, they could succeed. Universalizing values and interests promoted a theory of social change based on uplift in which real struggle between opposing groups was unnecessary. Similarly, the metonymies, in their ability to simplify complex issues, encourage a view of human experience as disconnected from social institutions and systems. Narratives of class conflict, by contrast, connect people's daily experiences to their material position within a particular system, which is seen as shaping various aspects of a society.

Class conflict was a central issue for wage-earning women of the WTUL, not only rhetorically but materially. In their protests against very real institutions and persons who exploited them, these women engaged in this conflict by constructing themselves as agents whose experiences and demands were collective in nature. Through both words and actions, wage-earning women emphasized class solidarity. They appealed not only to a common sisterhood but also a worker identity forged in opposition to the brutalities of industry. In a 1904 speech given to shirtwaist makers at Clinton Hall, in New York City, O'Reilly encouraged her audience to view themselves not individually but as part of a group: "We all know to day the day of individual effort is passed. The day of organised effort is here. . . . [T]hose of us who would accomplish anything in any line, industrial, social, must take advantage of the only powerful force today: organization" (3). Pauline Newman, O'Reilly's comrade and fellow WTUL activist, made a similar assertion to readers of *Life and Labor* in 1914: "To-day the individual is helpless. He is helpless because he is powerless. At this period of centralization one alone cannot accomplish much. If anything is to be done, it will be necessary to use collective forces, and united efforts" (1914, 312).

O'Reilly was particularly adept at arousing emotion and creating a forceful worker persona through which to build audience confidence. In an undated speech likely given to a working girls' club or female union local, O'Reilly spoke directly to her audience's experiences in "the factory, the mill, the mine or shop . . . [as] a cog in a wheel of the great industrial machine that supplies the needs of mankind" (n.d. "Loyalty Among Working Women," 4). Building to a climax, O'Reilly conveyed to her audience the unquestionable necessity of worker loyalty. There is "peril if we women fail to see that in this new life away from the home out from under the sheltering roof of the homestead, in the mill, in the factory . . . we owe an allegiance to the women beside us equally faithful to that which we give to the women in the home we call mother and sister" (5). Most important, perhaps, O'Reilly emphasized that "sisterhood . . . must be established side by side with the brotherhood of man" (5).

Often, activists had before them the task of convincing more reticent female coworkers of the importance of organization in the face of prevailing popular ideologies which portrayed unions as disruptive, incendiary, or a violation of individual freedom. Aware of the sentiments to be overcome regarding unionization, O'Reilly outlined her ideas comparing the "coercion of trade unions" to the coercion by "morganized competition" (a reference to the businessman J. P. Morgan and the coercive nature of the industrial workplace characterized by tyrannical foremen, machinery speed-ups, and extreme regimentation) forcing young girls to work endless hours or starve (n.d. "Coercion of Trade Unions"). In O'Reilly's mind, the distinction was clear: "The struggle [is] between the Unionist and Non-Unionis[t]. It is a struggle to decide whether all men and women shall be prevented from working under bad conditions, or whether all men and women shall be driven to do so" (n.d., "Coercion of Trade Unions"). In an appeal to workers reluctant to join forces with their coworkers, the WTUL distributed a flier around 1910 that depicted a young girl standing in front of a large and stern-looking man sitting behind a desk. The flier read: "Dealing with the Individual. Is this an even Bargain?" (papers of the National Women's Trade Union League Papers, reel 4). This image articulated the inequality—in other words, class difference—between worker and boss, and reinforced the notion that there is strength in numbers. The flier communicated that a worker acting alone could easily be manipulated or simply fired. The implied answer to the problem posed on the flier was mobilization for collective action against the powers of manufacturers and owners who relied on their labor in order to keep factories running at full speed.

The worker organization of the time period that most embodied class solidarity was the Industrial Workers of the World (IWW). The IWW organized unskilled workers, immigrants, blacks, female and male laborers, and housewives in their struggles against employers. The organization was known for its bottom-up organizing in which the workers themselves shared leadership and learned through firsthand experience. Cole notes how the rhetoric of solidarity functioned by identifying for listeners their role as the producers of society's wealth (1978, 122). During a strike of mill workers in Lawrence, Massachusetts, in which strikers were held back by soldiers (see Photo 4.4), IWW leaders rallied the group with this reminder: "Can they [industrialists] weave cloth with soldiers' bayonets or policemen's clubs? . . . Did they dig coal with bayonets in the miners' strikes or make steel or run trains with bayonets?" (Flynn 1955, 135).

The rhetoric of solidarity also convinced listeners of the necessity of collective action. "An injury to one is an injury to all," proclaimed a May 1909 issue of *Industrial Worker* (quoted in Cole 1978, 121). "The vision of the future, when all the workers in *all industries* will be united in *one union* should fire the heart of every man and woman worthy of the name. Then, and only then, will the workers control industry with a grip of steel, and the whining of the employers and their agents will be a mere breath against the storm!"

Solidarity was also expressed in songs that established group identity, motivated group action, and reaffirmed the workers' persistence in achieving equality. The IWW, often referred to as the "troubadours of discontent," were known for their songs which were published and distributed to thousands of members in *The Little Red Songbook* (Cole 1978, 233). Women of the WTUL also expressed solidarity through enthusiastic songs and chants such as "Song No. 1," which reinforced a belief in solidarity and emphasized (perhaps for the still somewhat wary) the necessity of the union: "Put your trust in union, and work with heart and mind; / Opposing all oppression, leaving every fear behind; / All of us believers in union" (1911). Forging a resolute group identity as the producers of society's wealth was a similarly important task, which was in part accomplished through "Song No. 2," written by a well-known writer and socialist, Charlotte Perkins Gilman. As the second verse goes: "The world's life hangs on your right hand, / Your strong right hand, your skilled right hand, / You hold the whole world in your hand. / See to it what you do!" (1911).[26]

If cross-class or reformist-oriented organizations could be faulted for their lack of attention to class issues, working-class organizations, especially the IWW, often focused exclusively on economic issues at the ex-

PHOTO 4.4   State militia confronting wool-mill strikers in Lawrence, Massachusetts, in 1912. Walter P. Reuther Library, Wayne State University, Detroit, Michigan.

pense of gender-specific concerns. Though the IWW was one of the few labor organizations that actively recruited women workers and workers' wives, it often fell short of acknowledging the special needs of women in a culture still greatly marked by sex differences.

The "rebel girl," Elizabeth Gurley Flynn, an IWW activist committed to both women's liberation and worker liberation, set herself the task of recruiting women by appealing to their concerns as wives, mothers, and homemakers *of the working class*. In her speeches and writings, Flynn talked about the "[l]oveless marriages, household drudgery, acceptance of loathsome familiarities, unwelcome childbearing . . . [that have] marred the mind, body, and spirit of women" (1916, 135). The task, according to Flynn, was to overcome sexist stereotypes and social conditioning that relegated women to the domestic sphere and to give women equal opportunities for involvement in IWW meetings and actions. Flynn also took up the cause of birth control, which she viewed as the "most fundamental of all the claims made by women" (quoted in Tax 1980, 156). More than a woman's issue, birth control was a class issue, a "needed reform that could lessen the poverty and hardship of working-class life, especially for women, and enable them to be freer to fight" (Tax 1980, 158).

The IWW was also one of the few labor organizations to include black and immigrant workers in its efforts. Particularly during its early years (1903–1915), the WTUL was not known for its inclusion of black women workers. The shirtwaist makers' revolt of 1909–10 brought the issue of union discrimination to a head as owners recruited black women to replace striking women. The League responded by soliciting the strikebreakers to join the union. The appeals were not warmly received but rather were seen as opportunistic on the part of League organizers who had previously excluded black workers from union involvement (Foner 1979, 339–141). Only in the mid- to late teens did the League's organ, *Life and Labor*, begin to address the concerns of black women workers in earnest. In contrast, the IWW established a policy of inclusion in its 1905 bylaws: "[N]o working man or woman shall be excluded from membership because of creed or color" (Foner 1976, 108). Five years later, the IWW began actively recruiting black members through leaflets, pamphlets, and through the IWW's Southern publication, *Voice of the People*. IWW members were encouraged to view race discrimination as yet another way for capitalists to "divide and conquer" the working class, to keep workers fighting among themselves while capitalists reaped the benefits. The IWW recruited black members through fliers such as the one that noted, "If you are a wage worker you are welcome in the IWW halls, no matter what your color. By this you may see that the IWW is not a white man's union, not a black man's union, not a red man's union, but a working man's union. All of the working class in one big union" (quoted in Foner 1976, 110, 111).

By creating solidarity rhetorically, wage-earning women articulated agency in collective terms thus underscoring the systemic nature of their experiences, which required actions extending beyond the limits of the liberal individual. Solidarity among women was not unproblematic but often was complicated by issues surrounding race, gender, and class. Portrayals in popular magazines such as *McClure's* stood in sharp contrast to the workers' own rhetorical self-definitions, focusing on select workers who were meant to stand in for the entire working class. These individuals demonstrated the success of ideals such as hard work and thrift which enabled individuals to better themselves within the current system. The emphasis on values and ideals elided underlying material institutions and the need for collective confrontation in order to challenge discriminations that were systemic and deeply entrenched.

Meanwhile, the actual words of wage-earning women and girls reveal a different reality: The vast majority of workers suffered at the hands of employers in factories and in company-owned towns, and they were angry about the starvation wages, dangerous work conditions, and "idleness of loafers" who benefited from their toils. Through speeches, testimonies, songs, union involvement, and not least of all, through their daily experiences on the shop floor, workers learned valuable lessons regarding the need for solidarity and a collective agency capable of confronting deeply entrenched systems and institutions.

Engaging Labor Power Through Physical Solidarity

Wage-earning women and girls also realized the importance of their physical presence in communicating their solidarity and power to the public and to their bosses. In describing a strike of garment workers led by the ILGWU Cloak and Suit Tailors' Local 9 in New York, Rose Schneiderman asserted that the women "did such splendid picket work that nobody else could get up to the shop, and the employer had to take them back" ("Report of Interstate Conference of the National WTUL" 1908, 21). The importance of worker unity also became startlingly clear on occasions when it was absent. The disappointing experience of waitresses who struck Conrad's lunch room in New York City in 1914 offers a clear example of the necessary difference between establishing rhetorical and material solidarity. The waitresses stood together in their dissatisfaction with pay cuts and fines. As O'Reilly recounted, "Every girl had some grievances" (1914, 247). Yet in order for the strike to be successful by achieving the girls' demands for wage raises, rest time, and reduced fines, workers needed more than symbolic agreement. Physical solidarity in the form of a walkout was necessary. But as O'Reilly related, "When the time came to walk out only seven girls could command the courage to do it. Six stayed put and lost the strike for the others and all respect for themselves" (247).

More often, workers demonstrated their willingness to walk out of the workplace arm in arm with their coworkers. In her testimony to the Chicago WTUL strike committee, Rosa Greenfield, a button worker in Chicago, told of her astonishment upon finding that her paycheck amounted to $1.50 for backing one hundred vests. She told the foreman that she would not work for $1.50 and she "talked to the other girls and told them to come out with me and so we all left" ("Meeting of the Strike Committee"). Marie Pofelski, a pocket maker who worked alongside Rosa Greenfield at the same Chicago factory, B. Kuppenheimer's, related her own experience as workers began to walk out: ". . . and then the great strike came,—not just the separate little strikes—but one whole strike. When the foreman heard us all talking about it, he said, 'Girls, you can have your pockets and your cent back again if you'll stay,' but just then there was a big noise outside and we all rushed to the windows[,] there we see the police beating the strikers,—clubbing them on our account and when we saw that, we went out" ("Meeting of the Strike Committee").

Broom makers in Chicago demonstrated similar solidarity in 1914. The foreman singled out workers who were suspected of attending a union meeting and ordered them "to go home and stay there" (Franklin 1914, 294). Much to the foreman's surprise, the "whole force turned and went with them" (294). These and countless other examples demonstrate the "sticking capacity"[27] of workers who readily expressed solidarity physically as well as rhetorically.

As their testimonies indicated, it was primarily through collective absence (or confrontation, as the case may be) that workers were able to force owners' hands. Striking waitresses in Minneapolis picketed the sidewalk in front of Dayton's department store where they worked and explained their grievances to potential customers entering the establishment. The women were so successful at "drawing customers away from the restaurant . . . that after a week the Dayton management asked for a conference and matters were settled satisfactorily" ("Department Store Waitresses Win Increase," 141). Corset workers also witnessed the power of physical solidarity in their September 1915 strike in Springfield, Massachusetts. As workers began to walk out of the factory, the Bay State Corset Company offered a two-dollar bonus to employees who would bring in strikebreakers. But the "pickets were so numerous that they could and did form a human chain a block square around the factory," thus preventing any scabs from entering. At this, "[T]he management began to see that some reply would have to be made to the demands of the girls," and thus a settlement was won (Field 1915, 169).

An extended testimony in the August 1914 issue of *Life and Labor* provides yet another inspiring example of the willingness with which workers exercised their power as producers. In the account, the narrator explained how she stood up to the boss who harassed the less assertive workers. The details of the confrontation brilliantly clarify the essential nature of extra-discursive protest actions.

> [The boss said,] "You mind your own business, making trouble here. You're satisfied with your pay, ain't you?" and I says, "Yes, I'm satisfied with my pay, but the other girls' pay is my business, too." He got mad, and he says to me, "Get out." And so I quit workin' and go home, and they told me after I was gone everybody in that shop quit workin', too, and says they won't do a stitch until I comes back. And so the boss he had to send for me, and we had a shop meetin' and a committee goes to the boss, and he raises the wages of the girls. Now we're organized fine, and everybody in our shop belongs to the union. ("Girls' Stories," 244)

Collective actions such as those of the waitresses, corset workers, and button workers extended beyond speech; they were persuasive insofar as they exerted *material* force that directly affected bosses' pocketbooks. Examining the impact of actions such as walkouts and strikes broadens our understandings of the role of objective structures in struggles for resistance and underscores the argument that words alone are not always enough to challenge work arrangements from which certain groups benefit materially.[28]

Such tactics resulted in tangible gains. Corset workers won a forty-eight-hour week for the same wages they had earned for fifty-four hours of work, charges for materials were reduced or dropped, and fines were abolished (Field 1915, 169). Shirtmakers in Philadelphia won increased wages, reduced hours, improved workplace conditions, and union recognition. Even office workers—considered "impossible to organize"—won an agreement with employers after a short walkout from their office in New York (Bean 1915, 7). These and countless other examples point to the concrete gains achieved through extraverbal tactics such as strikes and walkouts. In his detailed history of women in the American labor movement, Philip Foner notes that from the wave of strikes between 1909 and 1916, tens of thousands of female workers won reduced hours, at least 20 percent increase in pay, and guaranteed overtime pay. Perhaps most important, union membership, particularly in the garment trades, rose dramatically. Just prior to the famous Uprising of 30,000 in 1909, only 3,000 women belonged to unions in the garment industry. By late

1913, 63,872 women were listed as union members in New York State trade union records (Foner 1979, 373). Strong unions were central to maintaining newly won workers' rights and served as a stable ground and resource from which to launch future struggles.

By taking their collective identity "to the streets," vocalizing working-class solidarity, and establishing a physical presence, wage-earning women of the WTUL also defied the domesticating ideology found in magazines that targeted a working-class audience.

Upending the "Happy Home"

Through a rhetorical frame of domestication, mail-order magazines such as *Comfort*, *The People's Home Journal*, and *Home Life* privatized issues that were public in nature, and proposed apolitical and personalized solutions to problems whose remedy in truth required collective action. All three magazines regularly recognized their readers' desires for community and life betterment. *Comfort* provided numerous romance stories, while *The People's Home Journal* encouraged readers to become a part of the "Sunshine Society," to reach out to their neighbors, and to get their "heart . . . interested in the welfare of Others" ("Sunshine Work Now!," 1).

By acknowledging working-class hardships, mail order magazines opened a space in which to provide innocuous solutions as replacement for the collective confrontations occurring beyond their pages, which were successfully disrupting the industrial status quo. Hence, instead of joining a union, the *The People's Home Journal*'s Sunshine Society's regular columns encouraged readers to take faith in the transformative powers of the smile or an upbeat attitude. And, rather than depict physical confrontation with owners or foremen, *Comfort* demonstrated how couples overcame material hardships through their enduring love for one another or by making a happy home held together by smiles (Carpenter 1911; Fleming 1895; Townsend 1895). By emphasizing adjustments to one's inner self (attitudes, emotions), or one's private space (the home), these magazines advocated coping as a way to get by or make do within current social arrangements.

Activist wage-earning women of the early twentieth century, by contrast, called attention to the social nature of their work and home experiences, the interconnectedness between workplace and home front, and the ways these spheres were influenced by broad-reaching institutions and social relations. Further, activists emphasized the importance of solidarity to achieving *material change*, and painted vivid pictures of factory life that punctured images of a sunny society and a blissful home. Moreover, their persistent public presence in pickets, outdoor meetings, parades, and on street-corner soapboxes shattered the silence maintained by mail-order magazines when it came to women's public protest activities.

Solidarity for More Than Sunshine

"Sunshine doesn't fill your pay envelope" remarked a young glove maker who was on strike with 250 of her fellow workers at the Herzog factory in Chicago ("The Story of the Herzog Strike" 1915, 138). Such were the sentiments of tens of thousands of workers who transgressed gender norms, defied the orders of bosses, and risked imprisonment and beatings by police and company thugs in their struggles for social change that could be felt directly. For wage-earning activists, many of whom were young girls of fifteen or sixteen, the friendships and support experienced through organizations such as the WTUL were important and attracted those who may have been hesitant to became labor activists. But the goal of their solidarity did not stop at the metaphoric "gold in the smile" ("The Picture Before Us," 1913a). Rather, women of the WTUL organized for the kind of gold that would make a physical difference in their daily experiences: real wage increases, shorter hours, and a working experience free of the threat of bodily harm or death. Speaking for all workers, O'Reilly stated: "We have 9,000,000 aspiring souls, feeling, thinking, acting together to shorten the hours of labor, to establish a living wage, to improve the conditions of life and labor everywhere" (1911d). O'Reilly's demands emphasize how workers sought community in order to transform material conditions in addition to attitudes and emotional states.

In a speech to working girls around the early 1900s, Leonora O'Reilly encouraged her audience to see themselves as "part of the great economic world" (n.d., "Untitled Speech to a Working Girls' Club," 1). She specifically tied organization—i.e., trade union involvement—to material issues such as shortened hours, better wages, and safer conditions. Similarly, speaking to a group of shirtwaist makers in 1904, O'Reilly developed a theme of friendship and connected its positive connotations to the issue of trade unionism: "You have joined hands in the shop, you know as one link in the chain of industry you count for very little, you know you need the friendship or fellowship of the girl next [to] you and the girl next to her until your chain of fellowship shall be long and strong enough to encompass your trade" (O'Reilly 1904, 3). In a talk to college women, O'Reilly justified the need for unions to her potentially skeptical audience: "[T]he Trade worker sees by association benefits to be gained which he could not aspire to alone" (n.d., "Talk for College Women," 9). In these speeches, O'Reilly talked about how friendship fostered worker solidarity and aided workers in fighting for *economic* justice—"[I]n the chain of industry you count for very little." In contrast, *Comfort*, *Home Life*, and *The People's Home Journal* offered affective relations as a *domestic substitute* that worked at the level of attitudes and emotions—"[S]mile into someone's face. And give them something to smile about" ("Sunshine and Shut-Ins" 1911, 2). Where labor activists such as O'Reilly employed a collectivity to challenge the material systems that touched their lives, the mail-order magazines envisioned what could be called consolation communities in which difficulties would be mitigated by means of adjusting one's attitudes so that one fit into a system that remained in place.

Reconnecting Workplace Welfare to the "Comforts" of "Home Life"

Comfort, *Home Life*, and *The People's Home Journal* used the domestication frame to place heavy emphasis on the literal site of domesticity, the home, constructing the home as a site of tranquillity and bliss. For many working-class individuals, the home was indeed one of the few arenas of life where one could relax and enjoy some amount of autonomy. For many wage-earning women, however, images of a stable and comfortable home life did little to ameliorate the actual effects of endless hours spent in the factory. These activists knew that if they wanted to have the time or energy to enjoy being at home, they had to transform their experiences at work first.

When voicing their demands for change to bosses, legislators, and middle- and upper-class reformers, wage-earning women painted vivid portraits of their work experiences, and these rhetorically superseded the popularized images of the tranquil home. The testimonies provided in courts and to wealthy allies gave the workers a chance to detail their daily experiences and demonstrate the extent to which their work experiences permeated all areas of their lives. Anna Rudnitzky expressed the sentiments of thousands of young workers in a statement that appeared in *Life and Labor:* "Life means so much, it holds so much, and I have no time for any of it; I just work. . . . In the busy time I work so hard; try to make the machine run faster and faster because then I can earn some money and I need it, and then night comes, and I am tired out and I go home and I am too weary for anything but supper and bed" (Rudnitzky 1912, 99).

Rudnitzky's comments imply that wage-earning League activists like her felt the desire for cultural and recreational activities that would add quality and texture to their lives—if only they weren't so tired. Clearly they were aware that the shape and extent of their experiences outside the factory (in the home, at a movie house or museum) could not be separated from, indeed were directly affected by, their experiences inside the factory.

In a tone similarly marked by weariness—but not complete debility—Myrtle Whitehead, a member of the Crown, Cork and Seal Operatives Union of Baltimore, broaches the question of leisure in her article, "What About Vacations?" Working women need a vacation, Whitehead asserted, but their "hopes are useless." "Our wages have been so small and we have had to put every cent into the home to help support the family. . . . [O]ur employer is so rushed with work which must be finished before winter, that if we should take a week or two off we should probably be discharged" (1914). Whitehead's answer to her question was unequivocal: women must join the union. She concluded, "Let us, then, unite in sisterly love, to obtain justice, so that we may the better enjoy the life God gave us to enjoy."

In her description of the average wage-earning woman's living circumstances, "The Need for Co-operation Among Working Girls," Pauline Newman made a similar plea for the necessity of organization. Newman focused on the most basic right demanded by women, the right to earn a living wage: "What kind of a life . . . can they lead" without a decent wage, she asked. Her answer: "A life which is a mere existence, that is all. . . . They live on a five-cent breakfast, ten-cent lunch and a twenty-cent dinner; live in a dingy room without air and without comfort; wear clothes of cheap material. . . . Their whole life is cheap from beginning to end. Deprived of sunshine and fresh air, no time for recreation, no time for rest, they have only time for work" (1914, 313).

In the same year that Newman, Whitehead, and thousands of other working girls and women were affirming the need for life's basic *material* necessities, a *People's Home Journal* editorial, "The Picture Before Us," tells readers, "Income is not wages and salary alone. . . . The only safe securities are personality, the personal force, the gold mine of the mind. Everyone owns this mental gold mine, the undeveloped potentiality of the soul" (1914b). Juxtaposing this sage advice with the words of the workers themselves underscores the inadequacy—if not outright vacuity—of advice provided by popular magazines such as *The People's Home Journal*, *Comfort*, and *Home Life*.

In Leonora O'Reilly's fierce language, the conditions of workers was "wage slavery," conveying the notion that as long as workers toiled in their present conditions, they could not be free in any realm of life. In an essay written for the Socialist paper the *New York Call*, O'Reilly referred to the "horrible death dealing conditions workers are subjected to all over the world." Workers were "confined in fire traps, barred in . . . inflammable factories . . . poisoned by phosphorous and lead until their bones decay, in order to earn a scanty living" (1911a, 2). Written in a similar style, O'Reilly's February 1911 article in *The American Suffragette*, "Looking over the Fields," served as a harbinger for the deadly shirtwaist factory fire the next month:

> Production never ends; the producers are crushed in the process. Men, women, and even children of the modern proletariat, since the advent of machinery, bear their heavy cross of painful labor through the portal of the mill and factory along their via dolorosa, to the modern Calvary, where enforced labor, tearing of flesh, straining of nerve, breaking of bones, loss of limbs, mortal entanglement in machinery is their Crucifixion; while hunger gnaws the stomach and benumbs the brain (1911b, 8).

The hollowness of The Sunshine Society's advice to "scatter smiles" is brought into sharper relief when juxtaposed with O'Reilly's pointed language and vivid imagery.

The experiences of mining families in Michigan and Colorado point up the connections between home- and worklife even more markedly. Home for these families was not a safe haven to be autonomously molded into a space of tranquillity, but was wholly inseparable from the horrors of daily life in the mine. In mining communities from the Mesabi Range in northeastern Minnesota to Calumet, Michigan, and Ludlow, Colorado, homes and stores were owned and controlled by mining companies. As Mrs. M. H. Thomas, wife of a Ludlow miner, pointed out in "An American Pogrom," "A man dare not report a piece of unsafe roofing here, he would just be fired and blacklisted if he did" (1914, 172). Tax notes that in the Mesabi iron mines in Minnesota, bosses offered a favorable work spot below the ground to workers who would grant sexual access to the worker's wife or daughter (1980, 128).

In many of these communities, workers who struck for safer mining conditions were summarily evicted from their homes. Women and children were not immune to the violent tactics of company-hired gunmen, detectives, and even the National Guard. In Ludlow, striking workers, evicted from their homes, set up tent camps for their families. On April 20, 1914, National Guard gunmen set fire to the tent village, sending families fleeing to the hills. All in all, twenty-six women and children were killed in what came to be known as the Ludlow Massacre.

Not content to passively accept such abuses, working-class women in mining communities and company-owned towns organized as housewives and as workers. Often led by the indomitable Mother Jones, wives of strikers fought off scabs by beating them with rolling pins, throwing rocks, and banging pots and pans. The IWW devoted considerable attention to organizing wives of strikers, who, kept busy with homemaking and child-rearing, were all too often cut off from strike activity. "We knew that to leave [wives of strikers] at home alone, isolated from the strike activity, a prey to worry, affected by the complaints of tradespeople, landlords, priests and ministers, was dangerous to the strike," explained Elizabeth Gurley Flynn, a primary IWW organizer of women (Tax 1980, 255).

In their neighborhoods, women identified with each other on the basis of their common experiences as homemakers. They built neighborhood networks and, in the early years of the century, organized and protested rises in prices and rent hikes (Orleck 1995, 26). Though many defined themselves primarily in terms of the domestic sphere, women in working-class neighborhoods did not confine themselves to the home. In fact, the home itself was often transformed into a site from which public organizing and agitation sprang. Ardis Cameron notes that the success of the Lawrence textile strikers' uprising "depended on women's use of female domains to maintain order, get out the news, transport and distribute circulars and dodgers, prevent defeatist rumors, and organize demonstrations" (1985, 53). As homemakers and as workers, women and girls demonstrated, boycotted, and spoke in outdoor meetings and on street corners, thus creating a public presence and calling attention to the ways that they and their families were exploited for the "luxury of loafers" (O'Reilly 1911c).

Conclusion

This chapter compared wage-earning and middle-class women's protest rhetoric to the ideological frames of various popular magazines, and also distinguished between the strategies employed by activists from differing class backgrounds. Both middle-class and wage-earning activists employed rhetoric that refuted—and sometimes reflected—the naturalizing, universalizing, and domesticating ideologies advocated in mass-circulation magazines of the early twentieth century. Differences among activists' rhetorical emphases and strategies often stemmed from the very different worlds these women came from. Well-to-do allies of the WTUL often downplayed the necessity of class struggle and solidarity, instead emphasizing universal sisterhood and cultural uplift. In contrast, working-class activists stressed class differences and the need for collective actions that challenged the economic system which exploited them as workers.

Despite the existence of some class conflict within the WTUL, the efforts of League allies should not be underestimated. In addition to providing strike support and organizational and leadership skills, these middle- and upper-class reformers contributed essential funds that kept the organization alive in its beginning years. Even though the organizational efforts of the IWW and some independent worker-formed organizations played important roles in wage-earning women's struggles, the WTUL remained the primary organization of support for wage-earning women and girls who were systematically excluded from much AFL labor organizing.

Even though strategic and tactical differences among League activists did not always follow class lines; and even though League rhetoric did not always challenge dominant ideologies regarding women and their roles in society, generally, wage-earning activists' emphasis on class conflict represented a primary difference between the rhetoric of League allies and workers, as well as between the workers and the popular magazines. By revealing specific people and institutions behind social forces, wage-earning activists highlighted the human constructedness of exploitative work relations and thus countered the naturalizing frame used by the *Atlantic Monthly*. Similarly, by pointing to differing and conflicting human interests as stemming from different material circumstances, these women challenged the universalization frame used by *McClure's*. Through a public show of solidarity, working-class women defied the domestication frame used by *Comfort*, *The People's Home Journal*, and *Home Life*, which placed them in the home and privatized their problems.

The texts examined in this chapter expand the existing body of work on feminist protest rhetoric by including the unique strategies and tactics employed by activists who were influenced by their experiences as women *and* as workers. Activists such as Leonora O'Reilly, Rose Schneiderman, Pauline Newman, and countless others strove not only to transform oppressive images and cultural norms that regulated their lives as women, but also to improve the actual conditions that shaped their lives as workers such as better wages and safer workplaces.

Karlyn Kohrs Campbell's work on feminist rhetoric has played a key role in broadening notions of rhetorical effectiveness by emphasizing the unique difficulties that women faced as public speakers in the early twentieth century. Yet the emphasis on the rhetoric of predominantly middle-class white women is premised on an ideology of liberal individualism that elides the impact of material institutions on individuals' lives.[29] Wage earners of the WTUL, while fighting for equality explicitly as women, could not afford to ignore the ways that they were exploited as workers. Their daily experiences in the factory and tenement led them to articulate their demands in collective and material terms. They protested not only as women who were oppressed by sexual norms but as female wage earners who were collectively exploited as laborers.

Examining the protest tactics of wage-earning women provides a way to explore the nature of resistance undertaken through subjective agency within a context constrained, in part, by objective structures. Much current cultural and rhetorical scholarship emphasizes the ways that individuals resist through various micropolitical actions such as consumption behaviors, subversive readings, or lifestyle alterations. This individualized view of agency is debilitating in that it concedes the predominance of dominant hegemonic institutions and asserts, in effect, that collective confrontation is outdated or ineffective and therefore should be replaced with individualized strategic strikes in which individuals make the best of their given situation. Similarly, the consumption-based view of agency, a perspective that focuses on individuals as agents of consumption instead of as labor, downplays or completely ignores the role of material elements—structures and institutions existing external to but understood through human language—in subordinate groups' attempts at resistance or transformation. Rather, oppression and resistance are framed in individualized and discursive terms, and liberation is necessarily understood in terms of the skill of the autonomous speaker, or the ability to render ironic readings or playful parodies (see Fiske 1986, 1989; Butler 1990). This chapter argues for the continued relevance of a collective labor-based agency to be engaged both rhetorically and extraverbally in struggles against broad-reaching and deeply entrenched institutions of exploitation.

In this book a theory has been advanced regarding the relationship between subjective agency and objective structures. Three primary lessons can be drawn from an examination of the protest tactics of wage-earning and middle-class women of the early twentieth century:

1. Rhetorical intervention in the form of holding meetings, distributing fliers and pamphlets, giving speeches, and telling stories played a central role in shaping worker solidarity, motivating workers to struggle for improvement and giving workers the confidence necessary to take risks involved in social struggle.

2. Rhetorical intervention was often preceded by, accompanied by, or further fortified by firsthand experience on the shop floor. It was in and through women's experiences as workers that various types of rhetorical intervention held meaning for them. Often, firsthand experience was the initial motivator that propelled women and girls to participate rhetorically—in meetings, conversations etc. Other times, workers had to be persuaded—through conversations, speeches, pamphlets, fliers—of the necessity of collective struggle.

3. Workers' rhetorical interventions often were not sufficient to enact social change but necessarily had to be accompanied by extraverbal confrontation such as walkouts and strikes, in which

collective absence from the shop floor was the workers' most persuasive tool. Halting production in this manner spoke loudly and reached recalcitrant bosses in ways that a public speech may not.

Thus, a labor-based agency was formed and engaged through both rhetorical and extraverbal intervention. Traditional means of persuasion—speeches, pamphlets—were necessary to combat and upend popular hegemonic ideologies such as naturalization, universalization, and domestication, and to convince reticent workers to join the struggle. Yet words were not always necessary to convince workers of the need for struggle nor were they always sufficient to alter material conditions. As the countless examples provided throughout the chapter demonstrated, women were often awakened to the need to organize in and through their daily experiences on the shop floor. Witnessing or feeling directly the toil and unscrupulous discrimination of factory work was often sufficient to move workers to do something to alter the situation. Similarly, firsthand engagement in a strike or walkout had an extending persuasive effect: strikers remarked how their participation in a strike further deepened their commitment to the cause.[30] Finally, once persuaded—either through rhetorical intervention or from direct experience—workers became aware of the difficulty, if not futility, of fighting their battle exclusively on discursive grounds. In conjunction with outdoor meetings, speeches, testimonies, and pamphleting, wage-earning women communicated through extraverbal tactics that halted production and thus spoke loudly to manufacturers concerned with the bottom line.

The previous chapters have examined the relationships between popular portrayals of women as workers, mothers, and activists and the self-definitions offered by women themselves through their struggles for political and economic equality. The popular and protest texts were situated within the specific socioeconomic context which in part influenced the production and reception of the discourses. Chapters 1–3 explored how popular magazines responded to women's labor and suffrage struggles and how women's protest rhetoric in turn responded to or resisted popular portrayals by subverting the images of natural womanhood, universal sisterhood, or domesticated worker. The present chapter delved more deeply into women's protest rhetoric, elaborating class differences and examining the centrality of extra-discursive tactics through which wage earners engaged themselves physically as laborers.

Through these examinations, this project seeks to demonstrate that valuable lessons can be learned regarding the influences of popular culture and the nature of resistance that are relevant in the late twentieth century. In the final chapter parallels are drawn between early-twentieth-century popular rhetorics and those circulating in contemporary mass-media outlets in order to demonstrate the continued influence of such hegemonic ideologies, despite substantial changes in the nature of mass communication over the past 100 years. Further: In light of continued hegemonic ideologies that justify unequal relations, seek to compell conformity to the status quo, and quell dissent; and perhaps more fundamentally, in light of the continued existence of deeply entrenched and broad-reaching institutions that exploit groups at a material level, a labor-based agency is still of relevance, indeed, a necessity in late-twentieth-century society. Moreover, this labor-based agency must be engaged at the extraverbal as well as rhetorical level.

Notes

1. The WTUL speeches and pamphlets on which this chapter relies are archived in an extensive collection, "The Papers of the Women's Trade Union League and Its Principal Leaders." This collection is on microfilm and can be obtained through interlibrary loan service from the Schlesinger Library, Radcliffe Institute, Harvard University, Cambridge, Massachusetts, and also from the Library of Congress. The Leonora O'Reilly Papers, the Rose Schneiderman Papers, and the National Women's Trade Union League Papers are part of this collection. This chapter also relies on speeches and articles that appeared in *Life and Labor*, an organ of the WTUL, available through interlibrary loan service.

2. See for example Cathcart 1972, 1980; Wilkinson 1976, McGee 1975; Lucas 1980. These works are some of the most well known attempts at delineating the parameters of social-movement studies. While they differ in other regards, all emphasize the *discursive* behaviors of members of social movements.

3. See Dye 1975a, 1975b, 1980. See also the work of Robin Miller Jacoby (1975), who provides insights on the WTUL members' suffrage activities.

4. In recent years, feminists both within and outside the academy have debated issues surrounding how and when women may speak on behalf of other women (Alcoff 1988, 1991/92; Biesecker 1992; Bordo 1990; Combahee River Collective 1983; Di Stephano 1990; Weedon 1987). As many have usefully pointed out, in order to have a *woman's movement* that addresses the needs and concerns of *women*, we cannot afford to retreat to individualized subject positions in which each woman can only "speak for herself." Such a move is not only impossible but politically debilitating. As Alcoff points out, "What can we demand in the name of women if 'women' [as a group] do not exist and demands in their name simply reinforce the myth that they do?" (1991/92, 420). Yet in order to recognize the diversity among women and to rectify the class and race discrimination that has occurred within the women's movement, we must be mindful of how our location as speaker bears upon our words and shapes the meaning of what is said.

5. See Aune (1994). Aune notes that one of the major rhetorical problems of Marxism is that it "tends to see the need for revolution as self-evident, without considering that people might need to be persuaded to that belief" (14).

6. See also Foner (1977) for an extensive account of the first women labor activists including those from the Lowell textile mills.

7. See Foner 1979; Kessler-Harris 1975; Payne 1988; Tax 1980.

8. See Campbell 1989, v. 1 and Kraditor 1965 for the ways woman's movement orators employed "arguments from expediency" to link the cult of True Womanhood to women's political involvement.

9. The limited success of the uprising was due in part to the process of organizing and settling shop by shop, which undermined collective strength. Also, the WTUL had not been inviting to black shirtwaist workers before the strike, and thus had a difficult time gaining their support during the strike. Finally, the AFL and the ILGWU provided only limited support to the group of largely immigrant female strikers (Foner 1979).

10. Not all scholars agree on the nature and extent of class conflict within the WTUL. Payne (1988) offers a more positive perspective on the cultural activities of the WTUL and while she does not ignore class differences, she sees the League's emphasis on feminist (and religious and ethnic) solidarity as, in part, a successful move to overcome these differences. Additionally, Payne asserts that, "[w]ithin the League, there was only sparing recourse to the language of class conflict, a consideration that implicitly recognized that discord within the organization could not be reduced to a matter of class struggle" (60). Other historians have highlighted wage earning members who frequently voiced frustration at allies' emphasis on sisterhood and inattention to the ways that class confounded notions of gender solidarity (Dye 1975a, 1980; Orleck 1995; Tax 1980).

11. In *Reform, Labor, and Feminism*, Payne describes in detail the arguments and motivations of Robins' "sacred motherhood" (1988, 117–154).

12. It can be debated whether working-class women identified themselves primarily as women or as workers. Eisenstein (1983), Jacoby (1975), and Payne (1988) imply in their work that wage-earning women identified strongly with the norms of True Womanhood and most often viewed their work experiences as temporary stints before marriage. The accounts of Orleck (1995) and Tax (1980) provide evidence that for at least a few labor activists, class was a central if not overriding issue in their struggles for justice. I simply wish to point to the ways that women variously negotiated their struggles as women and as workers through their public arguments for change.

13. In her comprehensive study of the NWP, Ford notes that the "banners were very shrewd, and often quoted Wilson himself, as in 'Liberty Is A Fundamental Demand Of The Human Spirit.' On Lincoln Day the banners asked Wilson, 'Why Are You Behind Lincoln? Lincoln Stood For Woman Suffrage 60 Years Ago'" (1991, 126).

14. Basch 1990; Dye 1980, 88–92; Foner 1979, 324–346; Orleck 1995, 62; Tax 1980, 214–221.

15. At times, however, these actions on the part of the WTUL bordered on patronizing. A report by the Chicago WTUL strike committee emphasized the "twofold task of picketing with the girls and patrolling the streets for their protection . . . It is perhaps the most important service that any group of public spirited women can render their younger sisters in times of industrial struggle" ("WTUL of Chicago, Official Report of the Strike Committee," 10).

16. The testimony, which appears in the collection of Leonora O'Reilly's papers, is dated "1912 or 1913?"

17. At one point, allies offered Schneiderman, Lemlich, and Fannia Cohn opportunities for college educations. Each turned down the offers on the grounds that it would not be right to pursue a college education while the majority of women of their class lacked even an elementary education (see Orleck 1995).

18. *New York Call*, December 22, 1909, quoted in Basch (1990).

19. In *Diary of a Shirtwaist Striker*, Malkiel describes another well-known fundraiser that was put on by Alva Belmont at the Hippodrome in New York City on December 5, 1909: "Many [of the workers] came without dinner, but the collection baskets had more pennies than anything else in them—it was our girls themselves who helped to make it up, and yet there were so many rich women present. And I'm sure the speakers made it plain to them how badly the money is needed, then how comes it that out of the $300 collected there should be $70 in pennies?" (107, 108).

20. The cap maker Rose Schneiderman eventually occupied a position in the Roosevelt administration, the glove maker Agnes Nestor was on the federal Women's Committee, and the shoe worker Mary Anderson directed the Department of Labor's Women's Bureau (Tax 1980, 121).

21. See Cloud 1996; Hall et al. 1978, 181–217; Stabile 1995; Zinn 1990, 118–136.

22. The 1996 United Nations Human Development Report states that the combined wealth of 358 billionaires is equal to the total income of the poorest 45 percent of the world's population.

23. See Cloud (1999) for a clearly elucidated distinction between "identity" and "interests." Identities are "discursive constructions that enable us to articulate a sense of self based on mutually recognizable symbolic characteristics," while "interests are "desires and aspirations produced out of needs shared in the real, material world, in common by a class of people."

24. Indeed, uplift and assimilation became a reality for some of the WTUL wage-earning activists. In particular, Rose Schneiderman—at one time an outspoken socialist—rose through the WTUL ranks and eventually occupied a governmental post in the Roosevelt administration. See Tax 1980, 95–124.

25. This description of wage-earning women's protest rhetoric is not meant to imply that all wage earning activists employed this style in all situations. The history of working class activists' struggles for social change is rich and varied with women and girls variously interspersing traditional arguments with more transgressive arguments and tactics. Yet, the speeches, testimonies, and letters of working class women repeatedly point to their frustrations with more traditional approaches to change. And the hundreds of strikes and walkouts in which they participated indicate working class women's willingness to rely on more confrontational measures in order to achieve changes that affected their abilities to feed, clothe, and provide a home for their families.

26. Other songs include "The Maids' Defiance" (Tax 1980, 136) and "Toilers, Arise" (Dreier 1912). Slogans include "Don't be a scab" (Dreier 1912) and "An injury to one is the concern of all."

27. Melinda Scott used this phrase to describe the women of the hatting industry who stood by their male coworkers throughout the six-month struggle for workplace rights (1915).

28. In this context, it is interesting to note the connotation of the phrase "lip service" as in "The politicians are only giving lip service to the needs of the poor." The phrase implies that the words spoken are empty, meaning they don't necessarily have any effect on the material world, or the objective living and working conditions that people face day to day.

29. Barbara Biesecker (1992) offers a similar critique of Campbell, although her suggested method for social change differs substantially from that proposed here.

30. Rose Schneiderman tells of the transformation that took place during a strike of underwear workers in 1907. Before the strike, "The women looked upon each other as enemies because one might get a better bundle of work done than the other. But now, since they had organized and had fought together, there was a kinship among them" (quoted in Orleck 1995, 47).

5

Protest and Popular Culture: Bridging Past and Present

Though much in the way of workplace and communication culture has changed since Clara Lemlich called out for a general strike on a November day in 1909, important lessons can be learned from a study of protest and popular-culture rhetorics of the early twentieth century. The previous chapters sought to establish a two-part argument concerning the relationship between social movements and the popular media that portray them. First, popular images were examined in order to explore how the persuasive strategies of naturalization, universalization, and domestication were employed in order to perpetuate gender, race, and class inequalities even as space was made to acknowledge changing social relations and forces vying for economic and political transformation. Second, the self-definitions were examined of protesting women and girls who, in contrast to images promulgated in popular media, crafted themselves rhetorically as laboring agents in order to resist popular ideologies. Their actions provide a way to examine the relationship between "subjective agencies and objective structures" (Aune 1994) and the necessity of extra-discursive actions in attempts to alter structures and institutions that influence material well-being and that benefit from popular hegemonic ideologies in the first place.

In this final chapter, I hope to draw out two important lessons that can be learned from the historical study that was the subject of this book. The first concerns the persistence of popular ideologies; the second, the relevance of a laboring agency and extra-discursive tactics to bring about social change. Important changes as well as persistent similarities in both the workplace and in communication technologies will be accounted for in drawing parallels between early- and late-twentieth-century popular and protest rhetorics.

Lesson 1: The Persistence of Popular Ideologies

Despite important changes in the production, transmission, and reception of mass communication arising out of technological advances since the early 1900s, the early-twentieth-century magazines examined in Chapters 1–3 can deepen understanding of the origins of contemporary mass-communication portrayals of social dissent. Early-twentieth-century mass-media outlets continued in a more widespread and systematic manner the nascent trends in nineteenth-century magazines and newspapers. Early-1900s popular magazines laid the groundwork for contemporary hegemonic ideologies that diffuse, dematerialize, or redefine dissent so as to frame counterhegemonic struggles in terms consonant with the status quo.

Some contemporary scholars have called for new concepts and theories for conceptualizing society in an era variously tagged "postindustrial," "post-Fordist," or "postmodern." The premise of *Protest and Popular Culture* is that the continuities are greater than the discontinuities. The attempt here is to demonstrate the continued salience of frameworks of analysis that call attention to the dialectical relationship between hegemonic ideologies and a socioeconomic context that continues to exploit labor and control life-sustaining resources in much the same way as was the case in the early twentieth century. Indeed, now more than ever, in light of new media technologies that provide a plethora of messages globally and instantaneously, scholars must continue to explore how popular ideologies naturalize class, race, and gender disparities, universalize ideals and values in service of the status quo, and domesticate dissent in order to redirect challenges to social institutions onto personal spaces.

Postmodern Ahistoricity and an Ideology of Naturalization

A present-day society increasingly characterized by workplace uncertainty, social diversity and antagonisms, thirty-second-soundbite packaged politics, and a multiplicity of contradictory consumer-oriented messages has led postmodern scholars and popular pundits alike to claim the end of the "grand narrative." By this they imply the inapplicability of totalizing claims or all-encompassing theories to explain such concepts as truth, reality, or justice. Jean-François Lyotard, perhaps the most well known elucidator of the "postmodern condition," advocates a localized and textualized politics over attempts to understand or intervene in systemic relations and the connections among various economic, social, and cultural realms (1984).

Along with other scholars of a postmodern bent (Foucault, Derrida, and Laclau), Lyotard argues against prescriptives applied universally, instead embracing multiple justices applied individually and locally. In this view, history—seen as social relations shaped by historical structures in identifiable and systematic ways—disappears under the weight of a social reality marked by a play of differences, ever-shifting localities that throw the notion of a reality outside of representation into radical question. The postmodern perspective points up the value of questioning the social constructedness and hidden assumptions of social theories, and recognizes voices and perspectives that had previously been denied a space in Enlightenment, liberal, and other explanatory discourses. Despite the value of this inclusion of previously excluded voices, it is argued here that the postmodern incredulity toward explanatory narratives erases a necessary context in which to understand and ground struggles for social change.

Contemporary society is indeed marked by increasing fragmentation, multiplicity, diversity, and indeterminacy as exemplified both in the workplace and through communication technologies. Workplace downsizing, job cuts, and layoffs are creating a workplace environment of uncertainty. A 1998 study conducted by the economists Geoffrey Paulin and Brian Riordon concluded that by all economic measures, young adults today are worse off than those in the preceding generation (Jorgensen, 4). Over the past 20 years, the continued decline in manufacturing jobs and growth of service sector and contingent jobs have translated into lower wages, minimal healthcare, and little opportunity for advancement for today's young-adult workforce.

Within this economic context, media outlets and new media technologies arguably contribute to feelings of alienation and social fragmentation, and foster a sense that little can be done to change current social arrangements. For instance, television and the Internet have radically transformed information flow, affecting the ways that individuals view political and social issues. In his study of the influence of television on modern politics, the political-communication scholar Roderick Hart asserts that the medium's ahistoricity—it's in-the-moment, here-and-now technology—fosters a cynical attitude toward politics (Hart 1994, 84). Politics relies on history, but television (and television viewers) eschew history as boring. "By offering us so many matters to contemplate," Hart observes, "television makes it hard, or profitless, to find the connective tissues. Television makes us atheoretical, just as it makes us ahistorical. It invites us to dwell in the moment and nowhere else" (86).

At the same time, the regularity of television's scheduled programming conveys a sense of "social fixity," of a "social world impervious to substantial change" (Gitlin 1987, 246). Even the notion of television "seasons" connotes the inevitability inherent in nature's regular and predictable change in weather patterns (Gitlin 1987, 246). Gitlin asserts that the "standardization" of television programming "help[s] confirm audiences in their sense of the rightness and naturalness of a world that, in only apparent paradox, regularly requires an irregularity, an unreliability, which it calls progress" (246). Television's format works in conjunction with content to keep controversial issues off of the agenda and to reaffirm the status quo as inevitable, always already there. Thus it can be said that television as a medium promotes a *naturalized* view of society through its multiple fragmented messages, which erase an understanding of historical constructedness, and through its regularity of programming, which instills a sense of fixity—one cannot change what has always been there.

Television and other new media technologies have certainly altered our understandings of social relations and have arguably contributed to a sense of fragmentation, multiplicity, and ahistoricity. Such feelings are compounded by insecurity, uncertainty, antagonism, and cynicism stemming from very real events in the broader economic and political contexts. In the midst of this environment, must we concede that totalizing explanations of history are outmoded or inapplicable?

On the contrary, we may view the postmodern retreat from systemic explanations of oppression and emancipation as *playing into the hands* of the hegemonic ideology of naturalization. Naturalization relies on its ability to obliterate history, to make particular social relations appear as though they had always already been there. The postmodern abandonment of systemic explanations upholds naturalization's omission of history through its rejection of "modern assumptions of social coherence and notions of causality in favour of multiplicity, plurality, fragmentation, and indeterminacy" (Best and Kellner 1991, 4). In fact, the postmodern "incredulity toward metanarratives" (Lyotard 1984, xxiv) creates an ahistorical understanding of social relations, one that fails to fully acknowledge and theorize a history of class exploitation and struggle that is complex and dialectical, yet real, in the sense that relations of production exist outside representation and require for their transformation more than textual subversion.

In the face of late-twentieth-century technologies that continue to shape our understandings of society, politics, and public participation, it is crucial to continue the project of historical contextualization. Technologies such as television and the Internet, which rely on in-the-moment, spontaneous, and instantaneous presentation of ideas and images, further enhance the rhetorical aims and effects of naturalization by denying the viewer a sense of past and future change, and denying the need for and possibility of conscious action within an extra-discursive context that is entrenched but alterable. Rather than celebrate the ahistoricizing or fragmenting nature of communication technologies, or acknowledge them as harbingers of a new era, we must continue to provide theoretical grounding on which to locate relations and systems within a specific historical context shaped by human interests and needs. Toward this end, symbolic analyses should represent what Thompson calls a "depth hermaneutics," which includes a social-historical analysis (production of message), a discursive analysis (content of message), and an analysis of interpretation (reception of message) (Thompson 1990, 281–291).

Chapter 1 examined the *Atlantic Monthly*, a prestigious mass-circulation magazine, in the early 1900s for the ways that work and gender relations were framed by an ideology of naturalization. The chapter located the magazine within a specific context of social upheaval and rapid industrial growth in order to explore how the magazine's images and accounts of women, labor, and suffrage responded to and transformed events beyond the magazine's pages. Chapter 4 examined the protest rhetoric of women and who girls who variously relied upon and also subverted the ideology of naturalization in their own rhetorical endeavors. The *Atlantic*'s framing of social disparities as inevitable and as part of a natural order represents the origins of contemporary popular discourses that continue to naturalize workplace and gender inequalities. Put differently, the *Atlantic* initiated the widespread use of a rhetorical strategy suited for television some thirty years prior to the medium's development and naturalization as a rhetorical frame remains particularly relevant in studies of a medium that dehistoricizes social events and "cements the obduracy of a social world" through its standardized programming (Gitlin 1987, 246).

The Predominance of Symbols and an Ideology of Universalization

In late-twentieth-century society, mass-communication networks from print to new media technologies continue to expand and transform personal and work relationships as well as public affairs. Amidst the advent of what has been dubbed the Information Age, scholars—self-proclaimed postmodernists and others—advance the symbolic—words, images, codes—as that which most shapes social relations and the psyche. This stance reveals itself in a variety of ways across numerous disciplines. Ludic feminisms emphasize a "politics of representation" in which playful symbolic subversions and bodily performance (for example, Butler's cross-dressing) are seen to be predominant modes of resistance. Butler advances parodic performance in order to destabilize the socially constructed male/female binary that regulates sexuality (1990).

Others emphasize how female readers use popular-culture texts and images for their own subversive ends (Penley 1992; Radway 1984). In communication studies, scholars have explored the "self-production of culture" and the ways that subordinate groups empower themselves through various cultural and consumption practices such as resistant readings, symbolic identifications, and window shopping (Brown 1994; Brummett 1991; Brummett and Duncan 1992; Fiske 1986; 1987, 1989; Grossberg 1984, 1989). And critical organizational-communication scholars have been interested in examining how communication creates and recreates organizational realities for members (Mumby 1988), with a focus on the "nature of power in interest representation, and the systems of interaction in which domination or representation occurs" (Deetz and Mumby 1990, 12).

Few would gainsay the observation that late-twentieth-century society is characterized, if not epitomized, by hypermediation. Beginning with the proliferation of newspapers and magazines in the early 1900s, to the growth of radio, television, and now the Internet, mass-communication outlets continue to provide the means to get a multitude of messages out to millions of people globally, thus transforming social relations, understandings, and behaviors in previously unimaginable ways. Roderick Hart boldly asserts, "Television has changed politics itself," transforming how we talk about politics and encouraging feelings of cynicism that discourage genuine political participation (1994, 6). Thompson elaborates on the ways electronic media "create new opportunities for individuals to act in response to others who are spatially and temporally remote" (1990, 232). For instance, widespread television coverage of the Vietnam War contributed, at least to an extent, to the growth in participation of the antiwar movement (Thompson 1990, 233, 234).[1] We can, and certainly must, acknowledge and continue to explore the growing and pervasive influence of symbolic forms on politics and workplace relations. Yet such endeavors should not then lead us to abandon studying or ignore the continued influence of extra-discursive phenomena on mediated messages and on social relations.

Postmodern and ludic celebrations of the symbolic and the related retreat from issues of materiality bolsters the hegemonic ideology of universalization and its conservative overtones as elaborated in Chapter 2. Universalization elides material phenomena by emphasizing the power of values and ideals to overcome material disparities. Universalization represents an idealizing rhetoric which decontextualizes and personalizes social struggle by stressing individual character and values that seemingly enable a transcendence of race, class, or gender discriminations. What gets obscured through such rhetorical framings is the social nature of oppression and the need for extra-discursive actions in order to alter discriminations that are systemic in origin and have systemic effects. Similar to naturalization, universalization is a hegemonic concept that remains relevant despite changes in media technologies. Indeed, such technological changes can be seen to exacerbate or accentuate the ideology of universalization insofar as media outlets such as television and the Internet emphasize the predominance and pervasiveness of symbols through their abilities to repeat, juxtapose, and transmit messages at rapid-fire pace without opening a space to contemplate a reality beyond such orgiastic displays. We need not acquiesce to this hypermediation and conclude that extra-discursive phenomena have no bearing on mediated messages in politics, personal relations, or the workplace. In the face of an increasingly mediated society, it remains important to analyze universalization and its idealizing effects and to confirm the centrality of material institutions and systems that shape and influence values and ideas that operate in service of the economic and political status quo.

Chapter 2 examined the popular muckraking journal *McClure's*, a periodical that focused more pointedly than the *Atlantic Monthly* on portrayals of women's labor and suffrage struggles. More than the *Atlantic*, *McClure's* quite openly addressed gender and class oppression and often supported workplace reforms and sexual equality. *McClure's* relied on a frame of universalization, which allowed the magazine to discuss and even support controversial issues such as birth control and divorce without fundamentally challenging the structures that upheld class and gender privilege and sustained an inequitable distribution of resources. Biographical profiles were a format that supported the magazine's rhetoric of universalization. Focusing on individual workers encouraged a personalization and decontextualization of social circumstances and led to an emphasis on individual values and ideals at the expense of highlighting widespread discriminatory practices. Thus, though the magazine published articles about social disparities—and, some scholars argue, contributed to legislative reform—portrayals of certain individuals affirmed the centrality of ideals in transcending dire circumstances and thus elided material institutions and structures that systemically discriminated against groups and that required more than ideals to transform.

In light of contemporary society's reliance on information as commodity and the widespread fascination with and influence of the symbolic—image, identity, cyberspace—we would do well to recall the hegemonic effects of universalization and to uncover the ways that this rhetorical frame continues to shift attention from relevant material institutions and structures onto the metaphysical so as to absorb and redirect attempts to transform structures that exist outside discourse and that affect not only values and identities but access to life-sustaining resources.

Identity Politics and an Ideology of Domestication

Turn on the radio, flip on the television, or open a newspaper today and one finds a variety of social causes gaining recognition through mass-media outlets. Those advocating ecofeminism to antiwar protest to breast-feeding are struggling to get their voices heard in this media-driven age. In the context of an information-based society characterized by fragmentation, plurality, and a number of conflicting sites of domination, some contemporary scholars have abandoned the notion of a collective class-based struggle in favor of democratic alliances or "new social movements" that struggle on a localized and ad-hoc basis (Laclau and Mouffe 1985). New social movement theorists, siding with the postmodern affinity for discourse, emphasize the centrality of representation and identity (symbolic concepts) in the creation of new social movements and new forms of resistance among various groups, for example, feminists, gays and lesbians, peace advocates, environmentalists, etc. According to these scholars, mass confrontation that strives for material justice is inapplicable, outmoded, or even repressive.

On one hand, the new social movement perspective encourages scholars and activists to pay attention to potential exclusionary practices within democratic struggles. For example, the AFL denied support to women, immigrants, blacks, and unskilled workers. Similarly, the first and second waves of the woman's movement was marked by exclusion of or inattendance to the perspectives of poor, working-class, and black women. Yet including the needs and concerns of a host of groups that differ along gender, race, and other cultural axes does not imply the need to abandon the notion of unified social struggle for justice for all. Antonio Gramsci, when he considered the outlines of a political organization necessary for challenging and transforming capitalism, emphasized the importance of recognizing a host of democratic struggles even as he continued to stress the centrality of a struggle based on resistance to the prevailing mode of production: "The working class and its party cannot do without intellectuals, nor can they ignore the problem of grouping around themselves and giving a lead to all those elements who, in one way or another, are driven to rebel against capitalism" (1988 [1926], 157). Emphasizing the importance of collective struggle on the basis of class interest does not necessarily lead to suppression of difference. As Cloud notes, "The advantage of class as a category [for organization] is that it offers unity in struggle without uniformity; it allows solidarity without universalizing claims about identity or culture" (1999).

The conditions facing present-day workers and their struggles, successful and otherwise, for workplace justice point to the continued relevance of collective confrontations based on class discrimination. As

Chapter 4 demonstrated, the most effective tool that workers of any stripe—service, industrial, or pink-, blue-, or white-collar—hold is the power to halt production. This tool assumes and relies upon the power inherent in collective action. In contrast, new social movements theory represents an atomized approach to transformation which ultimately plays into the personalization and social disconnection of political issues perpetuated through an ideology of domestication. Domestication redirects social critique of economic institutions onto personal spaces—the home, the psyche—thus eclipsing the need for publicly expressed dissent and collective confrontation aimed at material structures and institutions.

New social movement theory's emphasis on cultural identity and differences between groups likewise leads to an individuated and personalized view of oppression and resistance that obscures the connections between different types of discrimination and the necessary linkage between cultural identity and class position (see Cloud 1999). We need not concede to a maneuver of personalization in theorizing and organizing for social change. Such a concession will further promote an ideology of domestication with its shift of social struggles away from public issues of interests toward personal issues of identity. It remains important to upend the atomizing effects of domestication by providing a rhetorical grounding on which to argue for the need for collective confrontation in altering deeply entrenched institutions that discriminate systematically.

Chapter 3 examined the ways three mail-order magazines that targeted working-class audiences domesticated issues that were social in origin and that required public confrontation in order to alter. Stories, advice columns, and regular features found in *Comfort*, *The People's Home Journal*, and *Home Life* encouraged readers to cope within their present circumstances by changing their home, their disposition, or their inner mind. Tactics of social protest and mass confrontation, which were successful in bringing about change in the real world, were replaced in the pages of the magazines by domestic activism. Domestication's persuasive force stems in part from the frame's ability to acknowledge working-class hardships even as it controlled anger regarding those difficult circumstances. Recognizing readers' daily experiences in dangerous factories or unsanitary tenements opened a space for the magazines to offer their own, albeit personalized, solution to working-class problems. This putative solution rhetorically replaced working-class solidarity and silenced the voices of female workers who were expressing their demands by the thousands in the world outside the magazines.

In the context of present-day democratic struggles that appear increasingly disconnected from one another and of new media technologies whose presentation style, format, and means of transmission exacerbate disjunction, disconnection, and separation, it is all the more important to continue to upend an ideology of domestication by emphasizing the social nature of oppression and resistance and by highlighting the systematic nature of discrimination and the ways that exploitation affects different groups in similar ways.

It can be seen that popular magazines of the early twentieth century represent some of the earliest mass-mediated attempts to represent and contain voices of dissent. The magazines examined in the previous chapters relied on naturalization, universalization, and domestication as overarching framings that directed content and shaped portrayals of women as homemakers, mothers, workers, and activists. Within the time period under examination, 1894 to 1917, images changed and the frames bent in response to events in the broader economic, political, and cultural contexts. Cultural hegemony is never a static process but one of constant negotiation and change. Any study of ideology must fully account for the effects of new media technologies that shape production, transmission, and reception of messages (Thompson 1990). A comprehensive and rigorous examination of late-twentieth-century mass media outlets such as television or the Internet would need to account for institutional codes, regulations, and behaviors that shape production, technological features that affect transmission, discursive features of the message itself, and specific contexts in which such messages are received.

This book argues that despite changes and advancements in production, transmission, and reception since the early twentieth century, the ideological strategies of naturalization, universalization, and domestication not only persist throughout contemporary media outlets but are enhanced by contemporary technological advances and are heightened by postmodern rhetorics that celebrate fragmentation, ahistoricity, and the predominance of symbols in late-twentieth-century society. It remains of importance for scholars to examine the ways that hegemonic frames have changed over time, particularly in the context of what Thompson calls the "mediaization of modern culture," or the "diffusion of symbolic forms through the various media of mass communication" (1990, 265). The three rhetorical frames examined in this book are certainly not the only ideological strategies employed for representing challenges to systems and relations of domination. They are, however, widespread and persuasive, and were first disseminated on a wide scale through early mass-circulation magazines. Examination of other ideological strategies, or combinations of strategies, used to portray and contain voices of dissent remains central to future studies of rhetoric and social change in an era of mass communication.

Lesson 2:
The Relevance of a Laboring Agency and Extra-discursive Tactics

The other half of the picture painted in this book related to the ways that members of target audiences constructed themselves in contrast to the popular mediated images perpetuated in magazines. Chapter 4 detailed the protest rhetoric and tactics of wage-earning and middle-class women in labor and suffrage organizations. These activists rhetorically crafted themselves as a collective laboring body through speeches, pamphlets, and testimonies. Women and girls upended naturalization's construction of work and gender disparities as inevitable. They pointed a finger at specific individuals who benefited from and perpetuated the discrimination they experienced as workers and as women. Further, through their aggressive confrontational tactics, women and girls subverted the construction of the cult of True Womanhood that held women to be naturally domestic and submissive. In addition, by highlighting how material institutions shaped their lives, activists confronted the idealizing effects of universalization. Often wage-earning activists distinguished themselves from their more wealthy sisters in an attempt to demonstrate class disparity that could not be overcome through cultural uplift, whose elimination would require extra-discursive confrontation. Finally, women and girls denied the relevance of domestication as a solution to their problems by continuously drawing connections between their worklife and the impossibility of creating such a tranquil domestic space. Activists contradicted the domestication ideology's silencing effect by making their presence as workers known in the streets through mass pickets and parades.

The activism of women and girls of the early twentieth century did not stop at rhetorical intervention. As Chapter 4 also detailed, wage-earning women—often with the help of middle-class allies—engaged themselves physically by walking out of factories en masse and halting production. This tactic extended beyond the symbolic realm to affect the material institutions, such as factories, and systems, such as piece-work wages and the sexual division of labor, that limited their ability to pay rent and put food on the table. Through collective absence, workers engaged themselves as the creators of wealth, thus employing the most powerful tool they held. Although a collective voice was often effective at gaining the attention of politicians, bosses, and the general public and was often employed in bargaining for fair wages and hours, symbolic tactics were not always enough to force the hand of those who held control. Extra-discursive tactics worked in conjunction with rhetorical tactics to provide the decisive blow to owners—who were unable to run factories and turn a profit without workers.

Examining extra-discursive protest tactics provides a corrective to traditional rhetorical and social movement studies, which tend to take a discourse-centered approach to social movements. Previous studies have tended to explore how language is employed in social protest in order to arouse attention, gain acceptance of ideas (Griffin 1952), mobilize and sustain action (Stewart 1980), or affirm selfhood (Gregg 1971). Similarly, new-social-movements cultural studies give a prominent place to discourse and use a localized approach to examining social struggle. Many of these studies emphasize identity formation and symbolic subversion, arguing that the nature of political agency has changed in the context of a "postmodern" or "postindustrial" society. Scholars have examined the ways that disenfranchised groups engage themselves as consumers in order to subvert dominant readings, formulate playful readings, engage desire and jouissance, and upend codes and rules in order to resist dominant modes and institutions.

Protest and Popular Culture, by contrast, attempts to redirect attention to the ways that disenfranchised groups craft and engage themselves as laboring agents. The approach taken in this project assumes the importance of class as site of both exploitation and emancipation and emphasizes the importance of social struggle based on material needs. Such an approach allows us to examine how marginalized groups effectively envision change, craft a rhetoric of possibility, and mobilize themselves physically within material constraints that affect access to basic life-sustaining resources. Though material structures are entrenched and far-reaching, they are not inalterable. The history of social struggle demonstrates how disenfranchised groups have not been content to make do within dominant constraints, but have actively and collectively struggled to transform such institutions. Struggle of this nature entailed material as well as rhetorical intervention and remains relevant to disenfranchised groups today, despite changes in the contemporary workplace.

Studies of domination and resistance within late-twentieth-century workplaces have been enhanced by a critical organizational perspective that asks: "Whose interests are being served by ... [organizational] goals? What role do they pla[y] in creating and maintaining structures of power and domination? What are the conditions that would allow for a more consensual determination of goals?" (Deetz and Kersten 1983, 155). These questions direct scholars to an examination of voice and representation within organizational decision making. In a similar vein, Deetz and Mumby argue that within organizations, "[D]ifferent discourses compete among each other to define the terrain of signification upon which the struggle over meaning occurs" (1990, 38). According to these scholars: "In modern, 'deindustrialized' society, the value of labor and [the] nature of the production process are not as significant as having information and the opportunity to engage in meaningful discourse regarding decisions. Analysis of the tension between capital and labor is less significant than that of the tension within systems allocating opportunities for expression" (29).

The experiences of women and girls detailed in Chapter 4 confirm that indeed voice and representation in organizational negotiation and decision making were important goals for workers. *Protest and Popular Culture* takes the critical organizational viewpoint one step further by underscoring a need to recognize the ways that material factors underpin and shape the nature of discursive struggle. Owners not only defined what counted as "quality work" or "fair piece rates," but backed these definitions with the power to fire workers who disagreed or did not comply. Chapter 4 demonstrated how wage-earning women and girls learned from firsthand experience that the right to complain resulted in little tangible benefits unless their demands were backed by collective actions that halted factory production. Thus, this book encourages scholars to recognize the limitations of "voice" as a goal of workplace transformation. Cloud usefully distinguishes between "voice" and "redress," noting that equal representation does not always result in tangible change for workers. "'Voice' can become a consolatory substitute for actual material gains in a struggle for justice" (Cloud 1999).

It cannot be denied that contemporary capitalism has changed since World War II and is increasingly characterized by flexible labor processes and information technologies. Nevertheless, some scholars ask whether the nature and extent of such changes warrant the abandonment of the analysis of concrete relations of production in favor of the analysis of discourse and identity as driving social forces. Ebert maintains the importance of material, concrete relations as influences on social life (1996): "[The] most important point to be made about the shifting patterns of production and employment is that they are all still grounded on the basic structural relations of capitalism—*the expropriation and exploitation of living labor (surplus labor) for profit*" (112; see Bina, Clements, Davis 1996; Callinicos 1990; Harvey 1989; Marshall 1997).

In these pages the story has been told of work and gender relations as they were portrayed and actually lived in early-twentieth-century America. Today, the realities of thousands of workers around the world paint an often strikingly similar picture of labor conditions and workers' interests and struggles. Whether they work in manufacturing jobs, information-based industries, or the service sector, workers earn a fraction of what corporate and factory owners and executives earn from their labor. Many work in dangerous or hostile environments and are subject to harassment because of their sex, race, age, or sexual orientation. In some instances, workers are not allowed to organize in order to get their grievances heard. Granted, all of these factors differ in degree of severity depending on the nature of the job and the location of the workers. The point is that workers' interests have not fundamentally changed. Millions of men and women in the United States and around the world continue to struggle not only for "opportunities for expression" and a voice in decision making, but more fundamentally for decent wages, forty-hour weeks, and safe working conditions free of harmful chemicals, pesticides, and faulty equipment.

The shift of emphasis to issues of identity and discursive struggle within social movement, cultural, and organizational studies was motivated in part by a desire to acknowledge how gender and race differences are employed through language to further divide and marginalize various groups and, in turn, how various subordinate groups have affirmed their identities and cultures as women, blacks, gays, etc. The previous analysis of popular culture and women's protest in the early 1900s explored gender oppression, but articulated a broad-reaching critique that investigated the interrelated nature of gender discrimination and a system of material exploitation, namely, industrial capitalism. Countless contemporary examples of gender representation and workplace oppression demonstrate the continued relevance of systemic critiques such as the one launched throughout this book.

Contemporary Parallels: Popular Media Portrayals

We can turn to a host of contemporary media outlets besides popular-culture magazines to examine the persistence of hegemonic ideologies and the ways these ideological frames have changed over time. In this section, late-twentieth-century magazines, popular television shows, and Hollywood movies will be examined to explore the workings of naturalization, universalization, and domestication in contemporary media.

Perhaps the most interesting insight to emerge from this discussion is that contemporary mass-media outlets appear to exacerbate or at least reinforce hegemonic ideologies rooted in early-twentieth-century popular magazines. Notwithstanding the call for "new categories, modes of thought and writing, and values and politics" (Best and Kellner 1991, 30), this project points to the relevance of "old" theories of domination and resistance in a capitalist society that relies on flexibility and change afforded through "new" technologies even as it perpetuates "old" social relations grounded in the exploitation of labor for profit.

Before proceeding, it is important to briefly discuss relevant changes in the production, transmission, and reception of mass-mediated messages and their effect on social structures. In his thorough analysis of cultural transmission in the modern age of mediaization, Thompson elaborates on the impact of various media technologies in the late twentieth century (1990). Corporate concentration and globalization of media industries have impacted both the production and transmission of mediated messages. Videocassette recorders, cable television, and direct satellite broadcasting are shaping reception as viewers are not tied to network program schedules and are given a dizzying array of shows to choose from. Perhaps most notably, new media technologies offer the "possibility of a more personalized and interactive form of communication, in the sense that they give recipients greater choice in the selection of channels and services and greater capacity to transmit messages of their own through the system" (214). Such is the case with the Internet, which provides an open forum for anyone with a computer, modem, and telephone line.

What is at issue for many scholars is not the fact of such changes but the extent to which they represent a new era of mass communication and signal profound changes for the ways that ordinary people understand themselves and their roles in society and the ways they participate in politics and public-sphere activities. Some hold out the promise that the Internet and new media technologies foster democracy by making public-sphere participation and decision making available to a wide array of people around the globe. Golding, on the other hand, points to the continuity in the relation between affluence and access and casts serious doubt on the Internet's democratic potentials (1998; see also 1996). What I wish to call attention to here is overarching ideological frames identifiable in late-twentieth-century media outlets that in many ways parallel those originating in early-twentieth-century popular magazines. Such a comparison calls attention to the persistence of hegemonic strategies over time, but also highlights the ways such discourses change in response to the broader context in an effort to "speak to" contemporary audiences and in order to neutralize dissent specific to the time period.

New Traditionalist and "Tough Girls": Negotiating Natural Motherhood in the Late Twentieth Century

The image of the naturally domestic and submissive woman reemerges at different points in history in response to changes in and challenges to gender and work relations. Chapter 1 explored how True Womanhood surfaced in response to the "feministic agitations" occurring outside the pages of the stately *Atlantic Monthly,* which exuded propriety in a period of great upheaval. World Wars I and II provide an interesting context in which to examine the notable flexibility and persistence of the image of the domestic woman in light of the great need of female labor in factories and offices in order to sustain the war effort during both conflicts. Lewis and Neville examine images of women in magazine advertisements between 1940 and 1946 in order to determine "whether advertisers made a concerted change in their shaping of women's images during and after World War II" (1995, 217). They found that though images of women in the workplace increased during the war years, "It appears [that] traditional female gender constructions in advertising based on a social and cultural system of male dominance persisted during the war" (223). Much like the *Atlantic Monthly*, magazine advertisements during World War II responded to contextual exigencies while maintaining a framing rhetoric that naturalized traditional sex role division (Lewis and Neville 1995, 224).

Film noir of the late forties and early fifties further reinforced women's traditional roles by juxtaposing the "nurturing madonna"—the True Woman—and her "evil twin," who embodied the consequences of women's role transgressions and desires for self-fulfillment (Paul and Kauffman 1995, 167). Powerful or independent-minded women were inevitably bound for evil ends. The twin images of evil vixen and the virtuous mother and wife supported naturalization's reinforcement of traditional gender roles in a manner much like that employed by the *Atlantic Monthly* thirty or forty years earlier. In the early 1900s, the *Atlantic Monthly* responded to women's protests for political equality with articles elaborating on the "unmixed evil" of woman suffrage, the "cataclysmal confusion" that would result from women's equality (Seawell 1910), and the "menace to family life" resulting from women's desires for independence (Deland 1910). Like the portrayal of transgressive women in the *Atlantic*, film noir characters make sex-role transgression undesirable, and even unnatural. The "masculine woman" (i.e., the independent, ambitious woman) is an anomaly of nature who, if allowed to roam free, will wreak havoc upon the time-honored workings of civilization.

Demonizing images of women have recurred throughout history in response to cultural fears stemming from change and transition in social identities and roles (see Rogin 1987). Hollywood films of the 1980s saw a reemergence of such images, particularly as personified in the power-hungry, selfish seductress who metaphorically or literally envelops or devours the male protagonist (Traube 1992). The 1989 hit *Fatal Attraction* perhaps best exemplifies the female-stalker story line in which a high-powered book editor relentlessly and viciously pursues the married man with whom she had a one-night stand. Juxtaposed against the mad lover is the domestic wife who stands by her man through the mayhem and murder that ensues. As in the magazine pieces of the early 1900s and the noir films of the late 1940s, the images of women in these contemporary films represent a response to the "women's movement, changes in family structure, and the increased participation of women in the work force" (Traube 1992, 121, 122).

In the late 1980s and early 1990s films have to a degree abandoned the madonna/whore story line. But there are other themes relating to images of women that are important to explore. For example, images of motherhood reemerge and change over time, as do the ways that motherhood is reconciled (or not) with issues surrounding work and sexuality (Kaplan 1994). Kaplan examines six films about mothers in order to show the disparities between film and the realities facing women today. "Films have not responded to the statistics concerning work and motherhood," she says, "nor have they dealt seriously with role conflicts and practical issues that arise when mothers, especially single ones, work" (261). Kaplan's larger project is to theorize reasons behind the "renewed sentimentalizing of motherhood discourse" (262), which she posits on the basis of the films (*The Good Mother*, 1988; *Fatal Attraction*, 1989; *Baby Boom*, 1988; *Three Men and a Baby*, 1988; *Look Who's Talking*, 1990–91; *Postcards from the Edge*, 1991). Kaplan notes that Hollywood's recent images of motherhood, much like the *Atlantic Monthly*'s reinstallment of the centrality of motherhood and family in the context of women's growing demands for political and economic independence, arise in an environment of "anxiety in relation to white women and the cultural changes in sex, family, and work spheres that are emerging in tandem with changes in the technological, economic, and industrial spheres" (258). An examination of early-twentieth-century mass-circulation magazines provides a window into the origins of mass culture's method of responding to cultural changes in sex roles which appear to threaten a "natural"—i.e., stable, controlled—order engendered in and through the nuclear family and the sexual division of labor.

Advertising of the late 1980s and early 1990s created the "New Traditionalist," perhaps the clearest reemergence of the figure of the True Woman to date. Part of a *Good Housekeeping* campaign to solicit advertisers, the New Traditionalist defined itself "by means of its similarities to and differences from the visions and assumptions of feminism" (Darnovsky 1991/92, 74). The New Traditionalist provided a site on which the rhetoric of naturalization could be reworked for a late-twentieth-century audience. As the label implies, the rhetoric of New Traditionalism splices old and new, "oppositions are affirmed yet reconciled" (Darnovsky 1991/92, 81) in terms consonant with the early-twentieth-century ideology of domesticity. The ads describe the New Traditionalist as a "contemporary woman whose values are rooted in tradition;" "the contemporary woman who has made a new commitment to the traditional values that some people thought were 'old-fashioned'" (81, 82). The black and white photos of the New Traditionalist underscore the overarching ideology of naturalization. Women are portrayed in domestic settings with buttoned-up collars with adoring children at their sides.

The New Traditionalist is always portrayed without her husband, which "establishes the separateness and the gendered character of the public and private spheres" (80). Figures in each photo are framed by flowers, leaves, or trees—natural elements that further reinforce the traditional association of woman with nature (76, 77).

Other ads, while not as blatant in reinforcing an ideology of domesticity, balance women's traditional roles with ideals and values associated with late-twentieth-century feminism. The Practical True Woman identified in mail-order magazines of the early 1900s represents the origins of the contemporary popular images so lucidly deconstructed by Bordo in her book *Unbearable Weight* (1993). Bordo explores how advertisements and articles in magazines negotiate between the feminine characteristics of nurturance and submissiveness and those of independence and self-control necessitated by women's participation in the public arena. What was true of work, gender, and popular culture in the early twentieth century is equally true today: "[E]ven as young women today continue to be taught traditionally 'feminine' virtues, to the degree that the professional arena is open to them they must also learn to embody the 'masculine' language and values of that arena—self-control, determination, cool, emotional discipline, [and] mastery" (Bordo 1993, 171).

The tensions between the "new" liberated woman and the "old" cloak of femininity are played out in Hollywood films featuring "tough girls" (Inness 1999). "Tough girls" such as Xena (*Xena: Warrior Princess*), Captain Janeway (*Voyager*), Ripley (*Alien*), Dana Scully (*X-Files*), and Sarah Connor (*Terminator*) are appearing more frequently in films and TV shows and are to a degree challenging traditional assumptions of masculinity and femininity. Despite the gender bending, however, the image of "toughness is often mitigated by . . . femininity" (Inness 1999, 5). The exception, according to Inness, is Xena, for whom toughness does not take a backseat to femininity. Ripley in the *Alien* movies and Sarah Connor in the *Terminator* movies leave less room for optimism (Bordo 1993; Goscilo 1987–88; Inness 1999). In those characters, shifting gender norms are accommodated, then reconciled in favor of time-worn portrayals of the self-sacrificing mother or the submissive helpmate. Inness points out that Sarah Connor in *Terminator* is tough, "but the film assures viewers that she is tough *only* because her family is being threatened" (1999, 125). Making a similar observation regarding the recuperative nature of the motherhood subtext, Goscilo states that "Sarah's pregnancy encompasses her heroism, in reassurance that maternity differentiates and secures the feminine, however strong a woman may become" (1987/88, 49). Certainly the 1980s and '90s tough girls have traveled a long way from the early 1900s *Atlantic Monthly* mother, who "through the serenity and wisdom of her own nature is dew and sunshine to growing souls" (Key 1913, 51).

Nevertheless, it is all the more significant that the motherhood under-current remains a force in the midst of female swift kicks and swashbuck-ling. The steady, if not at times inaudible, tune that continues to play in the background blends indelibly into the scenery, it becomes a natural part of the backdrop, unquestioned because it has always already been there. In the tough-girl world, the immovable presence of motherhood is recognized as that much more "natural." The image implies that despite trappings that seem to indicate the contrary, natural attributes always re-main and will rise to the surface.

Contemporary popular-culture advertisements and movies exemplify a strong parallel between early-twentieth-century naturalization as ex-plored in the *Atlantic Monthly* and a rhetoric of naturalization that in re-cent times has transmogrified to project the trappings of feminism. Other popular-culture texts more explicitly take on challenges of feminism by means of a frame of universalization, which provides a way to discuss potentially controversial issues while keeping the material structures and institutions that underlie social conflict beyond the boundaries of the discussion.

Popularizing a Movement: Feminism and Universalization

Mass media decision makers have long since realized the profit potential in feminism and have worked since the early 1900s to portray the move-ment's values, ideas, and activities in a manner consonant with the de-mands of big business. Universalization provides an appropriate overar-ching frame in which to deal head-on with the challenges of feminism. The ideology emphasizes values and ideals as the engines of history, em-bodies the concept of free will and choice, and upholds the ability to act autonomously unconstrained by external material institutions or struc-tures. These tenets discredit the influence of material institutions that shape human consciousness, limit choices, and constrain behavior within a context marked by social relations of domination. Thus the frame pro-vides a way to discuss issues concerning disparity and unrest while de-politicizing possible solutions.

Advertisements provide perhaps the most obvious avenue for univer-salizing feminism. Present-day ads sell not so much a product as an im-age—an ideal of limitless choice and freedom. Even as early as the 1920s, advertisements seized upon the image of the "New Woman" in an effort to associate their products with the liberation and freedom that she rep-resented (Ewen 1976, 159–176). To overcome the negative stigma associ-ated with women who smoked cigarettes in public, the American To-bacco company initiated an advertising campaign in which women lit "torches of freedom" (cigarettes). And drawing on then recent memories of suffrage parades down Fifth Avenue, the American Tobacco Company organized a group of women to march in the 1929 Easter Parade in New York City with their freedom torches lit for all to see.

Not much has changed in contemporary advertisements directed toward the "liberated woman." Goldman, Heath, and Smith provide an incisive critique of media co-optations of "feminism" in which they explore how the movement, its values, and its goals are reworked in advertisements to mean not a political movement but a stylistic choice: "Women's magazines attempt to redefine feminism through commodities, interpreting the everyday relations women encounter and negotiate into a series of 'attitudes' which they can then 'wear'" (1991, 336). Fashion magazines have taken up feminism's "unruliness," working various activist tactics and "bad girl" figures into the magazine's fashion ethos. Juxtaposed with the usual fashion spreads, feminism becomes yet another fashion to consider and the "image of the feminist 'bad girl'" takes on a much "blander, less ominous, and infinitely more confusing" association (Gambrell 1994–95, 141). A quick perusal of one 1997 issue of *Cosmopolitan*, one of the most popular women's magazines, reveals that wearing Tommy Girl cologne is "a declaration of independence" and sporting Chic Jeans means that the reader is "no slave to fashion."

Feminism's associated desires for self-control and freedom also become transferred onto the body, which in popular culture is upheld as the quintessential locus for exercising autonomy. Advertisements for sports equipment and drinking water convey a sense of limitless possibilities when it comes to appearance. As Bordo explains, however, "The rhetoric of choice and self-determination . . . efface . . . the inequalities of privilege, money, and time that prohibit most people from indulging" in practices such as cosmetic surgery and regular gym workouts (1993, 247). Similar to the argument being advanced in this chapter, Bordo draws a connection between the images and narratives elicited in popular culture and those characterizing postmodern academic discourses. Popular culture's valorization of the body as a site for engaging freedom and desire parallels postmodern discourses characterized by a "disdain for material limits and the concomitant intoxication with freedom, change, and self-determination" (Bordo 1993, 246). These similarities again point to the usefulness of theories of domination and resistance the origins of which can be found in early-twentieth-century popular texts. The "postmodern" era of late-twentieth-century society does not require us to set aside these theories but rather calls on us to apply them to a specific historical context that relies on flexibility and negotiation to perpetuate relations of domination along identifiable lines.

Popular television shows have also sidled up to feminism with portrayals most often falling within the parameters of liberal feminism. Such limited portrayals of a movement that is so varied and complex come as no surprise, given that the tenets of liberal feminism align most clearly with the tenets of liberal capitalism, which sustains the commercial needs of the television and advertising industries. Liberal feminism is grounded in an ideology of universalization, with its emphasis on equal access to traditionally male-dominated realms and its belief in autonomous action and hard work as sufficient to transcend social discrimination. Dow explores "television's fondness for representations stressing liberal, or equal opportunity, feminism" in her studies of the *Mary Tyler Moore Show* and *Murphy Brown* (Dow 1996, 37; see also Dow 1992). Her studies of representations of feminism in the popular television shows *Mary Tyler Moore Show* and *Murphy Brown* point to the shortcomings of these portrayals, which reinforce the division between private and public spheres and denigrate traditional female roles. In *Murphy Brown*, liberal feminist values are placed under "social control" through comedic scapegoating of the central character. Murphy Brown assumes an extreme form of liberal feminist values such as competitiveness and independence and thus exemplifies a "caricature of the consequences of liberal feminism" (1992, 149).

Popular-culture stories narrating the lives of women who manage to succeed despite great odds further reinforce the assumptions of individualism inherent in liberal feminism. *Lady Sings the Blues*, focusing on the accomplishments of singer Billie Holiday, "individualized Holiday and her accomplishments in ways that generally declined to implicate the society's racial practices in the problems and tragedies of her life" (Paul and Kauffman 1995, 172). Cloud examines the popularized construction of Oprah Winfrey as the figure "Oprah," a rhetoric of tokenism that operates hegemonically by negating the collective nature of black oppression and struggle and reinterpreting Oprah's experiences as a typical rag-to-riches story in which one overcomes poverty through individual efforts (1996). Features of a rhetoric of tokenism include "unquestioned faith in the American Dream and its accessibility to all people, the belief in a universal human nature, celebration of philanthropy as an appropriate means of social change (in contradistinction to political activism), and above all the exhortation to transcend racial or cultural conflict" (Cloud 1996, 124). A rhetoric of tokenism, as described by Cloud, can be viewed as one among many rhetorical strategies that promote an ideology of universalization.

Popular-media outlets not only have made feminism fashionable, even acceptable for a prime-time television audience, they have also shaped whose voices are considered to be the "voice of feminism" in the late 1990s. Mainstream media have been quick to home in on the assertions of feminist scholars such as Christina Hoff Sommers, Katie Roiphe, and

Camille Paglia, each of whom has in her own way propounded a variation of a "get-over-it-and-get-on-with-it" form of feminism deemed appropriate for today's "postfeminist" society.[2] In her study of contemporary press accounts of women's studies and feminist research,
McDermott observes that despite the variety of perspectives coming
from a host of feminists within and outside the academy, the media select
those such as Sommers and Roiphe to stand as representative of all feminist views (1995). Though this "is not a concerted 'media conspiracy,'
. . . it is far from benign; it promotes a version of women's studies that
trivializes feminist analyses of power . . . and casts feminism as a hegemonic bully on American campuses" (670–671).

Gitlin states of the *Mary Tyler Moore Show*: "Mary would not easily
have been conceived five or ten years earlier; less likely developed . . .
least likely scheduled; and probably not so ardently watched before
working women, the women's movement, and the sensitivity-culture
currents of the late sixties . . . disrupted the older values and, indirectly,
network executive culture" (1983, 215). Yet, a study of early-twentieth-
century mass-circulation magazines points to mass media's initial foray
into representations of women's activism. Predating Gitlin's observation
by nearly six decades, the political and, to a lesser degree, economic
struggles of wage-earning and middle-class women of the early 1900s
provided a context for media outlets that was ripe for broaching issues
previously untouched on a mass scale. Much like contemporary representations of feminism analyzed by Gitlin, Dow, and others, *McClure's*
addressed feminism as expressed in fiction and nonfiction and even ap-
pointed a "spokesman" for woman suffrage. And not unlike present-day
framings of feminism that emphasize individual choice and equal access
to male-dominated institutions, *McClure's* accounts were framed by an
ideology of universalization that personalized and decontextualized social issues through an emphasis on the values and character of individuals who were able to transcend oppression through individual effort.

Silencing Solidarity: Social Issues Remain "All in the Family"

Domestication, an ideological strategy that re-directs attention to private
spheres as sites for transformation, relied on depoliticization and silencing to portray social conflict and unrest. As was discussed in Chapter 3,
the persuasive force of domestication lies in its ability to recognize and
even affirm readers' feelings of disenfranchisement, anger, and despair.
Editors of *Comfort*, *Home Life*, and *The People's Home Journal* were attuned
to Gitlin's insight that media decision makers do not "simply manipulate
popular taste. . . . Rather, they shape and channel sentiment and taste,
which churn and simmer in the larger society, and express popular de-

sires in one form or another" (1987, 243). Having acknowledged reader's dis-ease, early-twentieth-century mail-order magazines then provided the antidote which directed attention away from social institutions and systems and onto personal spaces where transformation could be localized and contained.

The ideology of domestication prevailing in early-twentieth-century mail-order magazines laid the groundwork for contemporary media portrayals that continue to circumscribe social dissent within home and family. Gitlin has posited and explored a shift in TV programming to issues of "social relevance" that began in the 1970s in response to challenges posed by the civil rights, student, antiwar, and sex equality movements (1983, 1987). Television shows such as *All in the Family*, *The Jeffersons*, and *Good Times* openly tackled issues surrounding racism, the Watergate scandal, the Vietnam War, and the women's movement. Yet the moral of the story always reaffirmed a family's ability to cope with difficulty or dissent within the confines of the home sphere. The theme song of *Good Times* underscores the workings of domestication: "Keeping our heads above water, making the waves when you can, temporary layoffs, Good Times!, easy credit rip-offs, Good Times! . . . ain't we lucky we got 'em, Good Times!" Despite suffering the effects of an economic system that relies on and benefits from employee layoffs and credit rip-offs, the show's main characters are able to cope by way of the "good times" engendered within the family.

The generic characteristics of the situation comedy further reinforce the ideology of domestication. Situation comedies are "oriented toward resolution of conflict," usually center around a literal or metaphorical family that provides a core set of characters, and focuses on "stock storylines" (Dow 1996, 36, 37). Consequently, issues of social relevance tend to be addressed and resolved within the family with little or no collective conflict and little contextualization of the issue within a broader economic or political context. The relatively new sitcom *Wil and Grace* portrays how a gay male and his (heterosexual) female roommate–best friend pursue an "alternative" lifestyle while retaining a strikingly "traditional" family makeup. The issues facing the characters are usually apolitical, and Grace stands in as the mother figure who nurtures Wil when he is sick and comforts him on the anniversary of his breakup with a former boyfriend.

Cloud's analysis of therapeutic discourses offers insight on the ways that domestication operates in the larger political context of the post–Vietnam War era. The New Age movement, family values rhetoric, post-Marxist thought, and news about Persian Gulf War "support groups" are contemporary examples of therapeutic discourses that "encourage audiences to focus on themselves and . . . their private lives rather than to address and attempt to reform systems of social power in which they are embedded" (1998a, xiv). The ideology of domestication found in early–1900s mail-order magazines represents some of the earliest identified manifestations of therapeutic discourses, which have "restorative and conservative effects in the face of conflict and change" (Cloud 1998a, xiv). *Comfort, Home Life,* and *The People's Home Journal* contained responses to the waves of strikes and walkouts occurring across the United States during the first decades of the twentieth century, and contemporary therapeutic discourses represent a response to the upheavals of the late 1960s and early 1970s (xix). Studying origins and patterns of reemergence over time lends insight into the rhetorical function of this discourse and the ways it changes to adjust to and negotiate within a specific historical context.

Domestication is also supported by a more blatant silencing of controversial issues, which often occurs during periods of substantial and often quite effective collective protest. In the late 1940s and early 1950s, in the context of McCarthyism and the investigations of the House Un-American Activities Committee, Hollywood saw a remarkable decline in "social problem" films (Byars 1991, 113). Hollywood silenced working-class women and any "hint of working-class solidarity" and recast social issues as personal problems (Paul and Kauffman 1995, 168). Byars notes how films that dealt with "alcoholism, labor union corruption, drug addiction, and juvenile delinquency" displaced the issues from the public to the private realm, affirming that such problems could be "solved only by a return to traditional family values and structure" (114). Other scholars of 1950s Hollywood have made similar observations (Stead 1989; Biskind 1983). In short, films made in this era focused on the individual as the source and solution of conflict and left "no room for class criticism or for collective action" (Stead 1989, 170).

Numerous studies have explored newspaper and magazine portrayals of women between 1950 and 1990 and found that not a great deal changed during that period. A study of newspaper coverage of the early stages of the Second Wave of feminism of the late 1960s and early 1970s revealed a virtual news blackout of the issue (Morris 1973). Wholesale media omissions can be viewed as a form of social control, a way to reinforce the status quo through what is not said. Morris's study exemplifies the workings of a "third persona," as discussed in Chapter 3, a silencing (in this case, in news accounts) of socially relevant groups (feminist or women's liberation groups) in order to communicate (through absence) which behaviors are and are not socially acceptable. Another study of traditional and nontraditional women's magazines between 1950 and 1980 yields similar results. The upshot of an investigation by Busby and Leichty reveals that magazine portrayals of women contain little to no traces of feminist movement influences (1993). "Women's roles as decorative objects in advertising have continued to increase over time, despite social changes brought about by the feminist movement"; and "even the nontraditional women's magazines [*Ms.* and *Working Woman*] have carried and continue to carry a significant amount of advertising contrary to the tenets of the feminist movement" (258–259).[3] Rhode cites an array of studies pointing to contemporary media's underrepresentation of women, lack of attention to "women's issues," and inattention to and demonization of the women's movement (1995). In line with early-twentieth-century mail-order magazines, which made no mention of the formation and activities of the Women's Trade Union League, the more contemporary "*Washington Post* ran no story on the formation of the National Organization for Women and the *New York Times* placed its brief account beneath recipes for a traditional Thanksgiving" (690; see Beasley and Gibbons 1993, 7). Yet, as Rhode has noted, [w]hatever media leaders' reluctance to chronicle the rebirth of feminism in the 1960s and early 1970s, they had no such hesitation in reporting its demise" (1995, 691). In sync with the "press postmortems" (Rhode 1995, 691) decrying the end of feminism are the voices of "postfeminism" such as those of Hoff Sommers, Roiphe, and Paglia mentioned above. Ideological strategies of universalization and domestication work in tandem here to contain the challenges of a movement that seeks to draw connections between women's seemingly individual experiences and a broader society that discriminates systematically.

Countless examples of media portrayals in film, television, newspapers, and magazines from the 1920s to the present point to the persistence of ideological strategies that naturalize, universalize, and domesticate social disparities in an attempt to absorb and contain voices of dissent. The early-twentieth-century mass circulation magazines examined in Chapters 1–3 may not have provided the only source for such ideologies, but they do represent some of the earliest manifestations of these ideologies in mass-mediated popular-culture form. Technological advances in printing, reduced postal rates, and the increasing concentration of populations in urban areas all contributed to the growth and spread of magazines and newspapers as sources of information and entertainment. Continued changes in mass-media technologies have indeed shaped content, distribution, and reception of popular messages (Thompson 1990). Yet numerous similarities can be drawn between early- and late-twentieth-century media portrayals of social dissent and disparity. In many regards, recent technological advancements have served to exaggerate such hegemonic ideologies and have received further reinforcement from postmodern discourses and outlooks circulating both within and outside the academy.

In the midst of hegemonic ideologies that fragment social experience and personalize hardship, disenfranchised groups have rhetorically constructed and physically engaged a collective laboring agency in an effort not only to subvert dominant ideologies but also to transform institutions that oppress and exploit. The context of late-twentieth-century society has prompted some to give up mass struggle and material transformation in favor of localized politics that address identity and image; here, however, I wish to draw parallels between early- and late-twentieth-century workplaces in an effort to illustrate the valuable lessons to be learned from the wage-earning and middle-class women of the early 1900s who sustained mass actions and transformed not only their identity but their material surroundings.

The More Things Change the More They Stay the Same: The Late-Twentieth-Century Workplace

In this chapter I have argued that there are valuable lessons to be gleaned from a historical analysis of popular and resistant discourses. A primary argument connecting discussions of turn-of-the-century popular culture and protest rhetoric and that of the present day is that present-day society, despite notable changes in its workplace arrangements, cultural ideologies, and methods of domination and resistance, reflects important similarities to that of the early twentieth century. In this section, I will address workplace conditions more specifically, with an eye toward demonstrating the continued relevance of a frame for resistance that is collective and confrontational and that embodies extra-discursive tactics aimed at material transformation.

The economy of the 1970s to the present has often been characterized as "post-Fordist." "Fordism" refers to the mass production, assembly-line work, and scientific management practices developed by Frederick W. Taylor that are typically associated with manufacturing jobs. Post-Fordism is a term used to indicate what is perceived to be a fundamental shift in the nature of capitalist production.[4] Whereas Fordism refers to a system that is production-driven, a post-Fordist capitalist system is consumption-led and is shaped in part by new technologies in the workplace (Callinicos 1990, 134). "Computer-based distribution systems" and "flexible manufacturing systems" reduce overhead, prevent overstocking, and allow producers to target specific niches or specialized markets. In the post-Fordist workplace, the role of labor has changed from that of "semi-skilled machine-minder[]" to a "smaller multi-skilled core workforce capable . . . of participating actively in the labour-process" (Callinicos 1990, 135). Of relevance to this conversation is the post-Fordist viewpoint that such changes in production and work relations are part of a larger shift in economic, political, and cultural spheres which call for new understandings and approaches to social transformation (Clarke 1991, 155, 156). "New Times" is the name of the project, which eschews traditional Marxist frameworks emphasizing the influence of the mode of production in favor of a discourse-centered analysis that valorizes (enhances the value of) ideology and culture.

Indeed, workers from the 1970s to the present have felt the repercussions of workplace changes that have affected job stability and the ability to earn decent wages. At issue here is precisely what such changes represent and what they mean for labor organizing and resistance. Put differently, should these changes be characterized as "post-Fordist" or "business as usual"? "Post" implies "new," hence, the need for new categories, theories, and politics. In this vein, one scholar has said, "[S]uch new times require a new politics attuned to the economic, social and cultural diversity, one which can build a new collective political subject out of the plurality of subjectivities to replace the collapsing class-politics bloc of labourism" (Clarke 1991, 160). Not all scholars agree that a new approach is called for. Some continue to emphasize the persistence of capitalism's exploitation of surplus labor and thus the need for collective confrontation capable of challenging systemic disparities.

I will argue the "business-as-usual" view here: "post-Fordist" changes do not represent a fundamental shift in economic processes but rather stand as an entrenchment or exaggeration of capital/labor relations that call on us to revisit "old" understandings and methods of domination and resistance of a late-twentieth-century capitalist context. This context in many ways looks remarkably like that experienced by Leonora O'Reilly and her comrades in the early 1900s.

Scholars have effectively documented changes in workplace relations and economic production and distribution in the age of corporate restructuring and globalization (Bina, Clements, Davis 1996; Jenson and Mahon 1993; Rogers 1993). "Flexible" labor processes deemed necessary in the face of a more competitive global economy have increased the reliance on part-time and contract labor, have led to the "streamlining" of job classifications in order to create a "multiskilled workforce," and have created new payment systems based on company performance (Jenson and Mahon 1993, 7, 8). Late-twentieth-century capitalism has also seen a substantial growth in information- and service-based jobs. In 1900, 35.8 percent of jobs were characterized as blue collar, 17. 6 percent as white collar, and 9.1 percent as service. By 1993, those numbers had changed to blue collar, 25.5 percent; white collar, 57.9 percent; and service, 13. 8 percent. Thus, by 1993, white-collar and service jobs outnumbered blue-collar jobs by nearly three to one (Mogensen 1996, 178, 79).

Another change that has shaped workplace environments, particularly in the 1990s, involves a flattening of traditional hierarchies in favor of workplace "teams" and "quality circles." Increased worker participation and representation in decision making appear to have taken the place of top-down mandates and tight managerial oversight. A careful analysis of such trends indicates that there is nothing fundamentally new in their consequences for both business and labor. Since the early 1970s, corporations have seen a need for "restructuring" (plant closures and corporate mergers that maximize profit and keep labor costs low) in the context of a "globalized" economy where such moves are deemed necessary in order to remain "competitive" (i.e., reduce "workers' living standards to the lowest common denominator internationally"[5]).

"Flexible" labor operates in three ways, all of which result in lowering real wages for workers while increasing profits for company executives. (1) "Numerical" flexibility involves greater use of part-time, temporary, and contract laborers, which reduces employers' labor costs (no benefits or vacation and sick pay and lowered administrative costs, no pay for slack times). In 1997, 28 percent of workers aged twenty to thirty-five were temporary, part-time, or contract employees. An in-depth analysis of the conditions surrounding these work arrangements confirmed that, contrary to being a boon for workers (as maintained by those who tout the trend), "flexible" labor practices are "driven by *employers'* demand for . . . cheaper labor" and result in substandard work conditions for employees (Jorgensen 1999, 6). (2) Functional" flexibility means "streamlining" job classifications so that an individual worker performs multiple tasks for the same or reduced pay. (3) "Remuneration" flexibility entails "new payment systems [which] jettison cost-of-living adjustments" and replace them with lump sum payments based on a firm's or plant's performance (Jenson and Mahon 1993, 7, 8).

The most recent trend in "flexibility" for employers has come in the form of modular manufacturing in the automobile industry. "Modular" assembly is a way for auto employers to contract out labor typically performed in the plant. Nonunion auto suppliers provide "modules"—already-assembled portions of the car—to plants rather than separate parts to be put together by plant employees. The result is a cut in labor costs (a union auto worker earns an average eighteen dollars an hour whereas a worker for a supplier earns between eight and twelve dollars an hour) and the elimination of union jobs (Adams 1999, G3), thus the weakening of the union.

The shift from manufacturing to service-based industries has entrenched labor/capital disparities in similar ways. Callinicos points out that though the number of manufacturing jobs has fallen off in recent years, output has continually risen (1990). To say that the late twentieth century is characterized by a decline in the importance of manufacturing is somewhat misleading. A more insightful appraisal of the situation highlights that fewer workers are producing more—profits are rising while labor costs are kept low. Furthermore, emphasizing the shift from manufacturing to information industries obscures the rise in global manufacturing, particularly as U.S. steel, textile, and heavy machinery industries move overseas and to Mexican maquiladoras in search of cheap labor.

But what about those information-based industries? They do indeed represent a substantial percentage of employment in the late twentieth century. Even if we focus exclusively on these industries, however, we see striking parallels between the white-collar office jobs of the information sector and manufacturing jobs, which diminishes the notion that a significant shift has taken place in the nature of the workplace. "In many respects, the 'office of the future' resembles the factory of the past," notes Vernon Mogensen (1996, 178). Scientific management techniques have been applied to office environments in order to increase worker efficiency and to enhance managerial control over workers (Mogensen 1996, 180). Further, new office technologies, rather than freeing workers from tedious and repetitive tasks and giving them opportunities for creative input, have "accentuated the gap between skilled and unskilled workers" and have actually contributed to job loss (Mogensen 1996, 178). Worker knowledge once relied on by managers is now easily computerized, thus making various full-time positions obsolete. Furthermore, "[C]apital's ability to electronically shift work to cheaper and less organized labor markets undermines the worker's ability to organize, fight for safety and health protection, and maintain adequate wage and benefit levels" (Mogensen 1996, 178).

But what to make of the new more democratic workplace where management and labor share in decision making and cooperate in the context of teams? Some observers, rather than viewing cooperative labor-management relations as a boon for workers, have cautioned *against* the decline of antagonism that has traditionally marked labor-capital relations (Bina, Clements, Davis 1996; Cloud 1999). From management's perspective, labor participation and cooperation is an indispensable tool for enhancing worker productivity and remaining competitive in the global market (Bina, Clements, Davis 1996).[6] For workers, however, increased "voice" in workplace affairs can represent a "consolatory substitute for actual material gains in a struggle for justice" (Cloud 1999). In short, "[T]he 'new' approach to industrial relations [labor-capital teamwork] is not so new after all. [For business t]o be more competitive and more effective, workers have always been asked to participate in their own further subjugation under capital" (Bina, Clements, Davis 1996, 8).

Changes in the workplace associated with postindustrial information technologies, then, have not worked to labor's advantage. Indeed, recent studies by the U.S. Commerce Department and the United Nations point to a growing information or technology, gap which appears to be compounding the already documented income gap. According to the Commerce Department study, more than one in five of America's poorest families do not have a phone line to call a doctor much less to get Internet access (Scott 1999, D2). The study also revealed that blacks and Hispanics were less likely than whites of the same income group to be on-line (National Public Radio 1999). Taking a global perspective, the United Nations report drew clear links between wealth and technology, pointing out that a poverty-stricken country such as Cambodia only has one phone line per 100 people (Geewax 1999, A11). The idea of a "global village" appears dubious at best in light of such findings.

This review of so-called "post-Fordism" versus "business-as-usual" and the repercussions of new economic developments for both workers and corporate big-wigs supports a primary argument linking the chapters of this book: that despite important changes in communication technologies and economic arrangements which have affected the content, transmission, and reception of information and shaped the nature of and possibilities for democracy in the workplace and the public sphere, fundamental similarities have persisted, thus making it possible for us to analyze current developments with the same tools used in an historical analysis of popular culture and protest rhetoric.

The development of an "information gap" only compounds the effects of what countless statistics point to: an entrenchment of capital-labor relations based on extraction of surplus labor for profit. The twentieth century has witnessed a steadily growing gap between rich and poor. United for a Fair Economy recently released a report, *Shifting Fortunes: The Perils of the Growing American Wealth Gap*, which showed that between 1983 and 1995, the much touted economic "boom" benefited the richest 5 percent of Americans while the other 95 percent actually experienced a decline in net worth (Jackson 1999, A9). According to a recent United Nations Human Development Report, more than 25 percent of the world's population has seen their income fall over the last fifteen years, and approximately 30 percent of the world's labor force is either unemployed or underemployed. Meanwhile, the number of billionaires has almost doubled, to 358 individuals whose total wealth equals the combined income of the poorest 45 percent of the world's population. Profit margins continue to rise as owners and top executives reap the benefits while workers pay the price. American CEOs now earn 115 times what their employees earn (Gamboa 1999c, A7). Real wages have steadily declined since the early 1970s, and family members are working more hours than ever before. The average middle-class family is working 615 more hours a year than it was in 1979 (Gamboa 1999b, A8). An economist at the Economic Policy Institute put the matter plainly: "The typical American family is probably worse off than it was at the end of the 1970s" (Gamboa 1999b, A8).

As has always been the case, women and minorities carry a disproportionately heavy proportion of the hardship. Across the board and over time, blacks have earned less than whites and have faced resistance in promotion; and blacks with a high school degree are more likely to be unemployed than whites with the same education. An *Akron Beacon Journal*–Kent State University study of workers in Ohio showed that in 1997, black workers earned between 73 and 95 percent of white workers in the same age category (Gamboa 1999a, A9). Black families with household incomes below $40,000 are also more profoundly affected than whites by the information gap, as revealed in a 1998 Vanderbilt University study (Gamboa 1999a, A9).

The growth of information- and service-sector jobs has led to a widening of the gender gap as well as the race divide, with few women gaining access to positions of power or authority (Boyd, Mulvihill, and Myles, 1995; see also Callinicos 1990, 127). Boyd, Mulvihill, and Myles examined census data and conducted their own studies and concluded that the "service economy not only represents the continuation of female subordination, but also represents its consolidation" (199). Female workers are overrepresented in unskilled, low-paying, and often dangerous jobs and are subject to sexual harassment and physical abuse in the workplace and at home. At a most obvious level, persistent sex stereotypes of women as inferior or unserious workers continue to play a role in male/female wage differentials and operate to divide workers and lower the overall wage structure for both sexes. Revelations of the abuses endured by young women and girls in Nike plants in Vietnam are testimony to the often unabashed and horrific ways that capitalism benefits from racist and sexist divisions. A study conducted by Vietnam Labor Watch revealed that these workers are paid $1.60 a day and work twelve-hour days. They are subject to sexual harassment and physical punishment and are regularly driven to exhaustion. Meanwhile, Nike's quarterly revenues in 1996 were over $2 billion dollars. The experiences of these workers are not isolated, but stand representative of millions of male and female workers who are exploited in the workplace. Further, these examples point to the ways that gender and race differences interrelate with class exploitation as they are deployed to increase company profits.

Lest we be misled that such sweatshop conditions are distinct to "Third World" or developing nations, we need only turn to the state of the garment industry in the United States. The U.S. Department of Labor estimates that half of the 22,000 sewing businesses operating in the United States can be defined as "sweatshops," meaning they violate minimum wage and overtime laws and are often characterized by physically abusive environments. Conditions in these shops, located in large urban areas such as New York and Los Angeles, are remarkably similar to those faced by Leonora O'Reilly, Rose Schneiderman, and the thousands of other young women and girls during the early 1900s. In one New York City shop that employed mostly Latina women, "[T]he workers typically toiled at their sewing machines and presses for up to 60 hours a week in a room with wires hanging from the ceiling, three small fans that served as the only source of ventilation and no fire exists. Wages . . . often were arbitrarily cut or delayed. . . . Employees who missed a day would be illegally 'fined' $30, on top of losing a day's pay" (Branigin 1997, A1). Again, these examples argue forcefully for the continued need for critiques that engage the overarching system of resource production and distribution. Critics must recognize the continued centrality of labor relations and conditions in workers' lives—be they service-sector employees or garment sewers—and the extent to which worker struggles are not simply or primarily discursive struggles over meaning, but pertain directly to material need: fair wages, decent hours, and safe work conditions.

Sex and race discrimination are not confined to manufacturing jobs, but are widespread in service- and information-based industries. Conditions for female and minority workers are coming to light as a string of sexual harassment and discrimination lawsuits has made headlines. For example, Home Depot, the world's largest home-improvement chain, is involved in a sex bias lawsuit that charges that the company systematically failed to promote, train, or fairly compensate its female employees. Publix Super Markets Inc. recently settled lawsuits by promising to pay $81.5 million to women and $3.5 million to black employees who had charged the company with discrimination. According to the U.S. Equal Employment Opportunity Commission, employers in the Houston, Texas, area have been forcing pregnant workers to take unpaid sick leave, a violation of the Pregnancy Discrimination Act ("Discrimination Against Pregnant Women Alleged" 1997, B2). Even middle-class white women who have arguably made gains in the workplace are still relatively disadvantaged in traditional ways. They are still subject to a "second shift" of domestic maintenance and child rearing.

All of the above evidence underscores the need for scholars of communication to address the connections between symbolic exchange and the material institutions and practices that affect people's abilities to live decent and just lives. Workers continue to struggle over meaning making and interest representation, and these struggles certainly are not separate from their attempts to get fair pay and safe working conditions. Clearly, however, regardless of the ways that contemporary capitalism has changed since World War II, the "value of labor and the production process" have not lost significance, as Deetz and Mumby suggest, but are still of quintessential importance to workers.

In the midst of a merger mania sweeping the country's corporate land-scape, some consider themselves lucky just to hold on to their jobs. Many of those who don't manage to hold on to their jobs become part of a growing "contingent" workforce consisting of part-time, temporary, and contract laborers who are isolated from fellow workers, have little or no job security, and often no health insurance. As previously noted, in one month alone, nine mergers were announced of companies located in northeast Ohio, resulting in layoffs of thousands of blue- and white-col-lar workers. Nationwide the story is the same. The stock market rallied to an all-time high in the last week of November 1998, a week in which ten mergers were announced in one day. "Merger mania makes everybody feel good," noted Alfred E. Goldman, the director of market analysis at the financial-management firm A. G. Edwards & Sons—except perhaps the laid-off workers, such as the estimated 20,000 who are expected to be laid off as a result of the most unnerving merger of all, that between Exxon and Mobil. Or take Joe Cantale, a thirty-two-year veteran at a B. F. Goodrich plant in Cleveland, Ohio, who expects to lose his job as a result of a Goodrich merger with Coltec Industries. "How, at my age, will I go out and find a job with similar pay?" asks the fifty-one-year old factory maintenance worker. According to statistics, Cantale can expect to take an average 20 percent cut in pay—if and when he finds a new job (Drexler 1999, 12; see Bina, Clements, Davis 4).

While euphemistic terms such as "right-sizing," "synergy," and "global consolidation" spin justifications for mergers, Cantale and thou-sands of others know the reality of the situation: mergers reduce union jobs and extend the unemployment line for workers while top executives continue to collect 115 times the pay of their employees or ride fabu-lously generous golden umbrellas out of the world of work. An internal B. F. Goodrich memo acquired by the *Cleveland Free Times* revealed the company's stance toward union jobs: "In an ideal world, we would like to have production facilities that are union free," notes the memo, dated January 8, 1999 (Drexler 1999, 12). The automobile industry's proposed shift to modular manufacturing would also eliminate union jobs, as as-sembly-line positions would be sacrificed to work done by suppliers who send to auto factories already-assembled modules rather than separate parts. General Motors is planning modular manufacturing at its Saturn plant in Tennessee and at plants in Mexico, Ontario, Michigan, and Ohio (Slaughter 1999, 8).

Such developments, far from being reason to abandon traditional strategies for gaining workplace justice, point to the need, now more than ever, to consider anew strategies and tactics that proved effective in the past. We would do well to recall (or learn for the first time) the actual effects that mass labor protests of the teens and the thirties had on the workplace. Chapter 4 focused primarily on the experiences of women and girls who fought throughout the first decades of the twentieth century. Similar battles were waged in the thirties and forties as workers again turned to walkouts, general strikes, and a then new tactic, sit-down strikes, to achieve fair wages, hours, and workplace control (see Foner 1976, 1980; Boyer and Morais 1955). In 1936, to protest an imminent wage cut and the firing of union officials, Firestone rubber workers in Akron, Ohio, halted production and sat down on the job, initiating the first sit-down strike in labor history (Zinn 1980, 390). The sit-down strike had several advantages. Workers "were directly blocking the use of strikebreakers; they did not have to act through union officials but were in direct control of the situation themselves; they did not have to walk outside in the cold and rain, but had shelter; they were not isolated as in their work or on the picket line; they were thousands under one roof, free to talk to one another, to form a community of struggle" (Zinn 1980). Word quickly spread throughout the city and within a couple of weeks, ten thousand workers throughout Akron, Ohio, including those at Goodyear, were sitting down on the job. Within one month the strike was won. The idea of the sit-down soon spread, perhaps the most well known sit-down strike taking place at the Fisher Body plant in Flint, Michigan, in December 1936–February 1937.

Similar tactics gained momentum once again in the mid–1970s as workers faced rising prices, stagnant wages, and high unemployment. Brecher and Costello note that by June 1974 "a nationwide strike wave was under way, with more strikes than at any time since 1946" (1976, 123). Though union officials continuously aligned with management, wildcat strikes broke out across the country in industries that had previously seen little organization or action. As at the beginning of the century, coal miners and industrial workers continued to strike for basic safety measures on the job. Joining their ranks in swelling numbers were teachers and public-service workers for whom "bread and butter problems became the center of attention" during the 1970s (Zinn 1980, 563). Firefighters, police officers, sanitation workers, hospital workers, independent truckers, and teachers all put in time on the strike line in order to achieve improved wages (Zinn 1980, 562–569; Brecher and Costello 1976, 217, 218).

Though labor has faced a number of obstacles throughout the 1970s, '80s, and '90s—a steady decline in union membership, conservative union leadership, "restructuring" and "globalization," and concerted blows to organized labor as in the case of striking air traffic controllers who were summarily fired and replaced by strike breakers by President

Ronald Reagan in 1981—there are signs that give renewed hope for labor's cause as we enter the twenty-first century. Service-industry and white-collar workers continue to join labor's ranks. Previously unheard of organizing is currently taking place among physicians across the country. Just since 1997, the number of unionized physicians has grown from 25,000 to 45,000. Another surprise came when McDonald's workers in Macedonia, Ohio, organized the first strike against a fast-food chain in the spring of 1998. After five days of picketing, workers won an adjusted pay scale and one week paid vacations for full-time employees.

Another positive sign is that rank and file workers in the United States and around the world continue to buck conservative union leadership, often with far-reaching results. Teamsters for a Democratic Union initiated rank and file reform among the Teamsters, which culminated in the successful 1997 United Parcel Service strike (Moody 1999). The fifteen-day strike, which brought UPS operations down to 10 percent of capacity, resulted in improved wages and, not least important, renewed confidence in labor's "sticking capacity," to use Melinda Scott's apt phrase in reference to determined hatters striking in 1915.

Around the world, and often joining hands across borders, workers have turned time and again to the kinds of confrontational tactics that have proved so effective throughout labor's history. From Nike workers in Indonesia to auto workers in the United States to hospital employees in Korea, women and men continue to prove that the collective actions of strikes, walkouts, and demonstrations are not outmoded forms of struggle, but are effective, nay, indispensable in the context of contemporary capitalism. A few of the countless examples of labor activism around the world demonstrate that workers understand their power as the producers of wealth. Shoe workers in Nike plants in Indonesia walked out of factories, in defiance of a ban on independent labor organizing, they halted production and won wage raises. Government workers in Colombia held an eight-day general strike and won wage increases to match the inflation rate. And in an amazing show of solidarity, militancy, and worker confidence, women at a Phillips Van Heusen garment plant in Guatemala's maquiladora zone held numerous walkouts in order to win bonuses they were due and the right to collective bargaining. As the union organizer Maria Marroquin asserted, "We keep getting stronger every day. Now we know we have the support of other PVH workers in others plants where there are unions and contracts. United, we can win anything!" (O'Connor 1997, 12). In response to reductions in social programs, cutbacks in jobs ("downsizing"), and wage decreases around the world, workers are fighting back. Moody notes, "In many cases the strikes reflect the greater role of women in the workforce and in organized labor" (1997, 1).

In the late 1980s and early '90s, workers began forming alliances across borders in order to confront the effects of the North American Free Trade Agreement (NAFTA) and the intensification of globalization. Ford Motor Company workers in Mexico, the U.S., and Canada formed MEXUSCAN Solidarity Task Force to confront issues of abuse in Ford's Cuautitlán plant outside Mexico City (Moody and McGinn 1992, 44, 45). U.S. cannery workers similarly reached out to their counterparts in Mexico. In 1990, Green Giant laid off 382 Watsonville, California, employees who were paid $7.61 an hour and moved the jobs to a plant in Irapuato, Mexico, where workers were paid $.50 an hour. Watsonville workers promptly formed an organization, Trabajadores Desplazados (Displaced Workers), and visited cannery workers at the Irapuato plant in order to establish organizational connections (Moody and McGinn 1992, 48). After their visit, the Watsonville workers educated unions across the country regarding Green Giant's practices and sparked demonstrations and pickets in U.S. cities and in London where Green Giant's owner, Grand Metropolitan, is located (48). Similar ties have been established among communication workers in Canada and the United States. In 1990 Canadian Auto Workers and Communications and Electrical Workers of Canada supported the Communication Workers of America in their strike against Northern Telecom. And in December 1991, communication workers from Canada and the United States formed a permanent coalition with the Mexican union Sindicato de Telefonistas de la Republica Mexicana (Moody and McGinn 1992, 68, 69).

Alliances are formed and struggles waged on a near-daily basis around the globe despite the media blackout afforded to most labor activity. Turning to the sit-down tactic so effectively engaged for the first time nearly sixty years ago, Canadian auto workers occupied the Johnson Controls factory in Stratford, Ontario, on April 15, 1999. Workers were protesting recent layoffs and the company's decision to outsource to Mexico. The plant occupation was a success, as workers won their jobs back as well as a renewed sense of strength in solidarity. The words of one worker sounded remarkably like those of workers of the early 1900s who testified to the transformative effect that such collective actions had. "In the twenty-eight years that I have been a member of this local [Canadian Auto Workers Local 1325] I have never seen the membership so united," stated Diane Albrecht. "This action did more in one day than a lifetime of education could have accomplished" (Albrecht 1999, 6).

Even service-industry workers—thought by many to be "impossible to organize"—have taken to traditional protest tactics in efforts to win fair wages and work conditions. Teachers in the state of Washington turned to one-day walkouts and rallies in an effort to win wage increases to match the rate of inflation (Yao 1999). In Saskatchewan, over eight thousand nurses defied a court injunction and remained on strike for ten days in April 1999 in a protest against excessive work hours (Buswell-Robinson 1999). The nurses, many of whom worked ninety-six hours a week, were effective at shutting down nearly all healthcare facilities and eventually won the support of government employees and academic assistants at the University of Regina, who struck in solidarity.

Despite the changes in the late-twentieth-century workplace, nurses, longshoremen, steelworkers, airplane pilots, and countless others demonstrate the continued relevance of collective labor-based confrontations that encourage people to rally around the one thing they all have in common—the need to work in order to live. Indeed, what is theorized and abstracted by politicians and academics is common sense to most. Though the late twentieth century is marked by increased diversity, fragmentation, and hypermediation, the fact remains that a tiny percentage own and control the tools for producing a society's goods while the vast majority actually produce the food, appliances, cars, homes, and services necessary for the society to function and sustain itself. Just as the collective and coordinated labor of millions is relied upon in order to keep a society functioning, so is the collective halting of production the most effective way to alter work conditions that generate profits for a few at the expense of the many.

Final Thoughts

As I bridged the distance between early- and late-twentieth-century popular-culture ideologies, in this last section I have provided specific examples from the workplace context in order to support the larger argument that despite changes in the nature of communication and its impact on social relations, we have much to learn from historical frames and struggles prominent in the early 1900s. More specifically, the above examples (and others too numerous to include) point to the strikingly similar conditions faced by workers in the last decade of the twentieth century—conditions that have not been mitigated but exacerbated by various technological advances. As the twenty-first century arrives and we find ourselves surrounded by and embedded in the same disparities that divided us a century ago, some scholars are paying renewed attention to "traditional" or "old" theories and conceptualizations of domination and resistance in contradistinction to the calls for a "new" politics in an age variously dubbed post-Fordist, postindustrial, postmodern, postcolonial, and postfeminist (see Bina, Clements, Davis 1996; Callinicos 1990; Cloud 1999; Ebert 1996; Harvey 1989; Marshall 1997). *Protest and Popular Culture* contributes to this renewed focus and provides a case study from which to gain an understanding of the past so that we may have a better conception of what is needed for the future.

Throughout this conclusion, we have traveled quite a distance from the protest tactics and popular portrayals examined in the chapters of this book. Indeed, the purpose of this discussion is to demonstrate the remarkable continuities between past and present, the similarities that characterize the landscapes of both early- and late-twentieth-century popular and workplace contexts. *Protest and Popular Culture* uncovered the origins of mass communication strategies that mystified work and gender disparities, elided class conflict, and personalized dissent. The frames frequently employed in popular magazines promoted a worldview that obscured the influence of objective structures that discriminated and denied the presence of a laboring body capable of resisting and transforming such structures through collective action. The intent of this project is not to downplay important differences between the early and late twentieth century, but to redirect attention to past struggles in the belief that there is much to learn from history—both its successes and struggles.

Communication technologies will undoubtedly continue to evolve at break-neck speed as growing numbers of people log on to the Internet for the first time each day. As members of a society in which individuals must sell their labor in order to survive, we would do well to remain vigilant regarding what new communication technologies have to offer and how they shape interpersonal and work relationships, politics, and public affairs. Rather than celebrate or accede to the fragmentation, multiplicity, and simulacra, we must continue to ask who is benefiting and at whose expense. Rather than acquiesce to capitalism's divide-and-conquer strategy, accomplished by means of new social movements, identity politics, or individualized strategic strikes, we would do well to learn from activists such as Leonora O'Reilly of the early 1900s and Maria Marroquin, of the 1990s who called attention to the relevance of material structures in their lives and who engaged themselves collectively as laborers in order to transform not only the hegemonic ideologies of gender and class discrimination but, more fundamentally, the objective structures and systems that constrained their abilities to live decent and humane lives.

Notes

1. Thompson does not offer a wholesale celebration of television in its role as political motivator but rather notes the possibility of concerted action in response to mediated messages (1990). Thompson's analyses of mediated messages include an examination of the technological means of transmission as well as the

historical context of production and reception. For a more optimistic account than Thompson's of the role of television in fostering political understanding among viewers, see Brummett 1991.

2. Sommers distinguishes between "gender feminism" and "equity feminism" and asserts that "gender feminists" such Gloria Steinem, Catherine MacKinnon, and Susan Faludi are spreading "falsehoods" and "exaggerations" that are "muddying the waters of American feminism" (1994). Roiphe decries the upsurge in rape awareness groups, help lines, and speak-outs as reinforcing and even overdramatizing women's status as victims (1993). And Paglia criticizes "Betty Crocker feminism" as an outdated mind-set that erroneously holds to a view of contemporary society as patriarchal (1994). According to her, "[W]hat feminists call patriarchy is simply *civilization*, an abstract system . . . now co-owned by women" (26).

3. Busby and Leichty acknowledge that *Ms.* magazine no longer carries advertisements, but they explain that "its historical position as the first national magazine of the feminist movement and as the icon of the movement made it important for inclusion" in their study (252).

4. The term "post-Fordism" is often associated with writers of the journal *Marxism Today* who argue that a fundamental break in capitalist production and relations has rendered traditional Marxist concepts and understandings outmoded. "New times" scholars, as they refer to their project, call for a new politics such as that elaborated in the previous discussion of "new social movements." See Clarke 1991.

5. Burkett 1994, 13.

6. The carmaker Saturn is perhaps the best-known example of a company that espouses labor-management cooperation and teamwork. Saturn's version of "teamwork" consists of rotating shifts where employees move back and forth between day and night shifts every few days while select managers are granted day shifts only. "Rebalancing" refers to Saturn's practice of doing the same work with fewer workers (Slaughter 1999).

Bibliography

A few minutes with father. 1916. *Home Life*, Jan., 3.

A few words by the editor. 1909. *Comfort*, August, 3.

A few words by the editor. 1910. *Comfort*, March, 3.

A few words by the editor. 1911. *Comfort*, March, 3.

A few words by the editor. 1912. *Comfort*, Feb., 4.

A woman's luncheon. 1895. *Atlantic Monthly*, Aug., 194–205.

Abbott, Edith. 1908. The English working-woman and the franchise. *Atlantic Monthly*, Sept., 343–346.

Abbott, Lyman. 1903. Why women do not wish the suffrage. *Atlantic Monthly*, Sept., 289–296.

Abbott, Mabel. 1914. The waitresses of Seattle. *Life and Labor*, Feb., 48–49.

Adams, David. 1999. Auto parts industry undergoes shakeout. *Akron Beacon Journal*, Jan. 31, G1.

Adams, Martin. 1916. Woman's Party Convention: The first Woman's Party in the world organized in Chicago. *Home Life*, Aug., 7.

Addams, Jane. 1911a. A new conscience and an ancient evil, Chapter 1. *McClure's*, Nov., 3.

———. 1911b. A new conscience and an ancient evil, Chapter 2. *McClure's*, Dec., 232–240.

———. 1912a. A new conscience and an ancient evil, Chapter 3. *McClure's*, Jan., 338–344.

———. 1912b. A new conscience and an ancient evil, Chapter 4. *McClure's*, Feb., 471–478.

———. 1912c. A new conscience and an ancient evil, Chapter 5. *McClure's*, March., 592–598.

Albrecht, Diane M. 1999. Sit-in stops Johnson Controls from shipping jobs to Mexico. *Labor Notes*, June, 1.

Alcoff, Linda. 1988. Cultural feminism vs. poststructuralism: The identity crisis in feminist theory. *Signs: Journal of Women in Culture and Society* 13: 405–436.

———. 1991–92. The problem of speaking for others. Cultural Critique Winter: 5–32.

An American pogrom. 1914. *Life and Labor*, June, 171–173.

Anderson, Harriet. 1912. Woman. *Atlantic Monthly*, Aug., 177–183.

Anderson, Mary. 1914. National Suffrage Convention. *Life and Labor*, Jan., 12.

Armstrong, Elizabeth. 1909. Color in the home. *People's Home Journal*, Feb., 20.

Atkinson, Edward. 1903. Commercialism. *Atlantic Monthly*, Oct., 517–521.

Augusta, Clara. 1895. Taken into partnership. *People's Home Journal*, July, 12.

Aune, James Arnt. 1994. *Rhetoric and Marxism*. Boulder: Westview Press.

Austin, Jane G. 1903. The lady of Leigh. *People's Home Journal*, Nov., 1.

Baker, Paula. 1994. The domestication of politics: Women and American political society, 1780–1920. In *Unequal sisters: A multi-cultural reader in U.S. Women's History*, ed. Vicki L. Ruiz and Ellen Carol DuBois, 85–110. 2nd ed. New York: Routledge.

Baker, Ray Stannard. 1903a. The right to work: The story of the non-striking miners, *McClure's*, Jan., 323–336.

———. 1903b. Capital and labor hunt together: Chicago the victim of the new industrial conspiracy. *McClure's*, Sept., 451–463.

———. 1903c. The trust's new tool—the labor boss. *McClure's*, Nov., 30–43.

———. 1904a. A corner in labor. *McClure's*, Feb., 366–378.

———. 1904b. Organized capital challenges organized labor. *McClure's*, July, 279–292.

Barnes, Earl. 1912a. The feminizing of culture. *Atlantic Monthly*, June, 770–776.

———. 1912b. The economic independence of women. *Atlantic Monthly*, Aug., 260–265.

———. 1915. A new profession for women. *Atlantic Monthly*, Aug., 225–234.

Barr, Robert. 1894. The revolt of the _____. *McClure's*, July, 169–177.

Barrett, Michèle. 1980. *Women's oppression today: Problems in Marxist feminist analysis*. London: Verso.

Barrett, Michèle, and Mary McIntosh. 1982. *The anti-social family*. 2nd ed. London: Verso.

Barthes, Roland. 1957. *Mythologies*. Trans. Annette Lavers. New York: Hill and Wang.

Basch, Françoise. 1990. The shirtwaist strike in history and myth. Introduction to Theresa S. Malkiel [1910], *The diary of a shirtwaist striker*. Ithaca, N.Y.: ILR Press, 1–77.

Bean, Alice S. 1915. Organization of office workers: An impossible job! *Life and Labor*, Jan., 5–7.

Beasley, Maurine H., and Sheila J. Gibbons. 1993. *Taking their place: A documentary history of women and journalism*. Washington D.C.: American University Press.

Beecher, Henry Ward. 1895. Henry Ward Beecher's advice. *People's Home Journal*, Jan., 8.

Bell, Bernard Iddings. 1916. Woman and religion. *Atlantic Monthly*, March, 378–382.

Bennett, Emerson. 1894. Buried in a mine. *People's Home Journal*, March, 3.

Best, Steven, and Douglas Kellner. 1991. *Postmodern theory: Critical interrogations*. New York: Guilford Press.

Biesecker, Barbara. 1992. Coming to terms with recent attempts to write women into the history of rhetoric. *Philosophy and Rhetoric* 25:140–161.

Bina, Cyrus, Laurie Clements, and Chuck Davis. 1996. Beyond survival: Toward revitalization of labor. Introduction to *Beyond survival: Wage labor in the late twentieth century*, ed. Cyrus Bina, Laurie Clements, and Chuck Davis, 3–17. Armonk, N.Y.: M. E. Sharpe.

Biskind, Peter. 1983. *Seeing is believing: How Hollywood taught us to stop worrying and love the fifties*. New York: Pantheon Books.

Black, Edwin. 1970. The second persona. *Quarterly Journal of Speech* 56:109–119.

Booth, Katherine. 1909. The pretty girls' club. *Comfort*, May, 12.

Bordin, Ruth. 1981. *Woman and temperance: The quest for power and liberty, 1873–1900.* Philadelphia: Temple University Press.

Bordo, Susan. 1990. Feminism, postmodernism, and gender-skepticism. In *Feminism/Postmodernism*, ed. Linda J. Nicholson, 133–156. New York: Routledge.

———. 1993. *Unbearable weight: Feminism, Western culture, and the body.* Berkeley: University of California Press.

Boteler-Sanders, Grace. 1912. No quitter. *People's Home Journal*, Aug., 7.

Bowers, John Waite, and Donovan J. Ochs. 1971. *The rhetoric of agitation and control.* Massachusetts: Addison-Wesley.

Boyce, Neith. 1896. A woman's way. *Comfort*, Jan., 2.

Boyd, Monica, Mary Ann Mulvihill, and John Myles. 1995. Gender, power, and postindustrialism. In *Gender inequality at work*, ed. Jerry A. Jacobs, 178–206. Thousand Oaks, Calif.: Sage.

Boydston, Jeanne. 1994. To earn her daily bread: Housework and antebellum working-class subsistence. In *Unequal sisters: A multicultural reader in U.S. women's history*, ed. Vicki L. Ruiz and Ellen Carol DuBois, 44–56. 2nd ed. New York: Routledge.

Boyer, Richard O., and Herbert M. Morais. 1955. *Labor's untold story.* New York: United Electrical, Radio & Machine Workers of America.

Boylan, Grace Duffie. 1913. The shared mother. *People's Home Journal*, Dec., 16.

Branigin, William. 1997. Reaping abuse for what they sew. *Washington Post*, Feb. 16, A1.

Brecher, Jeremy, and Tim Costello. 1976. *Common sense for hard times: The power of the powerless to cope with everyday life and transform society in the nineteen seventies.* New York: Two Continents Institute for Policy Studies.

Breen, Richard, and David B. Rottman. 1995. *Class stratification: A comparative perspective.* New York: Harvester Wheatsheaf.

Brown, Eleanor. 1916a. Girls in the city: Professions for the gifted girl. *Home Life*, Oct., 15.

———. 1916b. Girls in the city: Some questions and answers. *Home Life*, Nov., 13.

Brown, F. Sewall. 1910. How Amy handled the bandits. *Comfort*, Aug., 17.

Brown, Mary Ellen. 1994. *Soap opera and women's talk: The pleasure of resistance.* Thousand Oaks, Calif.: Sage.

Brummett, Barry. 1991. *Rhetorical dimensions of popular culture.* Tuscaloosa: University of Alabama Press.

Brummett, Barry, and Margaret Carlisle Duncan. 1992. Toward a discursive ontology of media. *Critical Studies in Mass Communication* 9:229–249.

Brush, Mary Isabel. 1912. Business women in a business club: An organization that went in for city 'boosting' in place of 'civic art.' *Home Life*, April, 11.

Bryson, Valerie. 1992. *Feminist political theory: An introduction.* New York: Paragon House.

Budd, Mike, Robert M. Entman, and Clay Steinman. 1990. The affirmative character of U.S. cultural studies. *Critical Studies in Mass Communication* 7:169–184.

Buhle, Mari Jo. 1981. *Women and American socialism, 1870–1920.* Urbana: University of Illinois Press.

Burke, Kenneth. 1966. *Language as symbolic action: Essays on life, literature and method*. Berkeley: University of California Press.

Burkett, Paul. 1994. The strange U.S. economic recovery and Clintonomics historically reconsidered. *Capital and Class* 52 (Spring):13.

Burnett, Mary G. 1893. Mrs. Gladstone and her good works. *McClure's*, Aug., 235–241.

Burns, Agnes. 1917. Shirt makers win. *Life and Labor*, April, 63.

Busby, Linda J., and Greg Leichty. 1993. Feminism and advertising in traditional and nontraditional women's magazines 1950s–1980s. *Journalism Quarterly* 70(2): 247–264.

Buswell-Robinson, Cheryl. 1999. Nurses strike for better staffing and patient care. *Labor Notes*, June, 1.

Butler, Judith. 1990. *Gender trouble*. London: Routledge.

Byars, Jackie. 1991. *All that Hollywood allows: Re-reading gender in 1950s melodrama*. Chapel Hill: University of North Carolina Press.

Caine, Stanley P. 1974. The origins of progressivism. In *The Progressive Era*, ed. Lewis L. Gould, 11–34. Syracuse: Syracuse University Press.

Callinicos, Alex. 1990. *Against postmodernism: A Marxist critique*. New York: St. Martin's Press.

Calvert, Peter. 1982. *The concept of class: An historical introduction*. New York: St. Martin's Press.

Cameron, Ardis. 1985. Bread and roses revisited: Women's culture and working-class activism in the Lawrence strike of 1912. In *Women, work, and protest: A century of U.S. women's labor history*, ed. Ruth Milkman, 42–61. London: Routledge & Kegan Paul.

———. 1991. Landscapes of subterfuge: Working-class neighborhoods and immigrant women. In *Gender, class, race, and reform in the Progressive Era*, ed. Noralee Frankel and Nancy Schrom Dye, 56–72. Lexington, Ky.: University Press of Kentucky.

Cameron, Margaret. 1903. The committee on matrimony: A comedy in one act. *McClure's*, Oct., 659–665.

Campbell, Karlyn Kohrs. 1973. The rhetoric of women's liberation: An oxymoron. *Quarterly Journal of Speech* 59:74–86.

———. 1989. *Man cannot speak for her: A critical study of early feminist rhetoric*. Vol. 1. New York: Greenwood Press.

Carpenter, Elizabeth R. 1911. Love or money. *Comfort*, March, 32.

Cathcart, Robert S. 1972. New approaches to the study of movements: Defining movements rhetorically. *Western Speech* 36:82–88.

———. 1980. Defining social movements by their rhetorical form. *Central States Speech Journal* 31:267–273.

Chapman, Rev. J. Wilbur. 1913a. Problems of life, I: Temptation and how to meet it. *Home Life*, Aug., 8.

———. 1913b. Problems of life, II: Trouble and how to bear it. *Home Life*, Sept., 9.

Chase, Arthur M. 1912. The new woman and the old man: They meet in a most informal way. *Home Life*, March, 8.

Cheng, Vicki. 1997. Stewart our most important Martha since Washington. *Austin American Statesman*, July 4, E1.

Clark, Sue Ainslie, and Edith Wyatt. 1910a. Working girls' budgets: A series of articles based upon individual stories of self-supporting girls. *McClure's*, Oct., 595–614.

———. 1910b. Working girls' budgets: The shirtwaist-makers and their strike. *McClure's*, Nov., 70–86.

———. 1910c. Working girls' budgets: Unskilled and seasonal factory workers. *McClure's*, Dec., 201–211.

———. 1911. Women laundry workers in New York. *McClure's*, Feb., 401–414.

Clarke, John. 1991. *New times and old enemies: Essays on cultural studies and America*. London: HarperCollins Academic.

Cloud, Dana L. 1992. The limits of interpretation: Ambivalence and the stereotype in *Spenser: For Hire*. *Critical Studies in Mass Communication* 9:311–324.

———. 1994. The materiality of discourse as oxymoron: A challenge to critical rhetoric. *Western Journal of Communication* 58:141–163.

———. 1996. Hegemony or concordance? The rhetoric of tokenism in 'Oprah' Winfrey's rags-to-riches biography. *Critical Studies in Mass Communication* 13:115–137.

———. 1998a. *Control and consolation in American culture and politics*. Thousand Oaks, Calif.: Sage.

———. 1998b. "The rhetoric of < family values>: Scapegoating, utopia, and the privatization of social responsibility. *Western Journal of Communication* 62(4):387–419.

———. 1999. Get a little class: A programmatic essay (a.k.a. manifesto) on labor and communication. Paper presented at the annual convention of the Western States Communication Association, Feb. 22, Vancouver, B.C.

Cobble, Dorothy Sue. 1991. *Dishing it out: Waitresses and their unions in the twentieth century*. Urbana: University of Illinois Press.

Cole, Terry Wayne. 1978. *Labor's radical alternative: The rhetoric of the Industrial Workers of the World*. Ann Arbor, Mich.: University Microfilms International.

Combahee River Collective. A black feminist statement. In *This bridge called my back: Writings by radical women of color*, ed. Cherrie Moraga and Gloria Anzaldua, 210–218. New York: Kitchen Table/Woman of Color Press.

Comer, A. P. 1911. The vanishing lady. *Atlantic Monthly*, Dec., 721–734.

Comfort, Lucy Randall. 1902. Flossie Field's fortunes: The story of a poor girl. *Comfort*, June, 8.

Condit, Celeste Michelle. 1994. Hegemony in a mass-mediated society: Concordance about reproductive technologies. *Critical Studies in Mass Communication* 11:205–230.

Connelly, Mark Thomas. 1980. *The response to prostitution in the Progressive Era*. Chapel Hill: University of North Carolina Press.

Coontz, Stephanie. 1988. *The social origins of private life: A history of American families, 1600–1900*. London: Verso.

———. 1992. *The way we never were: American families and the nostalgia trap*. New York: Basic Books.

Cooper, Courtney Ryley. 1914. Contentment. *People's Home Journal*, Sept., 9.

Cott, Nancy F. 1987. *The grounding of modern feminism*. New Haven: Yale University Press.

Crothers, Samuel McChord. 1914. Meditations on votes for women. *Atlantic Monthly*, Oct., 538–546.

Cunningham, William J. 1909. Two views of the railroad question: Brotherhoods and efficiency. *Atlantic Monthly*, Sept., 289–302.

Curtis, Nettie Lounsbury. 1916a. Home life problems: The quarrelsome sex—I. *Home Life*, Sept., 7.

———. 1916b. Home life problems: Her personal income—II. *Home Life*, Oct., 7.

Darnovsky, Marcy. 1991/92. The new traditionalism: Repackaging Ms. Consumer. *Social Text* 9–10: 72–91.

Davies, Mary Carolyn. 1915. Little things. *People's Home Journal*, Nov., 12.

Davis, Angela Y. 1981. *Women, race, and class*. New York: Random House.

Davis, Jennie Melvene. 1902. Men, women and things. *Comfort*, Jan., 8.

Deacon, Desley. 1989. *Managing gender: The state, the new middle class and women workers 1830–1930*. Melbourne, Australia: Oxford University Press.

Dealing with the individual. n.d. National Women's Trade Union League Papers. Microfilm, reel 4. Schlesinger Library, Radcliffe Institute, Harvard University.

Deem, Melissa D. 1995. Decorum: The flight from the rhetorical. In *Argumentation and Values*. Proceedings of the Ninth SCA/AFA Conference on Argumentation, ed. Sally Jackson, 226–229. Annandale, Va.: SCA.

Deetz, Stanley, and Astrid Kersten. 1983. Critical models of interpretive research. In *Communication and Organizations: An Interpretive Approach*, ed. L. L. Putnam and M. E. Pacanowsky, 147–171. Newbury Park, Calif.: Sage.

Deetz, Stanley, and Dennis K. Mumby. 1990. Power, discourse, and the workplace: Reclaiming the critical tradition. *Communication Yearbook* 13:18–47.

Deland, Lorin F. 1912. The Lawrence strike: A study. *Atlantic Monthly*, May, 694–705.

Deland, Margaret. 1894. Philip and his wife. *Atlantic Monthly*, Jan., 1–20.

———. 1910. The change in the feminine ideal. *Atlantic Monthly*, March, 289–302.

Deming, Seymour. 1914. A message to the middle class. *Atlantic Monthly*, July, 1–14.

Department store waitresses win increase. 1918. *Life and Labor*, July, 141.

Discrimination against pregnant women alleged. 1997. *Austin American Statesman*, March 30, B2.

Di Stephano, Christine. 1990. Dilemmas of difference: Feminism, modernity, and postmodernism. In *Feminism/Postmodernism*, ed. Linda J. Nicholson, 63–82. New York: Routledge.

Dolson, Cora A. 1914. The simple life. *People's Home Journal*, June, 16.

Douglas, Charles Noel. 1903. None can take a mother's place. *Comfort*, Dec., 13.

Dow, Bonnie J. 1992. Femininity and feminism in *Murphy Brown*. *Southern Communication Journal* 57:143–155.

———. 1996. *Prime-time feminism: Television, media culture, and the women's movement since 1970*. Philadelphia: University of Pennsylvania Press.

Dreier, Mary. 1912. To wash or not to wash, ay, there's the rub: The New York laundry strike. *Life and Labor*, March, 68–72.

Drexler, Michael. 1999. Crash landing: B. F. Goodrich merger may eliminate 650 Cleveland manufacturing jobs. *Cleveland Free Times*, July 14–20, 12.

DuBois, Ellen Carol. 1978. *Feminism and suffrage: The emergence of an independent women's movement in America, 1848–1869.* Ithaca, N.Y.: Cornell University Press.

———. 1994. Working women, class relations, and suffrage militance: Harriot Stanton Blatch and the New York woman suffrage movement, 1894–1909. In *Unequal sisters: A multi-cultural reader in U.S. women's history,* ed. Vicki L. Ruiz and Ellen Carol DuBois, 228–246. 2nd ed. New York: Routledge.

Duffy, Karen. 1998. Fifteen fun, fearless, female ways to celebrate. *Cosmopolitan,* March, 170.

Dye, Nancy Schrom. 1975a. Creating a feminist alliance: Sisterhood and class conflict in the New York Women's Trade Union League, 1903–1914. *Feminist Studies* 2:24–38.

———. 1975b. Feminism or unionism? The New York Women's Trade Union League and the labor movement. *Feminist Studies* 3:111–125.

———. 1980. *As equals and as sisters: Feminism, the labor movement, and the Women's Trade Union League of New York.* Columbia, Mo.: University of Missouri Press.

Eagleton, Terry. 1991. *Ideology: An introduction.* London: Verso.

Easley, Ralph M. 1902. What organized labor has learned. *McClure's,* Oct., 483–492.

Ebert, Teresa L. 1996. *Ludic feminism and after: Postmodernism, desire, and labor in late capitalism.* Ann Arbor, Mich.: University of Michigan Press.

Ehrenreich, Barbara. 1981. The women's movements: Feminist and antifeminist. *Radical America* 93:92–101.

Eisenstein, Sarah. 1983. *Give us bread but give us roses: Working women's consciousness in the United States, 1890 to the First World War.* London: Routledge & Kegan Paul.

Engels, Frederick. 1890. Letters on historical materialism. In *The Marx-Engels reader,* ed. Robert C. Tucker, 760–768. 2nd ed. New York: W. W. Norton, 1978.

Enstad, Nan. 1999. *Ladies of labor, girls of adventure: Working women, popular culture, and labor politics at the turn of the twentieth century.* New York: Columbia University Press.

Entman, Robert M. 1991. Framing U.S. coverage of international news: Contrasts in narratives of the KAL and Iran Air incidents. *Journal of Communication* 41:6–27.

———. 1993. Framing: Toward clarification of a fractured paradigm. *Journal of Communication* 43:51–58.

Epstein, Barbara Leslie. 1981. *The politics of domesticity: Women, evangelism, and temperance in nineteenth-century America.* Middletown, Conn.: Wesleyan University Press.

Epstein, Cynthia Fuchs. 1978. The women's movement and the women's pages. In *Hearth and home: Images of women in the mass media,* ed. Gaye Tuchman, Arlene Daniels, and James Benet, 216–222. New York: Oxford University Press.

Etz, Anna Cadogan. [1910] n.d.. Some reasons why. In *Woman suffrage: Arguments and results,* ed. National American Woman Suffrage Association. New York: Kraus Reprint Co. Reprinted from collections of the Alderman Library, University of Virginia.

Ewen, Stuart. 1976. *Captains of consciousness: Advertising and the social roots of the consumer culture.* New York: McGraw-Hill.

————. 1996. *PR! A social history of spin.* New York: Basic Books.

Fagan, James O. 1909a. The industrial dilemma: Labor and the railroads. *Atlantic Monthly*, Feb., 145–153.

————. 1909b. The industrial dilemma: The railroads and education. *Atlantic Monthly*, March, 326–335.

————. 1909c. The industrial dilemma: The railroads and efficiency of service. *Atlantic Monthly*, April, 543–552.

————. 1909d. The industrial dilemma: The railroads and publicity. *Atlantic Monthly*, May, 617–627.

————. 1911a. Socialism and human achievement. *Atlantic Monthly*, Jan., 24–34.

————. 1911b. Socialism and national efficiency. *Atlantic Monthly*, May, 580–591.

Faludi, Susan. 1991. *Backlash: The undeclared war against American women.* New York: Crown.

Farrell, Amy Erdman. 1995. Feminism and the media: Introduction. *Signs: Journal of Women in Culture and Society,* spring:642–645.

Fawcett, Waldon. 1903. The tableware of the White House. *Comfort*, June, 3.

Fay, Charles Norman. 1912. The value of existing trade-unionism. *Atlantic Monthly*, June, 758–770.

Ferguson, Marjorie. 1990. Images of power and the feminist fallacy. *Critical Studies in Mass Communication* 7:215–230.

Field, Amy Walker. 1915. Victory for the Springfield corset workers. *Life and Labor*, Nov., 168–169.

Filler, Louis. 1939. *Crusaders for American liberalism.* New York: Harcourt Brace.

Finding fortunes. 1895. *People's Home Journal*, Jan. 13.

Finnegan, Margaret. 1999. *Selling suffrage: Consumer culture and votes for women.* New York: Columbia University Press.

Fiske, John. 1986. Television: Polysemy and popularity. *Critical Studies in Mass Communication* 3:391–408.

————. 1987. *Television culture.* London: Methuen.

————. 1989. *Understanding popular culture.* London: Routledge.

Fleming, May Agnes. 1895. The sisters. *People's Home Journal*, Jan., 5.

Fletcher, Henry J. 1894. The railway war. *Atlantic Monthly*, Oct., 534–541.

Flexner, Eleanor. 1959. *Century of struggle: The woman's rights movement in the United States.* Cambridge: Belknap Press of Harvard University Press.

Flynn, Elizabeth Gurley. 1916. Problems organizing women. In *Words on fire: The life and writing of Elizabeth Gurley Flynn*, ed. Rosalyn Fraad Baxandall, 134–138. New Brunswick, N.J.: Rutgers University Press, 1987.

————. 1955. *The Rebel Girl: An autobiography, my first life (1906–1926).* New York: International Publishers.

Flynt, Josiah. 1894. Old Boston Mary: A remembrance. *Atlantic Monthly*, Sept., 318–325.

Foner, Philip S. 1976. *Organized labor and the black worker, 1619–1973.* New York: International Publishers.

————. 1979. *Women and the American labor movement: From colonial times to the eve of World War I.* Vol. 1. New York: Free Press.

————. 1980. *Women and the American labor movement: From World War I to the present.* Vol. 2. New York: Free Press.

Foner, Philip S., ed. 1977. *The factory girls*. Urbana: University of Illinois Press.

Ford, Linda G. 1991. *Iron-jawed angels: The suffrage militancy of the National Woman's Party 1912–1920*. Lanham, N.Y.: University Press of America.

Forty million dollars for education. *Comfort*, Jan., 17.

Fowler, E. W. 1903. A strenuous courtship. *McClure's*, Nov., 15–27.

Fox, Richard Wightman, and T. J. Jackson Lears. 1983. Introduction to *The culture of consumption: Critical essays in American history, 1880–1980*, ed. T. J. Jackson Lears and Richard Wightman Fox. New York: Pantheon Books.

Franklin, S. M. 1914. The new broom: How it is sometimes made: Strike of the only girl broom makers in the United States. *Life and Labor*, Oct., 294–296.

Freedman, Estelle. 1979. Separatism as strategy: Female institution building and American feminism, 1870–1930. *Feminist Studies* 5:512–529.

French, Minnie Reid. 1912. Yansen: A story of the mines. *People's Home Journal*, Jan., 6.

Gamboa, Glenn. 1999a. Blacks bear brunt of wage gap. *Akron Beacon Journal*, June 20, A1.

———. 1999b. Economic boom deceives. *Akron Beacon Journal*, June 20, A1.

———. 1999c. Wages rise at same rate for top, bottom of scale. *Akron Beacon Journal*, June 2, A7.

Gambrell, Alice. 1994/95. You're beautiful when you're angry: Fashion magazines and recent feminisms. *Discourse: Journal for Theoretical Studies in Media and Culture* 17(2):139–158.

Gannett, W. H. 1911. Strike! *Comfort*, Jan., 3.

Garvey, Ellen Gruber. 1996. *The adman in the parlor: Magazines and the gendering of consumer culture, 1880s to 1910s*. New York: Oxford University Press.

Gatlin, Dana. 1915. Woman stuff. *McClure's*, Dec., 31.

———. 1916. More woman stuff. *McClure's*, June, 23.

Geewax, Marilyn. 1999. Global agenda: Bridging the growing technology gap. *Akron Beacon Journal*, July 23, A11.

George, W. L. 1913. Feminist intentions. *Atlantic Monthly*, Dec., 721–732.

———. 1915. Notes on the intelligence of woman. *Atlantic Monthly*, Dec., 721–730.

———. 1916. Further notes on the intelligence of woman. *Atlantic Monthly*, Jan., 99–109

Giebler, A. H. 1912. Pretty is as pretty does. *People's Home Journal*, Sept., 7.

Gilmore, Florence. 1914. A little mother. *Atlantic Monthly*, Sept., 381–384.

Girls in the city: The stenographer. 1916. *Home Life*, Sept., 17.

Girls' stories. 1914. *Life and Labor*, August, 243–244.

Gitlin, Todd. 1979. Prime time ideology: The hegemonic process in television entertainment. *Social Problems* 26:251–266.

———. 1980. *The whole world is watching: Mass media in the making and unmaking of the New Left*. Berkeley: University of California Press.

———. 1983. *Inside prime time*. New York: Pantheon Books.

———. 1987. Television's screens: Hegemony in transition. In *American Media and Mass Culture: Left Perspectives*, ed. Donald Lazere, 240–265. Berkeley: University of California Press.

Glanton, Eileen. 1998. Mergers boost stock market, investor spirit. *Akron Beacon Journal*, Nov. 29, G2.

Godfrey, Hollis. 1909. The food of the city worker. *Atlantic Monthly*, Feb., 267–277.
———. 1910. City housing: The problem at home. *Atlantic Monthly*, April, 548–558.
Golding, Peter. 1996. World wide wedge: Division and contradiction in the global information infrastructure. *Monthly Review* 48 (3): 70–85.
———. 1998. New technologies and old problems: Evaluating and regulating media performance in the 'information age.' In *The media question: Popular cultures and public interests*, ed. Kees Brants, Joke Hermes, and Liesbet van Zoonen, 7–17. London: Sage.
Goldman, Robert, Deborah Heath, and Sharon L. Smith. 1991. Commodity feminism. *Critical Studies in Mass Communication* 8:333–351.
Goodwin, Thomas Dwight. 1915. The wife. *People's Home Journal*, June, 8.
Gordon, Eleanor. 1911. Jenny. *People's Home Journal*, April, 7.
Goscilo, Margaret. 1987/88. Deconstructing *The Terminator*. *Film Criticism* 12 (2):37–52.
Gould, Lewis L. 1974. The Progressive Era. Introduction to *The Progressive Era*, ed. Lewis L. Gould, 1–10. Syracuse: Syracuse University Press.
Gould, Margaret. 1916. The fashionable figure—and how she gets it. *McClure's*, March, 32–33.
Gramsci, Antonio. 1926. Selections from political writings (1921–1926). In *A Gramsci reader: Selected writings 1916–1935*, ed. David Forgacs. London: Lawrence & Wishart, 1988.
———. n.d. Selections from prison notebooks. In *A Gramsci reader: Selected writings 1916–1935*, ed. David Forgacs. London: Lawrence & Wishart, 1988.
Gray, Herman. 1994. Television, Black Americans, and the American dream. In *Television: The critical view*, ed. H. Newcomb, 176–187. 5th ed. New York: Oxford University Press.
Gray, John H. 1903. The social unrest. *Atlantic Monthly*, April, 569–572.
Great American givers. *Comfort*, Jan., 6.
Greaves, Ethel. 1916. Girls in the city: Investigator of unskilled trades for women and girls. *Home Life*, July, 9.
Green, Helen. 1909. Pioneer goes suffragette. *McClure's*, Oct., 676–682.
Greenwald, Maurine Weiner. 1980. *Women, war, and work: The impact of World War I on women workers in the United States*. Westport, Conn.: Greenwood Press.
Gregg, Richard B. 1971. The ego-function of the rhetoric of protest. *Philosophy and Rhetoric* 4:71–91.
Griffin, Leland M. 1952. The rhetoric of historical movements. *Quarterly Journal of Speech* 38:184–188.
Grossberg, Larry. 1984. 'I'd rather feel bad than not feel anything at all': Rock and roll, pleasure and power. *Enclitic* 8:94–111.
———. 1989. MTV: Swinging on the (postmodern) star. In *Cultural politics in contemporary America*, ed. Ian Angus and Sut Jhally, 254–270. New York: Routledge.
Hale, Beatrice Forbes-Robertson. 1915. What women want. *McClure's*, Sept., 17–19.
Hall, Gertrude. 1893. The rose is such a lady. *McClure's*, June, 82.

Hall, Stuart, Chas Critcher, Tony Jefferson, John Clarke, and Brian Roberts. *Policing the crisis: Mugging, the state, and law and order*. 1978. New York: Holmes & Meier.

Hall, Stuart, and Martin Jacques. 1989. *New times: The changing face of politics in the 1990s*. London: Verso.

Halttunen, Karen. 1993. Early American murder narratives. In *The power of culture: Critical essays in American history*, ed. Richard Wightman Fox and T. J. Jackson Lears, 67–101. Chicago: University of Chicago Press.

Harding, Sandra. 1993. Rethinking standpoint epistemology: 'What is strong objectivity'? In *Feminist epistemologies*, ed. Linda Alcoff and Elizabeth Potter, 49–82. New York: Routledge.

Hariman, Robert. 1992. Decorum, power, and the courtly style. *Quarterly Journal of Speech* 78:149–172.

Hart, Roderick P. 1994. *Seducing America: How television charms the modern voter*. New York: Oxford University Press.

———. 1997. *Modern rhetorical criticism*, 2nd ed. Boston: Allyn and Bacon.

Hartsock, Nancy. 1983. The feminist standpoint: Developing the ground for a specifically feminist historical materialism. In *Discovering reality*, ed. Sandra Harding and Merrill Hintikka. Dordrecht, Netherlands: Reidel.

Hartz, Louis. 1955. *The liberal tradition in America: An interpretation of American political thought since the Revolution*. San Diego: Harcourt Brace Jovanovich.

Harvey, David. 1989. *The condition of posmodernity: An enquiry into the origins of cultural change*. Cambridge, Mass.: Basil Blackwell.

Hay, Walter Beach. 1910. The pretensions of Charlotte. *McClure's*, March, 539–544.

Hendrick, Burton J. 1903. A great municipal reform. *Atlantic Monthly*, Nov., 665–673.

Hennessy, Rosemary. 1993. *Materialist feminism and the politics of discourse*. New York, Routledge.

Henry, Alice. 1913. The vice problem from various angles. *Life and Labor*, May, 141–144.

Herrick, Christine Terhune. 1903. How to make work easy. *Comfort*, July, 12.

Higginson, Ella. 1910. Full many a flower. *People's Home Journal*, May, 10.

Hoerle, Helen Christene. 1915. One fearsome lady. *Home Life*, Dec., 7.

Hollander, Jacob H. 1912. The abolition of poverty. *Atlantic Monthly*, Oct., 492–497.

Holt, Henry. 1908. Competition. *Atlantic Monthly*, Oct., 516–526.

Horowitz, Daniel. 1985. *The morality of spending: Attitudes toward the consumer society in America, 1875–1940*. Baltimore: Johns Hopkins University Press.

Hume, Janice. 1997. Defining the historic American heroine: Changing characteristics of heroic women in nineteenth-century media. *Journal of Popular Culture*, 31.1:1–21.

Humphrey, Zephine. 1912. The lady of the garden. *Atlantic Monthly*, April, 526–530.

Hyman, Colette A. 1985. Labor organizing and female institution-building: The Chicago Women's Trade Union League, 1904–24. In *Women, work and protest: A century of U.S. women's labor history*, ed. Ruth Milkman, 22–41. London: Routledge & Kegan Paul.

Inness, Sherrie A. 1999. *Tough girls: Women warriors and wonder women in popular culture.* Philadelphia: University of Pennsylvania Press.

Irwin, Wallace. 1916. Home, mother and the cabaret. *McClure's*, March, 13.

Irwin, Wallace, and Inez Milholland. 1913. Two million women vote. *McClure's*, Jan., 241–251.

Jackson, Derrick. 1999. Giddiness over Dow too familiar. *Akron Beacon Journal*, April 6, A9.

Jacoby, Robin Miller. 1975. The Women's Trade Union League and American feminism. *Feminist Studies* 3:126–140.

Jameson, Fredric. 1979/80. Reification and utopia in mass culture. *Social Text* 1:130–148.

Jenson, Jane, and Rianne Mahon. 1993. North American labour: Divergent trajectories. In *The challenge of restructuring: North American labor movements respond*, ed. Jane Jenson and Rianne Mahon, 3–15. Philadelphia: Temple University Press.

Johnson, Agnes. 1916. Girls in the city. *Home Life*, Aug., 8.

Johnson, Anne Porter. 1915. Mother's face. *People's Home Journal*, Oct., 28.

Johnson, Leola A. 1995. Forum on feminism and the media: Afterword. *Signs: Journal of Women in Culture and Society*, Spring:711–719.

Johnston, Mary. 1910. The woman's war. *Atlantic Monthly*, April, 559–570.

Jones, Emma Garrison. 1894. Ruby. *People's Home Journal*, June, 1.

Jorgensen, Helene J. 1999. *When good jobs go bad: Young adults and temporary work in the new economy.* Policy report. Washington D.C.: 2030 Center.

Joslyn, Earl. 1894. The mistress of the foundry. *McClure's*, Aug., 261–271.

Joyce, Patrick, ed. 1995. *Class.* Oxford: Oxford University Press.

Kaplan, E. Ann. 1994. Sex, work, and motherhood: Maternal subjectivity in recent visual culture. In *Representations of motherhood*, ed. Donna Bassin, Margaret Honey, Meryle Mahrer Kaplan, 256–271. New Haven: Yale University Press.

Keller, Kathryn. 1994. *Mothers and work in popular American magazines.* Westport, Conn.: Greenwood.

Kellor, Frances A. 1916. Lo, the poor immigrant! *Atlantic Monthly*, Jan., 59–65.

Kemper, S. H. 1915. Woman's sphere. *Atlantic Monthly*, April, 496–500.

Kerr, Sophie. 1916. The gayest woman in Marchmont. *McClure's*, March, 27.

Kessler-Harris, Alice. 1975. Where are the organized women workers? *Feminist Studies* 3, 92–110.

———. 1981. *Women have always worked: A historical overview.* Old Westbury, N.Y.: Feminist Press.

Key, Ellen. 1912. Motherliness. *Atlantic Monthly*, Oct., 562–570.

———. 1913. Education for motherhood. *Atlantic Monthly*, July, 48–56.

———. 1916. War and the sexes. *Atlantic Monthly*, June, 837–844.

King, Barbara. 1895. Women and newspapers. *Comfort*, Dec., 17.

Kirk, Adrian. 1903. Masters of their craft. *McClure's*, April, 563–574.

Knox, Loren H. B. 1909. Our lost individuality. *Atlantic Monthly*, Dec., 818–824.

Knox, Noelle. 2000. Telecom acquisitions, mergers set record in '99. *Akron Beacon Journal*, Jan. 2, C10.

Kolko, Gabriel. 1963. *The triumph of conservatism: A reinterpretation of American history, 1900–1916.* London: Free Press of Glencoe.

Kozol, Wendy. 1995. Fracturing domesticity: Media, nationalism, and the question of feminist influence. *Signs: Journal of Women in Culture and Society,* Spring:646–667.

Kraditor, Aileen S. 1965. *The ideas of the woman suffrage movement, 1890–1920.* Garden City, N.Y.: Anchor Books.

Laclau, Ernesto, and Chantal Mouffe. 1985. *Hegemony and socialist strategy: Towards a radical democratic politics.* London: Verso.

Larned, J. N. 1911. Prepare for socialism. *Atlantic Monthly,* May, 577–580.

Laughlin, J. Laurence. 1913. Monopoly of labor. *Atlantic Monthly,* Oct., 444–453.

Lauck, W. Jett. 1912a. The cotton-mill operatives of New England. *Atlantic Monthly,* May, 706–713.

———. 1912b. The vanishing American wage-earner. *Atlantic Monthly,* Nov., 691–696.

Lazarsfeld, Paul F., and Robert K. Merton. 1948. Mass communication, popular taste, and organized social action. In *The communication of ideas,* ed. Lyman Bryson, 95–118. New York and London: Harper Brothers.

Lears, T. J. Jackson. 1981. *No place of grace: Antimodernism and the transformation of American culture, 1880–1920.* New York: Pantheon Books.

———. 1983. From salvation to self-realization: Advertising and the therapeutic roots of the consumer culture, 1880–1930. In *The culture of consumption: Critical essays in American history, 1880–1980,* ed., T. J. Jackson Lears and Richard Wightman Fox, 1–38. New York: Pantheon Books.

Let us read the news together. 1916a. *Home Life,* Aug., 3.

Let us read the news together. 1916b. *Home Life,* Dec., 4.

Let us read the news together. 1917a. *Home Life,* Feb., 4.

Let us read the news together. 1917b. *Home Life,* April, 4.

Leupp, Francis E. 1911. The problem of Priscilla. *Atlantic Monthly,* June, 762–770.

Levi, Ida. 1918. Hotel maids seek protection in organization. *Life and Labor,* April, 74–76.

Levine, Susan. 1983. Labor's true woman: Domesticity and equal rights in the Knights of Labor. *Journal of American History* 70:323–339.

Lewis, Charles, and John Neville. 1995. Images of Rosie: A content analysis of women workers in American magazine advertising, 1940–1946. *Journalism and Mass Communication Quarterly* 72(1):216–227.

Lewis, Frank W. 1909. Employers' liability. *Atlantic Monthly,* Jan., 57–65.

Lewis, Jocelyn. 1903. An educated wage-earner. *Atlantic Monthly,* Sept., 387–392.

Lincoln, Jonathan Thayer. 1909. Trade-unions and the individual worker. *Atlantic Monthly,* Oct., 469–476.

List, Karen K. 1986. Magazine portrayals of women's role in the New Republic. *Journalism History,* 13.2: 64–70.

———. 1994. The media and the depiction of women. In *Significance of the media in American history,* ed. James D. Startt and William David Sloan, 106–128. Northport, Ala.: Vision Press.

Lloyd, Henry Demarest. 1902. A quarter century of strikes. *Atlantic Monthly,* Nov., 656–674.

Lucas, Stephen E. 1980. Coming to terms with movement studies. *Central States Speech Journal* 31:255–266.

Ludlow, J. M. 1895. Some words on the ethics of cooperative production. *Atlantic Monthly*, March, 383–387.

Lyotard, Jean-François. 1984. *The postmodern condition*. Minneapolis: University of Minneapolis Press.

Mainly about men and women. 1912. *Home Life*, June, 3.

Malkiel, Theresa Serber. [1910] 1990. *The diary of a shirtwaist striker*. Cornell University: ILR Press.

Marlborough, Sylvia. 1909. The blazing finger of fate: A thrilling and true Hallowe'en romance. *Comfort*, Oct., 10.

Marshall, Carrie. 1902. The lost mine. *People's Home Journal*, March, 16.

Marshall, Gordon. 1997. *Repositioning class: Social inequality in industrial societies*. London: Sage.

Martin, George Madden. 1902a. The confines of consistency. *McClure's*, May, 61–71.

———. 1902b. A ballad in print o' life, *McClure's*. July, 207–213.

Martin, John. 1908. Social reconstruction today. *Atlantic Monthly*, Sept., 289–297.

Marx, Karl, and Frederick Engels. 1846. *The German ideology, part 1*, ed. C. J. Arthur. New York: International Publishers, 1986.

Mason, Ethel, and S. M. Franklin. 1913. Low wages and vice—are they related? *Life and Labor*, April, 108–111.

Matthaei, Julie A. 1982. *An economic history of women in America: Women's work, the sexual division of labor, and the development of capitalism*. New York: Schocken Books.

Matthews, Glenna. 1992. *The rise of public woman: Woman's power and woman's place in the United States, 1630–1970*. New York: Oxford University Press.

McCann, John Ernest. 1895. My Jenny. *McClure's*, June, 90.

McCraw, Thomas K. 1974. The Progressive legacy. In *The Progressive Era*, ed. Lewis L. Gould, 181–201. Syracuse: Syracuse University Press.

McCreary, Maud. 1918. My first trade union conference. *Life and Labor*, Nov., 245.

McCulloch, George Elmer. 1909. Mrs Piper's limit. *McClure's*, Aug., 431–436.

McDermott, Patrice. 1995. On cultural authority: Women's studies, feminist politics, and the popular press. *Signs: Journal of Women in Culture and Society*, Spring:668–687.

McFarlane, Arthur E. 1911. The inflammable tenement: How New York has placed two and a half million people in the worst fire-trap dwellings in the world. *McClure's*, Oct., 690–701.

McGee, Michael C. 1975. In search of 'the people': A rhetorical alternative. *Quarterly Journal of Speech* 61:235–249.

———. 1980. The "ideograph": A link between rhetoric and ideology. *Quarterly Journal of Speech* 66:113–33.

McKenna, Ethel MacKenzie. 1894. Ellen Terry. *McClure's*, April, 457–465.

McRobbie, Angela. 1994. *Postmodernism and popular culture*. New York: Routledge.

Meeting of the strike committee of the Women's Trade Union League of Chicago. 1910. National Women's Trade Union League Papers. Microfilm, reel 4. Schlesinger Library, Radcliffe Institute, Harvard University.

Meredith, Ellis. 1908. What it means to be an enfranchised woman. *Atlantic Monthly*, Aug., 196–202.

Merwin, Samuel. 1915a. The honey bee: The story of a woman in revolt, part one. *McClure's*, July, 40.

———. 1915b. The honey bee: The story of a woman in revolt, conclusion. *McClure's*, Aug., 41.

Michelson, Miriam. 1904. Prince Roseleaf and a girl from Kansas. *McClure's*, Feb., 339–350.

Milholland, Inez. 1913a. The liberation of a sex. *McClure's*, Feb., 181–188.

———. 1913b. The changing home. *McClure's*, March, 206–219.

———. 1913c. The woman and the man. *McClure's*, April, 185–196.

Milkman, Ruth, ed. 1985. *Women, work, and protest: A century of women's labor history.* London: Routledge and Kegan Paul.

Mitchell, John. 1902. The coal strike. *McClure's*, Dec., 219–224.

Mittelstadt, Louisa. 1914. Women must organize! *Life and Labor*, April, n.p.

Moffett, Cleveland. 1895. Life and work in the powder-mills. *McClure's*, June, 3–17.

Mogensen, Vernon. 1996. The future is already here: Deskilling of work in the "office of the future." In *Beyond survival: Wage labor in the late twentieth century*, ed. Cyrus Bina, Laurie Clements, and Chuck Davis, 177–197. Armonk, N.Y.: M. E. Sharpe.

Moody, Kim. 1997. Austerity fuels mass strikes around the world. *Labor Notes*, April, 1.

———. 1999. Twenty years of *Labor Notes*: Born in the storm, raised in the struggle. *Labor Notes*, March.

Moody, Kim, and Mary McGinn. 1992. *Unions and free trade: Solidarity vs. competition.* Detroit: Labor Notes.

Morris, Monica B. 1973. Newspapers and the new feminists: Black out as social control? *Journalism Quarterly* 50.37–42.

Mortimer, Ruth. 1909. A million a minute. *People's Home Journal*, Feb., 16.

———. 1911. The old house. *People's Home Journal*, Jan., 17.

Mott, Frank Luther. 1938. *A history of American magazines: 1850–1865.* Vol. 2. Cambridge, Mass.: Harvard University Press.

———. 1957. *A history of American magazines: 1885–1905.* Vol. 4. Cambridge: Harvard University Press.

Mouffe, Chantal. 1993. *The return of the political.* London: Verso.

Moulton, Louise Chandler. 1894. When she was thirty. *McClure's*, Jan., 141–147.

Mowry, George E. 1963. The Progressive profile. In *The Status Revolution and the Progressive Movement*, ed. Edwin C. Rozwenc and A. Wesley Roehm. Boston: D. C. Heath.

Mumby, Dennis. 1988. *Communication and power in organizations: Discourse, ideology, and domination.* Norwood, N.J.: Ablex.

Mumby, Dennis, ed. 1993. *Narrative and social control: Critical perspectives.* Newbury Park, Calif.: Sage Publications.

Murphy, John M. 1992. Domesticating dissent: The Kennedys and the freedom rides. *Communication Monographs* 59:61–78.

Mussey, Henry Raymond. 1912. Trade-unions and public policy: Democracy or dynamite? *Atlantic Monthly*, April, 441–446.

National Public Radio. 1999. Study shows low income and rural Americans will suffer from lack of online resources. *All Things Considered,* July 8.

Newman, Pauline. 1911. The strike of the buttonworkers of Muscatine. *The Progressive Woman.* National Women's Trade Union League Papers. Microfilm, reel 4. Schlesinger Library, Radcliffe Institute, Harvard University.

———. 1914. The need for co-operation among working girls. *Life and Labor,* Oct., 312–313.

Nichols, Francis H. 1903. Children of the coal shadow. *McClure's,* Feb., 435–444.

Nock, Albert Jay. 1914. Motherhood and the state. *Atlantic Monthly,* Aug., 157–163.

O'Connor, Liz. 1997. Women send a message of international labor solidarity to Phillips Van-Heusen. *Labor Notes,* April, 12.

Ohmann, Richard. 1996. Selling culture: Magazines, markets, and class at the turn of the century. London: Verso.

Ono, Kent A., and John M. Sloop. 1995. The critique of vernacular discourse. *Communication Monographs* 62:19–46.

O'Reilly, Leonora. 1904. Untitled speech to shirtwaist makers at Clinton Hall. Leonora O'Reilly Papers. Microfilm, reel 9. Schlesinger Library, Radcliffe Institute, Harvard University.

———. 1911a. Labor Day. Leonora O'Reilly Papers. Microfilm, reel 9. Schlesinger Library, Radcliffe Institute, Harvard University.

———. 1911b. Looking over the fields. *The American Suffragette.* Leonora O'Reilly Papers. Microfilm, reel 9. Schlesinger Library, Radcliffe Institute, Harvard University.

———. 1911c. Mexican meeting. Leonora O'Reilly Papers. Microfilm, reel 9. Schlesinger Library, Radcliffe Institute, Harvard University.

———. 1911d. Untitled. *Life and Labor,* Aug., 227.

———. 1911e. Why the working woman should vote. *The Woman Voter.* Leonora O'Reilly Papers. Microfilm, reel 9. Schlesinger Library, Radcliffe Institute, Harvard University.

———. 1912. Suffrage statement to N.Y. state legislature. Leonora O'Reilly Papers. Microfilm, reel 9. Schlesinger Library, Radcliffe Institute, Harvard University.

———. 1914. Five dollars a week and our meals. *Life and Labor,* Aug., 246–247.

———. [1914?]. Wage earners and the ballot. Leonora O'Reilly Papers. Microfilm, reel 9. Schlesinger Library, Radcliffe Institute, Harvard University.

———. 1915. Miss Ida Tarbell and woman suffrage. *Life and Labor,* Feb., 34–35.

———. 1917. Why an industrial section for votes for women. Leonora O'Reilly Papers. Microfilm, reel 9. Schlesinger Library, Radcliffe Institute, Harvard University.

———. n.d. Talk for college women. Leonora O'Reilly Papers. Microfilm, reel 10. Schlesinger Library, Radcliffe Institute, Harvard University.

———. n.d. Untitled speech to a working girls' club. Leonora O'Reilly Papers. Microfilm, reel 9. Schlesinger Library, Radcliffe Institute, Harvard University.

———. n.d. Religion of labor. Leonora O'Reilly Papers. Microfilm, reel 10. Schlesinger Library, Radcliffe Institute, Harvard University.

———. n.d. Loyalty among working women. Leonora O'Reilly Papers. Microfilm, reel 10. Schlesinger Library, Radcliffe Institute, Harvard University.

———. n.d. Coercion of trade unions. Leonora O'Reilly Papers. Microfilm, reel 10. Schlesinger Library, Radcliffe Institute, Harvard University.

———. n.d. From 1848–1911. Leonora O'Reilly Papers. Microfilm, reel 9. Schlesinger Library, Radcliffe Institute, Harvard University.

———. n.d. To be used in every lecture. Leonora O'Reilly Papers. Microfilm, reel 9. Schlesinger Library, Radcliffe Institute, Harvard University.

Orleck, Annelise. 1995. *Common sense and a little fire: Women and working-class politics in the United States, 1900–1965*. Chapel Hill: University of North Carolina Press.

Our home ideals: How we realized them. 1915. *People's Home Journal*, April, 26.

Our Sunshine Society. 1911. *People's Home Journal*, Aug., n.p.

Paglia, Camille. 1994. *Vamps and tramps: New essays*. New York: Vintage.

Pankhurst, E. Sylvia. 1913. Forcibly fed: The story of my four weeks in Holloway Gaol. *McClure's*, Aug., 87–93.

Parker, Carleton H. 1917. The I.W.W. *Atlantic Monthly*, Nov., 651–662.

Patterson, Florence L. 1915. The price of life. *People's Home Journal*, April, 16.

Paul, Jasmine, and Bette J. Kauffman. 1995. Missing persons: Working-class women and the movies, 1940–1990. In *Feminism, multiculturalism, and the media: Global diversities*, ed. Angharad N. Valdivia, 163–184. Thousand Oaks, Calif.: Sage Publications.

Payne, Elizabeth Anne. 1988. *Reform, labor, and feminism: Margaret Dreier Robins and the Women's Trade Union League*. Urbana: University of Illinois Press.

Peiss, Kathy. 1986. *Cheap amusements: Working women and leisure in turn-of-the-century New York*. Philadelphia: Temple University Press.

Penley, Constance. 1992. Feminism, psychoanalysis, and the study of popular culture. In *Cultural studies*, ed. Lawrence Grossberg, Cary Nelson, Paula Treichler, 479–494. New York: Routledge.

Peterson, Theodore. 1956. *Magazines in the twentieth century*. Urbana: University of Illinois Press.

Phelps, Elizabeth Stuart. 1896a. Chapters from a life. *McClure's*, March, 361–368.

———. 1896b. Chapters from a life. *McClure's*, April, 490–495.

Pike, Manley H. 1902. Engineer Nettie. *Comfort*, May, 3.

Piven, Frances Fox, and Richard A. Cloward. 1971. *Regulating the poor: The functions of public welfare*. New York: Pantheon Books.

Poole, Ernest. 1903. Waifs of the street. *McClure's*, May, 40–48.

Poyntz, Juliet Stuart. 1917. The Unity Movement—The soul of a union. *Life and Labor*, June, 96–98.

Quinones, Eric R. 1998. Cuts could follow Exxon, Mobil merger. *Akron Beacon Journal*, Dec. 1, D7.

Radway, Janice. 1984. *Reading the romance: Women, patriarchy, and popular literature*. Chapel Hill: University of North Carolina Press.

Ransome, Jean. 1912. The girl who comes to the city: She wishes to learn stenography. *Home Life*, March, 11.

Redd, Louise. 1917. The Women's Peace Party. *Home Life*, March, 17.

Rees, John, ed. 1994. *The revolutionary ideas of Frederick Engels*. International Socialism 65.

Reese, Stephen D. 1990. The news paradigm and the ideology of objectivity: A socialist at *The Wall Street Journal*. *Critical Studies in Mass Communication*
7:390–409.

Regier, C. C. 1957. *The era of the muckrakers*. Chapel Hill: University of North Carolina Press.

Report of interstate conference of the National Women's Trade Union League.
1908. National Women's Trade Union League Papers. Microfilm, reel 1.
Schlesinger Library, Radcliffe Institute, Harvard University.

Repplier, Agnes. 1915. Women and war. *Atlantic Monthly*, May, 577–585.

———. 1916. Americanism. *Atlantic Monthly*, March, 289–297.

Rhode, Deborah L. 1995. Media images, feminist issues. *Signs: Journal of Women in
Culture and Society*, Spring:685–710.

Richardson, Anna Steese. 1915. Safeguarding American motherhood. *McClure's*,
July, 35.

———. 1916a. A woman-made season: Beauty, brains and technique win. *Mc-
Clure's*, April, 22.

———. 1916b. Am I my husband's keeper? *McClure's*, May, 15.

———. 1916c. A man in her life. *McClure's*, June, 30.

———. 1916d. The business of being a lady. *McClure's*, Aug., 24.

———. 1916e. Outside the law: As told by the woman in the case. *McClure's*, Oct.,
28.

Roberts, Octavia. 1910. For the sake of her children. *McClure's*, March, 629–637.

Robins, Elizabeth. 1913. Woman's war: A defense of militant suffrage. *McClure's*,
March, 41–52.

Robins, Margaret Dreier. 1911a. How to take part in meetings. *Life and Labor*, June,
170–171.

———. 1911b. How to take part in meetings: Lesson II. *Life and Labor*, July, 202–203.

———. 1911c. How to take part in meetings: Lesson III. *Life and Labor*, Sept.,
272–273.

———. 1911d. Presidential address. *Life and Labor*, Sept., 278–280.

———. 1911e. How to take part in meetings: Lesson IV, The question of reconsid-
eration. *Life and Labor*, Oct., 297–299.

———. 1911f. How to take part in meetings: Lesson V, How to preside. *Life and
Labor*, Nov., 336–337.

———. 1911g. How to take part in meetings: Lesson VI, Nominations and election of officers. *Life and Labor*, Dec., 379–380.

———. 1912. Self-government in the workshop. *Life and Labor*, April, 108–110.

Rogers, Joel. 1993. Don't worry, be happy: The postwar decline of private-sector
unionism in the United States. In *The challenge of restructuring: North American
labor movements respond*, ed. Jane Jenson and Rianne Mahon, 48–71. Philadelphia: Temple University Press.

Rogin, Michael. 1987. *Ronald Reagan, the movie and other episodes in political de-
monology*. Berkeley: University of California Press.

Roiphe, Katie. 1993. *The morning after: Sex, fear, and feminism on campus*. Boston:
Little, Brown, 1993.

Rosen, Ruth. 1982. *The lost sisterhood: Prostitution in America, 1900–1918*. Baltimore: Johns Hopkins University Press.

Rudnitzky, Anna. 1912. Time is passing. *Life and Labor*, April, 99.

Rusnak, Robert J. 1982. *Walter Hines Page and "The World's Work," 1900–1913*. Washington, D.C.: University Press of America.

Russell, Ruth M. 1917. Doing the work of men. *Life and Labor*, Oct., 159.

Ryan, Mary. 1990. *Women in public: Between banners and ballots, 1825–1880*. Baltimore: Johns Hopkins University Press.

Sajbel, Maureen. 1995. 'She' visions: Sexy looks aren't anti-feminist statements in MTV special. *Los Angeles Times*, Nov. 2, E6.

Salter, William M. 1902. What is the real emancipation of woman? *Atlantic Monthly*, Jan., 28–35.

Scanlon, Jennifer. 1995. *Inarticulate longings: The Ladies' Home Journal, gender, and the promises of consumer culture*. New York: Routledge.

Schiller, Dan. 1981. *Objectivity and the news: The public and the rise of commercial journalism*. Philadelphia: University of Pennsylvania Press.

Schneiderman, Rose. 1908–9. Women's Trade Union League: Report of organizer. Rose Schneiderman Papers. Microfilm, reel 2. Schlesinger Library, Radcliffe Institute, Harvard University.

———. 1913. Address to suffrage school. Rose Schneiderman Papers. Microfilm, reel 2. Schlesinger Library, Radcliffe Institute, Harvard University.

———. 1915. The woman movement and the working woman. *Life and Labor*, April, n.p.

Schneirov, Matthew. 1994. *The dream of a new social order: Popular magazines in America, 1893–1914*. New York: Columbia University Press.

Schudson, Michael. 1978. *Discovering the news: A social history of American newspapers*. New York: Basic Books.

Scott, Dave. 1999. Phone line and online are bypassing some people. *Akron Beacon Journal*, July 19, D1.

Scott, Melinda. 1915. Untitled. Leonora O'Reilly papers. Microfilm, reel 3. Schlesinger Library, Radcliffe Institute, Harvard University.

Scott, Robert L., and Donald K. Smith. 1969. The rhetoric of confrontation. *Quarterly Journal of Speech* 55:1–8.

Scudder, Vida D. 1902a. A hidden weakness in our democracy. *Atlantic Monthly*, May, 638–644.

———. 1902b. Democracy and education. *Atlantic Monthly*, June, 816–822.

———. 1902c. Democracy and society. *Atlantic Monthly*, Sept., 348–354.

———. 1910. Socialism and sacrifice. *Atlantic Monthly*, June, 836–849.

———. 1911. Class-consciousness. *Atlantic Monthly*, March, 320–330.

Seawell, Molly Elliot. 1910. The ladies' battle. *Atlantic Monthly*, Sept., 289–303.

Sergeant, Elizabeth Shepley. 1910. Toilers of the tenements: Where the beautiful things of the great shops are made. *McClure's*, July, 231–248.

Shulman, Alix Kates, ed. 1983. *Red Emma speaks: An Emma Goldman reader*. New York: Schocken Books.

Simmons, Mona Joseph. 1913. Slate-women. *People's Home Journal*, Nov., 7.

Simon, Roger. 1991. *Gramsci's political thought: An introduction*. London: Lawrence & Wishart.

Simons, Herbert W. 1972. Persuasion in social conflicts: A critique of prevailing conceptions and a framework for future research. *Speech Monographs* 39:227–247.

Sinclair, Upton. [1906] 1985. *The Jungle.* New York: Penguin American Library.

Sklar, Kathryn Kish. 1995. Two political cultures in the Progressive Era: The National Consumers' League and the American Association for Labor Legislation. In *U.S. history as women's history: New feminist essays,* ed. Linda K. Kerber, Alice Kessler-Harris, and Kathryn Kish Sklar, 36–62. Chapel Hill: University of North Carolina Press.

Sklar, Martin J. 1988. *The corporate reconstruction of American capitalism, 1890–1916: The market, the law, and politics.* Cambridge: Cambridge University Press.

Slaughter, Jane. 1999. The ultimate in 'contracting out' comes to North America. *Labor Notes,* May, 8.

Smith, Anna. 1903. How women may earn money. *Comfort,* Jan., 18.

Smith, Ethel M. 1918. Low wages send cigar makers on strike. *Life and Labor,* May, 92–93.

Sommers, Christina Hoff. 1994. *Who stole feminism? How women have betrayed women.* New York: Simon & Schuster.

Song no. 1. 1911. Leonora O'Reilly Papers. Microfilm, reel 9. Schlesinger Library, Radcliffe Institute, Harvard University.

Song no. 2. 1911. Leonora O'Reilly Papers. Microfilm, reel 9. Schlesinger Library, Radcliffe Institute, Harvard University.

Squire, Belle. 1912. Woman's problem, the housekeeping money: One way to meet (and beat) the higher cost of living. *Home Life,* June, 9.

Stabile, Carol A. 1995. Resistance, recuperation, and reflexivity: The limits of a paradigm. *Critical Studies in Mass Communication* 12:403–422.

Stansell, Christine. 1994. Women, children, and the uses of the streets: Class and gender conflict in New York City, 1850–1860. In *Unequal sisters: A multicultural reader in U.S. women's history,* ed. Vicki Ruiz and Ellen Carol DuBois, 111–127. 2nd ed. New York: Routledge.

Statement on the strike of the 35,000 unorganized garment workers of Chicago. c. 1911. National Women's Trade Union League Papers. Microfilm, reel 4. Schlesinger Library, Radcliffe Institute, Harvard University.

Stead, Peter. 1989. *Film and the working class: The feature film in British and American society.* London: Routledge.

Steffens, Lincoln. 1902. A labor leader of to-day: John Mitchell and what he stands for. *McClure's,* Aug., 355–357.

———. 1903. The shame of Minneapolis. *McClure's,* Jan., 227–239.

Steghagen, Emma. 1913. A summer of strikes in Cincinnati. *Life and Labor,* Nov., 333–335.

Stern, Madeleine B., ed. 1980. *Publishers for mass entertainment in nineteenth century America.* Boston: G. K. Hall.

Stewart, Charles J. 1980. A functional approach to the rhetoric of social movements. *Central States Speech Journal* 31:298–305.

Stewart, Charles J., Craig Allen Smith, and Robert E. Denton, Jr. 1989. *Persuasion and social movements.* Prospect Heights, Ill.: Waveland Press.

Strong, Hero. 1895. The heiress of Heathcourt. *People's Home Journal,* March, 1.

———. 1903. In Shelton coal mine. *People's Home Journal*, Dec., 14.

———. 1910. The Kimberly Mills. *People's Home Journal*, June, 3.

Sullivan, Olive M. 1918. The women's part in the stockyards organization work. *Life and Labor*, May, 102.

Sunshine and shut-ins. 1911. *People's Home Journal*, Nov., 2.

Sunshine work now! 1911. *People's Home Journal*, Sept., 1.

Tax, Meredith. 1980. *The rising of the women: Feminist solidarity and class conflict, 1880–1917*. New York: Monthly Review Press.

Tentler, Leslie Woodcock. 1979. *Wage-earning women: Industrial work and family life in the United States, 1900–1930*. Oxford: Oxford University Press.

The beauty patch and its meaning. 1903. *Comfort*, July, 3.

The city housewife: The ins and outs of life in a flat. 1910. *Comfort*, March, 20.

The Comfort sisters' corner. 1910. *Comfort*, March, 7.

The forty-eight-hour week for women. 1917. National Women's Trade Union League Papers. Microfilm, reel 3. Schlesinger Library, Radcliffe Institute, Harvard University.

The People's Home Journal for 1911. 1910. *People's Home Journal*, Dec., 2.

The picture before us. 1912a. *People's Home Journal*, Feb., 5.

The picture before us. 1912b. *People's Home Journal*, June, 3.

The picture before us. 1912c. *People's Home Journal*, Aug., 3.

The picture before us. 1912d. *People's Home Journal*, Oct., 3.

The picture before us. 1913a. *People's Home Journal*, April, 5.

The picture before us. 1913b. *People's Home Journal*, Aug., 5.

The picture before us. 1913c. *People's Home Journal*, Oct., 5.

The picture before us. 1914a. *People's Home Journal*, Feb., 5.

The picture before us. 1914b. *People's Home Journal*, April, 5.

The picture before us. 1914c. *People's Home Journal*, July, 5.

The picture before us. 1914d. *People's Home Journal* Sept., 5.

The picture before us. 1914e. *People's Home Journal*, Oct., 5.

The picture before us. 1914f. *People's Home Journal*, Nov., 5.

The picture before us. 1914g. *People's Home Journal*, Dec., 7.

The picture before us. 1915. *People's Home Journal*, Sept., 5.

The story of the Herzog strike. 1915. *Life and Labor*, Aug., 138–139.

The Sunshine Society is yours. 1911. *People's Home Journal*, July, 2.

Thompson, Charlotte M. 1916. National efficiency: I—The home—the best training camp. *Home Life*, Sept., 14.

Thompson, John B. 1990. *Ideology and modern culture: Critical social theory in the era of mass communication*. Stanford: Stanford University Press.

Townsend, Virginia F. 1895. The story of Miss Leighton. *People's Home Journal*, Jan., 6.

Traube, Elizabeth G. 1992. *Dreaming identities: Class, gender and generation in 1980s Hollywood movies*. Boulder: Westview Press.

Tucker, William Jewett. 1913. The goal of equality. *Atlantic Monthly*, Oct., 480–490.

Universal Sunshine Society. 1912. *People's Home Journal*, Nov., 36.

Useful hints showing where time and material are economized in every part of the home. *Comfort*, March, 17.

Wakefield, Edward. 1894. Nervousness: The national disease of America. *Mc-Clure's*, Feb., 302–307.

Waldinger, Roger. 1985. Another look at the International Ladies' Garment Workers' Union: Women, industry structure and collective action. In *Women, work and protest: A century of U.S. women's labor history*, ed. Ruth Milkman, 86–109. London: Routledge and Kegan Paul.

Walton, Dorothy. 1919. Women and the steel strike. *Life and Labor*, Nov., 275.

Wander, Philip. 1984. The third persona: An ideological turn in rhetorical theory. *Central States Speech Journal* 35:197–216.

Weedon, Chris. 1987. *Feminist practice and poststructuralist theory*. Oxford: Basil Blackwell.

Welter, Barbara. 1966. The cult of true womanhood: 1820–1860. *American Quarterly* 18:151–74.

West, Rebecca. 1916. Women of England. *Atlantic Monthly*, Jan., 1–11

White, Eliza Orne. 1894. The queen of clubs. *Atlantic Monthly*, May, 653–660.

White, Mimi. 1987. Ideological analysis and television. In *Channels of discourse, reassembled*, ed. Robert C. Allen, 161–202. 2nd ed. Chapel Hill: University of North Carolina Press.

White, Stewart Edward. 1903. The foreman: A "blazed trail" story. *McClure's*, Aug., 391–397.

Whitehead, Myrtle. 1914. What about vacations? *Life and Labor*, Aug.

Wilkinson, Charles A. 1976. A rhetorical definition of movements. *Central States Speech Journal* 27:88–94.

Williams, Raymond. 1975. *Television: Technology and cultural form*. New York: Schocken Books, 1975.

———. 1977. *Marxism and literature*. New York: Oxford University Press.

Williamson, Judith. 1986. The problems of being popular. *New Socialist* 4:14–15.

Wilson, Christopher. 1983. The rhetoric of consumption: Mass-market magazines and the demise of the gentle reader, 1880–1930. In *The culture of consumption: Critical essays in American history, 1880–1980*, ed. T. J. Jackson Lears and Richard Wightman Fox, 39–64. New York: Pantheon Books.

Winston, Ambrose P. 1902. The trade union and the superior workman. *Atlantic Monthly*, Dec., 794–801.

Woloch, Nancy. 1994. *Women and the American experience*, 2nd ed. New York: McGraw Hill.

Women workers and their industrial future. 1919. *Life and Labor*, Nov., 289.

Women's Trade Union League of Chicago. Official report of the strike committee. 1910. National Women's Trade Union League Papers. Microfilm, reel 4. Schlesinger Library, Radcliffe Institute, Harvard University.

Wood, Ellen Meiksins. 1986. *The retreat from class: A new "true" socialism*. London: Verso.

Wood, James Playsted. 1971. *Magazines in the United States*. 3rd ed. New York: Ronald Press.

Wood, Julia T. 1996. Dominant and muted discourses in popular representations of feminism. *Quarterly Journal of Speech* 82:171–205.

Woodbridge, Elisabeth. 1915. The married woman's margin. *Atlantic Monthly*, Nov., 629–637.

Wright, Erik Olin. 1989a. Exploitation, identity, and class structure: A reply to my critics. In *The debate on classes*, ed. Erik Olin Wright, 191–211. London: Verso.

———. 1989b. Rethinking, once again, the concept of class structure. In *The debate on classes*, ed. Erik Olin Wright, 269–348. London: Verso.

Wyatt, Edith. 1910. Heroes of the Cherry mine. *McClure's*, March, 473–492.

Yao, David. 1999. Teachers replace "quiet and polite" letter-writing with rallies and strikes. *Labor Notes*, June, 16.

Young, R. E. 1902. Mrs Shanklin's ambitions. *McClure's*, July, 232–240.

Zaretsky, Eli. 1973. *Capitalism, the family, and personal life*. New York: Harper Colophon Books.

Zinn, Howard. 1980. *A people's history of the United States*. London: Longman Group Limited.

———. 1990. *The politics of history*. 2nd ed. Urbana: University of Illinois Press.

Zuckerman, Mary Ellen. 1998. *A history of popular women's magazines in the United States, 1792–1995*. Westport, Conn.: Greenwood Press.

Index